About this book

Today's global health crisis reflects widening inequalities within and between countries. As the rich get richer and the poor get poorer, advances in science and technology are securing better health and longer lives for a small fraction of the world's population. Meanwhile children die of diarrhoea for want of clean water, people with AIDS die for want of affordable medicines, and poor people in all regions are increasingly cut off from the political, social and economic tools they can use to create their own health and well-being.

The real scandal is that the world lacks neither funds nor expertise to solve most of these problems. Yet the predominance of conservative thinking and neoliberal economics has led the institutions that were established to promote social justice into imposing policies and practices that achieve just the opposite. They police an unjust global trade regime with a doctrinaire insistence on privatization of public services, and preside over the failure to curb disease by tackling the poverty that enables it to flourish.

Global Health Watch 2005–2006 is a collaboration of leading popular movements and non-governmental organizations comprising civil society activists, community groups, health workers and academics. It has compiled this alternative world health report – a hard-hitting, evidence-based analysis of the political economy of health and health care – as a challenge to the major global bodies that influence health. Its monitoring of institutions including the World Bank, the World Health Organization and UNICEF reveals that while some important initiatives are being taken, much more needs to be done to have any hope of meeting the UN's health-related Millennium Development Goals.

The report also offers a comprehensive survey of current knowledge and thinking in the key areas that influence health, focusing throughout on the health and welfare of poor and vulnerable groups in all countries. These issues range from climate change, water and nutrition to national health services and the brain drain of health professionals from South to North.

Global Health Watch 2005–2006 is above all a call for action, written in a clear, accessible style to appeal to grass-roots health workers and activists worldwide, as well as to international policy-makers and national decision-makers. Its resource sections advocate actions everyone can take, while its recommendations show how better global health governance and practice could work for Health for All rather than health for the privileged few.

'A very good reference work for people working in areas affecting the health of populations. It deals with some of the most important issues in today's world. I highly recommend it.' – *Vicente Navarro, Editor-in-Chief,* International Journal of Health Services

'Combines academic analysis with a call to mobilize the health professional community to advocate for improvements in global health and justice. I hope it will be read by many health professionals in rich and poor countries alike.' – *Professor Andy Haines, Director, London School of Hygiene & Tropical Medicine*

'Governments and intergovernmental organizations have structured our social world so that half of humankind still lives in severe poverty. These global poor suffer vast health deficits due to inadequate nutrition and lack of access to health care, safe drinking water, and clean sewage systems. Each year, some 18 million of them, including 10 million children under 5, die from preventable or treatable medical conditions – accounting for one third of all human deaths ... This greatest moral outrage of our time will continue until citizens reflect on its causes and firmly place the human rights of the global poor on the political agenda. *Global Health Watch 2005–2006* is a courageous and promising effort in this direction.' – *Thomas Pogge, Professorial Research Fellow, Centre for Applied Philosophy, Australian National University*

'*Global Health Watch 2005–2006* offers a critique of global trends that threaten health including the practices of multinational corporations, the false promise of the genetics revolution, the scandal of hunger in a world of plenty and the failure of UN institutions such as WHO to live up to their original mission to promote the health of poor people. *Global Health Watch* shows clearly that whether we are healthy or not is deeply rooted in our political, economic and social structures. More important, it also demonstrates, with practical suggestions, that another world is possible. It will become the essential guidebook for health activists who want to campaign for a kinder, more equitable, healthier and people-centred world.' – *Fran Baum, member of the WHO Commission on the Social Determinants of Health*
'A much-needed resource, unique, and reflecting the work of well-qualified authors from all continents. I applaud the effort – and the result.' – *Philip R. Lee, MD, Consulting Professor, Stanford University*

Global Health Watch 2005–2006

An alternative world health report

People's Health Movement
BANGALORE

Medact
LONDON

Global Equity Gauge Alliance
DURBAN

UNISA Press
PRETORIA

Zed Books
LONDON | NEW YORK

Global Health Watch 2005–2006 was first published by Zed Books Ltd,
7 Cynthia Street, London N1 9JF, UK and Room 400, 175 Fifth Avenue,
New York, NY 10010, USA in 2005
<www.zedbooks.co.uk>

and in South Africa by UNISA Press, PO Box 392, Pretoria, RSA 003
<www.unisa.ac/za>

in association with:

People's Health Movement: c/o Community Health Cell, #367 'Srinivasa
Nilaya', Jakkasandra 1 Main, 1 Block, Koramangala, Bangalore–560 034,
India

Medact, The Grayston Centre, 28 Charles Square, London N1 6HT, UK

Global Equity Gauge Alliance: c/o Health Systems Trust, 401 Maritime House,
Salmon Grove, Victoria Embankment, Durban 4001, South Africa

www.ghwatch.org

Cover photo credits: Thailand drought (Kittprempool/UNEP/Still Pictures);
India, Mumbai, slum with highrise buildings in the background (Ron
Giling/Still Pictures); USA, California, motorway juntion (NRSC/Still Pictures);
China, Hong Kong, the city at night (JP Sylvestre/Still Pictures); Mali near
Segou, healthcare in the Niger River area – village clinic (Jan Banning/Panos
Pictures); India, Calcutta, examining sick child at a hospital for the poor (Neil
Cooper/Panos Pictures).

Cover designed by Andrew Corbett
Set in Arnhem and Futura Bold by Ewan Smith, London
Index: ed.emery@britishlibrary.net
Printed and bound in Malta by Gutenberg Press

Distributed in the USA exclusively by Palgrave Macmillan, a division of
St Martin's Press, LLC, 175 Fifth Avenue, New York, NY 10010.

A catalogue record for this book is available from the British Library.
US CIP data are available from the Library of Congress.

ISBN 1 84277 568 5 hb
ISBN 1 84277 569 3 pb

Contents

Boxes, figures and tables | vi
Acknowledgements | ix Foreword | xv

Introduction	1
**Part A	Health and globalization**	9
A1 Health for all in the 'borderless world'?	11
**Part B	Health care services and systems**	53
B1 Health care systems and approaches to health care	55
B2 Medicines	100
B3 The global health worker crisis	119
B4 Sexual and reproductive health	134
B5 Gene technology	147
**Part C	Health of vulnerable groups**	161
C1 Indigenous peoples	163
C2 Disabled people	179
**Part D	The wider health context**	191
D1 Climate change	193
D2 Water	207
D3 Food	225
D4 Education	239
D5 War	253
**Part E	Holding to account: global institutions, transnational corporations and rich countries**	267
E1 World Health Organization	269
E2 UNICEF	293
E3 The World Bank and the International Monetary Fund	299
E4 Big business	307
E5 Aid	322
E6 Debt relief	332
E7 Essential health research	339
**Part F	Conclusions**	351
Index	361

Boxes, figures and tables

Boxes

A1	Women and export processing zones	20
A2	What is structural adjustment?	23
A3	Debt, corruption and the cost of doing business	26
A4	The international finance facility – sound investment or living off the future?	27
A5	NAFTA, the FTAA and the right of foreign companies to sue governments	34
B1.1	Countries in decline – health and health care in Africa, the former Soviet Union and Afghanistan	57
B1.2	Neoliberalism	61
B1.3	Public and private health care financing	62
B1.4	New Public Management	66
B1.5	Integrated Management of Childhood Illness	71
B1.6	The pitfalls of expanding anti-retroviral treatment in developing countries	73
B1.7	Global Public Private Initiatives (GPPIs)	74
B1.8	Millennium Development Goals for the financing of health care systems	85
B2.1	The concept of essential medicines	100
B2.2	Drugs for neglected diseases	102
B2.3	'Big Pharma' – profits and power	103
B2.4	The US–Australia free trade agreement	107
B3.1	The impact of HIV/AIDS on health worker retention and performance	124
B3.2	Strategies to retain health workers in rural areas in Thailand	129
B4.1	Resources	139
B4.2	Youth rights in Africa	143
C1.1	The International Decade of the World's Indigenous Peoples: a failure?	163
C1.2	Killings in Brazil	167
C1.3	Sustainable systems of food production	167
C1.4	Abuse of Indigenous people's health and rights in Cambodia	168
C1.5	Health status of Indigenous peoples in four countries	169
C1.6	Indigenous peoples' perceptions of health	171
C1.7	Traditional birthing centre, Ayacucho, Peru	172
C1.8	Indigenous organizations and networks	174
C1.9	National Indigenous health research as a catalyst for development	176

C2.1	The facts about disability	180
C2.2	A disabled man from Congo speaks out	184
C2.3	The independent living movement in the South – some examples	186
D1.1	The effect of transport on climate change and health	195
D1.2	The flexible mechanisms of the Kyoto Protocol	200
D1.3	Adaptation to climate change and equity	204
D2.1	The importance of water to health	208
D2.2	The public sector can do it just as well	214
D2.3	Regulating private water companies in the UK	215
D2.4	Water privatization hits the poor in the Philippines	216
D2.5	Civil society fights back	217
D2.6	Two flushes a day	218
D2.7	US citizens told to boil their water	219
D3.1	How nutrition underpins the Millennium Development Goals	225
D3.2	Genetic engineering and nutrition	230
D3.3	Regulating the food industry	236
D4.1	Education as a determinant of health outcomes: the example of HIV/AIDS	240
D4.2	Education and women's health	242
D4.3	Programmes that aim to empower	245
D4.4	Promoting life skills and better health through education	246
D5.1	The disastrous impact of war on the environment	256
D5.2	Military spending and the UN: whose priorities?	262
D5.3	An agenda for peace	263
E1.1	Milestones in WHO history	273
E1.2	WHO and the People's Health Movement	286
E2.1	UNICEF	293
E2.2	Who is Ann Veneman, the new head of UNICEF?	294
E5.1	Key privatization advisers	328
E6.1	Zambia: inflation or death?	335
E7.1	Essential national health research and national health research systems	340
E7.2	The value of national health research capacity in low and middle-income countries	342
E7.3	Bridging the 'know-do' gap	344
E7.4	Asking the social-political research questions	347

Figures

A1	Trends in G7 development assistance	25
A2	How debt servicing dwarfs development assistance	25
B1.1	Immunization coverage rates	71

B1.2	The circus of external agencies and initiatives	78
B1.3	Factors undermining the PHC approach	80
B1.4	Healthy life expectancy and private spending as per cent of total health spending	82
B1.5	Healthy life expectancy (HALE) and government expenditure on health as per cent of GDP	83
B2.1	The mismatch between expenditure on medicines and health need	101
B2.2	How much does it cost to develop a new medicine?	109
B3.1	The negative correlation between mortality rates and health worker availability	120
B3.2	Health worker density	122
B3.3	Inequity in public primary care expenditure, Cape Town	123
B3.4	The global human resources for health conveyor belt	126
B3.5	Nurse registration in the UK from selected low income countries 1998/9–2001/2	128
D3.1	Trends in child malnutrition in developing countries, 1990–2000	226
D3.2	Determinants of nutritional well-being	227
E4.1	Average company tax rates in the EU and OECD, 1996–2003	320
E5.1	The long-term trend in ODA from DAC donors	322
E5.2	Provisional figures for ODA as a percentage of GNI in 2003	323
E5.3	The growing gap: comparison of how aid per person in DAC donor countries has failed to keep pace with growth in wealth per capita	324
E5.4	Share of aid to poorer countries 2002	324
E5.5	Shares of bilateral aid to basic needs	325

Tables

A1	Key health concerns with WTO agreements	32
B2.1	Spending money to change policy: PhRMA's budget initiatives	110
B3.1	Density of doctors and nurses in rich and selected poor countries	121
D2.1	Top corporate players in the world water industry	211
D3.1	Corporate control of US food sectors	229
E5.1	Value (in £) of new DFID contracts awarded to Big Five consultants, 1997–2002	329

Acknowledgements

The following individuals have contributed to this report in different ways and to different degrees. Outside of the small secretariat, individuals gave their time for free or, in a few instances, received small honoraria. Most people made contributions to only parts of the *Watch* and cannot therefore be held accountable for the whole volume and the views expressed in this report may not represent the opinions of everyone who has contributed. Ultimately, the *Watch* represents a collective endeavour of individuals and organizations who share a desire to improve the state of global health and to express their solidarity with the need to tackle the social and political injustice that lies behind poor health.

Nancy Alexander, Citizens' Network on Essential Services, USA; Annelies Allain, International Code Documentation Centre, Malaysia; Ian Anderson, University of Melbourne and The Cooperative Research Centre for Aboriginal Health, Australia; K Balasubramaniam, Health Action International Asia – Pacific and PHM Sri Lanka; Lexi Bambas, Global Equity Gauge Alliance, South Africa; Fran Baum, Department of Public Health, Flinders University, Adelaide and People's Health Movement, Australia; Adele Beerling, The Netherlands; Richard Bourne, Commonwealth Policy Studies Unit, UK; Paula Braveman, Center on Social Disparities in Health, California, USA; Jaime Breilh, Center for Health Research and Advice, Quito, Ecuador; Nicola Bullard, Focus on the Global South, Thailand; Ana Maria Buller, Medact, UK; Belinda Calaguas, WaterAid, UK; Geoffrey Cannon, World Health Policy Forum, Brazil; Greice Cerqueira, Women's Global Network for Reproductive Rights; Chan Chee-Khoon, Citizens' Health Initiative and PHM Malaysia; Sudip Chaudhuri, Indian Institute of Management Calcutta, India; Andrew Chetley, Exchange and PHM UK; Mickey Chopra, School of Public Health, University of the Western Cape, South Africa; Karen Cocq, Municipal Services Project, Queen's University, Canada; Charles Collins, UK; June Crown, Medact, UK; Mawuli Dake, Ghana National Coalition Against Privatisation of Water, Ghana; Sylvia de Haan, Council on Health Research for Development (COHRED), Switzerland; Armando De Negri, Latin American Association of Social Medicine and International Society for Equity in Health, Brazil; Gilles de Wildt, Medact, UK; Karen Devries London School of Hygiene and Tropical Medicine, UK; Rena Diamond, Medact, UK; Brianna Diaz, El Salvador; Jack

Dowie, London School of Hygiene and Tropical Medicine, UK; Dela Dovlo, Population Council, Ghana; Lesley Doyal, School for Policy Studies, University of Bristol, UK; Peter Drahos, RegNet, Australian National University; Anwar Fazal, World Alliance for Breastfeeding Action, Malaysia; Pedro Francke, Forosalud, Peru; Lucy Gilson, Centre for Health Policy, South Africa and London School of Hygiene and Tropical Medicine, UK; Sarah Graham Brown, UK; Andy Gray, Department of Therapeutics and Medicines Management, Nelson R Mandela School of Medicine, University of KwaZulu-Natal, South Africa; Andrew Green, Nuffield Centre for International Health and Development, University of Leeds; Ted Greiner; Sophie Grig, Survival International, UK; Sara Grusky, Water for All Campaign, Public Citizen, USA; Ana Guezmes Garcia, Observatorio de Salud, Peru; Wendy Harcourt, Society for International Development, International Secretariat, Italy and Women in Development Europe, Belgium; Thomas Hart, Health Unlimited, Guatemala; John Hilary, War on Want, UK; Richard Horton, *Lancet*, UK; Nuria Homedes, School of Public Health, University of Texas, USA; Saleemul Huq, International Institute for Environment and Development, UK; Rachel Hurst, Disability Awareness in Action, UK; Carel Ijsselmuiden, Council on Health Research for Development, Switzerland; Alan Ingram, Department of Geography, University College London, UK; Sameer Jabbour; Lisa Jackson-Pulver, Muru Marri Indigenous Health, University of New South Wales, Australia; Anne Jellema, Global Campaign for Education, South Africa; Mira Johri, Université de Montréal, Canada; Laura Katzive, Center for Reproductive Rights, USA; Andrew Kennedy, Council on Health Research for Development, Switzerland; Regina Keith, Save the Children, UK; Pauline Kisanga, International Baby Food Action Network, Africa; Meri Koivusalo, STAKES, Finland; Charlie Kronick, Greenpeace, UK; Abhay Kudale, Maharashtra Association of Anthropological Sciences, India; Ron Labonte, Canadian Coalition on Global Health Research and Institute of Population Health, University of Ottawa, Canada; Didier Lacaze, Programa de Promoción de la Medicina Tradicional en la Amazonía Ecuatoriana, Ecuador; Michael Latham, Cornell University, US; Kelley Lee, Centre on Global Change and Health, London School of Hygiene & Tropical Medicine, UK; David Legge, La Trobe University, Australia and PHM Australia; Uta Lehman, School of Public Health, University of the Western Cape, South Africa; Jane Lethbridge, Public Services International Research Unit; Barry Levy, Tufts University School of Medicine, US; Abhay Machindra Kudale, the Maharashtra Association of Anthropological Sciences (MAAS), Pune, Maharashtra State, India; Maureen Mackintosh, The Open University, UK; Tim Martineau, Liverpool School of Tropical Medicine, UK; Martin McKee,

London School of Hygiene and Tropical Medicine; Philip McMichael, Cornell University, US; Jaime Miranda, EDHUCASalud, Peru; Howard Mollet, Reality of Aid and British Overseas NGOs in Development, UK; Raul Montenegro, Fundación para la defensa del ambiente, Argentina; Benon Mugarura, African Indigenous and Minority Peoples Organisation, Rwanda; Kathryn Mulvey, Corporate Accountability International, US; Richard Murphy, Tax Justice Network, UK; Ravi Narayan, People's Health Movement Global Secretariat; Clive Nettleton, Health Unlimited, UK; Antoinette Ntuli, Global Equity Gauge Alliance, South Africa; Nyang'ori Ohenjo, Centre for Minority Rights and Development, Kenya; Eileen O'Keefe, London Metropolitan University, UK; Marcela Olivera, Water for All Campaign, Public Citizen, US; Eeva Ollila, STAKES, Finland; Akinbode Oluwafemi, Environmental Rights Action; Caleb Otto, Senator for the Government of Palau; Natasha Palmer, London School for Hygiene and Tropical Medicine, UK; Rajeev Patel, University of KwaZulu-Natal, South Africa; Enrico Pavignani, independent public health consultant; Victor B Penchaszadeh, Mailman School of Public Health, Columbia University, New York, USA; Ann Pettifor, Advocacy International, UK; Jack Piachaud, Medact, UK; John Porter, London School for Hygiene and Tropical Medicine, UK; Jeff Powell, Bretton Woods Project, UK; Chakravati Raghavan, South-North Development Monitor; Mohan Rao, Centre of Social Medicine and Community Health, Jawaharlal Nehru University and PHM India; Jeff Reading, Canadian Institutes of Health Research and Institute of Aboriginal Peoples' Health University of Victoria, Canada; Gill Reeve, Medact, UK; Margaret Reeves, Medact, UK; Cecilia Rivera Vera, Observatorio de Salud, Peru; Greg Ruiters, Municipal Services Project, South Africa and Political and International Studies, Rhodes University, South Africa; Moyra Rushby, Medact, UK; Andy Rutherford, One World Action and PHM UK; Gregorio Sánchez, Centro Amazónico para la Investigación y Control de Enfermedades Tropicales, Amazonas, Venezuela; David Sanders, School of Public Health, University of the Western Cape and PHM South Africa; Claudio Schuftan, PHM, Vietnam; Malcolm Segall, Institute of Development Studies, University of Sussex, UK; Sovathana Seng, The Center for Indigenous Peoples Research and Development, Cambodia; Amit Sengupta PHM, India; Hani Serag, Association for Health and Environmental Development and PHM Egypt; Ted Schrecker, Institute of Population Health University of Ottawa, Canada; Ellen Shaffer, Center for Policy Analysis on Trade and Health (CPATH), USA; Abhay Shukla, Center for Inquiry into Health and Allied Themes and PHM India; Alaa Ibrahim Shukrallah, Association for Health and Environmental Development and PHM Egypt; Victor Sidel, Montefiore Medical Center/Albert Einstein College of Medicine and Weill Medical

Acknowledgements

College of Cornell University, US; Mohga Kamal Smith, Oxfam GB; Rafiki Soilihi, Comoros Islands; Vuk Stambolovic, Institute of Social Medicine, Medical Faculty Belgrade, Serbia and Montenegro; Carolyn Stephens, Department of Public Health and Policy, London School of Hygiene & Tropical Medicine, UK; Marjan Stoffers, Wemos, Netherlands; Robin Stott, Medact, UK; Ellen 't Hoen, Medecins Sans Frontiers, France; Riaz Khalid Tayob, Southern and East African Trade Information and Negotiations Institute, Zimbabwe; Jerome Teelucksingh, University of the West Indies, Trinidad; PV Unnikrishnan, ActionAid International, UK and Bangkok and PHM Global Secretariat; Balakrishna Venkatesh, India; Ellen Verheul, Wemos, Netherlands; Helen Wallace, GeneWatch, UK; Gill Walt, London School of Hygiene and Tropical Medicine, UK; Fiona Watson, Survival International, UK; Scott Winch, Sydney South West Area Health Service, Aborginal Health Unit, Australia; James Woodcock, London School of Hygiene and Tropical Medicine, UK; Jo Woodman, Survival International, UK; David Woodward, New Economics Foundation, UK; David Zakus, Centre for International Health, University of Toronto, Canada; Christina Zarowsky, International Development Research Centre, Canada; Pam Zinkin, International People's Health Council and PHM UK; Maria Hamlin Zuniga, International People's Health Council, Global Secretariat and PHM Nicaragua.

We would like to thank the following organisations for funding the production of *Global Health Watch, 2005–2006*, and associated advocacy activities. The views expressed in the Watch are not necessarily those of the funding agencies: Exchange (http://www.healthcomms.org), Global Equity Gauge Alliance (http://www.gega.org.za), Greenpeace Environmental Trust (http://www.greenpeace.org), International Development Research Centre (http://www.idrc.ca), Medact (http://www.medact.org), Medecins du Monde (http://www.medecinsdumonde.org), Medicos (http://www.medico-international.de), Nuffield Trust (http://www.nuffieldtrust.org.uk), People's Health Movement (http://www.phmovement.org), Save the Children (UK) (http://www.savethechildren.org.uk), Swedish International Development Agency (http://www.sida.se), WaterAid (http://www.wateraid.org), Wemos (http://www.wemos.nl)

The following organisations have contributed to the production of the Watch indirectly (through research support, peer-reviewing etc.): ActionAid International; Advocacy International; African Indigenous and Minority Peoples Organisation, Rwanda; Association For Health and Environmental Development, Egypt; Bretton Woods Project, UK; Canadian Institutes of Health Research and Institute of Aboriginal Peoples' Health, University of

Victoria, Canada; Centre for Health Research and Advice, Ecuador; Center for Reproductive Rights, US; Centre for Civil Society, School of Development Studies, University of KwaZulu-Natal, Durban, South Africa; Centre for Indigenous Peoples Research and Development, Cambodia; Centre for International Health, University of Toronto, Canada; Centre for Minority Rights and Development, Kenya; Center for Policy Analysis on Trade and Health (CPATH), USA; Centro Amazónico para la Investigación y Control de Enfermedades Tropicales, Venezuela; Citizens' Health Initiative, Malaysia; Commonwealth Policy Studies Unit, United Kingdom; Cooperative Research Centre for Aboriginal Health, Australia; Corporate Accountability International, US; Council on Health Research for Development (COHRED), Switzerland; Department of Geography, University College London; Department of Public Health, Flinders University, Adelaide, Australia; Disability Awareness in Action, UK; EDHUCASalud (Civil Association for Health and Human Rights Education), Peru; Environmental Rights Action, Nigeria; EQUINET, Southern Africa; Focus on the Global South, Thailand; Forosalud, Perú; GeneWatch; UK Ghana National Coalition Against Privatization of Water, Ghana; Global Campaign for Education, South Africa; Global Equity Gauge Alliance; Greenpeace, UK; Health Action International Asia – Pacific, Sri Lanka; Health Unlimited, UK; Health Unlimited, Guatemala; Indian Institute of Management, India; International Physicians for the Prevention of Nuclear War; Institute of Social Medicine, Belgrade Medical Faculty, Serbia and Montenegro; International People's Health Council; London School of Hygiene and Tropical Medicine; Maharashtra Association of Anthropological Sciences (MAAS), Maharashtra State, India; Medact, UK; Medecins du Monde, France; Municipal Services Project, South Africa; Muru Marri Indigenous Health Unit, School of Public Health and Community Medicine, Faculty of Medicine, University of New South Wales, Australia; New Economics Foundation, UK; Observatorio de Salud, Peru; One World Action, UK; People's Health Movement Global Secretariat ; People's Health Movement, India; People's Health Movement, Australia; People's Health Movement, South Africa; People's Health Movement, Vietnam; Programa de Promoción de la Medicina Tradicional en la Amazonía Ecuatoriana, Ecuador; SATHI Cell, Center for Enquiry into Health and Allied Themes, India; School of Public Health, University of the Western Cape, South Africa; Save the Children, UK; Society for International Development, International Secretariat Rome, Italy; Women in Development Europe, Belgium; South West Sydney Area Health Service Aboriginal Health Unit, Australia; Southern and East African Trade Information and Negotiations Institute; Survival International, UK; Tax Justice Network, UK; Training and

xiii

Research Support Centre, Zimbabwe; University of the West Indies, Trinidad; War on Want, UK; Water for All Campaign, Public Citizen, US; WaterAid, UK; Wemos, Netherlands; Women's Global Network for Reproductive Rights, Netherlands; World Alliance for Breastfeeding Action (WABA), Malaysia.

The secretariat would like to express their deep gratitude to Robert Molteno and Anne Rodford at Zed Books and to typesetter Ewan Smith and cover designer Andrew Corbett for their speedy and efficient facilitation of this edition of the *Watch*. Thanks also to Moyra Rushby and Gill Reeve and the rest of the staff and board of Medact as well as Antoinette Ntuli, Farana Khan and Halima Hoosen-Preston at GEGA and Ravi Narayan, Nisha Susan and Abraham Thomas at the PHM Global Secretariat for supporting us so well.

We would like to thank the following for permission to reproduce the illustrations: numbers 1, 2, 5 and 6 Community Health Cell; 3 JP Sylvestre/ Still Pictures; 4 Neil Cooper/Panos Pictures; 7 Gisele Wulfsohn/Panos Pictures; 8, 9 Crispin Hughes/Panos Pictures; 10 AK Moe/WHO; 11 US Dept. of Energy Human Genome Programme (http://www.ornl.gov/hgmis); 12 Penny Tweedie/Panos Pictures; 13 Rachel Hurst; 14 Kittprempool/UNEP-Still Pictures; 15 NRSC/Still Pictures; 16 Tom Kruse <t.kruse@albatross.cnb.net>; 17, 20, 21 P Virot/WHO; 18 Chien-min Chung/ Panos Pictures; 19 Heidi Bradner/Panos Pictures; 22 World Bank; 23 Corporate Accountability International; 24 http://www.babymilkaction.org; 25 Duncan Miller

Global Health Watch secretariat and editorial team:
Claudia Lema; David McCoy; Patricia Morton; Michael Rowson;
Jane Salvage; Sarah Sexton.

Foreword

New reports on different aspects of the state of the world's health appear daily. International and national organizations of all kinds produce vast amounts of data, statistics and analysis. But what is lacking in this flood of information is honest and transparent assessment of the actions and policies that affect health and health inequalities, for good or ill, presented in a format that is accessible and understandable by health workers and civil society groups. How far do all the health projects, programmes, technical cooperation, aid and loans actually improve the health of poor people round the world? And how far do the actions of transnational corporations, global financial institutions and international trade rules undermine it?

Recognizing this, the People's Health Movement, the Global Equity Gauge Alliance and Medact came together in 2003 to plan a review of the performance of the very institutions that normally write global reports. It was time to turn the tables by reporting and assessing the actions of international health agencies such as the World Health Organization and UNICEF, donor agencies, rich country governments, the World Bank, the International Monetary Fund and the World Trade Organization. It was time to produce an alternative world health report that would highlight the root causes of poor health and reveal the gap between humanitarian rhetoric and reality.

This first edition of the *Global Health Watch* is the result, designed to create a joint platform for civil society organizations and individuals working in health and health-related sectors, including gender discrimination, global trade environmental protection, access to water and food, the arms trade, the peace movement and disaster relief. *Global Health Watch 2005–2006* has achieved this, and we hope to continue and improve the collaboration between these actors.

The report has limitations. We tried to involve people from as many countries as possible, but lacked adequate input from many regions, including the Middle East and China. Many key issues relevant to health are covered, but not everything of importance. With a limited budget and a tiny secretariat, we were simply unable to cover everything. What we have created, however, is the prototype of an instrument to 'watch' how international and national governments, agencies, banks, corporations, rules and structures act and perform in improving or worsening health and health inequities. This edition does not provide a complete report on all the relevant events and institutions, but it is a foundation for subsequent Watches.

It is now time to start preparing for the next *Global Health Watch* in 2007. What will be said then about the key role and performance of WHO and other global health bodies? Will they be able to improve their performance while the United States continues to attack the multilateral institutions? Will the tobacco companies have found ways to undermine the implementation of the WHO Framework Convention on Tobacco Control? Will the World Bank still be undermining public health systems while trumpeting its commitment to poverty alleviation? What will have been the impact of humanitarian and development efforts in areas affected by the 2004 tsunami? And what will health and the health system be like in Iraq?

Politicians, governments, donor and humanitarian agencies, banks and multilateral institutions need to be held accountable. They need to be praised when they do well; told when they fail; and exposed when they consciously contribute to the problem. Independent evaluation of the role of civil society should also, perhaps, be included in future. Meanwhile we hope this report marks the beginning of an ongoing process to improve accountability in the international system, and contributes to our wider goal of Health for All as a right.

People's Health Movement
Global Equity Gauge Alliance
Medact

Introduction

Origins

The *Global Health Watch* comes out of one of the largest ever civil society mobilizations in health. Its roots lie in the influential and lasting campaigns of the 1970s and 1980s when activists across the world challenged the global health divide between North and South and rich and poor. They formulated practical proposals for change and influenced the content of the ground-breaking 1978 Alma Ata Declaration. Community-based health care, the essential drugs list and controls on the marketing of infant formula are just some of the results of this advocacy, which has changed the lives of millions of people for the better.

During the 1990s, many activists came together again to take up more of the continually emerging challenges in global health – and to tackle some of the most intransigent ones such as poverty and inequality. A People's Health Assembly, held in Savar, Bangladesh, in December 2000, was the first step towards launching a global social movement to attain the aim written into the Constitution of the World Health Organization (WHO): 'the enjoyment of the highest attainable standard of health is one of the fundamental rights of every human being without distinction of race, religion, political belief, economic or social condition'.

Some 1500 people from 75 nations attended the People's Health Assembly and collectively drew up and endorsed a People's Health Charter. The Charter is a call for action on the root causes of ill-health and many people's lack of access to essential health care, and set the agenda for the People's Health Movement that emerged out of the Assembly.

This first edition of the *Global Health Watch* takes up the Charter's call for action and suggests ways in which the global movement of people concerned with health can take its principles forward. In the process, it has brought together health activists, health professionals and academics from around the world to put together an alternative world health report. It is aimed primarily at all those around the world who work in health care or for health and who represent an important section of civil society. They usually have a certain standing in society that enables them to be influential in promoting action on global health.

But aren't there enough world health and development reports already? The

1

World Health Report, produced by the WHO; the *Human Development Report* compiled by the United Nations Development Programme; an annual report produced by UNAIDS; the annual State of the World's Children produced by UNICEF; and the *World Development Report* issued by the World Bank every year. The *Global Health Watch* is different, however. The paragraphs below outline how and why health workers from all over the world have expressed a need for such a report.

The politics of health

The co-existence of wealth and widespread, severe poverty suggests that the latter can be avoided. The cost of achieving and maintaining universal access to basic education, basic health care, adequate food, and safe water and sanitation for all has been estimated at less than 4% of the combined wealth of the 225 richest people in the world (UNDP 1998: 30). In many countries in which hunger is prevalent, there is enough productive land to feed their populations many times over. Alternative social, political and economic arrangements at a national and global level could change this stark reality.

The *Watch* therefore sets out an explicitly political understanding of the current state of health around the world. This is nothing new – public health has been recognized as a political concern for many years. As the famous nineteenth century German pathologist, Rudolf Virchow, explained, 'medicine is a social science, and politics is nothing more than medicine practised on a larger stage'.

UNICEF has devised a conceptual model for explaining child morbidity and mortality. It states that, amongst other factors, the political, social and economic systems that determine how resources are used and controlled need to be considered so as to determine the number and distribution of children who do not have sufficient access to food, child care, clean water, sanitation and health services (Figure Intro.1).

The UNICEF model is applicable to other aspects of health (for example, AIDS and maternal health) and echoes the analytical approach used by the *Watch* to highlight how the distribution of power, political influence and economic resources shapes the pattern of health globally.

Poverty and development as a public health issue

Poverty is the biggest epidemic that the global public health community faces. It underlies most cases of under-nutrition, fuels the spread of many diseases and deepens vulnerability to the effects of illness and trauma. Poor countries are unable to give their health and social services adequate resour-

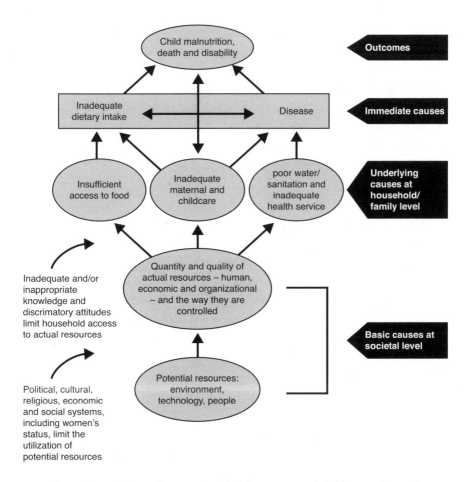

Figure Intro.1 Immediate and underlying causes of child mortality and morbidity (*Source:* Unicef 1998)

ces, resulting in a poverty of health systems that compounds poverty at the household and community levels.

The challenge of improving global health is therefore inextricably linked to the challenge of addressing widespread and growing poverty. According to the official statistics of the World Bank, the number of very poor people has increased by 10.4 percent between 1987 and 2001 to 2735 million – almost half the world's population (Chen and Ravallion 2004). Furthermore, there is reason to believe that the World Bank's methodology for measuring poverty is flawed and underestimates the true breadth and depth of poverty worldwide (Reddy and Pogge 2006). The extent of poverty demands that tackling it is at the centre of health programmes and health policy analysis, and that understanding its causes and engaging with the political and economic reforms is essential to abolishing it.

Health workers engage with the health effects of illiteracy; the lack of access to clean water and sanitation; hunger and food insecurity; the degradation of the environment; and militarism and conflict. These public health issues highlight the common challenges shared by health workers, teachers, engineers, geographers, farmers and biologists, to name just a few professions in fulfilling the universal right to health and dignity. The *Watch* aims to promote health as a theme that can bring together different sectors of civil society around a common agenda for human development and social justice.

Inequity

Increasing levels of poverty have been accompanied by growing inequality. The income gap between the fifth of the world's people living in the richest countries and the fifth of the poorest was 74 to 1 in 1997, up from 60 to 1 in 1990, 30 to 1 in 1960, and 11 to 1 in 1913. The world's 200 richest people more than doubled their net worth in the four years to 1998 to more than $1 trillion. The assets of the top three billionaires are worth more than the combined GNP of all least developed countries and their 600 million people (UNDP 1999).

Although inequality is commonly described in terms of differences between rich and poor countries, one fifth of the richest people in the world come from developing countries (Navarro 2004). Similarly, poverty and widening disparities are not confined to poor countries – inequalities have risen in wealthy nations over the past two decades.

An 'equity lens' is important because political and economic institutions are shaped in ways that can reinforce unfair advantages and widen socioeconomic disparities. International trade rules and regulations are stacked in favour of richer countries and multinational corporations; debt cancellation is given at the whim of rich nation creditors rather than as a response to the pressing needs of citizens of poorer countries. The conditionalities imposed upon poor governments by the World Bank and International Monetary Fund (IMF) are undemocratic and have included the privatization of public assets, thereby undermining public education and health care systems, and eroding social safety nets.

The *Watch* therefore emphasizes not just poverty, but also the relationship between rich and poor, between the powerful and the marginalized. Improving the situation of the world's poor cannot be achieved through aid or charity alone; profoundly unequal power relationships need to be tackled first and foremost. Health professionals can influence many of the decisions that will lead to a fairer distribution of wealth.

Human rights and responsibilities

Article 25.1 of the Universal Declaration of Human Rights states that 'everyone has the right to a standard of living adequate for the health of himself and of his family, including food, clothing, housing and medical care and necessary social services'. Article 12.1 of the International Covenant on Economic, Social and Cultural Rights recognizes the 'right of everyone to the enjoyment of the highest attainable standard of physical and mental health'.

Such declarations are a reminder that human rights encompass more than political and civil liberty human rights; they also incorporate social, economic and cultural rights. Universal human rights are not limited to a vote, free speech and freedom from oppression, but include a right to household food security, essential health care and other requirements that underpin human dignity.

Human rights discourse is often centred on the duties of states and governments. Violations committed against people by governments, under the guise of officialdom and the law, or with the complicity of the state, are rightly condemned because they not only deprive people of the objects of their rights (such as food and essential health care), but also attack and subvert the very notion of rights and justice. There is in addition an acceptance that governments are in breach of their duty if they fail to ensure in a reasonable manner the progressive realization of human rights through the use of resources under their control. Governments that allow corruption and fraud, for example, or inappropriate public expenditure on armaments when large sections of the population lack access to the basic means of survival and dignity, are committing human rights violations.

However, a moral conception of human rights implies that social, political and economic institutions must also be held to account. This is enshrined in Article 28 of the Universal Declaration of Human Rights, which states that 'everyone is entitled to a social and international order in which the rights and freedoms set forth in this Declaration can be fully realized'.

For example, while a legal right to adequate food is important, and while governments are obliged to ensure the progressive realization of this right, political and economic arrangements that determine how food is produced, controlled and sold may be as important, if not more so, in determining whether this right is fulfilled. Such arrangements might include historically unjust patterns of land ownership; the control of food production systems that leads to monopolies; the speculative hoarding of basic staple foods and excessively high food prices; or the dumping of heavily subsidized produce from rich countries onto poor ones in a way that decimates local agriculture and subsistence economies.

These examples suggest that even if governments do all they can, social, economic and political arrangements that keep people living below the poverty line when there are reasonable alternative arrangements should be considered violations of human rights, even if these arrangements are legal. This implies obligations not just on governments but also upon citizens and non-government actors to re-shape political and economic arrangements to ensure the fulfilment of rights.

Given global integration, governments, corporate actors and civil society have transnational duties and responsibilities towards the fulfilment of universal human rights. At present, the emphasis in human rights discourse is on the responsibilities of governments towards their own citizens. Transnational responsibilities for the fulfilment of human rights tend to be limited to avoiding or preventing direct violations of the civil liberties of citizens of another country, or merely invoke a weak humanitarian response to help out with aid and other forms of assistance. Economic cooperation with corrupt and undemocratic governments is not considered a human rights transgression, nor is the maintenance of trade rules that perpetuate or deepen severe poverty.

In sum, the *Watch* embodies a human rights perspective that emphasizes social and economic rights; identifies political and economic institutions, including the manner in which economic relationships are organized and structured, as being beholden to human rights declarations; and calls for a greater recognition of transnational responsibilities towards the fulfilment of human rights.

Mobilizing civil society and holding institutions to account

In light of the evidence that social, political and economic arrangements are failing to address the current state of ill-health, poverty and inequity adequately, a stronger mobilization of civil society committed to the fulfilment of human rights is needed. The *Global Health Watch* is explicitly linked to many civil society struggles for health and justice. Many of the individuals, networks and NGOs associated with this report participate in civil society mobilization, lobbying efforts, policy advocacy and development work on the ground. The *Watch* draws on their experiences and offers credible analysis to strengthen their work.

Part of the aim of this alternative world health report, therefore, is to present an analysis of the performance and effect of key institutions that have a responsibility for promoting global health. Health and development reports produced, for example, by the WHO, UNAIDS and the World Bank tend not to include themselves in the analysis of factors that are promoting or negatively impacting on health. The *Watch* hopes to fill this gap and provide another means of strengthening civil society's ability to engage with the determinants of ill health.

Overview of the *Global Health Watch*

The report is divided into six sections. Part A looks at how political and economic change at the global level influences people's health and well-being worldwide, noting how little control individuals have over these changes. It points to solutions for redressing global imbalances and shows how few of the promises made to developing countries in past years have been kept.

Part B carves out an agenda for the public sector's role in health, with a special focus on low- and middle-income countries. Its first chapter asserts that the Primary Health Care Approach adopted by the world's health ministers in the late 1970s is still relevant today, but that the public sector role in health is under threat, and that commercialization of health care has proceeded apace in the last two decades to the detriment of health. It points to the limitations of current efforts to address health priorities through selective health care interventions and pro-poor targeting. The chapter argues for a greater commitment to universal health care systems and for renewed investment in the public sector. Subsequent chapters on medicines and gene technology take up the theme of commercialization and suggest ways in which the public sector role can be strengthened. Other chapters explore two controversial issues – health worker migration in low-income countries that are short of health personnel; and the political struggle over sexual and reproductive rights, including analysis of how health care is connected to broader debates about poverty, politics and gender injustice.

Part C tackles the needs of two particular groups of people whose rights to health are frequently violated – Indigenous peoples and people with disabilities. These chapters describe their struggles for rights and outline what is needed to strengthen their claims on health and health care over the coming years.

Part D returns to the broader picture of health. The Primary Health Care Approach emphasized intersectoral action in health, recognizing that the determinants of health often lie outside the health care sector. Five chapters on education, war, environment, water and food security reveal the widespread threats to health in a diverse range of areas and circumstances, but also point to the potential for synergistic actions by governments and civil society actors that could improve livelihoods in several dimensions.

Part E scrutinizes the conduct of global institutions such as WHO, UNICEF

7

and the World Bank, and assesses the international actions of richer nations and big business. The analysis points to the need to redress imbalances of power at the international level; for richer nations to fulfil their promises on resource transfers to the developing world; for tighter regulation of powerful multinationals; and for better management of international institutions.

Part F concludes the *Global Health Watch* by drawing all the chapters together and making some general recommendations and possibilities for concerted action by civil society organizations.

What readers of the Watch can do

A central aim of the *Watch* is to strengthen existing campaigns and social movements by providing an alterative analysis of global health. The report also includes a number of demands that we make of governments, UN agencies and other actors. We hope that health professional associations and networks will become a more prominent voice in existing campaigns and movements to achieve a healthier and fairer world.

We encourage you to spread the word about the *Watch* widely. It is freely available on the web and on CD from the three co-ordinating organizations: People's Health Movement, the Global Equity Gauge Alliance and Medact. To comment on anything in this volume or make suggestions for the next *Global Health Watch* in 2007–8, please contact any of the co-ordinating organizations at ghw@hst.org.za.

Further information

People's Health Movement (www.phmovement.org)
Global Equity Gauge Alliance (www.gega.org.za)
Medact (www.medact.org)

References

Chen S and Ravallion M (2004). How have the world's poorest fared since the early 1980s? *World Bank Research Observer*, 19: 141–69 (http://wbro.oupjounals.org/cgi/content/abstract/19/2/141, accessed 12 May 2005).

Navarro V (2004). The World Health Situation. *International Journal of Health Services*, 34;1: 1-10.

Pogge T (2002). *World Poverty and Human Rights*. Cambridge, Polity Press.

Reddy S and Pogge T (2006). How not to count the poor. In: Anand S and Stiglitz J (eds.), *Measuring Global Poverty*. Oxford, OUP.

Unicef (1998). *The State of the World's Children 1998*. New York, Unicef.

UNDP (1998). *Human Development Report 1998*. Oxford, OUP.

UNDP (1999). *Human Development Report 1999*. Oxford, OUP.

PART A | Health and globalization

The processes of economic globalization are shaping people's health across the world – and not for the better. This first section of the *Global Health Watch* paints a negative picture of the impacts. The number of people in poverty has been increasing in some parts of the world, as has inequality between richer and poorer both within and between countries. The liberalization of international trade and investment has created unrestrained market forces that have enabled a few people to gain significant wealth but that have deepened immiseration and insecurity for the majority.

The current form of economic globalization did not come about by accident or 'naturally'. It has been influenced by and still relies upon a wide range of decisions and policies of national governments and international organizations that have acted largely in private interests rather than public ones. Part A therefore highlights how reforms of the global financial and trading systems are urgently needed to improve people's well-being – and even to keep economies going in future. For some countries, the existing set of international trade rules and practices has sucked them ever deeper into a poverty trap so that they have to export more and more raw materials at lower and lower prices, and thus gain little in the way of sustainable development. Despite the rhetoric of globalization, entrance to several markets in high-income countries is still largely restricted for many developing countries – the governments of the developed world may preach trade liberalization, but they tend to impose it on poorer countries while being very reluctant to lower their own trade barriers to outside competition.

The institutions of global governance – particularly the World Trade Organization – and their member countries need to recognize these imbalances of power and reform accordingly to create a genuine level playing field in international trade. Part A also shows that increasing transfers of resources from richer to poorer nations are a vital component of a globalization that works for the health of all.

A1 | Health for all in the 'borderless world'?

'The current path of globalization must change. Too few share in its benefits. Too many have no voice in its design and no influence in its course' – World Commission on the Social Dimensions of Globalization, 2004

In rural China, high school student Zheng Qingming kills himself by jumping in front of a train. Friends say it was because he could not afford the last US$ 80 of school fees, which meant he could not take the college admission test. The overall annual tuition is more than the average village family in his region earns in a year. Health care, like education, has become scarce and expensive since China embraced the market economy, and his grandfather had already spent the family savings on treating a lung disease.

In Zambia, Chileshe waits painfully to die from AIDS. The global funds and antiretroviral programmes are too little and too late for her. She was infected by her now dead husband, who once worked in a textile plant along with thousands of others but lost his job when Zambia opened its borders to cheap, second-hand clothing. He moved to the city as a street vendor, selling cast-offs or donations from wealthier countries. He would get drunk and pay for sex – often with women whose own husbands were somewhere else working, or dead, and desperately needed money for their children. Desperation, she thought, is what makes this disease move so swiftly; she recalls that a woman from the former Zaire passing through her village once said that the true meaning of SIDA, the French acronym for AIDS, was 'Salaire Insuffisant Depuis des Années' – too little money for too many years (Schoepf 1998).

In northern Mexico, a young girl named Antonia is suffering from severe asthma. She is falling far behind in school. Her parents do not have enough money to pay for specialists or medicines, and wonder whether her problems are connected to the industrial haze and foul-smelling water that come from the nearby factory. They cannot afford to move. All their savings were used up when corn prices plunged after the market opened to exports from the US, and it is not clear how they would make a living. How could so much corn grow so cheaply, her father Miguel used to wonder.

In a Canadian suburb two people die when a delivery van swerves into oncoming traffic and slams into their car. The van driver, Tom, survives. He either fell asleep at the wheel or suffered a mild heart attack. No one knows, and he cannot remember. It was his 15th day of work without a rest. When the assembly plant where he once worked relocated to Mexico, driving the van became one of his three part-time jobs, at just over minimum wage and with no benefits. He alternated afternoon shifts at two fast food outlets, did early night shifts at a gas station and drove the van late nights as often as the company needed him. With the recession over, they had needed him a lot lately.

Introduction

These vignettes show how recent, rapid changes in our global economy can imperil the health of millions. The first describes a real event (Kahn & Yardley 2004). The other three are composites, like those used in the *World Development Report 1995* (World Bank 1995), but in this case based on evidence that the remarkable accumulation of wealth associated with transnational economic integration ('globalization') has deepened the division between the rich and the rest.

Winners from globalization, in high- and low-income countries alike, comprise a global elite that sociologist Zygmunt Bauman (1998) calls 'tourists'. They have the money and status to 'move through the world' motivated only by their dreams and desires. 'Vagabonds', on the other hand, are those less privileged hundreds of millions: North Africans crossing the Mediterranean, Chinese hiding in Canadian-bound cargo ships, and more than a million Mexicans each year who try unsuccessfully to enter the US illegally. National borders are increasingly closed to them. Not all of globalization's losers become vagabonds, but their numbers may continue to rise as losers outnumber winners, because of how winners have set the global rules. The rules and institutions of globalization are 'unfair to poor countries, both in the ways they were drawn up and in their impact' (World Commission on the Social Dimensions of Globalization (WCSDG) 2004).

The causal pathways that link globalization with the illness or injury of particular individuals are often non-linear, involving multiple intervening variables and feedback loops. Individual circumstances and opportunities are still shaped by the policy decisions of national and local governments. For example, HIV prevalence rates during the 1990s fell in Uganda, but rose in South Africa: Uganda's early, active governmental response, including willingness to support and work with civil society organizations, contrasted with South African political leaders' reluctance to place HIV prevention and treatment high on the national agenda.

National policies still matter. But globalization may limit the ability of national and subnational governments to make policy choices that would

1 Medicine cannot deal with the many factors that cause ill-health.

lead to improvements in health, such as redistributing wealth, either directly or through public provision and financing of goods and services, and regulating the operation of markets and for-profit enterprises. The more steps in the pathway from globalization to the health of any particular individual, group or community, the more difficult it becomes to describe the web of causation. In order to address these difficulties we first describe globalization and extract a few health lessons from its history.

Globalization past and present

Globalization is best described as 'a process of greater integration within the world economy through movements of goods and services, capital, technology and (to a lesser extent) labour, which lead increasingly to economic decisions being influenced by global conditions' (Jenkins 2004). The focus of this chapter is on trade liberalization (increasing the cross-border flow of goods) and deregulation of national and international financial markets (facilitating rapid transnational movements of capital).

Historically, the transnational movement of people has been a crucial element of globalization, and to some extent remains so. Over 175 million people lived outside their country of birth in 2000. Remittances of foreign-born workers to their low- or middle-income countries of origin – some US$ 80 billion in 2002, more than double the amount in 1990 – have become an important source of foreign currency for many countries (Kapur and McHale 2003). Nevertheless, large-scale migration remains 'the missing flow in today's globalization' (Dollar 2002), mainly because of policy changes in one dominant nation, the US, 'which has switched from a protectionist welcoming immigrants to a free trader restricting their entrance' (Williamson 2002).

Globalization is not new. The history of humankind has been one of pushing against borders, exploring, expanding, trading, conquering and assimilating (Diamond 1997). By the 16th century the geographic and resource endowments of Europe, combined with new sailing and navigation technologies, ushered in the first truly global era of colonization and trade. Globalization came to a temporary halt in the early 20th century, with two world wars and the Great Depression. The ensuing devastation spurred the creation of new international organizations to promote reconstruction and development, in an effort to avoid the economic shocks that partly underpinned both wars. The UN would provide political oversight to global peace and development. The IMF would maintain global economic stability by helping countries with balance of payments problems. The World Bank would provide concessional (low interest) loans or grants for postwar reconstruction and, later, for global development. The General Agreement on Tariffs and Trade (GATT) would be a venue for negotiating the removal of protectionist barriers to international trade.

Globalization was back on track, even if its new rules and institutions represented the interests of the world's dominant, victorious nations, and even if international trade as a percentage of global economic output did not reach levels characteristic of the late 19th and early 20th centuries until the 1990s (Cameron and Stein 2000). The collapse of the USSR and the fall of the Berlin Wall, marking the end of an ideological counterweight to capitalism, arguably accelerated the pace of global market integration and certainly enhanced its legitimacy.

International trade in goods is only one dimension of globalization. Several other trends reveal how and why today's globalization differs from earlier eras.

The scale of international private financial flows resulting from capital market liberalization. Aided by technologies that allow round-the-clock global trade and new forms of finance capital such as hedge funds and derivatives, currency transactions worth US\$ 1.5–2 trillion occur daily. Much of this is speculative portfolio money chasing short-term changes in currency valuations, rather than foreign direct investment that may go into new productive capacity. The scale

14

of these transactions dwarfs the total foreign exchange reserves of all governments, reducing their ability to intervene in foreign exchange markets to stabilize their currencies, manage their economies and maintain fiscal autonomy (UNDP 1999). Each country experiencing a 'currency crisis' has seen increased poverty and inequality and decreased health and social spending, with women and children bearing the burden disproportionately (Gyebi et al. 2002).

The establishment of binding rules, primarily through the World Trade Organization. WTO (the successor to GATT) and other regional or bilateral trade agreements such as the North American Free Trade Agreement (NAFTA) have established enforceable supranational obligations on states, and have expanded to include services, investment and government purchases.

Countries have also entered into multilateral covenants and treaties on human rights and environmental protection. Notably, the 1948 Universal Declaration on Human Rights purportedly protects individuals and groups against state repression or discrimination, while obliging states to take 'progressive measures, national and international, to secure... universal and effective recognition and observance' of a package of rights including 'a standard of living adequate for the health and well-being of [oneself] and of his family, including food, clothing, housing and medical care and necessary social services, and the right to security in the event of unemployment, sickness, disability, widowhood, old age or other lack of livelihood in circumstances beyond his control' (Article 25). The 1966 International Covenants on Civil and Political Rights and on Economic, Social and Cultural Rights expanded these goals. Even though the latter are treaties and therefore binding on signatory countries that have ratified them (in the case of Economic, Social and Cultural Rights, conspicuously not including the US), they are unlike trade agreements in that no economic interests drive their enforcement through the limited mechanisms that are available.

Reorganization of production across national borders. This third trend is one of the most significant characteristics of the contemporary global political economy. Multinational enterprises (MNEs), several of which are economically larger than many nations or whole regions, are central to it (Anderson and Cavanagh 2000). At least a third of global trade is intra-firm trade between affiliated companies (WCSDG 2004), in which an MNE subsidiary in one country sells parts or products to a subsidiary in another country (Reinicke 1998). MNEs can now locate labour-intensive operations in low-wage countries (often in exclusive export processing zones); carry out research and development in countries with high levels of publicly funded education and investment in research; and declare most of their profits in low-tax countries. The result

15

is global tax competition and lower corporate tax revenues in all countries (Wade 2003).

These changes did not 'just happen', but required policy decisions by governments around the world from which the most affected citizens were often excluded. The breadth and depth of that exclusion generated a global social movement during the 1990s that was, if not actively hostile to globalization, at least profoundly sceptical about the claims of its cheerleaders. Protests during meetings of the WTO, the G8 countries, the World Bank and IMF and the World Economic Forum aroused considerable media attention. The quality of the campaigns' research and advocacy have compelled grudging acceptance of their legitimacy.

Health concerns have been slower to enter the globalization debate than environmental, social or economic issues (Deaton 2004), although the relation between health and globalization is far from new. Disease and pestilence have long followed trade routes from one part of the world to another. The economic costs associated with the 2003 outbreak of Severe Acute Respiratory Syndrome (SARS) alerted many high-income countries to the value of global infection control. But the increased spread of communicable diseases or unhealthy consumption by trade vector is only a small part of the globalization/health relationship. Of far more importance is how globalization affects such health determinants as poverty and inequality, and here we confront the dominant story of globalization's health benefits.

Globalization – a success story?

China, India and a handful of east Asian countries are often used to support a view of globalization which argues that sustained economic growth leads to higher standards of living and better health for all. China is increasingly cited as a model because it has experienced phenomenal economic growth since introducing selective internal economic reforms and beginning aggressive pursuit of export markets and foreign direct investment. Understanding the source of that growth and the reason China may rival the US as the world's largest economy within 20 years (Ramo 2004) is as easy as looking at the labels on merchandise at Wal-Mart, the giant US chain of department stores.

The story starts from the premise that increased trade and foreign investment improve economic growth, which increases wealth and reduces poverty, leading to improved health; greater wealth can sustain investment in public provision of such services as health care, education and water/sanitation; and improved education and population health accelerate economic growth, so the circle is completed. But much is left out of the story.

16

2 'I became sick because of my poverty.' 'Well, I became poor because of my sickness.' The two-way relationship between poverty and ill-health affects billions.

Consider, first, the impact of globalization on poverty, one of the most powerful predictors of poor health. It is claimed that globalization has reduced the number of people living in abject poverty (defined by the World Bank as living on less than a dollar a day) by 200 million since 1980 (Dollar 2002). This still leaves 1.2 billion people living on less than a dollar a day, and 2.8 billion, almost half the world's population, on less than two dollars a day (Chen and Ravallion 2004). Critics point to flaws in how the Bank measures poverty (Wade 2002), and raise questions about the validity of the purchasing power parity estimates used to measure cost of living differentials between countries (Reddy and Pogge 2003); use of questionable historical data (Wade 2004); the irrelevance of the dollar a day threshold to the realities of life in the developing world's fast-growing cities (Satterthwaite 2003); and lack of reliable data from China and India where almost all the poverty reduction has taken place (Wade 2002). All these factors mean that official figures on the extent of world poverty are likely to be under-estimates (Reddy and Pogge 2003). In India, for example, new research is finding that poverty and rural hunger probably increased during the 1990s (Patnaik 2004).

Even if recent growth in China and India has reduced the number of their

17

people living in extreme poverty, poverty increased in many regions including Sub-Saharan Africa, eastern Europe, central Asia and, until the early 1990s, Latin America. On the one or two dollars a day measure, the number living in poverty in Sub-Saharan Africa roughly doubled between 1981 and 2001 (Chen and Ravallion 2004). Modest economic growth in Latin America in 1990–7 cut poverty rates by 5%, but the Asian-precipitated recession in the late 1990s caused them to rise again, with almost 44% of the Latin American population living below official poverty lines in 2002 (UN-Habitat 2003a).

Why? Enthusiasts of globalization argue that countries that open themselves to the global economy grow, while those that retain outdated forms of protectionism languish (Dollar 2001). But reality is more complicated, in at least two respects.

First, those countries held up as model high-performing globalizers (China, India, Malaysia, Thailand and Vietnam) actually started out as more closed economies than the countries whose economies stalled or declined, mostly in Africa and Latin America (Dollar 2002). The sleight-of-hand lies in definition. David Dollar's globalizers are countries that saw their trade/GDP ratio increase since 1977; his non-globalizers are simply those that saw their ratio drop. But his non-globalizers were already twice as integrated into the world economy in 1977, a degree of integration his supposed globalizers did not reach until the late 1990s. There is, in fact, a long and contentious debate among development economists over the impacts of liberalization on growth and poverty reduction, much of it directly challenging Dollar's conclusions on theoretical, methodological and empirical grounds (e.g. Rodrik 2001, Rodriguez and Rodrik 2000). The problem for the non-performers was not their retreat from globalization, but their high dependence on natural resources and primary commodities (Milanovic 2003).

Second, the performing globalizers, notably China and India, experienced much of their poverty-reducing growth *before* they began to reduce their import tariffs and open themselves to foreign investment (Wade 2002). Like Japan, South Korea and Taiwan before them, China and India grew behind walls of import protection for their domestic producers, strict controls over banking and investment, and (at least in the case of China) direct and indirect subsidies for exporters. They liberalized trade only as they became richer. This was precisely how European and North American countries grew their wealth a century earlier (Chang 2002). New trade rules that deny low- and middle-income countries the opportunity to do the same today are kicking away the ladder.

So two key elements of the mainstream story – that liberalization reduces poverty and promotes growth – are shaky at best, and wrong as global generalizations. What, then, of the third, that globalization has no health-damaging effect on income inequalities? Health researchers dispute whether, or how, income inequalities that do not involve absolute poverty affect population health. Poverty, which is higher in countries with high levels of income inequality, may be the bigger problem whether poverty is defined in absolute or relative terms. But greater inequality of income or wealth makes it harder for economic growth to lift people out of poverty. Moreover, income inequalities continue to be associated with declines in social cohesion, public support for redistributive social policies (Deaton 2001, Gough 2001), and political engagement (Solt 2004), as well as with higher rates of infant mortality, homicide, suicide and generalized conflict (Deaton 2001).

This returns us to the story of the Chinese student who killed himself and its relationship to these trends. The key link is China's domestic market reforms, which while credited with rapid growth have also drastically increased economic inequalities. China's Gini coefficient (a standard measure of income inequality) was a low 29 in 1981 but reached 41 in 1995, similar to the US (Chen and Wang 2001). The rural-urban divide is increasing, regional disparities are widening and access to opportunities is becoming less equal: during the 1990s, only the incomes of the richest quintile of the population grew faster than the national average – again remarkably similar to the US (Chen and Wang 2001). Similar trends exist in India, Vietnam, Brazil and other countries experiencing rapid liberalization, rapid growth or both (although such inequalities often existed earlier, as legacies of colonialism). And in all these countries inequalities may be rising even in 'rich' regions, as they are in many industrialized countries (Cornia et al. 2004).

Many population health indicators, such as mortality of infants and children under five, actually improved over the past decade in countries where inequalities increased (China, Vietnam and India); however, immunization rates for one-year-olds saw significant worsening in all three countries (Social Watch 2004). But aggregate data hide important changes in intranational, interregional and other inter-group inequalities. Thus urban-rural and gender-related health inequalities in China increased (Akin et al. 2004, Liu et al. 2001), partly because market reforms not only increased economic inequality but also led to the collapse of employment- and community-based health insurance.

The government share of health expenditures fell by over half between 1980 and 1998, almost trebling the portion paid by families (Liu et al. 2003). This led to the growth of private delivery systems for those who could afford them, and increased cost-recovery schemes for services that were still under some form of public health insurance. The result was two-fold. There was a surge in the number of people who fell into poverty by exhausting their income and savings to pay for medical treatment – Qingming's grandfather was just one of 27 million rural Chinese in 1998 to whom this happened (Liu et al. 2003). There was also a dramatic slowdown in China's population health improvements (Deaton 2004), particularly infant mortality and life expectancy (Akin et al. 2004).

Similar trends are found in India, where rural poverty has deepened in many states. Women in the poorer states have shorter life expectancies and lower literacy rates (Abbasi 1999). Government expenditure on health care accounted for just 18% of health care spending, with the rest financed by users – making it one of the world's most privatized health care systems (WHO 2004). Predictably, the quality of public health services is low and deteriorating: the infant mortality rate for the poorest fifth of the population is 2.5 times higher than the richest fifth, and poorer children are almost four times as likely to die in childhood (International Institute for Population Sciences & ORC Macro 2004).

What if Qingming had completed his education and found employment in one of the many export processing zones (EPZs) to which 10–20 million rural

---

Box A1 Women and export processing zones

Had Qingming found work in an export processing zone (EPZ), his sex would have placed him in the minority. EPZ employers favour young, often single women, particularly in textile, garment manufacturing and electronics assembly: their fingers are thought to be more nimble than men's, and they receive only 50–80% of the wages paid to men (ICFTU 2003). Eighty per cent of China's EPZ employees are women (Durano 2002); the global average is 70–90% (Athreya 2003). EPZ employment for women is credited with increasing gender empowerment by providing them with income. This may sometimes be true, but women's earnings are often channelled back to the control of male family members, and many women's domestic responsibilities remain unchanged, creating a double burden of work (Durano 2002). To reduce costs, EPZs frequently employ women on part-time, casual or subcontracting arrangements that involve working at home. This gives women flexibility between their domestic and paid duties, but denies them the social protections that might come with regular forms of employment (Durano 2002).

Because they are located in countries with a large supply of cheap labour, EPZs rarely improve wage conditions for either women or men

---

20

Chinese migrate each year (AFL-CIO 2004)? EPZs have proliferated throughout the developing world in the past 20 years, with the free trade, foreign investment and export-driven ethos of the modern economy transforming them into 'vehicles of globalization' (ILO 1998). Between 40 million and 50 million workers were employed in some 5000 EPZs in 2004, 75% of them in China alone (Howard 2004; ILO 2004a). This migration to urban areas creates new health crises: public resources are rarely sufficient to provide essential housing, water, sanitation or energy. Indeed, the elements of globalization described here (the market reforms of liberalization, privatization and deregulation) are largely blamed for the worldwide growth of slums and the lack of public resources to cope with them (UN-Habitat 2003b). This UN report also finds that the rising wealth of globalization's winners creates inflationary pressure on most goods and services, particularly on land and housing, which only worsens conditions for the losers.

Qingming would also have been exposed to the hazardous working conditions associated with most EPZs. Some countries extend national labour laws

(ICFTU 2003). Workers are plentiful so there is little incentive for enterprises to train and retain their staff. Technology transfer, one of the key means by which low- and middle-income countries can improve their domestic economic efficiency and performance, is rare. Liberalization of financial markets means that little of the foreign currency that enters the EPZs stays in the host country. To attract foreign investment in EPZs, countries often offer extensive tax holidays (ILO 1998). By definition, these zones do not levy tariffs on imported materials, further limiting the tax benefits a country might receive for redistribution as health, education and other development investments. In many instances few locally produced goods are used in the EPZs. In 30 years of *maquiladoras* (as EPZs are called in Mexico), only 2% of the raw goods processed came from within the country (ILO 1998). Apart from the jobs created, and now departing to China, the EPZs have had virtually no impact on Mexico's overall economic development. They may help countries develop their internal economies, but only if there are strong 'backward and forward linkages' – requirements that companies in EPZs purchase raw materials from, and transfer new technologies to, the host country through partnerships with local firms outside the special zones (Wade 2002)

Health for all in a 'borderless world'?

and protections to them, but exceptions, violations and union-free policies are commonplace (ILO 1998). Hours are frequently long, the work is generally repetitive and arduous, and even minimal social safety nets are lacking. This leads to pervasive stress and fatigue (ILO 1998). Practices such as locking in workers have led to numerous deaths and injuries (ICFTU 2003). Hours of work and wages in China's EPZs are effectively unregulated; many people work 12–18-hour days, seven days a week, for months at a time. 'Death by overworking' – *guolaosi* – has become a common term in China. Workplace accidents reportedly killed 140,000 workers in 2003, or one in every 250 workers (AFL-CIO 2004).

China led the world in the amount of foreign investment it received in 2002, second only to the US in 2003 (*China Daily* 2004). It is more profitable to produce many kinds of goods in the world's largest supplier of cheap, non-unionized labour than almost anywhere else. Employment in Mexico's EPZs dropped from 1.3 million in 2000 to 1 million in 2002 as production shifted to China (AFL-CIO 2004).

Greater equality, employment security and safe working conditions – all essential to sustained population health – will perhaps in time return to China and to other rapidly liberalizing countries. But how long are those whose health is negatively affected by globalization expected to wait?

AIDS and poverty

As noted earlier, causal pathways that link globalization with the illness of individuals are not linear or straightforward. However, it is plausible to link Chileshe's HIV infection to the triumph of free markets in Zambia, actively promoted by international agencies dominated by high-income countries. In 1992, as part of a structural adjustment programme attached to loans from the IMF, Zambia opened its borders to imports including cheap, second-hand clothing. Its domestic, state-run clothing manufacturers, inefficient in both technology and management by wealthier nation standards, produced more expensive and lower quality goods. They could not compete, especially when the importers had the advantage of no production costs and no import duties. Within eight years, 132 of 140 clothing and textile mills closed and 30,000 jobs disappeared, which the World Bank acknowledged as 'unintended and regrettable consequences' of the adjustment process (Jeter 2002). Many of the second-hand clothes that flooded Zambia and other African countries ironically began as donations to charities in Europe, the US and Canada. Surpluses not needed for their own poor were sold to wholesalers who exported them in bulk to Africa, earning up to 300% or more on their costs (Jeter 2002).

The scale of this exchange is significant. Sales to sub-Saharan Africa from the US are worth about US$ 60 million annually (Jeter 2002); in 2001, Canadian exports of *salaula* ('rummaging through the pile', as used clothing is called in Zambia) were worth US$ 25 million (Industry Canada 2002).

For conventional economists, this is a textbook example of how and why trade liberalization works: consumers get better and cheaper goods, and ineffi-cient producers are driven out of business. However Chileshe and her husband paid a heavy price, one that cascaded throughout other sectors of Zambia's limited manufacturing base, with some 40% of manufacturing jobs disappear-ing during the 1990s (Jeter 2002). Large numbers of previously employed Zam-bian workers came to rely on the informal, ill-paid and untaxed underground

---

Box A2 *What is structural adjustment?*

The World Bank initiated structural adjustment loans in 1980 to help de-veloping countries respond to the impact of the 1979–1980 recession on their ability to service external debt. The Mexican debt crisis of 1982, the first of many around the world, saw the IMF and World Bank change into 'watchdogs for developing countries, to keep them on a policy track that would help them repay most of their debts and to open their markets for international investors' (Junne 2001). The mechanism of this trans-formation was the provision of new loans to help with debt rescheduling, provided countries agreed to a package of macroeconomic policies that included the following:

- reduced subsidies for basic items of consumption;
- trade and investment liberalization;
- reductions in state expenditures, particularly on social programmes such as health, education, water/sanitation and housing;
- rapid privatization of state-owned enterprises.

It is sometimes argued that structural adjustment failed because coun-tries failed to implement it fully, and their economies were so crisis-ridden when adjustment was imposed that deterioration might have been worse without it. Many economists and historians disagree. Many previously buoyant African countries began to slide into stagnation after adopting structural adjustment (UN-Habitat 2003b). Over half the countries under-taking structural adjustment underperformed relative to expectations (IMF 2004).

economy. The privatization of state enterprises eliminated a further source of revenues that might have been used to support social programmes such as education and health care.

Other causes for the public revenue decline included a continuous slide in world prices for copper, Zambia's main export; Japan's 1990s recession (it was Zambia's main importer of copper); high debt service costs; declining development assistance; and capital flight (WTO 1996, Lindsey 2002). Faced with public revenue declines and a donor preoccupation with 'cost recovery', Zambia began to impose user charges for schools and health services in the 1990s. Not surprisingly, this was followed by a rapid rise in school dropout and illiteracy rates, projected to double by 2015 (UN-Habitat 2003b), and costs became the main reason people failed to seek health care or did not follow up medical treatment (Atkinson et al. 1999).

The Zambian government is now seeking to undo many of these policies, to reimpose tariffs on *salaula*, and to reorient its development inwards. 'In a sense,' two officials recently wrote, 'Zambia is now a victim of its own honest policies. Trade in goods and services is now one of the mainstays of the economy, to the detriment of more productive activities and thereby employment opportunities' (Mtonga and Chikoti 2002). Or, as one of the Zambians interviewed by Jeter (2002) commented, 'The young people really love the [*salaula*] clothes they see ... but is this the way to develop your economy?'

Globalization played an important part in Chileshe's HIV infection. The web of connection between globalization and the HIV pandemic in Africa has many strands. Two of these include the debt crisis and the donors' response, particularly by the wealthy G7 countries (Canada, Germany, Italy, Japan, the UK and the USA).

Debt and aid

The long-standing debt crisis is a major factor in the inability of low-income countries to sustain or benefit from economic growth (UNCTAD 1999), or to invest in health-sustaining infrastructures. Worldwide, the amount of money returned to high-income countries dwarfs the amount received in development assistance: donor countries receive back many times over in debt repayments what they give in aid. Journalist Ken Wiwa, son of Ken Saro-Wiwa, the activist hanged for opposing Shell Oil's destruction of Nigerian homelands, noted: 'You'd need the mathematical dexterity of a forensic accountant to explain why Nigeria borrowed $5 billion, paid back $16 billion, and still owes $32 billion' (Wiwa 2004). The specific causes of debt crises vary from country to country and over time but the major contributors are as follows:

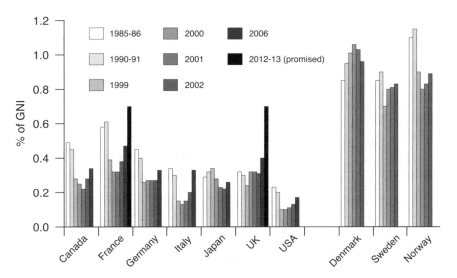

Figure A1 Trends in G7 development assistance, with selected comparison countries (*Source*: OECD 2004a, Chirac 2003, MacAskill 2004)

- The oil price shocks of 1973 and 1979–1980. All countries were affected, but low-income countries in particular had to borrow to pay the costs of suddenly expensive imported oil.
- Profligate lending by banks stuffed with new petrodollars, with few checks on the viability of the loans, or whether the money would simply disappear into the offshore bank accounts of corrupt political leaders.
- The rapid increase in inflation-adjusted interest rates during the early 1980s, resulting from US monetarist policies. Poor, indebted countries

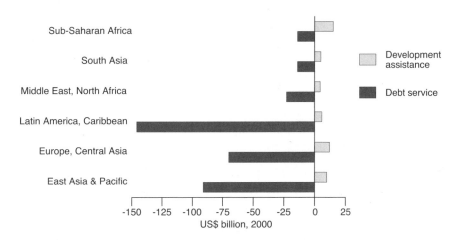

Figure A2 How debt servicing dwarfs debt assistance (*Source*: Pettifor and Greenhill 2002)

Health for all in a 'borderless world'?

Box A3 Debt, corruption and the cost of doing business

Transfers of resources to developing countries, as debt relief or direct grants, are increasingly accompanied by requirements that recipient countries demonstrate 'good governance', notably by reducing corruption. Superficially the logic of such requirements is unassailable. Transparency International, perhaps the most influential actor in civil society with regard to anti-corruption efforts (Serafini 2004), estimates that ten of the most notoriously corrupt leaders of the past 20 years, led by Indonesia's Suharto, the Philippines' Marcos and Zaire's Mobutu, embezzled US$ 29–58 billion from some of the poorest countries in the world (Hodess 2004).

The irony of such conditions, however, lies in the routine involvement of Western businesses in a range of corrupt practices. Western businesses in 1999 are said to have paid over US$ 80 billion in bribes to officials in low- and middle-income countries to gain market access (often for weapons purchases) and regulatory relaxation (often in the mining, logging and oil sectors). Such bribes inflate the costs of projects, and may increase the debts of low- and middle-income countries by creating an incentive for leaders to borrow for financially unsustainable but personally lucrative projects (Hawley 2000).

Multilateral initiatives to control corruption include an OECD Convention on Combating Bribery (which came into force in 1999) and the 2003 UN Convention Against Corruption. It potentially represents a major advance not only because of its provisions requiring domestic criminalization of various forms of corruption, but also because it specifically addresses the crucial issue of recovery of illegally obtained assets. However, although 113 countries had signed the convention by 2004, it had been ratified by only 13 and 30 ratifications are needed before it comes into force, even with respect to those countries that have ratified it.

Whatever multilateral agreements may be in place, implementation depends on legislation and enforcement at national and sometimes subnational level. Given the asymmetry of power relations in the world economy, it is especially important that industrialized countries both regulate the behaviour of firms under their legal jurisdiction, imposing sanctions that are meaningful when compared with the potential gains from engaging in corruption, and act aggressively to prevent financial institutions from handling proceeds from corruption.

had to borrow more just to keep up with suddenly very high interest payments.

- Falling world prices for the primary commodities that are the key exports (and foreign exchange earners) of many developing economies.
- Capital flight, which involved both theft by political leaders and legal choices by foreign investors and domestic economic elites to shift their assets abroad in order to avoid taxation and the prospect of currency devaluations (Ndikumana and Boyce 2003, Williamson 2004).

The health-damaging effect of debt service obligations, and the structural adjustment conditionalities attached to lending designed primarily around creditors' interests (also discussed in part E, chapters 3 and 6) were well known as early as 1987 (Cornia et al. 1987). Not until 1996, after much lobbying by international NGOs, did high-income countries respond collectively with the World Bank/IMF Heavily Indebted Poor Countries (HIPC) initiative. Almost

---

Box A4 The international finance facility – sound investment or living off the future?

The International Finance Facility (IFF) promoted by the UK is a special case of development financing. It proposes to transform the Monterrey (and subsequent) donor pledges for increased development assistance into bonds, repayable by the donor countries after 2015. The effect of issuing such bonds would be to double the amount of financing available for development within a few years. Coupled with debt cancellation it would bring international development financing closer to the estimates of the amount needed by low- and middle-income countries to meet their MDG targets.

The IFF proposal was first raised at the 2003 Evian summit as one of several possible financing instruments. Economic analyses conclude that this sudden increase in development assistance is not beyond the absorptive capacity of recipient countries (Mavrotas 2003). Almost 40 countries and numerous development agencies and NGOs support the proposal, which has been less warmly received by donor nations (Lister et al. 2004).

Chief among the many concerns is the possibility that repayments by donor countries could compromise the objective of meeting or sustaining aid levels at 0.7% of GNI after 2015. Such concerns do not negate the potential usefulness of the IFF, but they must be addressed if the proposal is to be meaningful as a contribution to improving global health equity.

half the HIPC countries' debt may remain unpaid and uncancelled at the conclusion of the initiative (Martin 2004). Despite recent promises of greater debt relief over the next 5 to 10 years, adequate debt cancellation for the world's poorest countries is still not on the global political agenda. Moreover, gains for poor countries in debt relief have come, in part, at the expense of declining amounts of other forms of development assistance (Killick 2004).

Development assistance is not a panacea. Aid has often served the political, strategic or commercial interests of donor nations, particularly in Africa (White and Killick 2001). Throughout the developing world, aid is often tied to the purchase of goods and services (in the form of technical cooperation) from donor countries, and similar criticisms are made of debt relief priorities. It has also financed large-scale, environmentally destructive projects with limited relevance to basic needs (Bosshard et al. 2003), or been stolen by corrupt officials (Vasagar 2004).

Some of these limitations are slowly being removed through commitments to untie aid and provide more aid as sector-wide budget support to government departments. At the same time, aid is increasingly accompanied by conditionalities that parallel those associated with debt relief. The 2003 US commitment to increase its annual aid spending to US$ 15 billion by 2006, by way of its Millennium Challenge Account, makes new funds conditional on 'sound economic policies that foster enterprise and entrepreneurship, including more open markets and sustainable budget policies' (UN Secretary-General 2002) – in other words, greater market and investment opportunities for US-based firms.

At least US$ 16.5 billion a year in new development assistance would be needed to ensure that highly-indebted poor countries could meet the basic needs of their people, even if their entire external debt were cancelled (Pettifor and Greenhill 2002). Many African countries will require aid contributions equal to 20–23% of their GDP over 2004–2015 if they are to finance achievement of the Millennium Development Goals and Targets (Sachs et al. 2004). Yet the value of aid as a percentage of most industrialized countries' GNP or GNI has been declining since the mid-1980s; only in the past two years has development assistance again begun to rise.

Trade and tortillas

So far we have examined the dominant story that globalization → growth → wealth → health, and found it wanting. We have argued that the collapse of African economies and health systems is partly explained by the fact that countries opened their economies to global competition without adequate ways to handle the consequent social and economic dislocations, and in some cases facing active hostility from international lending agencies to using existing resources and policy instruments. Antonia's story brings the issue of global trade rules as potential health threats into sharper focus.

It begins a century ago with Mexican land reforms that created subsistence and smallholding production plots. These plots were big enough to feed a family and earn some capital by selling to local markets, but did not provide (and were never intended to provide) economies of scale comparable to those of modern corporate farming practices. In the run-up to the North American Free Trade Agreement (NAFTA), the Mexican government ended its subsidies to 'small-scale producers of basic crops' including corn (Preibisch et al. 2002), the main ingredient of tortillas, Mexico's staple food. When NAFTA opened the Mexico-US border, corn from the US flooded the Mexican market. Large-scale agribusiness is massively subsidized in the US: in 2001, corn cost US\$ 3.41 a barrel to produce in the US, but sold on the world market for \$2.28 (Carlsen 2003). Currency crises and IMF conditional loans also played a role in the rapid decline of Mexico's corn prices. Following the collapse of the peso in 1995, the bail-out organized by the Clinton administration included a US\$ 1 billion export credit that obliged Mexico to purchase US corn. Predictably, Mexican imports of US corn to Mexico rose by 120% in a year (Carlsen 2003).

Mexican corn production stagnated while prices declined. Small farmers were hardest hit, becoming much poorer than they were in the early 1990s (Condesa Consulting Group 2004), despite efforts by the Mexican government to reintroduce some of the subsidies (ICTSD 2002). Some 700,000 agricultural jobs disappeared over the same period. The lack of demand for farm labour depressed wages by 2001 to less than half of what they were 20 years earlier. Rural poverty rates rose to over 70%; the minimum wage lost over 75% of its purchasing power; infant mortality rates of the poor increased; and wage inequalities became the worst in Latin America (Lichfield 2000, Schwartz 2002). Between 1984, when Mexico's 1982 debt crisis led to one of the first and most wrenching programmes of lender-driven economic adjustment, and 2000, the share of national income flowing to the poorest decile of the population fell from 1.7% to 1.5%, while the share of the richest decile increased from 33% to 39% (Schwartz 2002).

Adding insult to injury, as corn prices fell the price of commercially marketed tortillas almost tripled, because just two companies produce nearly all the corn products in Mexico. The Mexican government, apparently to ensure a cheap corn supply for these two companies, chose not to avail itself of NAFTA-approved regulations that would have severely limited the quantity of US corn crossing the border. Nor did it collect taxes on US corn imports amounting to over US$ 2 billion since 1994 (Henriques and Patel 2004).

Returning to Antonia, her asthma is unlikely to be treated effectively because Mexico's fragmented health care sector, despite recent improvements, still leaves half its population without access to health insurance (Barraza-Llorens et al. 2002). Her asthma may also result from exposure to air pollution from the factory or exhaust emissions from trucks taking its products north to the US. Even with the recent loss of more than 300 manufacturing plants to China (*The Economist* 2003), northern Mexico remains home to over 3000 manufacturing plants producing goods ranging from furniture and car parts to electronic components and textiles. As the cost of pollution control and health and safety standards rose in the US, and with the establishment of the NAFTA, many of the more hazardous and polluting links in the industrial production chain moved to the *maquiladoras* (Mexican export processing zones) (Frey 2003) – reflecting the market-driven rationality that underpins neoliberal economics. The environmental and occupational hazards associated with the *maquiladoras* include increased ground water and air pollution and the often illegal discharge of highly toxic chemicals. Despite a higher than average income level (Schwartz 2002), northern Mexico has higher than average infant and age-adjusted mortality and increased mortality and morbidity for infectious disease, partly due to the rapid expansion of poorly planned and serviced housing estates for the *maquila* workers.

A final danger for Antonia is the possibility that she might be tricked or kidnapped into the sex trade. Some 50,000 people annually, a third of them from Latin America, are sexually trafficked to the US by pimps and criminal gangs. Sex businesses are the largest sector of employment for women who have lost jobs as a result of globalization (Ugarte et al. 2003). The sex trade is a real element of globalization and a growing problem worldwide (Hughes 2000, Richard 2000). Antonia's story relates to a regional trade agreement, but attention should also be paid to the impacts of agreements administered by the World Trade Organization.

Globalization, health and the WTO

The WTO was formed in 1995 at the conclusion of the Uruguay round of talks on the General Agreement on Tariffs and Trade (GATT). Unlike most multilateral agreements, the 29 administered by WTO provide for a dispute settlement procedure (under the auspices of WTO) backed by enforcement provisions in the form of fines or monetized trade concessions. Any of the

147 member countries can now launch a complaint against other members they think are failing to live up to their WTO commitments. Key principles underpinning all WTO agreements are *national treatment* (foreign goods, investment or services are treated the same as domestic ones); *most favoured nation* (whatever special preferences are given to one trading partner must be given to all WTO member nations); and *least trade restrictive practices* (whatever environmental or social regulations a country adopts domestically must be those that least impede trade).

Several WTO agreements have specific bearing on the pathways linking globalization and health, as summarized in Table A1.

The *Agreement on Sanitary and Phytosanitary Measures* (SPS) requires that a country's food and drug safety regulations be based on a scientific risk assessment, even if the regulations do not differentiate between domestic and imported products (Drache et al. 2002). Canada, the US and Brazil initiated a WTO dispute to force the EU to accept imports of artificial hormone-treated beef: the EU does not allow the use of these hormones on its cattle. The WTO concluded that the EU failed to conduct a proper risk assessment (Charnovitz 2000). But the EU still does not accept such imports and is paying millions of dollars a year to the complaining countries in compensating trade sanctions.

At the same time, however, the agreement can be used in ways that may discriminate against developing countries. The EU has imposed a tougher standard than any other nation on aflatoxin contamination of dried fruits and nuts, resulting in an anticipated loss of US$ 670 million a year in agricultural export revenues for African countries (Otsuki et al. 2001). A compromise is needed between a country's sovereign right to the highest level of precautionary health protection and the financial inability of low-income countries to abide by stringent regulations.

The *Technical Barriers to Trade Agreement* (TBT) requires that all domestic regulations be 'least trade restrictive', treat 'like products' the same and be higher than international standards only if they can be justified on specific health grounds. Canada used this agreement to argue that France's ban on the use of asbestos products was discriminatory since asbestos was 'like' the glass fibre insulation France allowed. Canada lost this case – the only instance in which WTO mechanisms have favoured health over trade – because of the mass of evidence of the cancer-causing properties of asbestos (WTO 2000). (Article XX(b) of GATT permits exception to WTO rules 'necessary to protect human, animal or plant life or health.') Such conclusive evidence is rarely available. Both TBT and SPS demonstrate 'trade creep', a process in which trade rules limit how national governments can regulate their domestic health and

TABLE A1 Key health concerns with WTO agreements

Agreement	Health impacts from loss of domestic regulatory space
Agreement on Trade Related Intellectual Property Rights	Limited access to essential medicines. Higher cost of drugs drains money useful for primary health care.
Agreement on Sanitary and Phytosanitary Measures	Requires scientific risk assessments even when foreign goods treated no differently than domestic goods (i.e. there is no discrimination). Such assessments are costly and imperfect with many health risks associated with environmental and manufactured products.
Technical Barriers to Trade Agreement	Requires that any regulatory barrier to the free flow of goods be as 'least trade restrictive as possible'. Many trade disputes over domestic health and safety regulations have invoked this agreement. To date only one dispute favoured the exception allowing countries to abrogate from rules to protect health (France's ban on the import of Canadian asbestos products).
Agreement on Trade Related Investment Measures	Limits countries' abilities to direct investment where it would do most good for domestic economic development and employment equity, both important to population health.
Agreement on Government Procurement	Limits government's abilities to use its contracts or purchases for domestic economic development, regional equity, employment equity or other social goals with strong links to better population health.
Agreement on Agriculture	Continuing export and producer subsidies by the USA, EU, Japan and Canada depress world prices and cost developing countries hundreds of millions of dollars in lost revenue which could fund health-promoting services. Subsidized food imports from wealthy countries undermine domestic growers' livelihoods. Market barriers to food products from developing countries persist and deny them trade-related earnings.
General Agreement on Trade in Services	Locks in and could increase private provision of key health-promoting services, reducing equitable access by poorer families and groups.

environment affairs even if they treat products from other countries no differently than their own (Drache et al. 2002).

The *Agreement on Trade-Related Investment Measures* (TRIMS) prevents countries from attaching performance requirements (such as minimum levels of local content) to approvals of foreign investment. Such requirements have proved useful in the development of a viable domestic economy, partly by ensuring health-promoting employment and income adequacy for marginalized groups or regions. Their removal benefits investors from high-income countries much more than people in low- and middle-income nations (Greenfield 2001).

Similarly the *Agreement on Government Procurement* (AGP) requires governments to take into account only 'commercial considerations' when making purchasing decisions, precluding preferences based on environment, human or labour rights. Although this is a voluntary agreement that few low- or middle-income countries have signed, high-income countries are intent on making it mandatory and binding on all WTO members as part of their agenda for the Doha round of negotiations, begun in 2001.

The *Agreement on Agriculture* was designed to increase global trade in agricultural goods by reducing tariffs and phasing out export subsidies (financial assistance for food exports) and production subsidies (financial assistance for farmers). During a ten-year moratorium on trade challenges under this agreement that ended in 2004, many high-income countries failed to reduce their tariffs on agricultural products (World Bank/IMF 2002) and retained both tariff peaks (a higher-than-average import tax) on raw food imports and tariff escalations on finished food products (where more money can be made), taxing them at 2–3 times the rate of raw food imports (Watkins 2002). High-income countries also continued to pay huge subsidies to their domestic agricultural producers. Failure to reach an agreement on subsidy removal was the main reason for the collapse of the Cancún WTO ministerial talks in 2003. A 2004 WTO framework agreement to begin phasing out subsidies may remedy this impasse, but details are still subject to negotiation and the US says it will not begin to negotiate such reductions until after developing countries lower their agricultural tariffs (ICTSD 2004a). Incredibly, the 2004 agreement allows the US to retain a US$ 180 billion increase in domestic farm subsidies announced in 2002, as long as it can show they do not affect current levels of agricultural production (ICTSD 2004b).

The *Agreement on Trade-Related Intellectual Property Rights* (TRIPS) is unlike other WTO agreements in that it does not 'free' trade, but protects intellectual property rights, mostly held by companies or individuals in rich countries.

33

Health concerns about TRIPS centre on the role of extended patent protection on access to antiretrovirals and other essential drugs. These issues are addressed in detail in Part B, chapters 2 and 3.

Finally, the *General Agreement on Trade in Services* (GATS) is a complex framework agreement introduced at the conclusion of the Uruguay round. It was conceived, and continues to be defended, primarily as a vehicle for the expansion of business opportunities for multinational service corporations (Hilary 2001), almost all based in high-income countries, which are constantly looking for new opportunities. Service businesses include health care itself, health insurance, education, and water and sanitation services (Sanger 2001).

Some commentators argue that the effects of reducing barriers to trade and investment in such services on population health depend on domestic regulatory structures (Adlung and Carzaniga 2002). However, the 2000 *World Health*

Box A5 NAFTA, the FTAA and the right of foreign companies to sue governments

The WTO is not the only free trade regime with implications for government regulatory capacity or provision of essential public services. The North American Free Trade Area (NAFTA) and the proposed Free Trade Area of the Americas (FTAA) also have potentially profound health effects. NAFTA has a particularly problematic section, Chapter 11, which permits private foreign companies to deny democratically elected governments the ability to regulate in the public health interests of their citizens.

The following illustrations of this relate to Canada. The Canadian government let its legislation for plain packaging of tobacco products die after representatives of Phillip Morris International and R.J. Reynolds Tobacco International argued that it constituted an expropriation of assets, violating NAFTA investment and intellectual property obligations. The Canadian government similarly repealed its ban of the gasoline additive MMT, a known neurotoxin, and paid US$ 13 million in compensation after Ethyl Corporation argued, again on the strength of the NAFTA investment Chapter 11, that the ban had the effect of expropriating its assets even if there was no 'taking' in the classic understanding of expropriation. Both these NAFTA challenges achieved their goal of overturning a public health measure, although neither went to a dispute panel. More recently, a US-based water company is using NAFTA to sue the Canadian province of British Columbia for US$ 10.5 billion due to restrictions on bulk water exports legislated by

---

Report cautioned that 'few countries (with either high or low income) have developed adequate strategies to regulate the private financing and provision of health services' and that 'the harm caused by market abuses is difficult to remedy after the fact' (WHO 2000). The same caution should be applied to education, and especially to water and sanitation – where, as described in Part D, chapter 2, privatization experiences of the last decade have generated intense political resistance because of their negative effects on the poor.

GATS does not directly drive privatization, but functions as a trap-door that locks in existing (and future) levels of private provision of services. It may also indirectly create incentives for foreign investors and their actual or prospective host country joint-venture partners to lobby for privatization, because of the security it provides for investments in newly privatized services. The GATS exception for 'a [government] service which is supplied neither on a com-

the government. The declared intent of Canadian federal and provincial governments to prohibit international trade in water (primarily to the US) may be in violation of NAFTA (Shrybman 1999); states bordering the Great Lakes are currently drafting legislation to permit commercial diversion of water from the basin despite Canada's opposition, arguing that NAFTA gives them the right to do so. Of course, Canadian companies have also used Chapter 11 to challenge regulations in the US. Methanex Corporation, a Canadian-based producer of the gasoline additive MTBE, a suspect carcinogen, is suing for US$ 970 million because California banned its use in 1999.

With respect to health care, NAFTA provides that governments can expropriate foreign-owned investments only for a public purpose and if they provide compensation. This opens the door to NAFTA claims that measures to expand public health insurance in Canada (where prescription drugs, home care and dental care are currently privately insured), or to restrict private for-profit provision of health care services, amount to expropriation and that compensation must be paid to US or Mexican investors who are adversely affected.

From a health vantage point, NAFTA's Chapter 11 should be rescinded. Article 15 of the Chapter on Investment in the agreement on the FTAA, which would similarly allow investor-state suits, should be deleted. And no such provision should ever be adopted in the multilateral agreements administered by the WTO.

mercial basis, nor in competition with one or more service suppliers' (Article 1:3b) is often cited as evidence that concern over privatization is misplaced. This clause, however, may collapse under an eventual challenge, since most countries allow some commercial or competitive provision of virtually all public services (Pollock and Price 2003). There is further concern that Mode 4 of GATS (which applies to the 'temporary' movement of service workers between countries) could exacerbate the brain drain of health professionals.

Globalization comes home to roost

Our last vignette, about Tom the Canadian van-driver, reminds us that globalization destroys lives even in high-income countries whose leaders have been among its most ardent proponents. Other things being equal, their simple aggregate wealth means that high-income countries are better able to cope with the 'shocks' of global market integration. At the same time, globalization is leading to a blurring of boundaries – evident, for example, in the spread to industrialized countries of stereotypically 'Third World' forms of work organization such as piecework assembly of automobile parts by home-based workers in the US (Gringeri 1994). Trade liberalization could result in a neo-Victorian world order in which 'the First and Third worlds will not so much disappear as mingle. There will be more people in Mexico and India who live like Americans of the upper-middle class; on the other hand, there will be more – many more – people in the US who live like the slum dwellers of Mexico City and Calcutta' (Mead 1992). Early warning signs, like Tom's precarious work situation, are unmistakable in the US and elsewhere.

Trade liberalization accelerates the loss of work and income for less qualified workers in high-income (high-wage) countries, as those jobs shift to lower-wage nations (Dollar 2002). Simultaneously, the ability of corporate managers to relocate production (or to opt for a lower-cost supplier of outsourced activities) erodes workers' bargaining power to negotiate better wages or protect existing income and working conditions. Notably, full-time work in the industrialized countries has tended to be replaced by part-time, contract and temporary employment in the interests of lower costs and labour market 'flexibility'. 'Just as Japan perfected the just-in-time inventory system,' which reduces costs by ensuring that parts arrive at the point of production literally minutes before being needed, the US 'is well on its way to perfecting the just-in-time work force, notwithstanding the grim toll it takes on labour. The harsh truth is that it is a major productivity plus' (Wysockij 1995).

These trends are most conspicuous in the US, where labour markets are the least regulated in the industrialized world. Least skilled workers are losing ground on wages; work less regular shifts; and have poorer working conditions, fewer benefits such as pensions and health care, and less job security and job satisfaction (Fligstein and Shin 2003). Germany is facing a policy dilemma as high technology firms threaten to move to lower-wage countries with well-educated workforces, such as Hungary, leading German workers to accept longer working hours, lower pay and fewer benefits (Elliott 2004). The spread of insecure or precarious work is not confined to 'rust belt' manufacturing industries. The US, for example, has experienced a loss of over 400,000 high-tech jobs since 2001 as firms outsource work to lower-wage countries that have improved the education levels of their workforces (Srivastava and Theodore 2004).

The rising number of personal bankruptcies in the US is one of the consequences of the productivity gains from the 'just-in-time workforce', and an especially disturbing indicator of the spread of work-related insecurity and the associated stress. There were 1.5 million filings for bankruptcy in 2002 (Century Foundation 2004) and these numbers cannot tell us 'how much more of the middle class is near the fragile edge of economic failure' (Sullivan et al. 2000). In this detailed study of household bankruptcies, 68% of respondents identified job-related reasons for filing. On the other hand, incomes and entitlements are growing for those at the top of the economic pyramid (Smeeding 2002), most notably in the US but also other countries (WCSDG 2004), as illustrated by the growing gap between the pay of corporate chief executives and workers.

Meanwhile, social spending – at least since World War II the mechanism by which industrialized societies have provided safety nets against economic insecurity – has declined in high-income countries as a percentage of GDP over the 1980s and 1990s. Only four countries bucked this trend: Greece, Japan, Portugal and Turkey, and they were starting from a very low base. While the decline was slight in some countries (e.g. Switzerland, Iceland, Germany) it was dramatic in others: a drop of 28% in Ireland 1986–1998; 21% in the Netherlands 1983–1998; and 19% in Canada 1992–1999 (OECD 2004a). (Comparisons are for the year of highest social spending post-1980 to the most recent year of data.) Some of the biggest spending declines occurred in areas most important to health: health care, cash transfers to (generally low-income) families, supports to unemployed workers and programmes to increase labour market opportunities (OECD 2004b).

The decline in social spending partly results from revenue constraints created by tax competition among jurisdictions. MNE managers can relocate both production and profits to jurisdictions where tax treatment is more favourable and wealthy households can similarly relocate their assets, and sometimes themselves. The decline can also be attributed to the much-neglected effect of globalization on the waning *political* power of organized labour – 'the traditional counterweight to the power of business' (WCSDG 2004) and historically the base of progressive social movements and social democratic political parties. A large industrial working class still produces products for markets in North America and western Europe. But unlike the situation during the 30 years after World War II, globalization means that very large numbers of its members no longer live in these markets. Instead they live and vote (or cannot vote) in Mexico, Malaysia, Indonesia or China.

These points must be kept in mind when considering the view that even in a globalized world, 'the overall distribution of income in a country remains very much a consequence of the domestic political, institutional and economic choices made by those individual countries' (Smeeding 2002). There are certainly marked differences among the G-20 countries, an informal forum of 20 of the richest industrial nations and some middle income emerging-market countries. The most unequal distributions of income are found in Mexico, the Russian Federation, the US, the UK and New Zealand, while the most equal are in Sweden, Finland, Norway, Denmark, the Netherlands and Luxembourg. Canada, Taiwan and central European countries fall somewhere in the middle. Smeeding attributes these differences to stronger wage-setting institutions in the more egalitarian countries, a result of higher rates of unionization and a cause of better minimum wage standards, stronger collective bargaining rights and more progressive forms of income redistribution and state-supported welfare.

Others organize high-income countries into three different categories: the social democratic nations (such as the Scandinavian countries), in which labour institutions and social policies remain strong; the corporatist states (such as Germany and France), in which social insurance remains relatively generous and there is a strong emphasis on supporting families to provide essential welfare; and the liberal welfare state (primarily the Anglo countries of the UK, the US, Australia and New Zealand), in which means-testing and market-based systems predominate (Coburn 2004). Not only income inequalities but also disparities in key health indicators such as infant mortality increase along the continuum from social democratic to liberal welfare states. In 1996, infant mortality rates in the *poorest* neighbourhoods in Canada, a middling country closer to the corporatist than the liberal welfare states, were lower than the average rate for all neighbourhoods in the US; but rates in Canada's *richest* neighbourhoods were higher than the average rate for all of Sweden (Coburn 2004).

**3 Hong Kong at night: global competition has led to winners and losers
in developed and developing countries.**

What do these trends have to do with Tom, and with human health more
generally?

A reasonably secure job that provides an adequate income is one of the axi-
omatic determinants of health. Not only does decent work provide individuals
and families with the income to purchase the necessities for health; it is often
where people form the friendships and social networks that independently
and powerfully influence their health. It is a plus, of course, if the work is
relatively healthy or safe, including not only protection from accident hazards
and chemical and biological pollutants, but also a work regime that does not
exacerbate stress by combining high demands with low control over the pace
and conditions of work (Karasek and Theorell 1990).

These conditions are now only a faint hope for millions of workers like
Tom. 'Formerly well-paid, unionized...employees have been forced to seek
employment in the expanding service sector, where full-time jobs are scarce,
few employees have benefits or earn living wages, hours are irregular, and
many employees hold down multiple jobs in an effort to survive' (Polanyi et
al. 2004). One in five Canadian workers was employed part-time in 2003, one
in four of them involuntarily – that is, s/he claimed to be looking for full-time
work (Statistics Canada 2004). Counting temporary, self-employed and multiple (part-time) jobholders, like Tom, the number of Canadians in 'non-stan-
dard' and more precarious employment rises to one in three.

39

Even as labour income is stagnant or declining for many workers, their hours, workloads and work speed are rising rapidly, not only in Canada but in almost all OECD countries. Workplace stress, work-related mental health problems and physical illness are rising in parallel, as is the number of workers experiencing difficulty in managing both work and family life (Higgins et al. 2004). In ageing societies where social provision is being cut back, as in North America, increasing numbers of working people like Tom will have to meet the demands of elder care as well. The multiple dimensions of work-related insecurity are important sources of stress: workers are unsure not only about their present employment and income and prospects for the future, but also about the shrinking safety net of unemployment and welfare transfers (ILO 2004b). Canada's contribution to labour market flexibility has been a massive 60% decline in spending on supports for unemployed workers, as a percentage of GDP, in 1991–9 (OECD 2004a). Cutbacks in the national unemployment insurance system were a major factor in the government's ability to balance its budget after years of running deficits, but they made it much harder for Tom, and others like him, to collect benefits after they lost a job and to survive on them – reducing the percentage of unemployed workers eligible for benefits to levels not seen since the original legislation of the 1940s (Rice and Prince 2000).

It is not a great leap to Tom's accident from what the data tell us about the physical and mental health risks of part-time, insecure and precarious employment. In Canada the risks are increased by the post-NAFTA integration of North American labour markets. Above and beyond the 'offshoring' of jobs, Canada has increasing difficulty in setting social and labour market policies independently of the US. Especially in central Canada where Tom's accident occurred, manufacturing industry is tightly linked to suppliers and customers in the US and the price tag of independence – measured in job losses, capital flight and forgone tax revenues – is high and almost certainly rising. Canadian trends and policy responses therefore bear watching as early warning indicators of the challenges globalization will present for high income countries.

Conclusion

The fundamental health challenges inherent in our contemporary global political economy – equity and sustainability – have been central to the struggle for health for the past century. Addressing them requires some form of market-correcting system of wealth redistribution between as well as within nations. Globalization, as we know it today, is fundamentally asymmetric. 'In its benefits and its risks, it works less well for the currently poor countries and for poor households within developing countries. Because markets at the national level are asymmetric, modern capitalist economies have social contracts, progressive tax systems, and laws and regulations to manage asymmetries and market failures. At the global level, there is no real equivalent to national governments to manage global markets, though they are bigger, deeper and if anything more asymmetric. They work better for the rich; and their risks and failures hurt the poor more' (Birdsall 2002).

The national and global are linked. Globalization's present form limits the macroeconomic, development and health policy space in rich and poor nations alike. Liberalized capital markets 'sanction deviations from orthodoxy' (WCSDG 2004), that is, anything that limits the potential for profit, and have 'added to the speed at which, and the drama with which, financial markets bring retribution on governments whose policies are not "credible"' (Glyn 1995). Between nations, liberalized trade still benefits high- more than low-income countries; and its rules-based system is frequently ignored or undermined by countries such as the US when its outcomes are not in their interests. Developing world debt is 'perhaps the most efficient form of neocolonialism' (Bullard 2004). And the wealthy world's responses to disease crises sweeping many parts of the low-income world, while belatedly improving, are woefully inadequate and eclipsed by huge expenditures on attempts to make the world safer for the rich through increased militarization and decreased civil rights (Oloka-Onyango and Udugama 2003).

The discussion of whether globalization and openness is good or bad for the poor should move on to a discussion of 'the appropriate global social contract and appropriate global arrangements for minimising the asymmetric risks and costs of global market failure' (Birdsall 2002). What should the contents of such a global social contract look like? In somewhat idealist tones, the World Commission on the Social Dimensions of Globalization urged a rights-based approach in which the eradication of poverty and the attainment of the MDGs should be seen as the first steps towards a socioeconomic 'floor' for the global economy, requiring in part a more democratic governance of globalization (WCSDG 2004). Its recommended reforms to move the global political economy in this direction resemble those that have been proffered for at least the past 20 years, as follows:

- Increases in untied development assistance to the long-standing, albeit non-binding UN target of 0.7% of rich countries' gross national income, along with efforts to mobilize additional sources of funding.

- Accelerated and deepened debt relief relative to levels available under the enhanced HIPC initiative – although the report does not specifically recommend debt cancellation for countries not eligible under enhanced HIPC.
- Trade agreements that substantially reduce unfair barriers to market access, especially for goods in which developing countries have a strong comparative advantage such as agricultural products.
- Stepped up actions to ensure core human and labour rights for workers around the world, with particular emphasis on gender inequalities.
- A multilateral framework to manage the international flow of people, such as the brain drain of education professionals from poor to rich countries and its frequent corollary of brain waste after they migrate.
- Stronger voting rights for low- and middle-income countries at the World Bank and IMF.
- Building on existing frameworks for international tax cooperation as a vital element in strengthening the integrity of national tax systems in all countries, increasing public resources for development and facilitating the fight against tax havens, money laundering and the financing of terrorism.
- Increased coherence in the global economic, financial and health/human rights system, and heads of state to promote policies in international fora that focus on well-being and quality of life.

Policy initiatives that go further than the commission's recommendations are needed in at least two areas – the relation of trade agreements to human rights obligations and the internationalization of taxation and wealth redistribution.

On the first point, the UN special rapporteurs on globalization and human rights said it was necessary to move away from ad hoc and contingent approaches in ensuring that human rights, including the right to health, are not compromised by trade liberalization (Oloka-Onyango and Udugama 2003). The initial report from the UN's special rapporteur on the right to the highest attainable standard of physical and mental health outlined an expansive interpretation which explicitly included poverty-related issues (Hunt 2003). His subsequent examination of the WTO regime led to the conclusion that 'the form, pacing and sequencing of trade liberalization [must] be conducive to the progressive realization of the right to health' and that 'progressive realization of the right to health, and the immediate obligations to which it is subject, place reasonable conditions on the trade rules and policies that may be chosen' (Hunt 2004). High priority should be given to ensuring that both the content of trade agreements and the operations of the WTO (including its

42

dispute settlement mechanism, which was not considered in the 2004 report) and other trade policy institutions conform to this principle.

On the second point, recognition is growing of both the desirability and the difficulty of devising some mechanism of global income transfers. Yunker (2004) uses a global econometric model (the World Economic Equalization Programme, or WEEP) to simulate the effects over a 50–year period of a 'global Marshall Plan' to raise economic growth in the developing world using major increases in development assistance financed by national treasuries. While he is candid about the huge uncertainties inherent in such simulations, he concludes that if such a programme were implemented, 'the living standards of what are the poorest countries of today would have improved sufficiently, by the end of the period, to be comparable to those of the richest countries today'. This result, inconceivable in a business-as-usual scenario, is relatively insensitive to variations in key assumptions. However, it would require annual development assistance commitments by the rich countries on the order of 2–4% of GNI or GNP – far higher than the 0.7% target, now reached by only a few countries (see part E, chapter 5).

If such national commitments are unlikely, what international revenue-raising mechanisms might be considered? Taxes on arms trade and international air travel have been proposed, although neither would raise substantial revenue (US\$ 5–20 billion annually). A carbon tax on high-income countries only (at a rate low enough not to be a drag on consumption) would generate around US\$ 125 billion annually; the rationale for not imposing it universally is that some low-income countries with small populations could pay higher amounts of their income in such a tax than people in high-income countries, rendering it regressive rather than progressive. A currency transaction tax of 0.25% (the so-called Tobin tax) would generate over US\$ 170 billion annually, according to one estimate (others suggest it may be considerably less), and is perhaps the least difficult to implement.

Other suggestions to address the problem of MNEs and wealthy individuals shifting assets and operations around the world include the issuance of one tax identification number that ensured corporate or personal confidentiality, but would allow all jurisdictions believing they had a tax claim to levy it; and national withholding taxes on all capital leaving a country, to limit the possibilities for capital flight (Clunies-Ross 2004).

These policy options, even more than others we have described, face formidable political difficulties. They challenge the orthodoxy of neoliberal economics, and would involve fundamental shifts in the global distribution of wealth and power. History suggests that such changes demand radical (and not always non-violent) forms of political mobilization and action. Although history has not yet encountered such a demand on a global scale, it is worth recalling that the political difficulties of abolishing slavery (now achieved in many countries) and implementing maximum hours of work (now regulated in most of the industrialized world) were also once thought to be insurmountable.

References

Abbasi K (1999). Changing sides. *British Medical Journal*, 318:865–1208.

Adlung R, Carzaniga A (2002). Health services under the General Agreement on Trade in Services. In: Vieira C, Drager N, eds. *Trade in health services: global, regional and country perspectives*. Washington, DC, Pan American Health Organization.

AFL-CIO (2004). *Section 301 Petition* [to Office of the US Trade Representative] *of American Federation of Labor and Congress of Industrial Organizations*. Washington, DC, AFL-CIO.

Akin J, Dow W, Lance P (2004). Did the distribution of health insurance in China continue to grow less equitable in the nineties? Results from a longitudinal survey. *Social Science & Medicine*, 58:293–304.

Anderson S, Cavanagh J (2000). *Of the world's 100 largest economic entities, 51 are now corporations and 49 are countries*. Washington, DC, The Institute for Policy Studies (http://www.corporations.org/system/top100.html, accessed 25 February 2005).

Athreya B (2003). *Trade is a women's issue*. New York, Global Policy Forum (http://www.globalpolicy.org/socecon/inequal/labor/2003/0220women.htm, accessed 25 February 2005).

Atkinson S et al. (1999). The referral process and urban health care in sub-Saharan Africa: the case of Lusaka, Zambia. *Social Science & Medicine*, 49:27–38.

Barraza-Llorens M et al. (2002). Addressing inequity in health and health care in Mexico. *Health Affairs,* 21:47–56.

Bauman Z (1998). *Globalization: the human consequences*. Cambridge, Polity Press.

Birdsall N (2002). A stormy day on an open field: asymmetry and convergence in the global economy. In: Gruen D, O'Brien T, Lawson J, eds. *Globalisation, living standards and inequality: recent progress and continuing challenges, proceedings of a conference held in Sydney, 27–28 May 2002*. Canberra, Reserve Bank of Australia, 37–65 (http://www.rba.gov.au/PublicationsAndResearch/Conferences/2002/, accessed 1 February 2005).

Bosshard P et al. (2003). *Gambling with people's lives: what the World Bank's new 'high-risk/high-reward' strategy means for the poor and the environment*. Washington, DC, Environmental Defense, Friends of the Earth, International Rivers Network.

Bullard N (2004). The new elite consensus? *Global Social Policy*, 4(2):143–152.

Cameron D, Stein JG (2000). *Globalization triumphant or globalization in retreat: implications for Canada*. Ottawa, Department of Justice, Canada Research and Statistics Division (http://canada.justice.gc.ca/en/ps/rs/rep/RP2002–6.pdf, accessed 1 February 2005).

Carlsen L (2003). *The Mexican farmers' movement: exposing the myths of free trade*. Silver City, New Mexico, Americas Program, Interhemispheric Resource Center (http://www.americaspolicy.org/pdf/reports/0302farm.pdf, accessed 1 February 2005).

Century Foundation (2004). *Life and debt: why American families are borrowing to the hilt*. New York, Century Foundation (http://www.tcf.org/Publications/EconomicsInequality/baker_debt.pdf, accessed 1 February 2005).

Chang HJ (2002). *Kicking away the ladder: development strategy in historical perspective*. London, Anthem Press.

Charnovitz S (2000). The supervision of health and biosafety regulation by world trade rules. *Tulane Environmental Law Journal*, 13(2).

Chen S, Ravallion M (2004). *How have the world's poorest fared since the early 1980s?* Washington, DC Development Research Group, World Bank (http://papers.ssrn.com/sol3/papers.cfm?abstract_id=610385, accessed 1 February 2005).

Chen S, Wang Y (2001). *China's growth and poverty reduction: recent trends between 1990 and 1999*. Washington, DC, World Bank (http://econ.worldbank.org/files/2369_wps2651.pdf, accessed 1 February 2005).

China Daily (anon) (2004) Big FDI inflows pose no threat. *China Daily*, 28 April (http://www.china.org.cn/english/international/94243.htm, accessed 25 February 2005).

Chirac J (2003). President of France Jacques Chirac's Address to the UN General Assembly. *New York Times*, 23 September.

Clunies-Ross A (2004). Resources for social development. *Global Social Policy*, 4(2):197–214.

Coburn D (2004). Beyond the income inequality hypothesis: class, neo-liberalism, and health inequalities. *Social Science and Medicine*, 58:41–56.

Condesa Consulting Group (2004). *Mexico Agricultural Situation: Summary of Mexican government study on the effects of NAFTA on Mexican agriculture*, USDA Foreign Agricultural Service Report MX4070. Washington, DC, Global Agriculture Information Network (http://www.sice.oas.org/geograph/westernh/naftamexagri_e.pdf, accessed 25 February 2005).

Cornia GA, Addison T, Kiiski S (2004). Income distribution changes and their impact in the post-Second World War period. In: Cornia G, ed., *Inequality, growth, and poverty in an era of liberalization and globalization*, UNU-WIDER Studies in Development Economics. Oxford, Oxford University Press.

Cornia GA, Jolly R, Stewart F, eds (1987). Adjustment with a human face. In: *Protecting the vulnerable and promoting growth*. Vol. 1. New York, Oxford University Press.

Deaton A (2001). *Health, inequality, and economic development*. Geneva, Commission on Macroeconomics and Health, World Health Organisation (CMH working paper series WG1:3) (http://www.cmhealth.org/docs/wg1_paper3.pdf, accessed 1 February 2005).

Deaton A (2004). *Health in an age of globalization*. Princeton, Research Program in Development Studies, Centre for Health and Wellbeing (http://www.wws.princeton.edu/%7Erpds/downloads/deaton_measuringpoverty_204.pdf, accessed 1 February 2005).

Diamond J (1997). *Guns, germs and steel: the fates of human societies*. New York, W.W. Norton.

Dollar D (2001). *Globalization, inequality, and poverty since 1980*. Washington, DC, World Bank (http://econ.worldbank.org/files/2944_globalization-inequality-and-poverty.pdf, accessed 1 February 2005).

Dollar D (2002). Global economic integration and global inequality. In: Gruen D, O'Brien T, Lawson J, eds. *Globalisation, living standards and inequality: recent progress and continuing challenges, proceedings of a conference held in Sydney,*

27–28 May 2002. Canberra, Reserve Bank of Australia (http://www.rba.gov.au/PublicationsAndResearch/Conferences/2002/, accessed 1 February 2005).

Drache D, et al (2002). *One world one system? The diversity deficits in standard-setting, development and sovereignty at the WTO*. Toronto, Robarts Center for Canadian Studies, York University (Robarts Center Research Papers) (http://www.yorku.ca/robarts/projects/wto/pdf/oneworldonesystem_new.pdf, accessed 1 February 2005).

Durano M (2002). *Foreign direct investment and its impact on gender relations*. Women In Development Europe (WIDE) (http://www.eurosur.org/wide/Globalisation/IS_Durano.htm, accessed 25 February 2005).

Elliott L (2004). Deal on global trade holds out hope for poor nations. *The Guardian*, 2 August.

Fligstein N, Shin TJ (2003). *The shareholder value society: a review of the changes in working conditions and inequality in the US, 1976–2000*. Berkeley, University of California Berkeley Institute of Industrial Relations (Working Paper Series, no. iirwps-088-02) (http://repositories.cdlib.org/cgi/viewcontent.cgi?article=1026&context=iir, accessed 1 February 2005).

Frey RS (2003). The transfer of core-based hazardous production processes to the export processing zones of the periphery: the maquiladora centers of northern Mexico. *Journal of World-Systems Research*, 9(2):317–354.

Glyn A (1995). Social democracy and full employment. *New Left Review*, May-June: 33–55.

Gough I (2001). Globalization and regional welfare regimes: the East Asian case. *Global Social Policy*, 1(2):163–190.

Greenfield G (2001). The WTO agreement on Trade-Related Investment Measures (TRIMS). *Canadian Center for Policy Alternatives Briefing Paper Series: Trade and Investment*, 2(1):1–8.

Gringeri CE (1994). Assembling 'genuine GM parts': rural homeworkers and economic development. *Economic Development Quarterly*, 8:147–157.

Gyebi J, Brykczynska G, Lister G (2002). *Globalisation: economics and women's health*, London, UK Partnership for Global Health (http://www.ukglobalhealth.org/content/Text/Globalisation_New_version.doc, accessed 1 February 2005).

Hawley S (2000*). Exporting Corruption: Privatisation, Multinationals and Bribery*. Corner House Briefing 19. London (http://www.thecornerhouse.org.uk/item.shtml?x=51975, accessed 25 February 2005).

Henriques G, Patel R (2004). *NAFTA, corn, and Mexico's agricultural trade liberalization*. Silver City, NM, America's Program, Interhemispheric Resource Center (http://www.americaspolicy.org/pdf/reports/0402nafta.pdf, accessed 1 February 2005).

Higgins C, Duxbury L, Johnson K (2004). *Exploring the link between work–life conflict and demands on Canada's health care system*. Ottawa, Public Health Agency of Canada (http://www.phac-aspc.gc.ca/publicat/work-travail/report3/pdfs/fvwklfr-prt_e.pdf, accessed 1 February 2005).

Hilary J (2001). *The wrong model: GATS, trade liberalisation and children's right to health*. London, Save the Children (http://www.savethechildren.org.uk/temp/scuk/cache/cmsattach/986_wrongmodel.pdf, accessed 1 February 2005).

Hodess R (2004). Introduction. In: *Global corruption report 2004*. London, Pluto Press, 11–18 (http://www.globalcorruptionreport.org/download.htm, accessed 1 February 2005) .

Howard J. (2004). Global coherence, employment and labor standards. *Global Social Policy*, 4(2):136–138.

Hughes DM (2000). The 'Natasha' trade: the transnational shadow market of trafficking in women. *Journal of International Affairs*, 53:625–651.

Hunt P (2003). *Economic, Social and Cultural Rights: The right of everyone to the enjoyment of the highest attainable standard of physical and mental health: report of the Special Rapporteur.* New York and Geneva, UN Economic and Social Council, document E/CN.4/2003/58 (http://www.unhchr.ch/Huridocda/Huridoca.nsf/0/985430 2995c2c86fc1256cec005a18d7/$FILE/G0310979.pdf, accessed 25 February 2005).

Hunt P (2004). *Economic, Social and Cultural Rights: The right of everyone to the enjoyment of the highest attainable standard of physical and mental health: report of the Special Rapporteur – Addendum: Mission to the World Trade Organization.* New York and Geneva, United Nations Economic and Social Council, document E/CN.4/2004/49/Add.1 (http://www.unhchr.ch/huridocda/huridoca.nsf/0/5860D7D863239D82C1256E660056432A/$File/G0411390.pdf?OpenElement, accessed 1 February 2005).

Industry Canada (2002). *An overview of Canada's trade with Africa.* Ottawa, International Cooperation, International Business Branch, Industry Canada (http://strategis.ic.gc.ca/epic/internet/inibi-iai.nsf/en/bi18682e.html, accessed 25 February 2005).

ICFTU (International Confederation of Free Trade Unions) (2003). *Export processing zones – symbols of exploitation and a development dead-end.* Brussels, ICFTU (http://www.icftu.org/www/pdf/wtoepzreport2003-en.pdf, accessed 1 February 2005).

International Centre for Trade and Development (ICTSD) (2002). *Bridges Weekly Trade News Digest* . Geneva (http://www.ictsd.org/weekly/02–11–20/index.htm, accessed 25 February 2005).

International Centre for Trade and Development (2004a). *Bridges Weekly Trade News Digest.* Geneva (http://www.ictsd.org/weekly/04–03–24/index.htm, accessed 25 February 2005).

International Centre for Trade and Development (2004b). *Bridges Weekly Trade News Digest* . Geneva (http://www.ictsd.org/weekly/04–08–03/index.htm, accessed 25 February 2005).

International Institute for Population Sciences and ORC Macro [online database] (2004). *National Family Health Survey (NFHS-II) 1998–99* (http://www.nfhsindia.org/pnfhs2.html, accessed 25 February 2005).

International Labour Organization (1998). *Labor and social issues related to export processing zones.* Geneva, ILO (http://www.ilo.org/public/english/dialogue/govlab/legrel/tc/epz/reports/epzrepor_w61/index.htm, accessed 25 February 2005).

International Labour Organization [online database] (2004a). *EPZ employment statistics.* Geneva, ILO (http://www.ilo.org/public/english/dialogue/sector/themes/epz/stats.htm, accessed 25 February 2005).

International Labour Organization (2004b). *Definitions: What we mean when we say 'economic security'*, Socio-Economic Security Programme fact sheet. Geneva, ILO (http://www.ilo.org/public/english/protection/ses, accessed 1 February 2005).

International Monetary Fund (2004). *Does the IMF always prescribe fiscal austerity? Are targets too high?* Transcript of an IMF book forum, Washington, DC, International Monetary Fund, June 8 (http://www.imf.org/external/np/tr/2004/tr040608.htm, accessed 1 February 2005).

Health for all in a 'borderless world'?

Jenkins R (2004). Globalization, production, employment and poverty: debates and evidence. *Journal of International Development*, 16:1–12.

Jeter J (2002). The dumping ground: as Zambia courts western markets, used goods arrive at a heavy price. *Washington Post*, 22 April:A1.

Junne GCA (2001). International organizations in a period of globalization: new (problems of) legitimacy. In Coicaud JM, Heiskanen V, eds. *The legitimacy of international organizations*. Tokyo, United Nations University Press,189–220.

Kahn J, Yardley J. (2004). Amid China's boom, no helping hand for young Qingming. *New York Times*. Late Edition, 1 August: Section 1, Page 1.

Kapur D, McHale J (2003). Migration's new payoff. *Foreign Policy,* Nov/Dec:49–58.

Karasek R, Theorell T (1990). *Healthy work: stress, productivity and the reconstruction of working life*. New York, Basic Books.

Killick T (2004). Politics, evidence and the new aid agenda. *Development Policy Review*, 22(1):5–29.

Lichfield G (2000). Mexico: Revolution ends, change begins. *The Economist*, 28 October.

Lindsey B (2002). *Do cheap imports hurt poor countries?* (http://www.brinklindsey.com, accessed 25 February 2005).

Lister G, Ingram A, Prowle, M (2004). *Country case study: UK financing of international cooperation for health*. New York, Office of Development Studies, United Nations Development Programme (http://www.sti.ch/pdfs/swap385.pdf, accessed 1 February 2005).

Liu Y et al (2001). China: increasing health gaps in a transitional economy. In: Whitehead M, et al., eds. *Challenging inequities in health: from ethics to action*. New York, Oxford University Press,76–89.

Liu Y, Rao K, Hsiao WC (2003). Medical expenditure and rural impoverishment in China. *Journal of Health, Population and Nutrition*, 21(3):216–222.

MacAskill E (2004). Aim is to meet UN target by 2013. *The Guardian*, 30 July.

Martin M (2004). Assessing the HIPC initiative: the key policy debates. In: Teunissen J, Akkerman A, eds. *HIPC debt relief: myths and realities*. The Hague, Forum on Debt and Development (FONDAD),11–47 (http://www.fondad.org, accessed 1 February 2005).

Mavrotas G (2003). *The UK HM Treasury – DFID proposal to increase external finance to developing countries: the international finance facility*. Helsinki, United Nations University, World Institute Development Economics Research (UNU/WIDER) (WIDER Conference on Sharing Global Prosperity, Helsinki, 6–7 September, 2003) (http://www.wider.unu.edu/conference/conference-2003-3/ conference-2003-3-papers/IFFpaper-Final_new_-mavrotas.pdf, accessed 1 February 2005).

Mead WR (1992). Bushism found: a second-term agenda hidden in trade agreements. *Harper's Magazine,* September:37–45.

Milanovic B (2003). The two faces of globalization: against globalization as we know it. *World Development*, 31(4):667–683.

Mtonga CQ, Chikoti S (2002). *Zambia country paper on textiles and clothing*. Lusaka, Ministry of Commerce Trade and Industry, Government of Zambia (http://www. intracen.org/worldtradenet/docs/whatsnew/atc_lesotho_november2002/country_paper_zambia.pdf, accessed 1 February 2005).

Ndikumana L, Boyce JK (2003). Public debts and private assets: explaining capital flight from sub-Saharan African countries. *World Development*, 31(1):107–130.

Oloka-Onyango J, Udagama D (2003). *Economic, social, and cultural rights: global-*

ization and its impact on the full enjoyment of human rights. New York, United Nations, document E/CN.4/Sub.2/2003/14 (http://www.unhchr.ch/huridocda/ huridoca.nsf/AllSymbols/276821C18F7CDFF0C1256D780028E74B/$File/ G0314784.pdf?OpenElement, accessed 1 February 2005).

Organisation for Economic Cooperation and Development (OECD) [online database] (2004). *Public social expenditure by main category as a percentage of GDP (1980– 1998).* Paris, OECD (http://www.oecd.org/dataoecd/43/14/2087083.xls, accessed 25 February 2005).

OECD Development Assistance Committee (2005). Development cooperation: 2004 report. *DAC Journal*, 6 (1) [full issue].

Otsuki T, Wilson J, Sewadeh M (2001). *A Race to the Top? A Case Study of Food Safety Standards and African Exports.* Washington, DC, World Bank (http://econ. worldbank.org/files/1424_wps2563.pdf, accessed 25 February 2005).

Patnaik U (2004). *The republic of hunger.* New Delhi, Economic Research Foundation (http://www.networkideas.org/featart/apr2004/Republic_Hunger.pdf, accessed 1 February 2005).

Pettifor A, Greenhill R (2002). *Debt relief and the millennium development goals.* New York, UNDP .

Polanyi M, Tompa E, Foley J (2004). Labor market flexibility and worker insecurity. In: Raphael, D, ed. *Social determinants of health. Canadian perspectives.* Toronto, Canadian Scholars' Press, Inc., 67–77.

Pollock AM, Price D (2003). New deal from the World Trade Organization ... may not provide essential medicines for poor countries. *British Medical Journal*, 327: 571–572.

Preibisch KL, Rivera Herrejon G, Wiggins SL (2002). Defending food security in a free-market economy: the gendered dimensions of restructuring in rural Mexico. *Human Organization*, 61(1):68–79.

Ramo JC (2004). *The Beijing consensus.* London, The Foreign Policy Centre (http:// www.fpc.org.uk/fsblob/240.pdf, accessed 1 February 2005).

Reinicke W (1998). *Global public policy: governing without government?* Washington, DC, Brookings Institute.

Rice J, Prince M (2000). *Changing politics of Canadian social policy.* Toronto, University of Toronto Press.

Richard AO (2000). *International trafficking in women to the United States: a contemporary manifestation of slavery and organized crime.* Washington, DC, US Central Intelligence Agency (DCI exceptional intelligence analyst program intelligence monograph, http://www.cia.gov/csi/monograph/women/trafficking.pdf, accessed 25 February 2005).

Rodriguez F, Rodrik D (2000). *Trade Policy and Economic Growth: A Skeptic's Guide to the Cross-National Evidence*, Discussion Paper 2143. London, Centre for Economic Policy Research.

Rodrik D (2001). *The Global Governance of Trade as if Development Really Mattered.* New York, Bureau for Development Policy, United Nations Development Programme (http://www.undp.org/mainundp/propoor/docs/pov_ globalgovernancetrade_pub.pdf, accessed 25 February 2005).

Sachs JD, et al (2004). Ending Africa's poverty trap. *Brookings Papers on Economic Activity,* no. 1:117–240.

Sanger M (2001). *Reckless abandon: Canada, the GATS and the future of health care.* Ottawa, Canadian Centre for Policy Alternatives.

Satterthwaite D (2003). The millennium development goals and urban poverty reduction: great expectations and nonsense statistics. *Environment & Urbanization*, 15:181–190.

Schoepf BG (1998). Inscribing the body politic: AIDS in Africa. In: Lock M, Kaufert P, eds. *Pragmatic women and body politics.* Cambridge, Cambridge University Press.

Schwartz MJ (2002). Discussion. In: Gruen D, O'Brien T, Lawson J, eds. *Globalisation, living standards and inequality: recent progress and continuing challenges, proceedings of a conference held in Sydney, 27–28 May 2002.* Canberra, Reserve Bank of Australia,147–178 (http://www.rba.gov.au/PublicationsAndResearch/Conferences/2002/ , accessed 1 February 2005).

Serafini J (2004). Foreign Corrupt Practices Act. (Survey of white collar crime). *American Criminal Law Review*, 41:721–750.

Shrybman S (1999). *A legal opinion concerning water export controls and Canadian obligations under NAFTA and the WTO.* Vancouver, West Coast Environmental Law (http://www.wcel.org, accessed 25 February 2005).

Smeeding TM (2002). Globalisation, inequality and the rich countries of the G-20: evidence from the Luxembourg Income Study (LIS). In: Gruen D, O'Brien T, Lawson J, eds. *Globalisation, living standards and inequality: recent progress and continuing challenges, proceedings of a conference held in Sydney, 27–28 May 2002.* Canberra, Reserve Bank of Australia,179–206 (http://www.rba.gov.au/PublicationsAndResearch/Conferences/2002, accessed 1 February 2005).

Social Watch (2004). Fear and want: obstacles to human security. *Social Watch Report 2004.* Montevideo, Instituto del Tercer Mundo.

Solt F (2004). *Economic inequality and democratic political engagement.* Houston, Rice University (http://www.unc.edu/~fredsolt/papers/Solt2004MPSA.pdf, accessed 1 February 2005).

Srivastava S, Theodore N (2004). *America's High Tech Bust:* Report to the Washington Alliance of Technology Workers, Communications Workers of America, Local 37083. Chicago, Center for Urban Economic Development, University of Illinois at Chicago (http://www.uic.edu/cuppa/uicued/AmericasHighTechBust.pdf, accessed 1 February 2005).

Statistics Canada (2004). *The Canadian labour market at a glance: 2003.* Ottawa, Labour Statistics Division, Statistics Canada (Catalogue no. 71–222–XIE) (http://www.statcan.ca/english/freepub/71-222-XIE/71-222-XIE2004000.pdf, accessed 1 February 2005).

Sullivan TA, Warren E, Westbrook JL (2000). *The fragile middle class: Americans in debt.* New Haven, Yale University Press.

The Economist (anon) (2003). Mexico's economy: the sucking sound from the East. 35–36, 26 July.

Ugarte MB, Zarate L, Farley M (2003). Prostitution and trafficking of women and children from Mexico to the United States. In: Farley M, ed. *Prostitution, trafficking, and traumatic stress.* New York, The Haworth Maltreatment & Trauma Press: 147–165.

Universal Declaration on Human Rights (1948). New York, UN (http://www.un.org/Overview/rights.html, accessed 25 February 2005).

United Nations Conference on Trade and Development (UNCTAD) (1999). *Trade and development report 1999: fragile recovery and risks, trade, finance and growth.* New York and Geneva, United Nations (http://www.unctad.org/en/docs/tdr1999_en.pdf, accessed 1 February 2005).

United Nations Development Programme (1999). *Human development report 1999: globalization with a human face*. New York, Oxford University Press.

United Nations Human Settlements Programme (UN-Habitat) (2003a). *State of the world's cities: trends in Latin America and the Caribbean*. Nairobi, UN-Habitat (http://www.unhabitat.org/mediacentre/documents/sowc/RegionalLAC.pdf, accessed 25 February 2005).

UN-Habitat (2003b). *Slums of the world: the face of urban poverty in the new millennium?* Nairobi, UN-Habitat.

UN Secretary-General (2002). *Outcome of the International Conference on Financing for Development*. New York, United Nations (Report no. A/57/344 – 57th Session) (http://www.un.org/esa/ffd/a57-344-ffd-outcome.pdf, accessed 1 February 2005).

Vasagar J (2004). EU freezes $150m to aid 'corrupt' Kenya. *The Guardian Weekly*, London, 30 July – 5 August:10.

Wade RH (2002). Globalisation, poverty and income distribution: does the liberal argument hold? In: Gruen D, O'Brien T, Lawson J, eds. *Globalisation, living standards and inequality: recent progress and continuing challenges, proceedings of a conference held in Sydney, 27–28 May*. Canberra, Reserve Bank of Australia, 37–65 (http://www.rba.gov.au/PublicationsAndResearch/Conferences/2002/, accessed 1 February 2005).

Wade RH (2003). Bridging the digital divide: new route to development or new form of dependency. *Global Governance*, 8:443–466.

Wade RH (2004). Is globalization reducing poverty and inequality? *World Development*, 32(4):567–589.

Watkins K (2002). Making globalization work for the poor. *Finance & Development*, 39(1).

White H, Killick T (2001). *African poverty at the millennium: causes, complexities, and challenges*. Washington, DC, IBRD/World Bank.

Williamson J (2002). *Winners and losers over two centuries of globalization*. Helsinki, UN University World Institute for Development Economics Research (WIDER Annual Lecture 6) (http://www.nber.org/papers/w9161.pdf, accessed 1 February 2005).

Williamson J (2004). *The Washington Consensus as policy prescription for development*. Washington, DC, World Bank (World Bank Practitioners for Development lecture, 13 January) (http://www.iie.com/publications/papers/williamson0204.pdf, accessed 1 February 2005).

Wiwa K (2004). Money for nothing – and the debt is for free. *The Globe and Mail*, 22 May, A19.

World Bank (1995). *World development report 1995: workers in an integrating world*. New York, Oxford University Press.

World Bank/International Monetary Fund (World Bank/IMF) (2002). *Market Access for Developing Country Exports – Selected Issues*. Washington, DC, International Monterey Fund, September 26 (http://www.imf.org/external/np/pdr/ma/2002/eng/092602.pdf, accessed 1 February 2005).

World Commission on the Social Dimension of Globalization (WCSDG) (2004). *A fair globalization: creating opportunities for all*. Geneva, ILO (http://www.ilo.org/public/english/wcsdg/docs/report.pdf, accessed 21 February 2005).

WHO (2000). *World health report 2000: Health Systems: improving performance*. Geneva, WHO (http://www.who.int/whr/2000/en/whr00_en.pdf, accessed 1 February 2005).

WHO (2004). *World health report 2004: changing history*. Geneva, WHO 2004 (http://www.who.int/whr/2004/en/report04_en.pdf, accessed 1 February 2005).

World Trade Organization (1996). *Zambia's economic and trade reforms start to show benefits*. Geneva, WTO (http://www.wto.org/english/tratop_e/tpr_e/tp37_e.htm, accessed 1 February 2005).

WTO (2000). European communities – measures affecting asbestos and asbestos containing products: report of the panel. Geneva, WTO (http://www.worldtradelaw.net/reports/wtoab/ec-asbestos(ab).pdf, accessed 1 February 2005).

Wysocki B (1995). The outlook: foreigners find U.S. a good place to invest. *The Wall Street Journal,* 7 August.

Yunker JA (2004). Could a global Marshall Plan be successful? An investigation using the WEEP simulation model. *World Development*, 32(7):1109–1137.

PART B | Health care services and systems

This section of the *Watch* is focused on the governance, organization and delivery of health care services.

Easy access to health care is critical for all people, and the ability to receive timely care when we are sick and at our most vulnerable is highly valued. The first chapter in this section discusses the critical determinants of access to health care and the reasons why this right is violated for many. It raises questions about the relationship between access and equity, and points to principles of health care financing that should be adopted by governments and international health agencies.

The chapter calls for a recommitment to the principles of the Alma Ata Declaration and calls for a new agenda of policies and actions that will develop health care systems capable of delivering on the principles of the Declaration.

These include reversing the growth and malign effects of the commercialization of health care over the last three decades; reasserting the role of government and non-market, trust-based relationships within health care systems; shifting the focus from narrow and selective health programmes towards a more holistic approach to health care systems development; balancing short-term, emergency responses with more long-term sustainable planning; and designing health care system that promote a multi-sectoral agenda of health promotion rather a limited medical model of clinical care.

A further chapter on the global market for health workers highlights the direct impact of the broader global political economy on health care systems in developing countries. Not only are the health care systems of developing countries under-resourced and over-burdened, but they face having their most precious assets poached and drained away by the pull of rich country health care systems. As the single biggest item of expenditure in a health care system, the world's response to the health personnel crisis of developing country health care systems must be placed under close scrutiny.

The effects of commercialization are discussed further in the second chapter on medicines. The role of Big Pharma – which portrays itself as a force for good – is placed under the microscope and reveals not just a significant deficiency in the current system for financing research and development, but also the existence of disturbing and unhealthy relationships between Big Pharma and regulatory authorities mandated to protect public health, the medical profession and the research community.

This theme is carried over into a chapter that looks at the developments in gene technology in health care. The process of unravelling the human genome is raising questions about who owns life itself and threatens to accentuate an individual-focused, biomedical conception of health at the expense of a more efficient public health approach.

Finally, a chapter on sexual and reproductive health highlights the on-going need to link health care to broader cultural, economic and political relations within society – in this case, in terms of gender. Advocacy which challenges injustices in access to health care needs to link with a broad range of different actors beyond the bounds of the health professions.

B1 | Health care systems and approaches to health care

Introduction

An estimated 30,000 children die every day, mainly from preventable and easily treatable causes (Black, Morris and Bryce 2003). Millions of people do not have access to health care because health care systems in many countries are either non-existent or moribund. In many countries in Sub-Saharan Africa and in war-ravaged countries such as Afghanistan, health care systems are in a state of collapse. Life expectancy in two regions, Sub-Saharan Africa and the republics of the former Soviet Union (FSU), is deteriorating. In the FSU, although health status and health care systems are better than in Africa, health status is deteriorating at the same time that health care systems are struggling to ensure universal access to care (Box B1.1). In middle- and high-income countries, health care systems also struggle with widening disparities in health and health care consumption; uncontrolled rises in health care costs; profit-driven inefficiencies; and a deterioration in trust between citizens and providers.

Instead of focusing on particular diseases or issues such as HIV/AIDS, 'mental health' or 'child health', this chapter is focused on developing an agenda for health care systems development. In doing so, it advocates looking back to the 1978 Alma Ata Declaration on Health (WHO/UNICEF 1978) and the pledge made to achieve 'Health for All' through the *Primary Health Care (PHC) Approach.*

The principles of the PHC Approach are as relevant today as they were nearly 30 years ago and provide a guide not just for the organization of health care systems, but also for how health care systems should act as an engine for promoting health and development more generally, and as an instrument for promoting equity and empowering the poor. Section 1 of this chapter reasserts these principles.

Section 2 goes on to explore how the principles of the PHC Approach have been undermined by various policies and events in five thematic areas:

1) macro-economic factors;
2) health sector reform, neoliberalism and the commercialization of health care;
3) 'selective' health care and verticalization;

4) selective and efficiency driven cost-effectiveness analysis; and

5) public sector failures.

It would be impossible to provide a detailed chronological or historical account of how health care systems have been undermined in recent decades, not least because the ways in which health care systems have developed or deteriorated have varied from country to country. However, the wide-ranging factors and policies that have undermined the PHC Approach are discussed so as to produce guiding principles for health care systems development in the future. The chapter then sets out in section 3 a case for the central role of governments and the public sector within health care systems, and concludes by outlining an agenda of principles and priorities for the revitalizing of health care systems in section 4.

1 Remembering Alma Ata and the Primary Health Care Approach

The Alma Ata Declaration, sponsored by WHO and UNICEF, arose from the observation of failings in health care systems, as well as the positive results from health programmes in countries such as Nicaragua, Costa Rica, Guatemala, Honduras, Mexico, India, Cuba, Bangladesh, the Philippines and China (Commission on the Social Determinants of Health 2005). The term 'Primary Health Care Approach' came to be associated with the health care elements of the Declaration and can be summarised as follows:

- First, it stresses a *comprehensive* approach to health by emphasizing 'upstream interventions' aimed at promoting and protecting health such as improving household food security, promoting women's literacy and increasing access to clean water. This places a greater emphasis on preventive interventions and counters the biomedical and curative bias of many health care systems, and promotes a multi-sectoral approach to health.
- Second, it promotes *integration* – of different clinical services within health facilities, of health programmes and of different levels of the health care system. This recommendation was partially in response to the limitations of 'vertical', stand-alone disease control programmes and to the observation that hospitals in many countries were not adequately involved in strengthening primary-level health care.
- Third, it emphasizes *equity*. This recommendation would, for example, aim to correct the neglect of rural populations, as well as socially and economically marginalized groups, within many health care systems.
- Fourth, it advocates the use of *'appropriate' health technology*, and health care that is socially and culturally acceptable.

*Box B1.1   Countries in decline – health and health care in Africa,
the former Soviet Union and Afghanistan*

Life expectancy in many Sub-Saharan Africa (SSA) countries has now dropped below 50 years. Much of this is due to HIV/AIDS, fuelled and compounded by high levels of poverty, food insecurity and conflict. While the burden of disease has been increasing, health care systems have been deteriorating. The best evidence of this is stagnating or decreasing rates of child immunization and maternal mortality – two indicators that are particularly sensitive to the functioning of health care systems. Immunization coverage rates peaked at 55% in 1990 and stagnated throughout the 1990s. By 2000, only 53% of children in the SSA region were immunized against diphtheria, tetanus and whooping cough (WHO, UNICEF and World Bank 2002). Of 41 SSA countries, only six had maternal mortality ratios of less than 500 per 100,000 live births in 2004 (UNFPA 2004). In 35 countries, at least one woman died for every 200 live births. Seventeen countries had a maternal mortality ratio of 1000 or more – one death per 100 live births. In 12 countries, the maternal mortality ratio worsened between 1994 and 2004 (UNFPA 2004, WHO, UNICEF and UNFPA 2001).

In all 15 of the new republics of the former Soviet Union, life expectancy at birth fell between 1990 and 2000. Although there are several reasons for this reversal of human development, an underlying problem has been the effects of post-Soviet political and economic change upon the health care systems of these countries (see: http://www.ghwatch.healthformersoviet union)

More than 20 years of conflict have contributed to the destruction of Afghanistan's health care infrastructure (Waldman and Hanif 2002). In 2002, 60% of Afghans had no access to basic health services and two-thirds of Afghanistan's districts lacked maternal and child health services (Transitional Islamic Government of Afghanistan 2002). The maternal mortality ratio is 1600 per 100,000 live births – every 20 to 30 minutes a woman dies because of pregnancy-related complications (Ahmad 2004). The government has very weak institutions and a lack of both military and administrative control in large parts of the country which remain under the control of warlords and local commanders (World Bank 2004).

• Fifth, it emphasizes appropriate and effective *community involvement* within the health care system.

- And sixth, it adopts a strong *human rights perspective* on health by affirming the fundamental human right to health and the responsibility of governments to formulate the required policies, strategies and plans of action.

Significantly, the Alma Ata Declaration also placed the challenge of 'Health for All' within a global and political context by calling for peace, reduced military expenditure and a 'New International Economic Order' to reduce the health status gap between developing and developed countries.

Since 1978, however, the term 'PHC Approach' has been frequently misunderstood and confused with the 'primary level' of the health care system. It is also often wrongly associated with cheap, low-technology care supposedly best suited to developing countries. In fact, the PHC Approach refers to a set of concepts and principles that are as relevant and applicable to a university teaching hospital as to a rural clinic; to a poor African country as to an industrialized European country; and to a highly specialized doctor as much as to a community-based lay health worker.

In the years immediately after Alma Ata, the District Health System (DHS) model was formulated as an organizational framework for a health care system to deliver the PHC Approach. For many health care practitioners, the PHC Approach and DHS model formed the conceptual and organizational pillars respectively for the attainment of Health for All. The DHS model (WHO 1988; WHO 1992) consists of:

- a health care system organized on the basis of clearly demarcated geographical areas (known as 'health districts'), ideally corresponding to an administrative area of government.
- the health district as the basis for the seamless integration of community-based, primary level and Level 1 hospital services. Level 1 hospitals were considered a vital hub in which to locate medical expertise, pharmaceutical supply systems, and transport to support a network of clinics and community-based health care.
- health districts sharing the same administrative boundaries as other key sectors (such as water, education and agriculture).
- a district-level health management team with the authority and capacity to manage the comprehensive and integrated mix of community-based, clinic and Level 1 hospital services; to facilitate effective multi-sectoral action on health; and to work with local private and non-government providers.

Guidance was provided on the size of 'health districts' based on a balance between being small enough to facilitate community involvement and context-specific health planning, but large enough to justify investment in a decentralized management structure. Central and intermediate-level policy makers and managers would ensure national coherence and coordination, common standards and equitable resource distribution amongst districts.

2 The demise of health for all

Macro-economic factors Health care systems require the availability of basic physical and human infrastructure throughout a country if they are to be effective and equitable. Countries need to invest in the development of this infrastructure, but many have no resources to do so.

Low- and lower middle-income countries need to spend at least US$30–40 (2002 prices) each year per person if they are to provide their populations with 'essential' health care (Commission on Macroeconomics and Health 2001). This sum is about three times the current average spending on health in the least developed countries and more than current spending in other low-income and lower middle-income countries. More to the point, it is over five times the average *government* health spending of the least developed countries and about three times that of other low-income countries. Estimates of this kind are fraught with methodological limitations and assumptions, but they indicate the size of the resource gap facing most developing countries.

The causes of impoverished health care systems are varied. Many countries with low levels of health care expenditure are in fact able to invest much more than they do. However, many macro-economic factors (discussed in part A) that help to keep poor countries poor, by extension, keep levels of health care expenditure low.

Historically, a key macro-economic event was the hikes in oil prices during 1979–1981, which precipitated an economic recession in industrialized countries, prompting governments in those countries to raise interest rates. The combination of recession in the industrialized world, higher oil prices and raised interest rates precipitated a macro-economic crisis in many developing countries, especially in Latin America and Sub-Saharan Africa. These countries experienced reduced export demand, declines in primary commodity (non-fuel) prices, deteriorating real terms of trade, lower capital inflows and soaring debt service payments. Many countries had negative economic growth, reduced government revenue and increasing poverty.

The effects on health care systems, so soon after the bold and visionary aspirations of the Alma Ata Declaration, were nothing short of disastrous. Most health care systems have never had a chance to recover from these effects which included:

59

- declines in real public health expenditure and increasing donor dependency;
- deterioration of health facilities and equipment;
- shortages of drugs and other supplies;
- dwindling patient attendance at public facilities as the quality of care worsened; and
- a catastrophic loss of morale and motivation of public health workers as the value of their salaries plummeted and as expenditure constraints undermined their ability to work (Segall 2000).

Demoralization, cynicism and unethical behaviour grew among public sector health workers. This included treating patients uncaringly, levying 'under the counter' charges, 'moonlighting' in the private sector and stealing drugs for private use (Bassett, Bijlmakers and Sanders, 1997). Public sector downsizing and resignations led to health workers migrating to the private sector, adding to the growing numbers of informal and unregulated drug vendors, 'pavement doctors' and other private practitioners. As public services deteriorated, households resorted increasingly to over the counter drug purchases and the use of private practitioners (Segall 2000). While informal health care practice has always existed in developing countries, this economic crisis resulted in its significant expansion independently of any health sector reforms, a process that is called 'passive privatization'.

The macro-economic crisis also had an indirect effect on health care systems. It provided the IMF and the World Bank with an on-going opportunity to intervene in and shape the health sector of poorer countries through structural adjustment programmes and conditionalities attached to grants, loans and debt relief.

Health sector reform, neoliberalism and the commercialization of health care
'Health sector reform' is the term used to describe a set of policies initially promoted by the World Bank and IMF, often through structural adjustment programmes, from the mid 1980s onwards. These have included imposing tight and reduced fiscal limits on public health care expenditure; promoting direct cost-recovery (user fees) and community-based financing; and transferring or out-sourcing functions to the private sector. Later, the ascendance of neoliberalism (Box B1.2) added an ideological impetus to the privatization of health care. More recently, the World Trade Organization (WTO), together with a number of bilateral and regional trade agreements (usually involving the United States), have influenced the design of health care systems by reducing

the capacity of governments to regulate health care markets, encouraging cross border 'trade' in health care, and facilitating the entry of corporate health businesses to operate more freely within health care systems of other countries (Hilary 2001, Shaffer et al. 2005).

The following sub-sections discuss three aspects of these effects on health care systems: the growth in user fees; the segmentation of health care systems; and the 'commercialization' of health care.

Box B1.2 Neoliberalism

The term 'neoliberalism' is used in different ways. Its origins may be in economic theory, but it is used in this chapter to describe a particular orientation to public policy. The US government under President Ronald Reagan and the UK government under Prime Minister Margaret Thatcher were at the heart of the emergence of neoliberalism in the 1980s. It was then propagated globally by institutions such as the IMF and World Bank.

Neoliberalism is taken to mean the vigorous promotion of markets – networks in which buyers and sellers interact to exchange goods and services for money – combined with a reduction in government or multilateral regulation. It was initially associated with promoting the maximum freedom of movement for finance capital, goods and commercial services, but now embraces the promotion of a minimally regulated market economy in sectors that used to be considered the responsibility of the state. These include sectors that provide essential services and public goods such as health care, education, social security, water and sewerage, and policing and prison services.

Concerns with neoliberalism relate to the weakening of governments' ability to discharge their public duties such as reducing poverty; protecting the public and environment from unregulated economic activity; and providing a fair framework for the redistribution of wealth and profits.

USER FEES AND THE DENIAL OF ACCESS TO ESSENTIAL HEALTH CARE One effect of health sector reform was the promotion of a greater privatization of health care financing (Box B1.3), including out-of-pocket payments for health care in the public sector (Akin, Birdsall and Ferranti 1987), partly to offset reduced levels of public expenditure. Such privatization added to the growth in user charges that arose from the 'passive privatization' of health care and the increase in informal, under-the-counter charges in the public sector.

The impact of this transfer of responsibility for health care financing onto households has been disastrous, particularly for the poor. It has deterred people from accessing health care and resulted in untreated sickness and avoidable death (Whitehead, Dahlgren and Evans 2001, Theodore 1999, World Bank 1999, Yu, Cao and Lucas 1997 and Fu 1999). User fees have also discouraged people from taking full doses of their medication; evidence is emerging that they undermine adherence to anti-retroviral treatment and increase the risk of drug resistance (WHO 2004). Even when health care is nominally free, financial barriers may still put health care beyond the reach of many families. Maternity services in Bangladesh, for instance, are free but in practice are accompanied by hidden and unofficial payments; for more than one fifth of families, these payments are the equivalent of 50–100% of their monthly income (Nahar and Costello 1998).

User fees also generate poverty, or deepen the poverty of those who are already poor. In rural North Vietnam, an estimated one fifth of poor households

---

Box B1.3 Public and private health care financing

Private financing takes many forms. Private health insurance is often paid by individuals, but some private sector employers contribute to their employees' private health insurance. In some places, households contribute to a community-financing scheme, which pools funds that are managed on behalf of all members of the scheme. User charges refer to out-of-pocket payments that service users make directly to providers. Medical savings accounts are promoted as a mechanism for households to build up a reserve of money to enable them to meet the cost of user fees in the future.

Public financing is generally based on general tax revenue or national health insurance. In developing countries, external grants and aid from donors can constitute anything between 20% and 80% of total public sector health care spending.

Public and private sources of financing often co-exist – for example, community-financing schemes may complement public funds used to pay the salaries of some health workers, while private medical insurance may receive tax breaks that amount in practice to a public subsidy.

were in debt primarily because of paying for health care (Ensor and Pham 1996). Patients who borrow money to pay for treatment can end up paying extortionate interest rates. To offset the cost of borrowing, households may cut down on their food consumption, sell off precious assets such as land or cattle, or withdraw children (particularly girls) from school to save on school fees (Whitehead, Dahlgren and Evans 2001, Tipping 2000).

It is argued that exemption schemes can protect the poor from user fees. But such schemes are rarely effective (Russell and Gilson 1997) and can encourage extortion and patronage when service providers are poorly remunerated. Neither is there any evidence that user fees prevent the 'frivolous' overuse of health services – for most people, cost barriers result in an *under*-use of health care services.

Given the evidence that user fees are a major and widespread barrier to essential health care, as well as a cause of long-term impoverishment, it is paradoxical that the poorer a country, the more likely its people will face out-of-pocket health care expenditure. In stark contrast, high-income countries tend to have 'socialized' financing systems based on general taxation, national health insurance or mandated social health insurance (Mackintosh and Koivusalo 2004).

THE SEGMENTATION OF HEALTH CARE SYSTEMS The 'segmentation of health care systems' refers to the phenomenon of separate health care systems for richer and poorer people, as opposed to one universal health care system for all. The World Bank in particular has advocated that governments in poorer countries should focus their scarce public resources on providing a free 'basic' or 'minimum' package of preventative and curative services for the poor, while withdrawing from the direct provision of other services. By encouraging the relatively rich sections of society to use the private sector, it argues that the public sector will be able to redirect its resources to those most in need (IFC 2002, Gwatkin 2003). In some middle- and high-income countries, tax breaks on private insurance are used to entice higher-income groups away from publicly provided services. Health care systems in some countries are being segmented even further by the processes of globalization – in India, Mexico and South Africa private providers cater to foreign 'medical tourists' from high-income countries or from high-income groups in low- and middle-income countries.

The assumption behind these policies is that it is more efficient and equitable to segment health care according to income level – a public sector focused on the poor and a private system for the rich that allows the public sector to focus on the poor. But there is no evidence that such a system is more equitable or efficient. The greater likelihood is that it would result in increased inequality as the middle-classes opt out of public sector provision, take their financial resources and stronger political voice with them, and leave the public service as a 'poor service for poor people'.

Even if private medical services are entirely privately financed, they still draw on a limited pool of health professionals and, in developing countries, on limited foreign exchange for the import of drugs and equipment. A large private medical sector weakens the public provision of health care, especially as the ratio of resources to patient load is more favourable in the private sector – it sucks out more health care resources than it relieves the public sector of workload.

However, the notion of a public sector for the poor has strong advocates. If higher income groups can be segmented out, there is more opportunity to provide health care as a profitable, commercial product to these groups. Segmentation is therefore attractive to private investors in health care, especially in countries where there is a large enough or rich enough upper- and middle-class market to sustain the development and financing of a private health sector. Latin America, Asia and transitional Europe – all regions with histories of social health insurance and direct public health care provision – are now seeing rising levels of private insurance and corporate investment (Stocker , Waitzkin and Iriat 1999), as governments come under pressure from the private sector and trade-related policies to break up universal social security funds, and to open up the market to foreign investment. Finally, some health care providers, who benefit from providing care to the privileged and better resourced market, will challenge any reforms aimed at universalizing health care systems, often claiming that they would reduce standards of care and invoking the rights of individuals to the best care they can afford. The implication is that equity is a secondary concern.

Besides separating out higher income groups from lower income ones, a parallel public and private health care system can result in private sector 'cherry-picking' – private medical insurance schemes will adopt strategies to recruit low-risk consumers, corner healthy and profitable markets, and leave the sick and the elderly dependent on the public sector. Private medical schemes worked this way in South Africa until the post-apartheid government enacted legislation to enforce 'community rating' (whereby insurance premiums cannot be weighted according to individual risk) and a nationally prescribed minimum level of cover to make it harder for private companies to dump patients arbitrarily onto the public sector when their health care costs became too great.

These trends towards segmentation of a health care system, structured through health care financing arrangements, appear to be driven by a policy to institute health care systems that reflect and reinforce socio-economic inequities rather than to mitigate them.

THE COMMERCIALIZATION OF HEALTH CARE The growth of private sector health care provision in developing countries has largely been a consequence of 'passive privatization'. The collapse of the public sector has led to the emergence of a disorganized, unregulated and even chaotic provider market in many developing countries, particularly at the primary level of health care. The incapacity of public services has also resulted in governments and donors relying upon NGOs, UN agencies, charities, religious groups and humanitarian organizations to plug the gaps in public provision not only in primary care but also in essential hospital services and in response to humanitarian emergencies.

In middle- and high-income countries, the private provider market is also heterogeneous and may include non-profit, charitable organizations; single, stand-alone private hospitals or group practices; employer-based health maintenance organizations; and large corporate or business entities with public shareholders. Private providers also operate in more formal markets that include intermediary agents such as insurance companies. Such provision may emerge as a consequence of demand from consumers as well as from active encouragement through policy-levers, such as tax subsidies to the private sector or the use of public money to out-source functions, including to the for-profit, income-maximizing private sector (see Box B1.4).

The heterogeneous group of private providers operate in many different contexts. For millions of people, private providers provide a lifeline to health care in the absence of any effective public alternative. At the same time, however, private health care is clearly associated with profit, exploitation and preferential service of higher income groups. What is at issue, therefore, is not simply private provision, but a certain type or aspect of private health care provision – that of market-and income-driven provision when payments for health care are directly linked to provider income or shareholder profit.

What is relevant is the influence of such provision on provider behaviour that results in inefficient, inequitable and poor quality care (Woolhandler and Himmelstein 2004, Devereaux et al. 2002, Evans 1997). Such behaviour includes pricing health care to maximize income rather than to maximize access and benefit; 'over-servicing' (for example, conducting unnecessary and inappropriate laboratory tests and diagnostic investigations); inducing demand for health care that is unnecessary or inappropriate; providing sub-optimal (cheaper) health care in order to maximize net income; and providing inappropriate care in order to market a supposed difference from other providers (for example, advocating injections as better quality care when oral treatment or simple health advice would be better).

Commercialization also affects the nature of health care itself. It encourages a commodification of health care and a bias towards biomedical and curative interventions because it is easier to market and sell tangible health care products and services. Such commercialization benefits, and is therefore encouraged by, the medical profession, pharmaceutical companies and the

---

Box B1.4 New Public Management

New Public Management (NPM) is a term used to describe private sector solutions to public sector constraints. It is based on the idea that the monopoly power of government, and the lack of competition to government departments and civil servants that would otherwise compel them to be efficient and accountable to service users, are responsible for bureaucratic rigidity, corruption and inefficiency.

One NPM solution is to introduce competition between different public sector departments and 'internal markets' (purchaser-provider splits) within the public sector. Another is to restrict the role of government from being a funder and supplier of services to that of a funder and contractor of services. Public sector bureaucracy would then shrink as it moved away from public management via bureaucratic control to 'management by contract' of independent private sector providers, semi-independent parastatal agencies or local government bodies. In some instances, public sector entities are 'corporatized' (granted a greater degree of autonomy) and expected to enter the provider market to compete for government contracts and tenders.

The extent to which NPM has achieved its stated goals is contested (Stewart 1998, Evans 1997, Maynard 1998, Khalegian and Das Gupta 2004). Critics point to the high transaction costs associated with the management of internal markets; the use of internal markets as a staging post towards the eventual privatization of public services; the emphasis on competition over collaboration; and the emergence of an inappropriately excessive 'target-driven' culture (see http://www.ghwatch.org/targetcultureNHS).

medical-industrial complex. Public health measures to prevent illness and promote good health are easily neglected in the process.

Although commercial behaviour is associated with for-profit private providers, it can occur in the public sector as well. The under-financing of public health care systems and the growth in informal (under-the-counter) charges have resulted in the neglect of patients who cannot afford fees and a higher quality of care given to those who can. Similarly, public hospitals that have been granted greater autonomy, including the responsibility of raising some or all of their own finance, become motivated by the imperative to raise income and to balance their accounts. Managers and clinicians have a further incentive to prioritize the maximization of income if they can exceed civil service pay-scales. Although these hospitals remain publicly-owned, their character and nature mimic those of the private sector operating in a market.

Market-driven health care often does not promote efficiency or quality for several obvious reasons (Bloom 1991, Roemer 1984, Arrow 1963, Rice 1997). First, most patients do not have enough knowledge to make informed choices about the relative quality or merits of different health care providers, nor are they willing, able or assertive enough to negotiate on price and quality, especially when care is urgent, when sickness results in vulnerability, or when illiteracy and poverty are prevalent. Most people do not want 'choice' in health care, but an assurance that their local and accessible health care provider will provide good, if not the best, quality care. Instead, commercialized health care eats away at provider-patient trust, adding to the stress of being sick or injured. A trusting, caring and compassionate relationship between patient and health worker is in itself a therapeutic intervention that is corrupted by the market-based relationship between consumer and provider.

Second, the theory that provider competition will drive up quality and efficiency does not apply in many settings, particularly when it would be either unaffordable or wasteful to have several providers competing with each other. Rather than managing available health resources in a strategic way to achieve equitable coverage, competition results in duplication and inequity as for-profit providers gravitate towards affluent populations (McPake 1997). The promotion of choice and competition implies a need to differentiate the standard of care rather than to ensure high quality care for all.

Third, commercialized health care systems often have significant transaction costs accompanying attempts to manage or regulate the market (Himmelstein et al. 1999). Similar cost issues accompany the management of public contracts with private providers, especially those providers motivated to maximize income, who may strive to make short-cuts or manipulate data to achieve their contract specifications at the lowest cost, even at the expense of patients and the public good. To counteract this, purchasers end up spending large amounts of money on systems designed to catch out contractees in a 'cat and mouse' game of detection and deception, or end up being drawn into costly contract disputes.

Fourth, market-based systems with multiple independent providers are inefficient because of the loss of economies-of-scale in the purchasing, supply and distribution of drugs and equipment (Robinson and White 2001). They can pose barriers to developing important public health instruments that need to be applied consistently and universally, such as disease surveillance systems, if they are to be effective.

Finally, competition harms collaboration between different providers, often an important ingredient of good quality care, especially in relation to referrals between different kinds of specialists or between different levels of the health care system. Fragmented performance contracts can also undermine collaboration within health care systems. In China, for instance, competition *within* the public sector harmed the inter-provider cooperation that was necessary for effective disease surveillance (Liu and Mills 2002).

Selective health care and verticalization 'Selective health care' refers to a limited focus on certain health care interventions, as distinct from comprehensive or holistic health care. The most common argument in favour of selective health care is that, until health care systems are adequately resourced and organized, it is better to deliver a few proven interventions of high efficacy at high levels of coverage, aimed at diseases responsible for the greatest mortality (Walsh and Warren 1979).

Selective health care tends to be associated with 'vertical programmes' – generally meaning separate health structures with strong central management dedicated to the planning, management and implementation of selected interventions – partly because of a lack of adequate health care infrastructure, but also because it often reflects a scientific and biomedical orientation that emphazies the delivery of 'medical technologies' amenable to vertical programmes. Just as smallpox was eradicated through a concerted global effort, for instance, it is argued that diarrhoeal disease, malaria and other common diseases can be tackled in a similar way.

By the early 1980s, WHO, UNICEF and major bilateral donors, notably US-AID, had endorsed this approach, epitomized by the 'Child Survival Revolution' launched in 1982. This prioritized seven child health interventions: growth monitoring, oral rehydration therapy (ORT), breastfeeding, immunization, family planning, food supplements and female education, which collectively became known as the acronym GOBI-FFF.

In many ways, the logic of prioritizing cost-effective interventions to reduce child mortality is sound, and the practice can even be considered successful. Many countries made substantial progress in reducing child mortality following the launch of GOBI-FFF: the average number of under-5 deaths fell from 117 per 1000 in 1980 to 93 per 1000 in 1990, while immunization coverage expanded rapidly between 1980 and 1990 (UNICEF 2001).

However, there are problems with vertically-organized selective health care interventions (Smith and Bryant 1988, Rifkin and Walt 1986, Newell 1988, Unger and Killingsworth 1986). In the case of the 'child survival revolution', it has been argued that the focus on a limited set of technological interventions detracted attention from a more comprehensive approach to child health. For example, treating children with acute diarrhoeal disease would not be accompanied by interventions to improve childcare, feeding or access to water. Complex health problems with underlying social and economic determinants were recast as problems to be treated or prevented through the delivery of effective technologies. The participatory and bottom-up orientation of the PHC Approach has been downgraded, and the socio-political orientation of Alma Ata, with its emphasis on community empowerment and socio-economic equity, replaced by an approach that treated poorer communities more as passive recipients of health care than as active participants.

Questions have also been raised about the appropriateness of certain technologies. In the case of diarrhoeal disease, for example, the biomedical orientation resulted in the promotion of manufactured oral rehydration salts rather than more appropriate and accessible rehydration fluids that could be prepared locally (Werner and Sanders 1997).

In many countries, the selective health care approach has manifested itself as a set of multiple, parallel programmes operating in separate and fragmented 'stovepipes', disrupting the development of comprehensive health systems and the delivery of integrated essential health care. Multiple and centralized lines of command, frequently originating from within donor or international health agencies and often uncoordinated, tended to subvert local and more appropriate health planning. Information systems often comprise separate reporting forms sent directly to the central level without informing local service development. In Laos, 'Primary Health Care' itself was a separate programme, competing for resources with the immunization, malaria and TB programmes (Toole et al. 2003).

Multiple, vertical programmes can also lead to the de-skilling of primary health care workers as their focus narrows to achieving selected targets rather than addressing the immediate and pressing needs of sick people when they present to health care services. Instead of training scarce health workers to provide essential and appropriate health care, such programmes train them to be efficient conduits of medical technology. Thousands of family planning volunteers have been deployed in many countries, for instance, but many opportunities to promote health were lost because their training focused on the single technical issue of contraception and did not include other elements of community health promotion, such as nutrition and hygiene education (Toole et al. 2003).

Vertically organized health services are inconvenient to service users. The need to make several visits to access different services constitutes a significant barrier to access, while the inability of some selective programmes to address co-existing conditions could result in untreated morbidity – for example, family planning workers being unable to treat sexually transmitted infections; or ante-natal care providers being unable to provide immunization services (Brown 2000).

Although selective health care is often advocated on the grounds that basic health care infrastructure is inadequate, it is rarely implemented in conjunction with a plan to strengthen such infrastructure at the same time. As a result, many selective and vertical programmes have short-lived results because they are not followed by the establishment of permanent health services to sustain the on-going control and prevention of disease. Worse still, they may actually undermine the development of health care systems. Mass immunization campaigns, for example, have often been prioritized to such an extent that other services have been disrupted and the long-term development of sustainable routine immunization services hindered.

The inadequate development and protection of basic health care infrastructure, and the lack of sustained donor funding for child health, is more apparent now than a decade ago. In spite of the child survival revolution, 11 million children die each year from mainly preventable causes. Globally, the target set by the World Summit for Children in 1990 to reduce child mortality below 70 deaths per 1000 live births by the year 2000 (or a one-third reduction if it yielded a lower mortality rate than this target) has not been met (UNICEF 2001). In many countries, immunization coverage rates are stagnant or declining (see Figure B1.1). In others, the reduction in child mortality rates has slowed down (Black, Morris and Bryce 2003).

Some argue that the gains in child health made between 1980 and 2000 were a result of tackling illnesses that are most amenable to vertical interven-

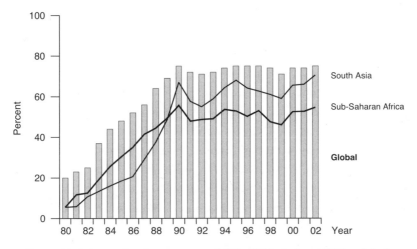

Figure B1.1 Immunization coverage 1980–2001, 3 doses DPT – global and by region (*Source*: WHO/UNICEF/World Bank 2002)

tions, and that any further improvements will need major efforts to strengthen the overall quality of health services (Box B1.5). Moreover, reductions in child mortality may not be sustained unless national health systems take over some of the roles played by donors and international NGOs in funding and deliver-

---

Box B1.5 Integrated Management of Childhood Illness

WHO and UNICEF have promoted the Integrated Management of Childhood Illness (IMCI) to reduce child mortality and morbidity. IMCI has a proven efficacy (Schellenberg et al 2004) and governments in more than 100 countries have committed themselves to implementing it. However, a systematic multi-country evaluation of IMCI has shown that, in most countries, fewer than 10% of all health workers providing child care have been trained, and that the rate of training was not sufficient to achieve high coverage in the foreseeable future (Amaral et al, forthcoming). Barriers to scaling up and sustaining high-quality care over time include the cost of training, problems caused by health workers being removed from clinical duties for a significant period to attend training courses, the limited availability of trainers and high rates of staff turnover – up to 40% in a two-year period in some countries (Bryce et al. 2003). IMCI programmes, no matter how good in theory, will struggle to make a widespread and long-lasting impact unless they are integrated into a comprehensive strategy for health systems development, especially in terms of human infrastructure.

Approaches to health care

71

ing services, highlighting the ephemeral nature of gains secured by vertical initiatives.

Today, selective approaches are a prominent feature of the international health policy landscape. Despite rhetoric about the need to improve coordination between different disease-based programmes and to complement vertical initiatives with a health systems development agenda, the multitude of single-focus or single-disease initiatives is reminiscent of the heyday of vertical programmes in the 1980s. At the country level, recipient governments are expected to dance to the tune of an international agenda rather than developing targets, policies and plans based on their own circumstances. Health care responses to high morbidity and mortality reflect a biomedical and 'technological' bias (vaccines, medicines or new technologies such as insecticide treated bednets) while a coherent and financially-backed agenda for the long-term and sustainable development of equitable health systems remains absent.

The Millennium Development Goals are also placing health services under pressure to achieve the MDG targets through selective interventions. It has been calculated that making 15 preventive interventions and eight treatment interventions universally available in 42 counties would achieve the MDG child mortality target (Jones et al. 2003). The pressure on governments to apply for and disburse quickly resources from new financing instruments, such as the Global Fund to fight AIDS, TB and Malaria (GFATM), so as to show the positive impact of such bodies, could also undermine cohesive health systems development (Box B1.6).

According to one group of child health experts, although many of the current disease-specific initiatives relate at least indirectly to child survival, and in this sense have expanded the resources available to child health, 'the result is a set of fragmented delivery systems, rather than a coordinated effort to meet the needs of children and families' (Bellagio Study Group on Child Survival 2003). They note that 'in today's environment of disease-specific initiatives, cross-disease planning, implementation, and monitoring are hard to establish and maintain'. Paradoxically, the threat of narrow, disease-based programmes disrupting health care systems is most acute where such systems are already fragile and under-resourced (Victora et al. 2003).

Many of the selective health care initiatives now operate as Global Public Private Initiatives (Box B1.7), introducing a much higher level of involvement from the commercial/private sector. This brings in private financing and private sector 'know-how', but at the same time provides the commercial sector with further public subsidies, and the opportunity to capture a share of the resulting market for their products.

Box B1.6 *The pitfalls of expanding anti-retroviral treatment in developing countries*

On the back of inspiring civil society campaigns to reduce the price of anti-retroviral treatment (ART), millions of dollars are now being directed at expanding access to these medicines. However, there are several pitfalls in this largesse that are particularly relevant to countries with under-resourced, disorganized and inequitable health care systems (McCoy et al 2005).

One is that access to ART could be expanded at the expense of other vital health care services, or could divert resources away from the prevention of HIV transmission. A focus on ART could also 'over-medicalize' the response to HIV/AIDS, and turn attention away from the political, social and economic determinants of the epidemic.

A second pitfall is that ART programmes may take inappropriate 'short-cuts' to achieve ambitious coverage targets and compromise on the quality and long-term outcome of care. Insufficient community and patient preparation, erratic and unsustainable drug supplies, and inadequate training and support of health care providers could result in low levels of treatment adherence, tending to an increased threat of drug resistance.

A third pitfall arising out of the pressure to achieve quick results is the use of non-government supply and delivery systems for ART because of their ability to set projects up quickly. Apart from the additional burden of coordinating and monitoring multiple non-government treatment services, this approach can weaken the capacity of the public sector health care system still further by draining skilled personnel into the better-paid independent sector.

Finally, ambitious ART coverage targets may lead to a preferential targeting of easier-to-reach, higher-income groups, typically those living in urban areas, and thereby widening existing health care inequities. A treatment-focused approach that inadequately addresses the basic needs of households, such as food security and access to water, will limit the capacity of the poor to benefit from ART.

Narrow, 'selective' or disease-based programmes or initiatives are not inherently bad, nor are they always influenced by undue commercial considerations. For some health interventions, for example those related to the control

73

Box B1.7 Global Public Private Initiatives (GPPIs)

There are currently about 80 GPPIs, the overwhelming number of which are linked to a specific disease or to the development of a new drug or vaccine. Examples include the Global Fund for HIV/AIDS, TB and Malaria; Roll Back Malaria; Stop TB; Global Alliance for Vaccines and Immunization; Global Polio Eradication Initiative; and the Global Alliance for the Elimination of Lymphatic Filariasis. WHO and UNICEF are the principal international governmental or multilateral actors involved, but the World Bank also plays a prominent role. On the private side, the Bill and Melinda Gates and Rockefeller Foundations are prominent, as are several for-profit pharmaceutical companies. Some NGOs are also involved, particularly with GPPIs they have helped to launch. However, certain groups are systematically under-represented, particularly poorer countries' governments and civil society organizations. On the whole, decision-making power sits in the hands of multilateral institutions and the commercial sector. (*Source*: Wemos 2004)

---

of vectors for infectious diseases such as mosquitoes, or those related to the control of acute disease outbreaks, a vertical and centralized approach may be entirely appropriate. Today, however, there is a growing proliferation of initiatives and programmes that collectively undermine national planning and coordination; a biomedical, technological bias towards health improvement; inappropriate public-private 'partnerships'; and the lack of more long-term and sustainable approaches to health systems development.

The rise of selective and efficiency-driven cost effectiveness analysis Cost effectiveness analysis (CEA) is a tool designed to rank the relative worth of different health care interventions. In 1993, the World Bank published a ranking of common health care interventions according to their cost effectiveness and used it to propose a minimum package of services for use in low- and middle-income countries (World Bank 1993). Its proposal appears rational at one level, but reinforced a selective approach to health care and undermined equity.

First, the Bank proposed that only this package should qualify for public funding – services outside the package that it deemed were not cost effective were considered discretionary and would have to be funded by individuals out-of-pocket or through insurance. Middle-income countries could be less restrictive than low-income ones in determining the content of a minimum package, although the same principles would apply. A closer inspection of the package reveals its serious shortcomings. At best, the minimum package would avert no more than one third of the estimated burden of disease in low-income countries and less than a fifth in middle-income countries. Examples of care that would be excluded from public funding in poorer countries include: emergency treatment of moderately severe injuries; treatment of childhood meningitis; and treatment of chronic conditions including diabetes, cataract, hypertension, mental illness and cervical cancer (Segall 2003).

Secondly, the health maximizing approach used by the Bank relied on a limited definition of health outcome. Consider the case of a single-handed poor farmer who develops a disabling inguinal (groin) hernia. His condition would be excluded from publicly funded treatment because the number of 'disability-adjusted life years' that would be gained by the farmer would not represent good value for money. What is not considered is how the hernia could undermine the farmer's ability to provide for his family, thus impoverishing them and thereby undermining their health. The calculation of 'disability-adjusted life years' gained would be different if these considerations were taken into account.

The World Bank also tended to apply CEA to discrete interventions rather than those interventions that have more complex direct and indirect impacts on health. Water provision is a good example. Access to adequate volumes of clean water not only reduces the incidence of diarrhoeal disease, intestinal worms, skin and eye diseases, but also improves child and maternal health indirectly by enabling women (who are usually the ones collecting water) to spend more time on other activities such as child care or household and economic tasks. However, the Bank did not classify improving access to clean water as a cost-effective health intervention.

Finally, although priority setting exercises are sound in principle, the Bank defined the goal of efficiency to mean the maximization of *aggregate* health gain for a given expenditure. The issue as to which people or population groups gained additional health was less important as the policy focus moved away from the prioritization of people in greatest need to the prioritization of interventions that would contribute most to aggregate health gain. The links between this approach with the Bank's stated intention to help the poor were only indirect. First, the interventions for inclusion in the minimum package were also selected according to the estimated population burden of disease they would address – as the poor constitute a high proportion of the population and make a substantial contribution to the total burden of disease, their disease patterns would be influential in the selection of interventions. Second, many of the diseases associated with poverty are amenable to simple and cost-effective interventions. However, from the standpoint of equity, resources should be allocated first towards tackling the health problems of poor people and only then between different programmes or interventions.

Public sector failure In many countries, the principles of Alma Ata have also been undermined by public sector failures. Illegitimate and corrupt governments that steal from the public purse, practise and tolerate human rights abuses, and allocate inappropriately high budgets to the military or to projects that benefit the elites of society are clearly one root cause of public sector failure – although these characteristics are by no means the sole preserve of poor countries. Corrupt and abusive regimes undermine the attainment of health for all and clearly require political solutions arising from within the countries themselves.

But corruption, abuse and state expenditure are far from being the consequence of local factors alone. Enabling all countries to have stable and effective governments that can improve people's health requires an international response to address the various ways in which richer countries or institutions endorse and support corrupt governments: the arms trade; banks and tax havens harbouring money that elites have looted from poor countries; Western corporations paying bribes; foreign government interference and collusion with illegitimate regimes; and the 'legitimate' and illegitimate economic transactions involving the purchase of natural resources (diamonds, minerals, oil, timber) from repressive and undemocratic countries (Pogge 2002).

Within countries, the ways in which societies organize themselves through their political systems and how these systems support health and development is clearly important. Some research suggests an independent positive association between health and democracy, political rights and civil liberties (Franco, Alvarez-Dardet and Ruiz 2004). However, the underlying mechanisms for the association between democracy and health are complex and may also depend on how democracy and rights are formulated and thought of – millions of people in the United States, for instance, have the political freedom to vote in a rich country but this is not a sufficient requirement for their access to health care. At the same time, countries without democratic political systems, such as China and Cuba, have achieved good and equitable health outcomes due to their commitment to ensuring universal access to the basic requirements of good health (Commission on the Social Determinants of Health 2005). The ways in which different social, political and economic systems influence the capacity for health systems to function effectively and

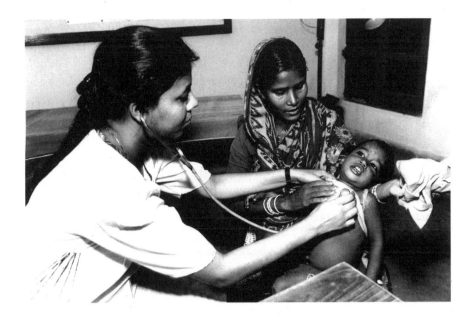

4 Effective clinical care is vital to the health and well-being of children.
But the mother of this child will also need to be given appropriate advice
and practical support on child care and nutrition.

equitably need more discussion and research amongst the international public health community.

Health care systems can also fail people as a result of bureaucratic failures. Rigid civil service rules and regulations combined with poor management and leadership can impair innovation, motivation, efficiency and community responsiveness. Civil servants can bend the rules or use their positions to serve their own personal needs. Many countries do not have the capacity for effective administration – for example, there may be no experts in the field of 'personnel management' working in the entire Ministry of Health in spite of the central importance of people to health care systems. Government health departments have vast responsibilities and varied challenges; they simply cannot succeed without a minimum degree of management and administrative capacity and competence at all levels of the health care system. At present, however, efforts are inadequate to ensure this level of capacity and competence.

In countries in which donor funds contribute a significant proportion of public health expenditure, public sector failure must be regarded as 'donor and international agency failure' as well. The influence of donors and international agencies on the functioning of the Ministries of Health in developing countries can be enormous – and is often not positive. One problem is the lack of coordination amongst donors and other external agents, more so now with the recent proliferation of global health initiatives. Ministries of Health in developing countries are faced with a circus of multiple external initiatives and programmes (often focused narrowly on specific diseases or interventions), donors, creditors and international NGOs (Figure B1.2) – this is hardly conducive to nationally-led decision-making; coordinated and coherent policy-making and planning; long-term development; or stable and efficient administration.

Furthermore, external policies and programmes imposed from the outside are inadequately tailored to local contexts. Policies, approaches and conceptual tools are often produced within donor circles and then applied worldwide – but supposedly 'owned' by recipients. Many agencies are staffed by individuals who have little or no understanding of local culture and history, a problem compounded by high staff turnover (Pfeiffer 2003).

Even in countries where a formal sector-wide approach (SWAp) has been established to create a health sector strategy shared by all stakeholders and to enable greater government leadership, the role of government can often be cosmetic (Hill 2002, Foster, Brown and Conway 2000), while international agencies preserve their own priorities, working styles, reporting formats, data collecting forms, financial procedures and short funding cycles. Only where there is firm government leadership, a clear vision based on a good understanding of health care problems on the ground, and a demand from NGOs and civil society for more national coordination, are countries able to resist the imposition of top-down, blueprint models of health development.

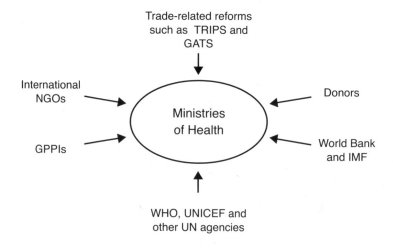

Figure B1.2 The circus of external agencies and initiatives

3 Resurrecting the 'public' in health care systems

The previous sections have outlined the key processes that have undermined the PHC Approach, while recognizing that different factors and forces have had different effects in different contexts. Figure B1.3 below illustrates the interactions and pathways that have hindered equity and efficiency within health care systems. Reversing these trends sustainably and effectively requires addressing all these factors simultaneously – simple, quick fixes will not suffice or be effective. It requires the involvement of more than health care providers, managers and health sector policy makers – many of the solutions involve political, social and economic interventions.

There is a need to resurrect and revitalize the 'public' within health care systems as part of an agenda for change. The goals of such an agenda should be to restore a proper balance and relationships between the public and private sectors as well as between public health care (population and community-based approaches to health) and individual private health care.

For several years, a prevailing view in certain media and amongst many policy makers has been that the private sector is better than the public sector. This is usually accompanied by another view that suggests that incentives formed through market dynamics result in 'better' and more efficient performance of health care systems than those of bureaucratic systems. While there are certainly problems within the public sector that need addressing, the record of public sector success is substantial. Added to this are the achievements of non-government actors, universities and charities, which may not be part of the public sector but which operate with a public ethic rather than one driven by competition, self-interest or market signals.

Public sector social welfare has been the bedrock of European social and economic development since the Second World War. Furthermore, low-income countries like Sri Lanka, Costa Rica and Cuba have had well-performing public health services for decades. The rapid and equitable decline in maternal mortality in Malaysia after independence from Britain in 1957 was due to government leadership (Pathmanathan et al 2003). Publicly-funded research in national institutes of science and universities has laid the foundations for many, if not most, developments in the medical sciences. Hundreds of thousands of public servants across the world are currently helping to make societies work in hundreds of different ways through bureaucracies – forms of organization characterized by a clear division of labour; clearly defined authority and responsibility; and administration and decision-making based on transparent rules.

For health care systems, several arguments point to the need for the public sector to take a central role. The first is that people have a right to health care

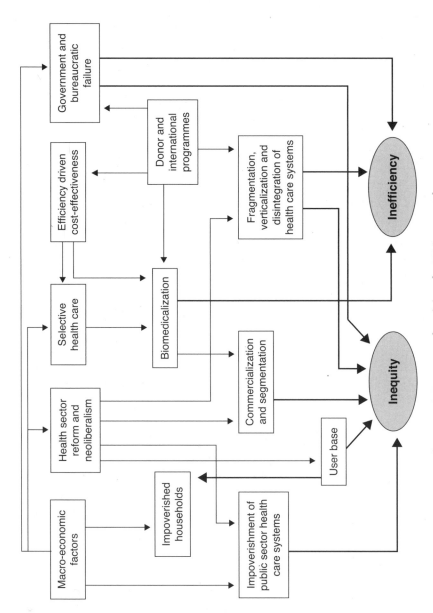

Figure B1.3 Factors undermining the PHC approach

that is not dependent on their ability to pay or on the vagaries of the market. Governments are critical to ensuring that these rights are fulfilled. Public sector health services are people's ultimate recourse for health care, especially poorer people. But public services must not become marginalized as 'poor care for the poor'. Societies should strive instead to use the health care system to promote social solidarity and to mitigate the effects of socio-economic disparities; they must be bold enough to make the idea of universal public-funded health care systems not just acceptable but aspirational.

Second, equitable and efficient health care systems require careful organization – fragmented, disorganized and market-driven health care systems are inefficient and inequitable. Public sector provision allows for direct planning of the location and types of health facilities and the organization of a coherent service to respond to the health care needs of a population. It allows the right balance to be struck between public health and clinical services, and between preventive and curative services.

Third, an adequately financed public service offers the best means of breaking the link between the income of health care providers and the delivery of health care – arguably one of the most critical conditions for the development of ethical behaviour and values within health systems and for avoiding the harm associated with 'commercial behaviour'.

This is not to deny any role for non-government actors. In many countries, the lack of public sector capacity is so great that a dependence on non-government providers is unavoidable. Non-government actors can also enhance community involvement within health programmes, help ensure public sector accountability and support public sector development. It is the role of commercially-driven private sector actors and the weakening of the public sector that has clashed most fundamentally with the aim of cost-effective and equitable health for all.

These arguments are based on socially-determined values. But there is also evidence that the larger the role of the public sector in health care systems, the better the outcome (Mackintosh and Koivusalo 2004). Healthy life expectancy (HALE), for instance, is significantly higher, and child mortality significantly lower, in countries with lower levels of private health expenditure relative to public expenditure (Figure B1.4); this remains the case after allowing for level of economic development and the influence of AIDS in Sub-Saharan Africa.

Countries that spend more of their GDP on health through public expenditure or social insurance also have significantly better health outcomes in terms of HALE and child mortality (see Figure B1.5). Better health in richer countries is therefore associated with higher incomes *and* with more public and so-

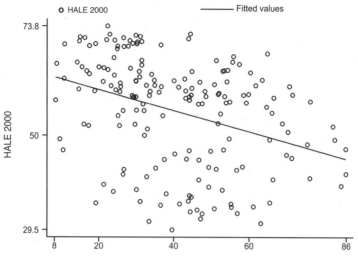

Figure B1.4 **Association between healthy life expectancy and private health care expenditure as a percentage of total health care expenditure, 2000** (*Source*: **Mackintosh and Koivusalo forthcoming 2005**)

cial health expenditure relative to GDP. Conversely, countries that apportion more of their GDP to private health expenditure do not display better health outcomes in terms of HALE or child mortality, after allowing for the effect of higher incomes on health outcomes. In fact, there is a mild (non-significant) association with worse outcomes (Mackintosh and Koivusalo 2004).

These observations are corroborated by Demographic and Health Survey (DHS) data from 44 low- and middle-income countries (Mackintosh and Koivusalo 2004) suggesting that:

- The proportion of deliveries with a skilled birth attendant is positively associated with higher government health expenditure as a share of GDP.
- Countries with a high proportion of children with acute respiratory infections (ARI) or diarrhoea who are treated privately generally have a lower proportion of children who are treated for these conditions at all, suggesting that higher levels of private provision are associated with higher levels of exclusion from health care.
- The percentage of children from the poorest 20% of households who were treated for ARI was more comparable (more equitable) to the percentage of children treated for ARI from the richest 20% of households in countries with a lower level of private primary care provision, suggesting that a greater privatization of primary care is associated with greater inequality.

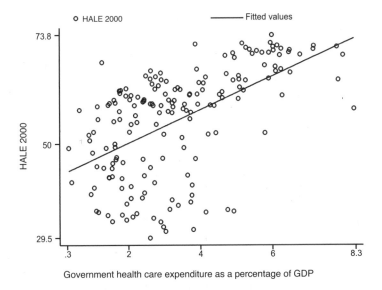

Figure B1.5 Association between healthy life expectancy and government health care expenditure as a percentage of GDP, 2000 (*Source*: Mackintosh and Koivusalo forthcoming 2005)

4 Agenda for health systems development

This section sets out an agenda to repair the damage to the public sector, uphold the role of accountable government in health care provision and reassert the principles of the PHC Approach. Its ten recommendations are not stand-alone options but need to be implemented together, and tailored to the particular social, political and economic realities of a given country.

Valuing and revitalising the public sector health worker – the lifeblood of health services Changing and improving how health personnel behave and function is so central to the rebuilding of health services, especially in developing countries, that it cannot be treated as just another administrative or bureaucratic task.

The performance of public sector health workers is affected by many factors and calls for a concerted, coordinated programme of health worker support and development. The re-establishment of a living wage is one requirement if health workers are to behave ethically and function effectively – countries must make up lost ground in the deterioration of public service salaries. Ensuring the right number and mix of types of health personnel (for example, increasing the number of nurses, medical auxiliaries and community health workers relative to doctors) can help countries to create payrolls that are sustainable, efficient and inclusive of incentives for trained staff to work in under-served areas.

But improved health worker performance cannot be achieved through money alone. The problems of demoralization and demotivation are more complex and require a multi-dimensional programme involving:

- adequate supplies of essential equipment, consumables and medicines to enable health workers to exercise their skills;
- systematic quality improvement programmes, including the training of staff in health service quality, interpersonal relations and responsiveness of care;
- support for health workers, especially those who work in isolated and difficult circumstances;
- a participatory style of health service management; and
- an incentive structure of professional rewards for good performance.

At the same time, clear rules and sanctions must signal that theft, unethical practices, and uncaring and abusive behaviour towards patients, especially the poor, women, elderly and ethnic minorities, will not be tolerated. Disciplinary procedures, however, must be consistent, fair and transparent.

There are also a range of management tools and processes that can be employed to promote commitment, good performance and ethical behaviour within public sector bureaucracies – these include non-financial incentives such as peer recognition and public praise of good performance; and opportunities to advance career and learning prospects. Ensuring improved performance through a combination of rules, public accountability and non-financial incentives requires much more emphasis to counter the prevailing focus on economic and market-based incentives.

Resources to achieve health for all For many countries, the need for adequately financed public sector health care systems is the paramount objective. The outright cancellation of unpayable debt, fair trade reform, increased and improved levels of overseas development assistance and the creation of new forms of global financing (see part A, part E, chapters 5 and 6, and part F) have to be part of any agenda for global health care systems development and should be reflected more prominently in the lobbying of international health agencies, including those of the major philanthropic foundations operating in the health and development sector. External financing must, however, be guaranteed with medium- to long-term commitments, and directed in ways that will strengthen Ministries of Health.

Within countries, governments should strengthen their capacity to increase their tax revenue in a progressive and fair manner. All countries should aim to raise an amount of tax revenue that is at least 20% of their GDP. Success in mobilizing public finance for health will then depend on the negotiating skills and credibility of the Ministry of Health, as well as an ability of social movements and other non-government actors to make effective demands on the political system. Civil society must also be encouraged and supported to monitor government budgetary allocations.

Financing health for all Health financing policies should aim to create a single national pool of funds, with the capacity for cross-subsidization between

---

Box B1.8 Millennium Development Goals for the financing of health care systems

The health-related MDGs have mostly been formulated in terms of outcome indicators. These are important, but do not chart a path to achieve the outcome goals. The following suggested targets for health systems financing may serve to explore how to map out such a path:

- countries to raise the level of tax revenue to *at least* 20% of their GDP;
- public health expenditure (including government and donor finance) to be at least 5% of GDP;
- government expenditure on health to be at least 15% of total government expenditure;
- direct out-of-pocket payments less than 20% of total health care expenditure;
- expenditure on district health services (up to and including Level 1 hospital services) at least 50% of total public health expenditure, of which half (25% of total) should be on primary level health care;
- expenditure on district health services (up to and including Level 1 hospital services) at least 40% of total public and private health expenditure;
- a ratio of total expenditure on district health services in the highest spending district to that of the lowest spending district of not more than 1.5.

These indicators would complement service output and outcome indicators such as immunization coverage, rates of skilled attendance at deliveries, TB completed-treatment rates, and maternal, peri-natal and child mortality rates.

high-income and low-income groups, and risk sharing between, for example, the young and the elderly. The more the system can be prevented from becoming polarized in terms of finance, the more it can ensure that better-off people do not separate themselves out institutionally from the public sector and distance themselves from the poor or from problems in the system (Mackintosh 2001).

To move towards more universalized health care systems, many countries should amalgamate existing forms of pooled financing and gradually reverse the segmentation of health care systems. The development of large-scale private insurance markets should be avoided at all costs. Where they exist, governments may pass laws to enforce community rating and prescribed minimum benefits, and insist on payment systems that discourage over-servicing and supplier induced demand.

Health systems should also work towards abolishing user fees for essential health care. This must be planned carefully and carried out in stages, depending on the medium- to long-term financing plan of the health care system.

Recommendations to make health care systems more equitable and to mitigate the harms of commercialized health care through financing reforms will meet varying levels of opposition from vested interests. Local civil society organizations and progressive international health NGOs can help to counter such opposition, while governments can promote public discussion on health sector financing reforms, ensuring the presence and voice of the poor in such discussions. WHO can promote and document a regular appraisal of health care financing systems on a country-by-country basis, making it easier for civil society to gauge the kind of reforms required in their countries.

Regulating and shaping the private sector In most of the poorest countries, the bulk of health care provision is carried out by the private sector, much of it in the form of small-scale, disorganized private dispensaries and clinics. Many governments do not have the capacity either to regulate the sector or to improve the quality and safety of care provided. Governments and donors must give issues of private sector regulation and quality assurance a much higher profile in their health policies and plans. Poor country governments with limited resources need to use their political and legal muscle to shift disorganized and commercialized health care markets towards a more equitable and efficient direction. The long-term goal must be a coherent primary level health care system operating under a clear national regulatory framework that governs standards quality and provider remuneration.

Private providers should also develop their own mechanisms to enhance professionalism, good clinical practice and ethical behaviour. However, self-regulation in the private sector is often weak and must be complemented by government and civil society intervention. Governments could consider working with the non-profit private sector – good non-government providers can develop and publicize standards for access and quality, and help undercut providers of a lower standard.

Other policy instruments to regulate the private sector include licensing requirements, formal accreditation and price controls. Licences can also be used to negotiate explicit returns in the form of arrangements for the public sector to use private sector facilities and equipment at a reduced cost, or for the private sector to provide services for free or at low-cost to patients referred from the government sector (Mackintosh and Tibandebage 2004). These recommendations should be implemented in the context of broader reforms to universalize the health care system and constrain commercial behaviour.

A key requirement for strengthening the public sector relative to the private sector is to reduce the disparity in incomes between public and private providers. This disparity should be regularly measured and monitored to draw attention to the need for active measures to reduce the gap.

Governments should revoke any commitments they have made to liberalize their health care and health insurance markets through the World Trade Organization's General Agreement on Trade and Services (GATS) or regional and bilateral trade agreements, and should reverse any agreements that undermine their ability to regulate the health care sector.

Making the public sector work – strengthening management Much more investment needs to be directed at strengthening public sector health management capacity at all levels of the health care system. Too often, however, management-strengthening initiatives are ineffective, short-lived and decontextualized, reflecting a general neglect of public administration in the development sector. Key elements of health systems management are highlighted below.

RESOURCE MANAGEMENT AND PLANNING Ministries of Health need to show where the money is spent, on whom and on what. A diagnostic health sector review, which characterizes health and health care inequalities and which describes resource levels and distribution, expenditure flows and the relative positions of public and private health sectors, including the role of non-government actors, is a necessity (Segall 1991). Plans to reallocate and redistribute resources can follow on from a transparent evidence base.

Structural imbalances, such as the relative over-development of large city hospitals and under-development of primary and secondary level care in rural areas, are best addressed through a series of 3–5 year planning cycles. To ensure equitable resource allocation between geographic areas, decisions about financing and major resource allocation should be centralized and based on an equitable, population-weighted needs-based formula. Countries should be wary of decentralizing health financing, as this may increase inequity as richer areas spend more money and absorb more resources.

PRIORITIZING INTERVENTIONS With respect to programmatic areas, resources should be titrated against the level of priority: higher priority programmes (for example, basic maternal and child health services) will be more intensely resourced, while those of lower priority will be less well resourced. This is a flexible system of rationing that has been termed *dilution* – as distinct from the blanket exclusion of interventions (through 'essential packages' World Bank style) that has been termed *denial* (New, 1996). From an equity perspective, resources should first be allocated according to the relative health care need of people, and only then should considerations of cost-effectiveness be applied to the selection of treatments – this is in contrast to the selection of people for treatment which will happen if priorities are primarily set in terms of interventions.

IMPLEMENTING PHC PROGRAMMES Central to improving health outcomes is the effective provision of medical services in conjunction with a multi-sectoral approach to promote and protect health. Health care systems can act as the engine for such a model of health care through the appropriate design of PHC programmes. Such programmes would include the delivery of cost-effective medical care, aided by essential medicines lists and rational, standard treatment guidelines, as well as interventions to promote and protect health, such as improving access to clean water; ensuring household food security; providing for adequate shelter and housing; and raising levels of literacy. The design of PHC programmes must also incorporate the involvement and empowerment of communities. The revitalization of community health worker programmes may form a part of this. Too many health programmes are still implemented in a top-down, technocratic manner with an over-emphasis on medical services.

HEALTH SYSTEMS AND OPERATIONAL RESEARCH Enhancing the role of research in strengthening health care systems is often discussed but rarely implemented. Much more investment is required in health systems and problem-solving operational research relative to biomedical research and research

5 To make health care systems more equitable and effective, both the geographic and social distance between health professionals and communities must be shortened.

that is geared towards academic publications. However, health systems and management research needs to become more embedded in health management and planning activities and not run as a parallel activity. Policy makers and health managers should lead the development of research agendas more than they do at present. There is also a need to invest more in the development of health information and disease surveillance, and the capacity and time for staff of public health care systems to conduct their own research.

APPROPRIATE TIMEFRAMES In many countries with urgent health needs, longer timeframes are needed to plan, implement, integrate and sustain health efforts. Today, timeframes set by international agencies and donors are often unrealistic and too short. They can lead to, for example, an over-dependence on top-down vertical approaches rather than approaches that simultaneously build the longer-term capacity and sustainability of health care systems. The frequent changing of international priorities and the short-term funding cycles of donors also needs to change towards adopting realistic and sustainable timeframes.

Political and social mobilization Those living in urban areas (especially the more affluent) and the higher levels of the medical profession benefit from the high technology and urban bias of resource distribution and will lobby against any measures to change this. Many parts of the private sector have reasons to block movement in the direction of the PHC Approach. These vested interests can be overcome only by a political effort, which includes the mobilization of those who are disadvantaged by the current system and their political and civil society representatives. Where communities face a commercially driven health care sector, they need to lobby for a regulatory framework to hold providers and the health system accountable. Where neo-liberal reforms are undermining public systems and shifting state obligations onto communities, they need to mobilize in support of the public sector.

The need to engage with actors and policies from beyond the local area poses a particular challenge. Social movements may need to bring together the concerns of several communities and find ways of presenting collective views and concerns at the national or international level. This form of community involvement requires an advanced level of organization, capacity building and civil society networking. Examples include the Treatment Action Campaign in South Africa, which challenged the patent monopolies of drug companies on anti-retroviral drugs and the failures of the South African government to provide treatment for HIV/AIDS, and the mobilization of civil society against the privatization of health services in El Salvador.

The role of international NGOs in acting as a conduit for the demands and needs of poor people in developing countries is important. International NGOs in developed countries should help develop the capacity of Southern-based NGOs and work with and through them. UN agencies must find ways to create a more prominent involvement of Southern-based NGOs, academics and health institutions in shaping the international health policy agenda.

Public and community involvement in health care systems For public sector bureaucracies to work effectively, efficiently and fairly, they need to be held accountable – internally through rules and codes of ethical conduct but, equally importantly, externally to communities and the public.

The spectrum of appropriate community involvement includes community mobilization to assert rights, challenge policies and present alternatives; monitoring of services by communities; involvement in planning and decision-making; and involvement in the implementation of PHC programmes and services. All too often, the role of civil society organizations within health care systems is given inadequate attention, or is used to cover up other agendas such as transferring government responsibility onto communities or rubber-stamping central decisions.

Appropriate community involvement should also be enhanced by health care systems through effectively empowered community structures and forums (such as district health committees, clinic committees and hospital boards), as well as by inculcating a culture of consultation and respect for lay people. Health care systems can disseminate information about local health services and the rights of service users, as well as publicize disparities in key indicators such as maternal mortality and immunization coverage to encourage a social commitment towards reducing inequity. However, because communities are themselves stratified, health workers need to make sure that community involvement does not entrench privilege.

More effective assistance from donors and global initiatives Donor and international health agencies must improve the quality, coordination and appropriateness of their programmes and initiatives. They must learn to develop a better understanding of local contexts and to adopt policies that place the long-term self determination and development of Ministries of Health and the citizens of recipient countries at the heart of all decision-making. Donors must reaffirm the generic principles of a coordinated sector-wide approach to health systems development. More investment should be aimed at developing, retaining and motivating public sector staff, and donors must be prepared to fund the recurrent costs of public sector health care systems in the poorest countries for at least the medium-term. Donors should also divert more funding away from agencies based in donor countries towards the public sector and NGOs in recipient countries.

Donor programmes and international health initiatives must translate the rhetoric of implementing disease-based programmes in ways that strengthen health care systems in practice. Disease-specific initiatives must explicitly explain and demonstrate *how* they are strengthening the overall development of comprehensive health care systems. Philanthropic agencies must recognize the need to balance investment in medical technologies with the need to invest in human resources, health systems and multi-sectoral approaches to health promotion and disease prevention.

Donors must avoid self-promotion and no longer insist that governments show quick results from their grants. Donor funding should be judged instead by the performance of the overall health care system over time. Donors should adopt a more incremental, problem-solving approach to health sector development, rather than the blueprint approach currently favoured by foreign technocrats. Technical assistants need to be selected with greater attention to the appropriateness of their skills; their willingness to learn the local cultural and historical contexts before prescribing remedies; and their commitment to developing the self-sufficiency and capacity of local counterparts.

Donor programmes and international health initiatives should develop mechanisms to uncover transgressions in the management of aid on the part of both recipient governments and donor agencies. The auditing of the performance of donors and international health agencies should be encouraged and conducted by independent institutions that do not have any conflicts of interest in doing so.

Finally, donors and international health agencies should fund and foster more partnerships between high-performing middle- and low-income countries that have been able to show above average health status and health care performance (such as Thailand, Sri Lanka, Cuba and Costa Rica) and other countries with struggling health care systems.

An organizational framework for the health care system – the District Health System The DHS model (described in section 1) provides an organizational framework for many of the other recommendations. It creates a decentralized system to allow health plans and programmes to be tailored to the needs and characteristics of the local population and topography. It provides a platform for the integration of policies and priorities emanating from different programmes and initiatives at the central level, and for getting the appropriate balance between top-down and bottom-up planning. Districts can form the basis for resource-allocation decisions informed by a population-based assessment of need, and can help central levels of the health care system to identify areas requiring additional capacity development or support.

The DHS represents a particular type of decentralization – one that promotes integration between hospitals, clinics and community-based health care within a single, coherent national health system – in contrast to the decentralization of neoliberal health sector reforms, which fragments the health care system. The organization of the health care system on a geographic basis adopts a more inclusive, population-based approach to health rather than the organization of health care according to segmented, socio-economic groups.

The DHS also provides an architecture for facilitating community involvement in health and organizing the comprehensive and multi-sectoral approach of Alma Ata. District-level health management structures could evaluate and monitor the quality of care provided in the private sector. The DHS could therefore be part of a strategy to reshape the performance and culture of the private health sector.

Establishing a DHS model implies more than just the demarcation of health

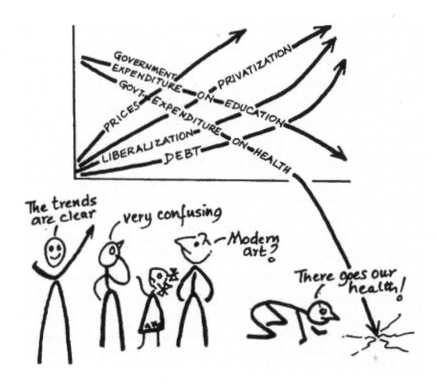

6 The demise of health for all and equity.

district boundaries. Most important is that district-level health management structures have the authority, status, skills and competencies to plan for and manage health care delivery for their local population without constant interference from central dictates and demands. Central-level policy makers and managers in turn have to change their function from directly managing health care services to developing guidelines, facilitating capacity development, providing support, and supervising and monitoring.

Although WHO has recently called for the revitalization of the PHC Approach, it did not set out an accompanying strategy for the organization of health care systems – instead it seems to advocate tacking on the PHC Approach to the various health sector reforms that have taken place since the 1980s.

Rebuilding trust The final recommendation involves promoting trust as a conceptual basis for encouraging a higher level of ethical behaviour within health care systems. Trust matters to health care systems for two reasons. First, it represents a moral value in itself, which is important because health care systems are social institutions that reflect and shape societal values and norms (Loewy 1998, Mooney 1998). The design of health care systems – from financing and resource allocation mechanisms to the governance arrangements of clinical practice – influence the values that they signal to society. In this way, trust sustains the legitimacy of public health policy and action and stands as an important and much-neglected counter-balance to the pressures of commercialization (Gilson 2003).

Second, trust facilitates the co-operation among people and organizations that is fundamental to the provision of health care. Trust is a key element of the provider-patient relationship – it is essential that patients can trust providers to behave ethically and have their best interests at heart (Davies 1999, Mechanic 1996). Trust also facilitates patient communication, underpins the provider's role in encouraging patients to change their behaviour, and enables greater patient autonomy in decision-making.

Health care systems can actively nurture trust and ethical behaviour by acting against violations of trust and promoting norms or values, such as truthfulness, attitudes of solidarity, and a belief in fairness. To this end, they should develop the institutions that are able to influence the behaviour of providers, managers and insurers, including standards of professional conduct, clinical protocols and best-practice guidelines; systems to monitor adherence to standards and protocols; licensing and disciplinary procedures; an explicit recognition of rights to health care (Giddens 1990); and actions that constrain profit-seeking behaviour, such as capping prices, countering the use of informal payments or requiring free treatment of emergency cases.

Management practices can also enhance levels of trust and ethical behaviour. Improved communication and a two-way flow of information can increase levels of trust, as can establishing transparent procedures by which community members can monitor and evaluate health care practices. Transparent expenditure reviews can ensure probity in the use of funds and act as a bulwark against the misuse of resources. The accreditation of providers, especially if conducted in a spirit of cooperation, is another mechanism to promote good performance according to specified standards as well as to build trust and shared values. Transparent and fair decision-making practices also act as a source of self-esteem and intrinsic motivation that can build commitment and trust for the employer organization.

Political, social and health sector leadership that promotes ethical behaviour, good quality care and values of fairness and justice is important in shaping a culture of trust and ethics within health care systems. These actions will need to be complemented by international action and debate to signal to health systems and society at large that trustworthy behaviour matters, pointing to an important role for WHO and other international health agencies. Rather than seeing health systems as machines through which bio-medical interventions are delivered, health leaders must recognize them as social institutions comprised of chains of people, relationships and understandings.

References

Ahmad K (2004). Health and money in Afghanistan. *Lancet* 364:1301–02.

Akin J, Birdsall N, Ferranti D (1987). *Financing health services in developing countries: an agenda for reform.* Washington, World Bank.

Amaral J et al. (forthcoming). Effect of Integrated Management of Childhood Illness (IMCI) on health worker performance in Northeast-Brazil. *Cadernos de Saude Publica.*

Arrow K (1963). Uncertainty and the welfare economics of medical care. *American Economic Review* 53: 941–73.

Bassett M, Bijlmakers L, Sanders D (1997). Professionalism, patient satisfaction and quality of health care: experience during Zimbabwe's structural adjustment programme. *Social Science and Medicine* 45; 12:1845–1852.

Bellagio Study Group on Child Survival (2003). Knowledge into action for child survival. *Lancet,* 362:323–27.

Black R, Morris S, Bryce J (2003). Where and why are 10 million children dying each year? *Lancet* 361:2226–34.

Bloom G (1991). Managing health sector development: markets and institutional reform. In: Colclough C and Manor J, eds. *States or markets: neoliberalism and the development policy debate.* Oxford, Oxford University Press.

Brown A (2000). *Integrating vertical programs into sector-wide approaches: experiences and lessons.* London, Institute for Health Sector Development.

Bryce J et al. (2003). Reducing child mortality: can public health deliver? *Lancet* 362:159–64.

Commission on Macroeconomics and Health (2001). *Macroeconomics and Health: Investing in Health for Economic Development.* Geneva, WHO.

Commission on the Social Determinants of Health (2005). Action on the social determinants of health: learning from previous experiences. A Background paper prepared for the Commission on Social Determinants of Health (http://www.who.int/social_determinants/en/, accessed 19 March 2005).

Davies H (1999). Falling public trust in health services: Implications for accountability. *Journal of Health Services Research and Policy* 4:193–194.

Devereaux P et al. (2002). Comparison of mortality between private for-profit and private not-for-profit hemodialysis centers: a systematic review and meta-analysis. *Journal of the American Medical Association* 288:2449–57.

Ensor T, Pham S (1996). Access and payment for health care: the poor of Northern Vietnam. *International Journal of Health Planning and Management* 11:69–83.

Evans R (1997). Health care reform: who's selling the market, and why? *Journal of Public Health Medicine* 19:45–9.

Evans R (1997). Going for the gold: the redistributive agenda behind market-based health care reform. *Journal of Health Politics, Policy and Law* 22:427–66.

Foster M, Brown A, Conway T (2000). *Sector-wide approaches for health development: a review of experience*. WHO, Geneva (http://whqlibdoc.who.int/hq/2000/WHO_GPE_00.1.pdf, accessed 24 March 2005).

Franco A, Alvarez-Dardet C, Ruiz M (2004). Effect of democracy on health: ecological study. *British Medical Journal* 329:1421–3.

Fu W (1999). *Health care for China's rural poor*. Washington, World Bank.

Giddens A (1990). *The consequences of modernity*. Cambridge, Polity Press.

Gilson L (2003).Trust and the development of health care as a social institution. *Social Science and Medicine* 56:1453–1468.

Gwatkin D (2003). Free government health services: are they the best way to reach the poor? (http://poverty.worldbank.org/files/13999_gwatkin0303.pdf, accessed 24 March 2005).

Himmelstein D et al. (1999). Quality of care in investor-owned vs not-for-profit HMOs. *Journal of the American Medical Association* 282:159–63.

Hilary J (2001). *The Wrong Model: GATS, trade liberalisation and children's right to health*. London, Save the Children (UK) (http://www.savethechildren.org.uk/temp/scuk/cache/cmsattach/986_wrongmodel.pdf, accessed 24 March 2005).

Hill P (2002). The rhetoric of sector-wide approaches for health development. *Social Science and Medicine* 54:1725–1737.

IFC (2002). *Investing in private health care: Strategic directions for IFC*. Washington DC, International Finance Corporation.

Jones G et al. (2003). How many child deaths can we prevent this year? *Lancet* 362: 65–71.

Khalegian P and Das Gupta M (2004). *Public Management and the Essential Public Health Functions*. World Bank Policy Research Working Paper 3220. Washington, World Bank.

Liu X, Mills A (2002). Financing reforms of public health services in China: lessons for other nations. *Social Science and Medicine* 54:1691–8.

Loewy E (1998). Justice and health care systems: What would an ideal health care system look like? *Health Care Analysis* 6:185–192.

Mackintosh M and Koivusalo M (2004). *Health systems and commercialisation: in search of good sense*. Geneva, UNRISD (http://www.unrisd.org/unrisd/website/projects.nsf/(httpProjects)/E90A28B15B255697C1256DB4004B2D63?OpenDocument, accessed 24 March 2005).

Mackintosh M and Koivusalo M (forthcoming 2005). Health systems and commercialization: in search of good sense. In Mackintosh M, Koivusalo M eds. *Commercialization of Health Care: Global and Local Dynamics and Policy Responses*. Palgrave, Basingstoke.

Mackintosh M (2001). Do health systems contribute to inequalities? In: Leon D, Walt G, eds. *Poverty, Inequality and Health: An International Perspective*. Oxford, OUP.

Mackintosh M and Tibandebage P (2004). Inequality and redistribution in health care: analytical issues for developmental social policy. In: Mkandawire T, ed. *Social Policy in a Development Context*. Basingstoke, UK, Palgrave and UNRISD.

Maynard A (1998). Competition and quality: rhetoric and reality. *International Journal for Quality in Health Care* 10:379–84.

McCoy D et al. (2005). Expanding access to anti-retroviral therapy in sub-Saharan Africa: avoiding the pitfalls and dangers; capitalising on the opportunities. *American Journal of Public Health* 95:18–22

McPake B (1997). The role of the private sector in health services provision. In: Bennett S, McPake B, Mills A. *Private Health Providers in Developing Countries: Serving the Public Interest?* London, Zed Books.

Mechanic D (1996). Changing medical organization and the erosion of trust. *The Milbank Quarterly* 74:171–189.

Mooney G (1998). Beyond health care outcomes: the benefits of health care. *Health Care Analysis* 6: 99–105

Nahar S, Costello AM de (1998). The hidden cost of 'free' maternity care in Dhaka, Bangladesh. *Health Policy and Planning* 13:417–422.

New B (on behalf of the Rationing Agenda Group) (1996). The rationing agenda in the NHS. *British Medical Journal* 312:1593–1601.

Newell K (1988). Selective primary health care: the counter-revolution. *Social Science and Medicine* 26:903–6.

Pathmanathan Indra et al. (2003). *Investing in Maternal Health: Learning from Malaysia and Sri Lanka*. Washington DC, World Bank.

Pfeiffer J (2003). International NGOs and primary health care in Mozambique: the need for a new model of collaboration. *Social Science and Medicine* 56:725–738

Pogge T (2002). *World poverty and human rights*. Cambridge, Polity Press.

Rice T (1997). Can markets give us the health system we want? *Journal of Health Politics, Policy and Law* 22:383–426

Rifkin S, Walt G (1986). Why health improves: Defining the issues concerning 'comprehensive primary health care' and 'selective primary health care'. *Social Science and Medicine* 23: 559–66.

Robinson M, White G (2001). The Role of Civic Organizations in the Provision of Social Services: Towards Synergy. In: Mwabu G, Ugaz C, White G eds. *Social Provision in Low-Income Countries – New Patterns and Emerging Trends*. Oxford, OUP.

Roemer M (1984). Private medical practice: Obstacle to health for all. *World Health Forum* 5:195–210.

Russell S, Gilson L (1997). User fee policies to promote health service access for the poor: a wolf in sheep's clothing? *International Journal of Health Services* 27:359–79.

Schellenberg J et al (2004). Tanzania IMCI Multi-Country Evaluation Health Facility Survey Study Group. The effect of Integrated Management. of Childhood Illness on observed quality of care of under-fives in rural Tanzania. *Health Policy and Planning* 19:1–10.

Segall M (1991). Health sector planning led by management of recurrent expenditure: an agenda for action-research. *International Journal of Health Planning and Management* 6:37–75.

Segall M (2000). From cooperation to competition in national health systems – and back?: impact on professional ethics and quality of care. *International Journal of Health Planning and Management* 15:61–79.

Segall M (2003). District health systems in a neoliberal world: a review of five key policy areas. *International Journal of Health Planning and Management* 18:S5–S26.

Shaffer E et al. (2005). Global trade and public health. *American Journal of Public Health* 95: 23–34.

Smith D, Bryant J (1988). Building the infra-structure for primary health care: an overview of vertical and integrated approaches. *Social Science and Medicine* 26: 909–17.

Stewart J (1988). Advance or retreat: from the traditions of public administration to the new public management and beyond. *Public Policy and Administration* 13:27.

Approaches to health care

Stocker K, Waitzkin H and Iriart C (1999). The exportation of Managed Care to Latin America. *New England Journal of Medicine* 340:1131–36.

Theodore K (1999). *Health sector reform and equity in Jamaica: report to the Pan-American Health Organisation.* Washington DC, PAHO.

Tipping G (2000). *The social impact of user fees for health care on poor households: commissioned report to the Ministry of Health.* Hanoi, Vietnam, Ministry of Health.

Toole M et al. (2003). Harnessing the new global health resources to build sustainable health systems. Melbourne, Centre for International Health, Burnet Institute (http://www.burnet.internationalhealth.edu.au/freestyler/gui/files/Health %20syste ms%20paper%2C%20April%202004.pdf, accessed 24 March 2005).

Transitional Islamic Government of Afghanistan (2002). *Afghanistan National Health Resources Assessment.* Prepared by Management Sciences for Health, HANDS and JICA (http://www.msh.org/afghanistan/3.0.htm, accessed 20 March 2005).

UNFPA 2004. *State of the world population 2004.* Geneva, UNFPA (http://www.unfpa. org/swp/swpmain.htm, accessed 24 March 2005).

Unger J, Killingsworth J (1986). Selective primary health care: a critical review of methods and results. *Social Science and Medicine* 22:1001.

UNICEF (2001). *Progress since the World Summit for Children: a statistical review.* New York, UNICEF (http://www.unicef.org/pubsgen/swethechildren-stats/sgreport_ adapted_stats_eng.pdf, accessed 28 March 2003).

Victora C, Wagstaff A, Schellenberg J et al. (2003). Applying an equity lens to child health and mortality: more of the same is not enough. *Lancet* 362:233–41.

Waldman R, Hanif H (2002). *The public health system in Afghanistan.* Afghanistan Research and Evaluation Unit (available at: http://www.areu.org.af/publications/ waldman_health.pdf, accessed 17 December 2004).

Walsh J and Warren K (1979). Selective primary health care: an interim strategy for disease control in developing countries. *New England Journal of Medicine* 301: 967–74.

Wemos (2004). *Good Intentions with Side Effects: Information on Global Public Private Initiatives in Health.* 2004. Amsterdam, Wemos (http://www.wemos.nl/documents/ Goodintentionswithsideeffects.pdf, accessed 29 March 2005).

Werner D, Sanders D (1997). *Questioning the solution: The politics of primary health care and child survival.* California, HealthWrights.

Whitehead M, Dahlgren G, Evans T (2001). Equity and health sector reforms: can low-income countries escape the medical poverty trap? *Lancet* 358:833–36

WHO/UNICEF (1978). *Declaration of Alma Ata: International Conference on Primary Health Care, 6–12 September 1978.* Geneva, WHO (http://www.who.int/hpr/NPH/ docs/declaration_almaata.pdf, accessed 15 March 2005).

WHO (1988). *The Challenge of Implementation: District Health Systems for Primary Health Care.* Geneva, World Health Organization.

WHO (1992). *The hospital in rural and urban districts: a report of a WHO study group on the functions of hospitals at the first referral level.* WHO Technical Report Series No. 819. Geneva, World Health Organization

WHO (2004). *World Health Report 2004 – Changing History.* Geneva, WHO.

WHO, UNICEF and UNFPA (2001). *Maternal Mortality in 1995 – Estimates developed by WHO, UNICEF, UNFPA* (http://www.who.int/reproductive-health/publications/RHR_ 01_9_maternal_mortality_estimates/index.en.html, accessed 24 March 2005).

WHO, UNICEF and World Bank. (2002) *State of the world's vaccines and immuniza-*

tion. Geneva: WHO (http://www.unicef.org/publications/files/pub_sowvi_en.pdf, accessed 24 March 2005).

Woolhandler S, Himmelstein D (2004). The high costs of for-profit care. *Canadian Medical Association Journal* 170:1814–5.

World Bank (1993). *World Development Report 1993: Investing in Health*. Washington DC, World Bank.

World Bank (1999). *The Kyrgyz Republic: participatory poverty assessment*, prepared for the global synthesis workshop poverty programme. Washington DC, World Bank.

World Bank (2004). *A guide to government in Afghanistan*. Washington DC, World Bank.

Yu H, Cao S, Lucas H (1997). Equity in the utilisation of medical services: a survey in poor rural China. *Institute of Development Studies Bulletin* 28:16–23.

Approaches to health care

B2 | Medicines

Introduction

Essential medicines are those that satisfy the priority health care needs of the population. Between 1.3 and 2.1 billion people remain without access to them despite decades of effort (WHO 2004a). Improvement is slow: the proportion of the world's population with access to essential medicines, defined in Box B2.1, improved from an estimated 63% to only 70% between 1987 and 1999. Almost 80% of those without access live in low-income countries, and 20% in middle-income countries. Such figures conceal major differences within countries, and do not adequately convey a sense of which medicines are lacking. Annual expenditure on medicines in 2000 varied from US$ 396 per head in high-income countries to only US$ 4 in low-income countries. At the same time, medicines accounted for a higher percentage of total health expenditure in low-income (19%) and middle-income countries (25%) than high-income countries (14%).

Box B2.1 The concept of essential medicines

Essential medicines, according to WHO, are those that satisfy the priority health care needs of the population, with due regard to evidence on efficacy and safety, and comparative cost-effectiveness. They are intended to be available at all times in the context of functioning health systems, in adequate amounts, in the appropriate dosage forms, with assured quality and adequate information, and at an affordable price (WHO 2004b).

Countries and health care systems should apply these principles to select a list of essential medicines, linking it to evidence-based treatment guidelines, for use in professional training, supervision and audit.

The impact of an essential medicines list depends on how the health system is structured and governed. In most countries the ministry of health can use regulatory procedures to ensure that all public sector providers adhere to it and its accompanying rational treatment guidelines. However, this may be subverted in systems with a large and unregulated private sector. The lists can also be used by insurance agencies to set standards and guidelines for reimbursement or coverage of care.

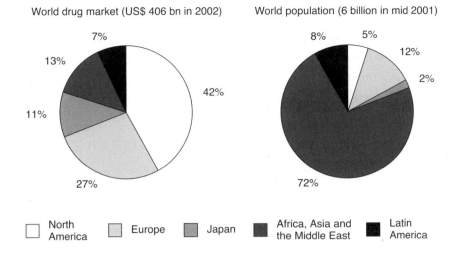

World drug market (US$ 406 bn in 2002)

7%
13%
11%
27%
42%

World population (6 billion in mid 2001)

8%   5%
12%
2%
72%

☐ North America   ☐ Europe   ☐ Japan   ■ Africa, Asia and the Middle East   ■ Latin America

Figure B2.1 The mismatch between expenditure on medicines and health need (Source: McCoy 2003)

The deeply unjust mismatch between expenditure on medicines and health need (Figure B2.1) mirrors global socio-economic disparities. 42% of global expenditure on medicines is spent on 5% of the world's population living in North America, while only 20% is spent on the majority of the world's population with the highest burdens of disease in Africa, Asia, the Middle East and Latin America.

Critics claim that the high prices of patented drugs are not a major barrier to access. Many essential medicines that are cheap and off-patent remain unavailable or inaccessible to millions of people, primarily a reflection of impoverished health care systems and communities. However, for millions of people, the lack of access to essential medicines is also a function of excessively high prices – as illustrated by the high prices of patented antiretroviral medicines.

Escalating levels of expenditure on medicines may reflect high volumes, high prices, inappropriate choices and irrational prescribing. For example, in Canada, the medicines share of total spending grew from a low of 8% in the late 1970s to 16% in 2002. A similar trend is evident in the health care system in the US, where medicine costs may soon exceed payments to doctors as the largest item on the health bill after hospital costs.

Finally, as new diseases and health threats emerge and pathogens develop resistance to medicines, and because many existing essential medicines are toxic or limited in their effectiveness, access to essential medicines is also determined by the success or otherwise of the research and development (R&D)

Medicines

of new medicines. The presence of so many prevalent and serious diseases without effective and affordable treatment (see Box B2.2) demonstrates a major failure of the pharmaceutical R&D system.

This chapter looks at three important issues related to the pharmaceutical sector. The first is the international intellectual property rights system and other trade-related impediments to access and rational medicine use. The sec-

---

Box B2.2 Drugs for neglected diseases

Despite advances in science, technology and medicine, the largely market-driven system for allocating resources to pharmaceutical research and development ignores diseases that affect the poor, including several that constitute a significant portion of the global burden of disease. Instead, the system is more geared towards directing investment towards new and expensive 'lifestyle' medicines such as Viagra, which claim to address the needs of the affluent minority of the world's population. Global and national strategies to correct this market failure are therefore necessary.

The pipeline of drugs for neglected diseases has been virtually empty for decades. Only 16 of the 1393 new chemical entities (drugs or medicines) registered in the US and Europe in 1975–1999 were for 'tropical diseases' that afflict people in developing countries, and five of them emerged from veterinary research. The result is a critical shortage of effective drugs for many diseases that mainly affect the poor, such as leishmaniasis, Chagas disease, trypanosomiasis (sleeping sickness), malaria and TB.

Existing medicines may be excessively toxic, difficult to administer or too expensive. For example, leishmaniasis, which is endemic in 88 countries and affects an estimated 12 million people, with 1.5–2 million new cases annually, is mainly treated with pentavalent antimony. This drug, discovered a century ago, has serious side-effects, requires prolonged treatment and is losing its efficacy in some regions due to increasing parasite resistance.

Owing to individual or governmental lack of funding to purchase them, some medicines have been withdrawn from the market despite the need for treatment, e.g. eflornithine for African sleeping sickness. Continued access to this was only facilitated when it emerged that it could also be used in an unrelated condition prevalent in developed countries, hence providing an economically viable market. (*Source* Trouiller et al. 2002)

Box B2.3 'Big Pharma' – profits and power

'Big Pharma' is a collective term used to describe the world's major pharmaceutical corporations, which are hugely influential in the control of the trade in medicines, and in shaping global trade rules and regulations. They include Pfizer, Bristol-Myers Squibb, Bayer, Merck, Pharmacia, Johnson & Johnson, Abbott Laboratories, Novartis, American Home Products, Eli Lilly, Schering-Plough, GlaxoSmithKline and Allergan.

The combined worth of the world's top five drug companies is twice the combined GNP of all Sub-Saharan Africa, and their influence on the rules of world trade is many times stronger because they bring their wealth to bear directly on the levers of western power. Their role in shaping international rules on patents by working hand in hand with the US government and European Commission has been extensively documented (Drahos and Braithwaite 2004).

Pharmaceutical profits, whether calculated as a percentage of assets or as a percentage of revenues, are among the highest of any commercial sector. The combined 2002 profits of the 10 biggest pharmaceutical companies, listed in *Fortune* magazine's annual review of the largest US businesses, were US$ 35.9 billion – comprising more than half the US$ 69.6 billion profits netted by the entire roster of Fortune 500 companies. These profits are reflected in the incredible earnings of top executives. For example, the former chairman and CEO of Bristol-Myers Squibb made US$74,890,918 in 2001, not counting his US$76,095,611 worth of unexercised stock options (Families USA 2001).

With such profits at stake, it is no surprise Big Pharma invests a huge amount of money in protecting them. Drug companies have the largest lobby in Washington, and contribute copiously to political campaigns. Well over $100 million went to paying for issue ads, hiring academics, funding non-profits and other activities to promote the industry's agenda in Washington (Public Citizen 2003). In 2002, the drug industry hired 675 different lobbyists from 138 firms – nearly seven lobbyists for each US senator. Drug industry lobbyists include 26 former members of Congress and all told, 342 of them have 'revolving door' connections with the federal government.

ond is the corrupting influence of profit-driven pharmaceutical companies on health professionals, academics and regulatory bodies. The third is the need to reshape the way pharmaceutical R&D is funded and incentives offered. The

Medicines

chapter recognizes that the pharmaceutical sector has largely been shaped by a powerful and politically influential corporate sector intent on protecting its own interests (see Box B2.3). Civil society needs to mobilize when these interests conflict with the social aims of equity and health for all, and the chapter concludes with recommendations for action.

Intellectual property rights, monopolies and high prices

The price of new medicines is largely governed by an intellectual property rights (IPR) regime that grants patents to any company that registers a new medicine. Patents are granted by governments and give a company monopoly power to manufacture and sell a medicine free of competition from any other manufacturer in that particular country. This monopoly power allows the patent-holder to set a price many times greater than the cost of production. Patents are usually granted for a fixed period after which other companies are permitted to manufacture generic versions of the same medicine.

Big Pharma argues that patents are vital incentives to companies to invest in pharmaceutical research and development. It also says the revenue from profitable products can be used to support research into new treatments for diseases, 'including those which particularly affect the developing world' (IFPMA 2005).

Initially, IPRs were governed internationally by the Paris Convention and administered by the World Intellectual Property Organization (WIPO). However, in 1986, the developed countries, led by the United States, brought IPR issues into the realm of trade policy and negotiations. Although certain developing countries argued that IPRs were not free trade issues, the developed countries, supported by Big Pharma, pushed through the Agreement on Trade Related Aspects of Intellectual Property Rights (TRIPS) in 1994 under the auspices of the World Trade Organization (Drahos and Braithwaite 2004). Developing countries gave up their resistance to the Agreement in the face of the overwhelming influence of the US, EU and Japan. The power imbalance of negotiations is reflected by the fact that only about ten developing countries actually sent intellectual property experts to the TRIPS negotiations (Matthews 2002).

TRIPS stipulates that by January 2005, all member states of the WTO must grant patents on all medicines for a period of 20 years. Whereas patents were previously granted by governments on a country-by-country basis, there is now a single and standard patent agreement that applies to all countries. A particular concern is the potential impacts on countries, such as India and China, that are important sources of generic medicines, including antiretrovirals. There is presently a campaign against the amendment to Indian patent

7 Selling medicines at the back of a bus.

law which will potentially destroy the generic drugs manufacturing capacity in India (Sen Gupta 2005).

A degree of flexibility has been built into TRIPS, following intensive lobbying by civil society and some developing country governments. This led to the fourth WTO ministerial conference adopting the Doha declaration on the TRIPS Agreement and Public Health in 2001 (WTO 2001). This says that TRIPS should be implemented in a manner that supports the right of countries 'to protect public health and, in particular, to promote access to medicines for all'. Paragraph 5 provides a list of policy flexibilities that can be used to overcome intellectual property barriers to access to medicines. It asserts the freedom of each member state to determine the grounds on which compulsory licences can be granted without the consent of the patent-holder, and confirms that the agreement in no way limits countries' capacity to allow parallel trade in patented medicines. (A compulsory licence is granted to allow a third party to manufacture a patented product without the authorisation of the right holder; a parallel import is a good sold by the patent-holder and resold in another country without the patent-holder's permission.) Finally, the Doha declaration extended the deadline for TRIPS compliance for the 30 least developed countries until 2016.

The Doha declaration left one issue unresolved. A country without local manufacturing capacity would not be able to make use of a compulsory or government-use licence to improve access to medicines (Correa 2002). The WTO therefore decided in 2003 to allow for a temporary waiver of the requirement that medicines produced under a compulsory licence should be predominantly for the domestic market (Correa 2004). With this waiver, a compulsory licence could be granted to a company to manufacture generic versions of a medicine for export to another country. For this to happen, two compulsory licences may be required, one each in the importing and exporting countries.

In practice it is difficult for developing countries to make use of these flexibilities (Baker 2004a, DFID 2004). To start with, a variety of burdensome administrative tasks have been created to limit the potential for compulsory licensing (Baker 2003). According to 20 civil society groups, WTO took a 52-word mechanism endorsed by the EU in 2002 and created a 3200–word maze of red tape 'plainly designed to frustrate and undermine the objective of protecting public health and promoting access to medicines to all' (Joint NGO Statement 2003).

Developing countries are furthermore subjected to enormous economic and political pressures not to use the TRIPS flexibilities. These pressures include threats of litigation by companies and trade sanctions by governments. The US government, for example, has used bilateral trade agreements, the threat of sanctions, and associated diplomatic and political pressures to undermine countries that produce generic medicines and/or consider importing them (Oxfam 2002).

TRIPS-plus

The TRIPS agreement, despite the flexibilities permitted by the Doha declaration and the 2003 WTO decision, has harmed efforts to improve access to essential medicines. Even worse has been the development and implementation of a variety of 'TRIPS-plus' agreements and policies aimed at killing off the flexibilities and eroding further the capacity of governments to regulate the pharmaceutical sector and the price of medicines.

US bilateral policy on patents and medicines is hugely influenced by the giant pharmaceutical companies' quest to stave off generic competition for lucrative patented drugs (Oxfam 2002), and the US has pursued a TRIPS-plus

---

Box B2.4 The US-Australia free trade agreement

The free trade agreement between Australia and the US undermines Australian public health while protecting US pharmaceutical corporate interests. It prohibits compulsory licensing except in three circumstances, whereas TRIPS permits compulsory licensing in any circumstances if certain conditions are met (Drahos & Henry 2004). Another stipulation involves patent term extensions for pharmaceuticals beyond those required by TRIPS. The agreement also gives patent owners greater control over the importation or reimportation of their products to obstruct parallel importation, unlike TRIPS, which expressly steers away from setting a standard on parallel trade.

Australia's pharmaceutical benefits advisory committee recommends the listing of medicines that will be subsidized by a programme operated by the federal government. Pharmaco-economic analysis and reference pricing are used to determine the benefits of a new drug while monopsony power (where the product is bought or used by only one customer) is used to counter the price-setting monopoly power of pharmaceutical patent-holders. As a consequence, medicine prices obtained by the Australian pharmaceutical benefits scheme are 3–4 times lower than those in the US (Lokuge et al. 2003). However, under pressure from US trade negotiators, the Australian government has agreed to the creation of an independent review body to examine medicines rejected by the committee. This follows a longer history of aggressive action by US pharmaceutical companies, including legal challenges to the committee's decisions and political lobbying for removal of committee members (Henry & Birkett 2001).

agenda through a series of bilateral and regional trade agreements (MSF 2004). These include free trade agreements (FTA) with the Americas, Central America, Jordan, Singapore, Chile, Australia and Morocco. The US is now negotiating an agreement with Thailand, opposed by Thai civil society, whose TRIPS-plus provisions will obstruct affordable antiretroviral treatment for nearly 10,000 people with AIDS. An agreement is also under negotiation with the Southern African Customs Union.

TRIPS-plus agreements and policies include limiting the potential for governments to award compulsory licences and embark on parallel importing. Another stipulation involves patent term extensions beyond those required by TRIPS. They are also being used to slow down access to generic medicines by conferring exclusive rights to pharmaceutical companies for the patient data used to secure regulatory approval. Although the TRIPS agreement is not overly prescriptive on protection of undisclosed data submitted to regulatory authorities by manufacturers, US bilateral trade agreements include granting exclusive rights on these data for at least five years. Since generic manufacturers rely on pharmaceutical test data to demonstrate that their products are safe and effective, data exclusivity means that they will have to repeat many costly clinical trials when they want to register a new generic medicine. This will significantly delay the introduction of generics even when there are no patents in effect.

Finally, bilateral trade agreements are being used to erode the power and role of national authorities for the regulation of medicines and the structures responsible for medicines selection. Regulation of medicines is one of the most important health stewardship functions of government. An effective framework should include a competent process for ensuring that medicines that are produced, sold and dispensed are safe and effective; that monitoring and surveillance systems exist to identify problems with safety; and that clinical trials conducted by the pharmaceutical sector are ethical, transparent, methodologically sound and free of bias. As outlined before, a complementary process involves those structures that ensure that the clinical use of medicines is informed by the periodic development and updating of treatment guidelines and essential medicines lists.

Such a framework should apply to both brand and generic medicines, and needs to be efficiently managed and robust enough to withstand pressure from pharmaceutical manufacturers, insurance companies and treatment activist groups alike. The challenges facing developing country regulators are particularly acute given neoliberal reforms and the lack of public sector capacity (Hill and Johnson 2004). The use of trade agreements to undermine public health and governments' regulatory capacity is particularly worrying given growing evidence that Big Pharma routinely places profit margins above the imperative to protect patient safety, and has become a corrupting influence on public health, academic and clinical practice. These issues are discussed later.

Dispelling the myth that patents promote efficient and innovative pharmaceutical R&D

Pharmaceutical companies repeatedly claim that patent protection is 'the goose that lays the golden egg' – that the companies' monopoly power is a price worth paying because it leads to new medicines. However, this argument is built on a number of myths that, when exposed, point to a moral and logical need for fundamental reform of how pharmaceutical research is financed and rewarded.

Firstly, Big Pharma portrays its industry as a highly risky one in a competitive market, just able to cover its enormous R&D costs but managing

---

How much does it really cost to manufacture a drug?

In November 2001, the Tufts Centre for the Study of Drug Development, which is 65% funded by the industry, came out with a figure of $802m. Public Citizen, a consumer organisation, did a detailed analysis of the figure and concluded that it was inflated by about 75%. In addition, none of the 68 drugs Tufts considered had been developed with the help of government money, unlike the case with many other medicines.

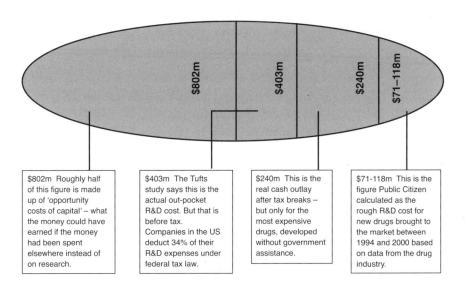

$802m Roughly half of this figure is made up of 'opportunity costs of capital' – what the money could have earned if the money had been spent elsewhere instead of on research.

$403m The Tufts study says this is the actual out-pocket R&D cost. But that is before tax. Companies in the US deduct 34% of their R&D expenses under federal tax law.

$240m This is the real cash outlay after tax breaks – but only for the most expensive drugs, developed without government assistance.

$71-118m This is the figure Public Citizen calculated as the rough R&D cost for new drugs brought to the market between 1994 and 2000 based on data from the drug industry.

Figure B2.2 How much does it cost to develop a new medicine?
(*Source: Guardian* 2003)

109

nonetheless to deliver a stream of innovative medicines in the public interest. However, as mentioned earlier, their profits are substantial. Pharmaceutical companies have also been guilty of exaggerating the cost of developing a new medicine (see Figure B2.2).

Furthermore, much of the truly innovative research that feeds into the manufacture of medicines is not undertaken by the corporate sector but by publicly funded research institutions and universities. Nearly half of the biomedical research spending in the United States is supported by either the government or non-profit sector, the outputs of which enter the public domain to the benefit of the commercial sector. Others were first developed by smaller biotech companies and then licensed to the large companies.

In contrast, a system which relies only on patent protection to fuel innovation can easily become distorted and inefficient (Baker and Chatani 2002). First, patent protection encourages an overemphasis on the production of copycat drugs that add little value to health outcomes. The US Food and Drug Administration said 76% of the drugs it approved in the 1990s were duplicative rather than breakthrough drugs (US Food and Drug Administration 2001). Second, patent protection gives manufacturers a big incentive to persuade doctors and patients to use their medicines rather than others – resulting in high spending on marketing and over-prescribing. Third, the legal and lobbying costs associated with securing and enforcing patents, which can include side

TABLE B2.1 Spending money to change policy: Pharmaceutical Research and Manufacturers of America budget initiatives

PhRMA Initiatives	Budget (US$m)
Pharmaceutical lobbying at the US federal and state level	121.4
Fighting price controls and protecting patent rights in foreign countries and in trade negotiations	17.5
Fighting a union-driven initiative in Ohio to lower drug prices for people with inadequate insurance cover	15.8
Lobbying the US Food and Drug Administration	4.9
Payments to research and policy organizations sympathetic to the industry	2.0
Funding a standing network of economists to speak against US drug price controls	1.0
Changing the Canadian health care system	1.0
TOTAL	163.6

Source: Pear 2003

payments to generic producers to keep competition out of the market, have become enormous (Box B2.3). The US industry recently spent US$ 163 million in a year on trying to change patent laws across the globe (Table B2.1). Fourth, restricting the dissemination of research findings is another cause of inefficiency – scientific progress is impeded by the financial incentives to prevent the disclosure of research findings until patents are filed. Lastly, the existence of large mark-ups provides a strong incentive for the production of unauthorized medicines. When medicines can be manufactured at prices between a tenth and a hundredth of the patent-protected price, there are enormous incentives to make black-market versions or counterfeits.

In contrast, alternative incentive systems for research continue to be effective and efficient. Innovative, high quality scientific developments can flourish for the benefit of all with good management and leadership (Baker 2004). The Human Genome Project shows that with good management and leadership; clear plans and goals; regular inter-action between funders, managers and technical experts; and a competitive atmosphere with peer review, open data and information exchange, researchers on academic salaries in the public domain can produce innovative and high quality scientific developments for the benefit of all (also discussed in part B, chapter 5).

The corruption of ethics and trust

There is growing concern about Big Pharma's unethical behaviour and lack of transparency. It is increasingly entering into financial arrangements with academic and research institutions that threaten the objectivity and credibility of clinical research (Medawar and Hardon 2004). In contracts with academic researchers, the companies may insist on controlling how the research is done and reported, and whether the results will be published. Furthermore, a growing number of clinical trials are being managed by investor-owned businesses that are even more beholden to the drug companies because the companies are their only clients.

The contact between pharmaceutical companies and researchers has become pervasive, as shown by the decision by the highly respected *New England Journal of Medicine* to drop its requirement that authors of review articles of medical studies must not have financial ties to the companies whose medicines were being analysed (Drazen and Curfman 2002). The journal could no longer find enough independent experts. The new standard is that reviewers can have received no more than US$10,000 from companies whose work they judge. Many see this as an unacceptable compromise, evidence of a scientific establishment corrupted by bias and conflicts of interest. In addition, this decision only applies to review articles. The authors of scientific studies are often funded by private drug companies with a stake in the results.

In other cases, papers are ghost-written by pharmaceutical company staff or contractors. Scientists at universities are often allowed to have stock options in companies benefiting from the research they are conducting. Researchers on industry payrolls may be persuaded to suppress unwanted results, and those who defy their corporate sponsors may lose their funding. Lastly, where university research was once oriented to producing independent and public knowledge, it is now increasingly locked up in patents.

This type of corruption and bias also extends to prescribing doctors and medicine regulatory authorities (Angell 2004, Avorn 2004, Kassirer 2005). Big Pharma spends lavishly to influence doctors who write the prescriptions. It funds and thereby influences much of the continuing medical education doctors need to renew their licences, and subsidizes scientific meetings of medical societies where it hawks its wares and often sponsors its own programmes.

Pharmaceutical companies have also been able to purchase influence in regulatory bodies: half the US Food and Drug Administration's budget for evaluation of new drugs comes from pharmaceutical company user fees, making it dependent on the industry it regulates – an obvious conflict of interest. A significant number of staff in regulatory authorities also have long and close connections with the pharmaceutical companies. The executive head of the regulatory authority in the UK, for example, was an employee of SmithKlineBeecham for over 20 years.

Even more alarming is the absence of effective laws and regulations to force drug companies to reveal all their clinical trial data. The FDA and its European counterparts have no right to demand to see any data that drug companies do not wish to reveal. This selective and biased release of scientific data, which should be made illegal, is potentially harmful to patients and also has a corrosive effect on the ethics and values of scientific inquiry. Regulatory bodies are also under political pressure to speed up the licensing of new medicines in order to minimize the loss of potential profits due to delays in marketing a new drug.

Proposals for a new agenda

TRIPS and international trade agreements Intellectual property rights related to essential medicines and other essential health technologies should not be governed by the WTO and trade agreements, but by public health considerations and public health institutions – elevating human rights and social considerations above the narrower considerations of commercial trade. In

8 Informal supply: lack of regulation of pharmaceutical markets is a key problem for many poor countries.

the long term, civil society should work towards the annulment of the TRIPS agreement related to medicines and the creation of a more just framework. Similarly, civil society and health professional associations should campaign for the annulment of all TRIPS-plus agreements and policies related to medicines in bilateral and regional trade agreements.

In the interim, NGOs and health agencies must work with governments to make maximum use of the existing TRIPS flexibilities. Countries exempt from being TRIPS-compliant until 2016 must not be pressurized into introducing new patent laws before then, or enacting new laws that undermine their capacity to make use of the flexibilities, as some are doing. Governments have a better chance of withstanding pressure from Big Pharma and the political establishments of the US and EU with public support and civil society involvement. Efforts are also required to develop governments' technical and legislative capacity.

Keeping the generic supply pipeline open The generic medicine manufacturing capacity in countries such as India, China, Brazil and Thailand must be maintained. The application of the TRIPS flexibilities is one important mechanism. Continued support must be given to WHO's efforts in pre-qualifying quality products and producers so as to speed up the process by which generic medicines can be registered for use in countries. So far, the WHO system has proved effective and efficient.

The administrative and paperwork requirements for the TRIPS compulsory licensing flexibilities should also be streamlined, particularly in cases where the response to public health emergencies can be strengthened by rapidly increasing access to generic medicines. WHO could be funded to provide advice and assistance to countries needing to use the flexibilities.

A new paradigm for funding and stimulating pharmaceutical R&D New ways to fund and stimulate pharmaceutical R&D are needed to achieve the goal of universal access to essential medicines and avoid the huge inefficiencies and corruption of the current system. Four innovative proposals could stimulate R&D while reducing the difference between the sales price and actual cost of production (Baker 2004b). These are:

- a mandatory employer-based research fee to be distributed through intermediaries to researchers;
- zero-cost compulsory licensing patents, in which the patent-holder is compensated based on the rated quality of life improvement generated by the drug, and the extent of its use;
- an auction system in which the government purchases most drug patents and places them in the public domain; and

- financing pharmaceutical research through a set of competing, publicly supported research centres.

These proposals could remove the need for excessive spending on marketing, provide adequate financing for expensive biomedical research, reduce incentives for wasteful copycat research and for data protection and scientific secrecy, minimize the risk of political interference in setting research priorities, and be administratively feasible at the international level.

A proposed Medical Research and Development Treaty, which proposes a new paradigm that includes minimum national obligations for supporting medical R&D, with flexibility regarding the business models and intellectual property rules, should be supported (http://www.cptech.org/workingdrafts/rndtreaty.html, accessed 8 March 2005).

More directly, the Drugs for Neglected Diseases Initiative (http://www.dndi.org, accessed 8 March 2005) aims to raise financing directly to build a balanced research portfolio of long, medium and short-term projects to fill identifiable gaps in the drug development pipeline for key neglected diseases.

Strengthen the transparent and ethical regulation of pharmaceutical companies Profit-motivated pharmaceutical companies, whether Big Pharma or generic manufacturers, cannot be left to operate without a strong regulatory framework to promote rational medicine use and patient safety. The erosion of independent national and international regulatory structures and powers must be reversed. Civil society must play a further watchdog role that holds pharmaceutical companies and government regulators accountable to high standards of ethical practice. WHO, working in collaboration with NGOs such as Health Action International and Public Citizen, should produce a periodic scorecard of the competence and probity of national medicine regulatory bodies as a mechanism for monitoring progress.

Laws, policies and agreements should be established to make the full disclosure of all clinical trials data an obligation. Failing this, any breaches of patient safety arising from the deliberate disclosure of clinical trials data should be treated as criminal acts and be prosecuted.

Legitimize price control options Domestic regulations to control drug prices are an important mechanism to promote access. In countries where public expenditure on health care is relatively high, government- or public-funded health insurance can keep medicine costs low by negotiating cheaper prices with pharmaceutical manufacturers. In countries where public health expenditure is low, retail sales constitute the majority of pharmaceutical sales and direct price control mechanisms are necessary to place a ceiling on profitability, unit prices or distribution chain costs. However, such interventions are under attack as part of the neoliberal drive to deregulate the sector and weaken the monopsony power of governments (the power of a large buyer to negotiate lower prices). In India, a country with low public expenditure on health care, the number of medicines under price control declined from 342 in 1979 to 73 in 1995, and there is a proposal to reduce it further to 25. Such trends need to be reversed and governments need to be proactive to stabilize medicine prices.

End the corruption of academic research institutions As public institutions of learning and inquiry, universities and research centres must be protected from the corrosive effect of commercial influences. As a first step in this direction, the US National Institutes of Health and the Canadian Institutes for Health Research have recently commissioned studies to assess the integrity of clinical research in their countries and make policy suggestions for its preservation and enhancement. Similar initiatives should be widely supported, and their recommendations given serious consideration.

Revitalize Essential Drug Programmes The term 'essential drug programme' (EDP) was common in the international health literature 20 years ago, when countries were encouraged to set up national committees to define cost-effective treatment guidelines as a means of promoting rational prescribing. Today health sector reform, neoliberal deregulation and the commercialization of health care systems have resulted in a more market-driven pattern of medicine prescribing. As a consequence there is over-prescribing (with growing costs, a growing incidence of negative side-effects and the development of antimicrobial resistance) and inefficient prescribing (using more expensive medicines when cheaper versions would do). It is time for WHO to revitalize the essential medicines concept and find ways of integrating it in increasingly fragmented and commercialized health systems. Consumer and health professional organizations should insist on independent and periodic surveys of prescribing practices in public and private health care sectors.

References

Angell M (2004). *The truth about the drug companies: how they deceive us and what to do about it*. New York, Random House.

Avorn J (2004). *Powerful medicines: the benefits, risks, and costs of prescription drugs*. New York, Random House.

Baker B (2003). *Vows of poverty, shrunken markets, burdensome manufacturing and other nonsense at the WTO* (http://www.healthgap.org/press_releases/03/092703_HGAP_BP_WTO_Cancun.html, accessed 6 March 2005).

Baker B (2004a). *Processes and issues for improving access to medicines: willingness and ability to utilise TRIPS flexibilities in non-producing countries.* London, DFID Health Systems Resources Centre.

Baker D (2004b). *Financing drug research: what are the issues?* Washington DC, Center For Economic and Policy Research.

Baker D, Chatani N (2002). *Promoting good ideas on drugs: are patents the best way?* Briefing paper. Washington DC, Center for Economic and Policy Research.

Correa C (2002). *Implications of the Doha declaration on the TRIPS agreement and public health.* WHO/EDM/PAR/2002.3. Geneva, WHO.

Correa C (2004). *Implementation of the WTO general council decision on paragraph 6 of the Doha declaration on the TRIPS agreement and public health.* WHO/EDM/PAR/2004.4. Geneva, WHO.

DFID (2004). *Access to medicines in under-served markets. What are the implications of changes in intellectual property rights, trade and drug registration policy?* DFID/HSRC overview paper. London, DFID Health Systems Resources Centre.

Drahos P, Braithwaite J (2004). Who owns the knowledge economy: political organizing behinds TRIPS. Corner House briefing 32 (http://www.thecornerhouse.org.uk/item.shtml?x=85821, accessed 6 March 2005).

Drahos P, Henry D (2004). The free trade agreement between Australia and the United States. *British Medical Journal*, 328:1271–2.

Drazen J, Curfman G (2002). Financial associations of authors. *New England Journal of Medicine*, 346:1901–2.

Families USA (2001). *Off the Charts: Pay, Profits and Spending in Drug Companies* (http://www.familiesusa.org/site/PageServer?pagename=media_press_2001_drugceos, accessed 6 March 2005).

Guardian [anonymous] (2003). How much does it really cost to manufacture a drug? *Guardian* Special report: AIDS. London, *Guardian*, February 18 (http://www.guardian.co.uk/aids/graphic/0,7367,898105,00.html, accessed 14 March 2005).

Henry D, Birkett D (2001). Changes to the pharmaceutical benefits scheme. *Medical Journal of Australia*, 74:209–210.

Hill S, Johnson K (2004). *Emerging challenges and opportunities in drug registration and regulation in developing countries.* London, DFID Health Systems Resources Centre.

IFPMA (2005). *Intellectual Property and Patents.* International Federation of Pharmaceutical Manufacturers and Associations, Geneva (http://www.ifpma.org/Issues/issues_intell.aspx, accessed 6 March 2005).

Joint NGO Statement on TRIPS and public health. WTO deal on medicines: a 'gift bound in red tape' (2003) (http://www.cptech.org/ip/wto/p6/ngos09102003.html, accessed 6 March 2005).

Kassirer J (2005). *On the take: how medicine's complicity with big business can endanger your health.* Oxford, Oxford University Press.

Lokuge B, Faunce T, Denniss R (2003). *A back door to higher medicine prices? Intellectual property and the Australia-US Free Trade Agreement.* Canberra, The Australia Institute.

Matthews D (2002). *Globalising Intellectual Property Rights: The TRIPS Agreement.* London, Routledge.

Medicines

117

Medawar C and Hardon A (2004). *Medicines out of control?* Netherlands, Aksant.

MSF (Médecins sans Frontières) (2004). *Access to medicines at risk across the globe: what to watch out for in free trade agreements with the United States.* Briefing note (http://www.accessmed-msf.org/documents/ftabriefingenglish.pdf, accessed 6 March 2005).

McCoy D (2003). *Health sector responses to HIV/AIDS and treatment access in southern Africa: addressing equity.* Discussion Paper 10. EQUINET (http://www.equinet africa.org, accessed 14 February 2005).

Oxfam (2002). *US bullying on drug patents: one year after Doha.* Briefing paper 33. Oxford, Oxfam.

Pear R (2003). Drug companies increase spending on efforts to lobby Congress and governments. *New York Times*, June 1 (http://www.nytimes.com/2003/06/01/national/01LOBB.html?tntemail1, accessed 8 March 2005).

Public Citizen (2003). *The Other Drug War 2003: Drug Companies Deploy an Army of 675 Lobbyists to Protect Profits* (http://www.citizen.org/documents/Other_Drug_War2003.pdf, accessed 6 March 2005).

Sen Gupta (2005). *Indian Patent Act – Jeopardising the Lives of Millions.* Bangalore (http://www.phmovement.org/india/articles/indianpatentact.html, accessed 6 March 2005).

Trouiller P et al. (2002). Drug development for neglected diseases: a deficient market and a public-health policy failure. *Lancet*, 359:2188–2194.

US Food and Drug Administration (2001). *NDAs approved in calendar years 1990–2001 by therapeutic potentials and chemical types* (http://www.fda.gov/cder/rdmt/pstable. htm, accessed 6 March 2005).

WHO (2004a). *The world medicine situation.* WHO/EDM/PAR/2004.5. Geneva, WHO.

WHO (2004b). *What are essential medicines?* (http://www.who.int/medicines/rationale. shtml, accessed 14 February 2005).

WTO (2001). *Declaration on the TRIPS agreement and public health.* Fourth WTO ministerial conference, Doha, Qatar (http://www.wto.org/english/thewto_e/minist_e/min01_e/mindecl_trips_e.htm, accessed 6 March 2005).

B3 | The global health worker crisis

At last there is explicit recognition of the fact that many countries worldwide face a health worker crisis. In 2004 the 57th World Health Assembly passed a resolution on the international migration of health personnel, recognizing that the migration of skilled health workers from poor countries to rich countries represented a serious challenge for health systems in developing countries, and asked WHO to undertake a number of tasks. It even asked the DG to consult the UN and specialized agencies on the possibility of declaring a year or a decade of Human Resources for Health Development. The Joint Learning Initiative, established by WHO and other agencies to develop a series of working papers on the human resource crisis, launched its final report at the Inter-Ministerial Summit on Health Research in Mexico, 2004. At regional and country level, public health professionals and NGOs are recognizing the need to strengthen human resource management systems if they are to make any headway in reaching the MDG targets. The realization that health worker problems in Africa are directly linked to policies in rich countries such as Canada, the UK and the US has resulted in global coalitions of NGOs and academics from different continents attempting to address the problem holistically.

This chapter's focus is on the global dimension of health migration, although it recognizes that the agenda for coherent and comprehensive health systems development discussed in part B, chapter 1, must place human resources at its centre.

The lifeblood of health care systems

Medicines, clean water, diagnostic equipment and the physical infrastructure of clinics and hospitals are all essential components of a functioning health care system. However, it is the nurses, porters, drivers, laboratory technicians, pharmacists, doctors, cleaners and health managers that are central to drawing together the full mix of inputs to provide high quality and effective services. All aspects of a health care system ultimately depend on people (human resources) to run smoothly and well.

The prospects for achieving 80% coverage of measles immunization and skilled attendants at birth are greatly enhanced where health worker density exceeds 2.5 per 1,000 population. However, 75 countries with 2.5 billion people fall below this threshold (JLI 2004). Figure B3.1 illustrates a positive association between health worker density and infant, under-five and maternal mortality in different countries. This does not mean that the density of health workers is the sole determinant of health outcomes – other determinants (e.g. socio-economic development) improve outcomes and are also likely to contribute to greater availability of health personnel.

However, despite the obvious centrality of health personnel, the planning, production and management of human resources for health has been for decades (and in many respects still is) the least developed aspect of health systems policy and development. The technical knowledge of diseases far outstrips the application of practical knowledge of how to plan, develop and care for human resources. Human resource directorates in governments, as in international organizations, are undervalued and underfunded. Donors and agencies are part of the problem. 'Many classify human resources as recurring expenditures, not as an investment. Amazingly, buildings are considered cap-ital assets, while human capital is considered a recurring burden' (Chen 2004). Furthermore, fears of inflation have led the international financial institutions to advise poor countries to cap spending on wages. This approach is slowly beginning to change, as the scale and seriousness of the health worker crisis begin to be appreciated.

WHO has collected global data on health workers for many years, but has only recently started to pay it closer attention. There is often very inadequate information on who works in the health system, especially among the groups of staff who are not doctors. Routinely, for example, even in rich countries, statistics fail to differentiate between a qualified nurse and an unqualified

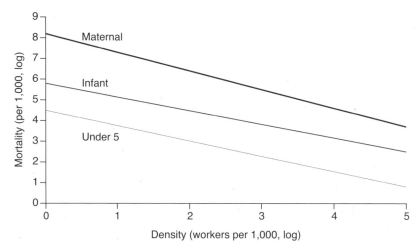

Figure B3.1 The negative correlation between mortality rates and health worker availability (*Source: JLI* 2004)

TABLE B3.1 Density of doctors and nurses in rich and selected poor countries

	WHO norm	Rich countries	Sample of 8 African countries
Nurses per 100,000 population	100 minimum	Several hundred to over 1000	8.8 – 113.1
Doctors per 100,000 population	20 minimum	200 – 400	3.4 – 13.2

Source: JLI 2004

nursing auxiliary. Without such data, planners, managers and educators are working in the dark since they do not really know how many staff they have, let alone how many are needed in future and what kind of work they should do.

The health worker crisis

For many people, especially in developed countries, access to competent health workers is not usually an insoluble problem. Those with money can always buy health care from private providers, from abroad if necessary. However, for the poor with the highest burdens of disease, competent health workers may not be available or accessible even to manage such common conditions as diarrhoeal disease, acute respiratory infections and childbirth. The sheer lack of health personnel in some countries is staggering, especially when compared to developed countries, or to recommended norms (see Table B3.1). In Malawi, there is one doctor per 50,000–100,000 people, compared to one per 300 in the UK.

The inequitable global distribution of numbers of health personnel is strikingly illustrated by Figure B3.2, which shows how countries with the highest disease burden have the lowest health worker density, particularly in Africa. Asia, with about half the world's population, has access to only about 30% of the world's health professionals. To make matters worse, 'the predominant flow of health professionals is from developing countries, where they are scarcest relative to needs, to developed countries, where they are more plentiful' (Woodward 2003). There is a global shortage of more than four million health workers; Sub-Saharan countries must nearly triple their current number of workers – adding the equivalent of one million – if they are to tackle the health MDGs (JLI 2004).

In addition to the overall lack of staff in many countries, health personnel

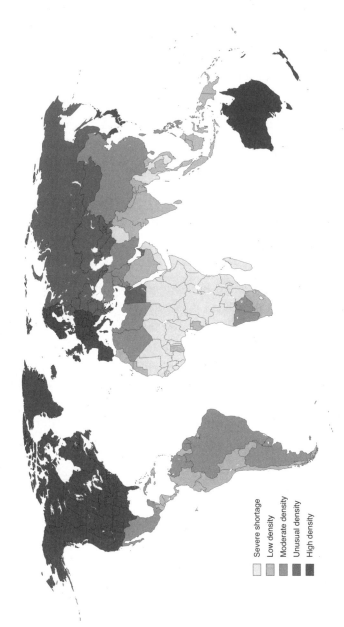

Figure B3.2 Health worker density (*Source: JLI 2004*)

Severe shortage
Low density
Moderate density
Unusual density
High density

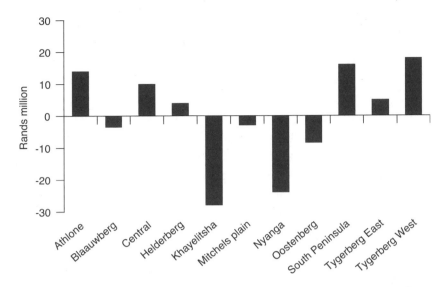

Figure B3.3 Inequity in public primary care expenditure, Cape Town (zero line represents an average equitable expenditure) (*Source*: Sanders et al. 2004)

are also often poorly distributed. Typically, rural and remote communities are served by fewer doctors and nurses than urban communities; this may be associated with a disproportionate concentration of health workers at the secondary and tertiary levels of the health system. Attracting skilled professionals to rural areas has long been a challenge, including in developed countries such as Canada, Australia and the US, which have become reliant on foreign-qualified doctors and nurses to staff facilities in rural and remote areas.

As increasing numbers of people move to urban conglomerations, there is growing evidence of acute disparities between different parts of the same city, with health services relatively understaffed in slums. Figure B3.3 shows the wide variation in public sector health care expenditure in Cape Town, with black townships hugely under-resourced compared to suburban areas (Sanders et al. 2004). The lower the funding allocation, the more likely it is that fewer staff will be employed, and with fewer qualifications.

There are also differences in the availability of health personnel in different segments of a health care system. Private health care services, particularly those tailored to the rich, are typically better staffed than services for the poor. In some countries there is also a growing divide between public sector services and better staffed nongovernment health care providers serving the poor. The channelling of large sums into HIV/AIDS programmes in relatively stand-alone structures and systems, many delivered through donor agencies and NGOs that offer higher salaries than the public sector, drains staff from the public sector and thereby weakens mainstream health services – though sometimes the labour market competition can drive up terms and conditions for all.

Finally, there is a need to consider the human worker crisis in terms of quality. In many developing countries, health workers are demoralized and demotivated as a result of the collapse of public health financing, decline in salary levels and increase in workload, in some cases arising from the HIV/AIDS epidemic (see Box B3.1). Staff who feel demoralized and demotivated may be tempted into various forms of petty corruption, extortion (e.g. under-the-counter charges) and taking on second jobs.

The fragmentation of health care systems and the collapse of public sector bureaucracies in many developing countries have also resulted in inadequate health support systems (e.g. erratic and unreliable medicine supply systems, poor transport management etc.) which means that even motivated health workers may not be as effective as they could be. Meanwhile the commercialization and commodification of health care, and the erosion of trust within health care systems, have resulted in a deterioration in professional ethics and standards of care.

Box B3.1 The impact of HIV/AIDS on health worker retention and performance

Health workers have had to bear a triple burden in the HIV/AIDS epidemic. First, they themselves have increasing morbidity and mortality. In South Africa, for example, prevalence amongst nurses has been estimated at 16–20% (Shisana et al. 2002). Second, they are caring outside work for sick and dying family and community members for whom they are often are the first port of call. Third, they shoulder the increasing burden of disease at work, having to deal with many more patients, and also much sicker and incurable ones – heavier workloads compounded as rates of absenteeism rise, and as more health workers leave because of illness or migration. This leads to accelerated burnout and decreased productivity.

Fear of infection is an additional stress factor. Despite overwhelming evidence that the risk of infection is low for health workers, characterizing the risk as low is unhelpful because 'health workers are likely to perceive the situation as one of "risk" or "no risk" and when exposed to possibly infected blood are not going to consider gradations of risk' (Gerber, quoted in Horsman and Sheeran 1995). The close association of health workers with the disease can result in social contagion and stigmatization – studies

The global brain drain

The brain drain of skilled health workers from poor countries to richer ones is a major dimension of the health worker crisis in many developing countries. There has been an upsurge in migration of health workers since the late 1980s. For example, the number of non-European Union nurses registering with the Irish Nursing Board rose from less than 200 a year to more than 1800 between 1990 and 2001. In the UK, the proportion of overseas-trained nurses admitted to the professional register each year rose from just over 10% in 1990 to more than half in 2001 (Buchan and Sochalski 2003). The countries that experience high levels of out-migration are often those that can least afford to lose skilled personnel, such as Zambia, where an estimated 550 of the 600 doctors trained since independence have gone abroad. The migration of teachers and academics from poor countries has also damaged countries' capacity to train new health workers.

The migration pattern generally follows a hierarchy of wealth, from poorer to wealthier countries, and from rich countries where terms and conditions are inadequate to other rich ones (the UK, for example, is seeing a drain of nurses

report that health workers treating HIV patients feel shunned by friends and neighbours, and that exposure to people living with HIV and AIDS is affecting family relations (Horsman and Sheeran 1995).

Helping health workers to cope with this triple burden should include giving them the material tools required to provide effective clinical care. Training programmes can strengthen their capacity to cope with the workload psychologically and emotionally.

The Mildmay Centre for Palliative Care in Uganda is an example of an innovative training programme which has implemented educational programmes to help improve care, with an emphasis on building local capacity. Participants include health workers (doctors, nurses, counsellors, social workers, volunteers, community health workers and so on); government and NGO staff (including policy-makers and the media); students and teachers in schools; workers; and men, women, children and adolescents living with HIV/AIDS. The mobile clinical training team takes training to the rural districts, visiting health centres run by the MOH, conducts a needs assessment, and develops a training programme. Trainees spend a week at the training centre, and then, over a year, are given follow-up and further training (UNAIDS 2000).

to the US, including some recruited from poorer countries). There is also migration from rural to urban and public to private, increasing inequity along the way (see Figure B3.4). There are a number of drivers. There is a growing demand for health care from the ageing populations of the developed world. At the same time there is inadequate local production of health workers in some of these countries – the US, for example, will need over a million more nurses by 2010 (US Bureau of Labor Statistics 2004). Active recruitment – proactive hiring and advertising in low-income countries by recruitment agencies acting on behalf of rich country health systems – has also encouraged migration.

These demand pressures have been reinforced by globalization and commercialization. Research in Ghana shows that technological change, notably the Internet, has dramatically increased knowledge of jobs and conditions elsewhere, and developed world health journals with recruitment advertising are widely available. Commercial investment in recruitment agencies is also facilitating migration, making obtaining visas, jobs and accommodation much easier (Mensah et al. 2005).

The international brain drain is also driven by a variety of other factors such as the widespread collapse of health systems in many low-income coun-

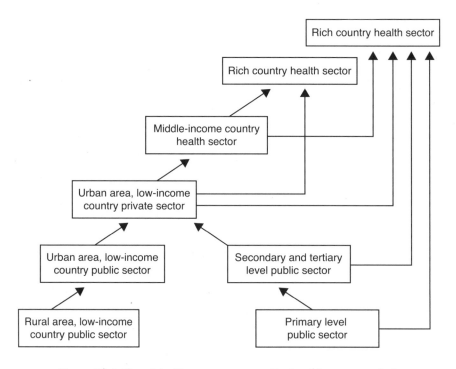

Figure B3.4 The global human resources for health conveyor belt
(*Source*: Padarath et al. 2003)

126

tries, which have resulted in low-paid health workers struggling to survive financially. Bad working conditions, poor management, lack of continuing education opportunities and poor prospects are often cited. Migration may also be a consequence of broader problems such as war and civil violence, high levels of crime and a lack of education opportunities for the children of health workers.

A shortfall of health personnel can quickly trigger a downward spiral in the quality of care that is hard to reverse. The loss of institutional memory carried by experienced staff, for example, cannot be replaced with new and junior staff. As more staff leave, the workload and stress on those remaining increases, potentially a catalyst for them to leave as well. The migration of even a small number of highly skilled personnel can have a dramatic impact on under-resourced health care systems: the only referral unit for spinal injuries for an entire region of South Africa was closed in 2000 when its two anaesthetists were recruited to Canada (Martineau et al. 2002).

Policy responses

Investments in training by poor countries are lost in the process of migration, especially if health professionals do not return: low-income countries train doctors and nurses each year and then see the benefits from that investment redistributed to the wealthy nations. This redistribution is a perverse subsidy from the very poor to the rich. What can policymakers do to reverse it?

Ethical recruitment One policy response in wealthy countries has been to limit 'active recruitment' by their health services through introducing – in consultation with many governments from staff-short countries – a code of practice prohibiting hiring and advertising in developing countries unless there is a government agreement that allows it. The UK introduced a voluntary code that covered its national health service, which has now been extended to the private sector (reflecting the huge shortage of UK nurses willing to work in private nursing homes for elderly people). Yet registration of nurses in the UK from a number of low-income countries in Sub-Saharan Africa has been accelerating since the code was introduced in 1999 (see Figure 5).

It has been ineffective partly because it is voluntary, and thus often ignored. Active recruitment is in any case only one part of the process through which health care labour markets are becoming integrated. Increasing globalization, primarily through technological changes, and commercialization, through the growth of labour market intermediaries such as recruitment firms, are making the process of finding a job and migrating much easier. These labour market

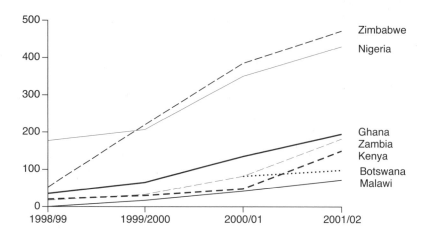

Figure B3.5 Nurse registration in the UK from selected low-income countries 1998/9–2001/2 (*Source*: Buchan et al. 2003)

changes are cumulative and self-reinforcing. Policies which work against their grain are not likely to succeed (Mensah et al. 2005).

South Africa has gone further and introduced a ban on registration of doctors from other African and Commonwealth countries, as an act of solidarity with its poorer neighbours. While this has reduced the entry of doctors from countries like Malawi, Ghana, Zambia and Tanzania, the overall effect on the outflow of doctors from those countries is unclear – doctors may simply have migrated elsewhere. Such measures also raise issues about professionals' right to freedom of movement.

Government service It is widely accepted in developed and developing countries alike that governments that invest in the training of health personnel are entitled to receive a return on that investment. Bonding measures that enforce public service have often worked well, especially in helping to increase the numbers of health professionals serving in deprived areas. Commentators have noted that bonding policies have played a role in the health gain of some 'high-performing' developing countries such as Thailand and Malaysia.

Bonding works in contexts where it is perceived as fair and legitimate. However, evidence suggests that in a number of staff-short, low-income countries facing large health worker migration, coercive measures work poorly (Mensah et al. 2005). Salary differentials are often so great – and working conditions so bad – that there is little incentive to honour the bond. Coercive measures may also backfire by creating incentives to leave – and not to return (Mensah et al. 2005, Bueno de Mesquita and Gordon 2005).

Division of labour Some countries are beginning to alter the composition of their health workforce to make them less vulnerable to recruitment from abroad, for example by making more use of paramedical staff, medical assistants, community health workers and unqualified staff. The rethinking of the health division of labour that this promotes may result in a better fit between population needs and workforce skills, and may be more resistant to international out-migration. One review concludes that expansion of the numbers and roles of staff whose qualifications are not internationally recognized has been 'a quiet success story, providing large numbers of health workers who keep the system running in a number of countries' (Hongoro and McPake 2005).The downside can be deskilling of the workforce, and a reinforcement of the current bias towards tertiary care, with the assumption that staff who work in primary health care/rural areas/ poor countries need less training than those in hospitals/cities/rich countries.

Incentive schemes Countries are also responding to out-migration with retention strategies designed to mitigate the push factors that promote external migration. These include strengthening financial and non-financial incentives for health workers to stay in developing countries, or in rural areas (see Box B3.2).

Incentive schemes need strong management and must be applied fairly. A very popular scheme in Ghana – welcomed by all health workers when it started in 1999 – was the additional duty hours allowance which doubled or trebled take-home money overnight and reduced strikes for some time. Yet it has been subject to arbitrary local decision-making, and some health workers

---

Box B3.2 *Strategies to retain health workers in rural areas in Thailand*

The government of Thailand has had considerable success in ensuring a reasonably fair distribution of health personnel across the country over the last 40 years. The recruitment of students from rural areas has played an important role. Nurses, midwives, junior sanitarians and paramedics are recruited and trained locally and then assigned to placements in their home towns. Students recruited by the ministry of health receive heavily subsidized tuition and free clothing, room and board, and learning materials during their studies. In return, they agree to work in the public sector for 2–4 years. (*Source*: Wibulpolprasert and Pengpaibon 2003)

have been excluded: in 2004 grievances led to a 10–day countrywide nurses' strike demanding a 70% increase in the allowance for nurses (Mensah et al. 2005). Further research is needed on the incentives that will work best – an important and neglected area.

Restitution Incentives cost money, which is why there have been calls for financial support to come from wealthy countries that benefit from the training investment made by poorer countries. While health worker migration takes place between most countries, it is the flow from staff-short, low-income countries to the developed world which leads to a perverse, or unjust, subsidy.

A recent study tried to measure the size of the subsidy in the case of Ghanaian-trained workers employed in the UK's national health service (Mensah et al. 2005). First it could be measured by calculating the training costs the UK has saved. Multiplying the numbers of Ghanaian doctors and nurses registered in the UK by an approximate current cost of training in the UK gives a figure of around US$ 200 million. Alternatively – and more appropriately – the value put on the benefits from the services of the Ghanaian staff could be assessed. One measure of value is salaries paid to those staff by the UK NHS, which yields a figure of around US$ 70 million a year (Mensah et al. 2005). The calculations are crude, but they illustrate the order of magnitude of the perverse subsidy.

Such figures – perhaps supplemented by others such as costings of 'health benefits lost' in Ghana or the training investment lost in the country of origin – could inform a financial restitution effort focused on rebuilding health systems in Ghana and similar staff-short countries, with good working conditions for health professionals and good quality health care.

Serious debate about restitution began at the 2004 World Health Assembly and needs sustained attention. Objectors point to remittances sent by migrant workers. These are valuable and substantial, but they do not go back into the health systems from which the investment has been lost. Others argue that restitution would not be well used. Yet Ghana and other countries have established financial channels for managing aid to health services that could be adapted to manage flows of restitution funds. The management problems can be solved case by case.

The most serious objection to restitution – though the least presented – is that it represents a tax on migrants and would jeopardize their right to freedom of movement. To deal with this problem, restitution payments should be detached from links to individual migrant staff. Instead, the extent of reliance in the UK on staff from a particular low-income country should inform and motivate government decisions to increase transfers of funds to rebuild

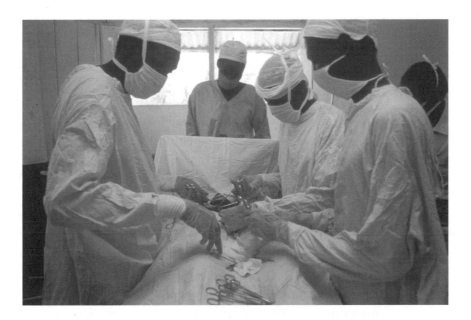

9 African surgeons are operating in a global labour market.

that country's health system in a manner that tackles the root causes of out-migration. This would also acknowledge wealthy nations' obligations under international human rights law to help fulfil the right to health of people in other countries (Bueno de Mesquita and Gordon 2005).

Restitution can come in other forms. There are many links between rich and low-income countries' health systems and staff, and these partnerships should be built on when they are effective and genuinely support capacity in poorer countries, with the objectives of improving conditions in poorer countries, increasing incentives to stay and return and allowing for career-enhancing migration. The Ghanaian diaspora in the UK for example plays an active role in contributing funds for health care in Ghana. Professional associations in origin and destination countries could support each other in the fight for better pay and conditions. One of the most serious effects of health worker migration is the 'beheading' of the system – the loss of leadership and high-level skills. Health professional academia could therefore be involved in supporting research and development, the capacity for local leadership and badly needed postgraduate specialization opportunities (Mensah et al. 2005).

Conclusions

This chapter has argued for positive policies to address health worker shortages in the world's poorest countries. Developing nations should be supported

131

to undertake greater experimentation, from the development of new health worker roles, through to financial and other incentives which improve health worker motivation and build the public sector ethos (Hongoro and McPake 2005).

Rich countries should do something in return. 'Ethical recruitment' policies can help ameliorate but cannot solve the problem. The developed world should help poor countries to strengthen their health systems and enable them to provide incentives for health workers. Restitution would be one way of providing the funding (and other types of capacity) to enable them to do this. Professional associations and health service bodies in the developed world can also play their part in restitution efforts, in a way that strives to develop local capacity effectively. Harmful policies such as caps on public sector wages imposed by the international financial institutions should be abandoned.

WHO's current work in the field of human resources for health should be supported and enhanced where appropriate, and it can play a key advocacy role. Its efforts to improve data collection through strengthening country capacity in collecting, managing, and evaluating such information should be a priority, and should focus on a number of key indicators such as health worker to population ratios, geographic variations in health worker density, and trends related to the balance of public and private sector health staff. Civil society in all countries should insist on such data being collected and publicized by ministries of health. Civil society in rich countries should also highlight health worker shortages in their own countries and campaign for them to be redressed.

WHO could also encourage countries to experiment with a system of compensation, involving effective partnerships to strengthen health systems in poorer countries. This would be in line with the 2004 resolution's call to 'establish mechanisms to mitigate the adverse impact on developing countries of the loss of health personnel through migration, including means for the receiving countries to support the strengthening of health systems, in particular human resources development in the countries of origin'.

References

Buchan J, Parkin T, Sochalski J (2003). *International nurse mobility: trends and policy implications*. Geneva, WHO.

Bueno de Mesquita J, Gordon M (2005). *The international migration of health workers: a human rights analysis*. London, Medact (http://www.medact.org, accessed 22 February 2005).

Chen L (2004). *Harnessing the power of human resources for achieving the MDGs*. High Level Forum on Health MDGs, WHO, Geneva.

Hongoro C, McPake B (2004). How to bridge the gap in human resources for health. *The Lancet*, 364:1451–1456.

Horsman J, Sheeran P (1995). Health care workers and HIV/AIDS: a critical review of the literature. *Social Science and Medicine*, 41 (11).

Joint Learning Initiative (JLI) (2004). *The health workforce in Africa: challenges and prospects*. WHO, World Bank and Rockefeller Foundation. Global Health Trust.

Martineau T, Decker K, Bundred P (2002). *Briefing note on international migration of health professionals: levelling the playing field for developing country health systems*. Liverpool, Liverpool School of Tropical Medicine.

Mensah K, Mackintosh M, Henry L (2005). *The 'skills drain' of health professionals from the developing world: a framework for policy formulation*. Medact, London (http://www.medact.org, accessed 22 February 2005).

Padarath A, Chamberlain C, McCoy D, Ntuli A, Rowson M, Loewenson R. Health Personnel in Southern Africa: Confronting maldistribution and brain drain. Equinet, Harare, South Africa (http://www.equinetafrica.org/Resources/downloads/HRH Review.pdf, accessed 2 March 2005).

Sanders D, Lehmann U, Ferrinho P (2004). *Health sector reform: some implications for human resources*. Paper presented at WHO Consultation on Health Sector Reform and Reproductive Health. Geneva, December.

Shisana O et al (2002). *The impact of HIV/AIDS on the health sector*. HSRC (http://www.hsrcpublishers.ac.za).

UNAIDS (2000). *Summary Booklet of Best Practices in Africa: issue 2*. Geneva, UNAIDS.

US Bureau of Labor Statistics (2004). *Monthly Labor Review*, February (http://www.bls.gov/news.release/ecopro.toc.htm, accessed 8 March 2005).

Wibulpolprasert S, Pengpaibon P (2003). 'Integrated strategies to tackle the inequitable distribution of doctors in Thailand: four decades of experience'. *Human Resources for Health*, Nov 25;1(1):12.

Woodward D (2003). *Trading health for profit: the implications of the GATS and trade in health services for health in developing countries*. Geneva, WHO.

B4 | Sexual and reproductive health

The first global agenda for sexual and reproductive health and rights was agreed at the UN International Conference on Population and Development, Cairo 1994 (referred to in this chapter as 'Cairo'). It marked a paradigm shift away from a narrow, technical, medical approach based on delivery of services and numbers rather than well-being – placing rights at the centre of population and development, and defining reproductive health as 'a state of complete physical, mental and social well-being ... in all matters relating to the reproductive system and to its functions and processes ... Reproductive health implies that people are able to have a safe and satisfying sex life and have the capacity to reproduce and to have the freedom to decide if, when and how often to do so' (UNICPD 1994).

This broader approach to reproductive health moved the Cairo agenda into political and economic debates over access and rights to knowledge, resources and appropriate services, making it highly contested (Lohmann 2003, Petchesky 2003, Sen and Barroso 1996). The macroeconomic conditions of the 1990s, described in part A, worked against it. Women and health movements in civil society and their allies in UN and national bureaucracies have undertaken strong campaigns to link public health, gender equality and development policy, and advocated nationally and internationally for the upholding of rights to be backed by the appropriate knowledge, services and funds.

This chapter maps out the economic and political debates determining the sexual and reproductive health and rights agenda, in order to understand where we are now and make proposals for moving forward. It reviews the Cairo consensus as the global normative rights framework, presents some of the reasons for the difficulties in meeting it, and concludes with recommendations for activists. In the spirit of the Global Health Watch it is strongly critical of the current mainstream approach to development, while advocating strategic engagement with governments and multilateral institutions.

The Cairo consensus

The term 'reproductive rights' emerged in the 1980s on the second wave of feminism largely generated by the women's movements in North America, Europe, Australia and Latin America. The consensus focused on women's liberation and autonomy, violence against women, the fight for abortion and 'our body ourselves' (what was called 'body politics'). Women from the South expanded the concept to embrace maternal health and morbidity, childbearing and child-raising. The formation of the Cairo consensus was complex, bringing together the North and South agendas developed through regional and international meetings led by networks of southern-based women such as the Women's Global Network for Reproductive Rights, DAWN and the International Women's Health Coalition (Correa 1994, Petchesky 2003, Antrobus 2004).

These movements have different emphases but many shared concerns, and the global reproductive health and rights movement managed with the support of UN agencies (particularly UNFPA) and some governments to establish a consensual women-centred and rights-based framework. In Latin America women's health movements emphasized quality reproductive and sexual health services in the face of religious and state oppression and in the context of citizenship needs. In Asia women were concerned with population control and coercion, maternal mortality, the health of the girl child and all forms of violence against women. Activists in Africa were concerned with poverty and survival issues, maternal mortality and morbidity, sexually transmitted diseases and HIV/AIDS. European and North American women focused on autonomy and expression, the medicalization of reproductive health and the rising cost of services. Middle Eastern women were concerned with access and rights to holistic reproductive health care throughout the life cycle. Central and Eastern European women focused on public health, gender equality and women's rights issues (Bandarage 1997, IRRAG 1998, Harcourt forthcoming).

Cairo presented a rights-based framework for population stabilization, discrediting old population control programmes. Its goal is to make reproductive health care services universally accessible through primary health care no later than 2015. The new consensus discredits the targeted approach to population control, rejects incentives and targets in family planning and underlines the need for comprehensive reproductive health services. It also defines health services as encompassing family planning care during pregnancy, prevention and screening of sexually transmitted diseases, basic gynaecological care, sexuality and gender education and referral systems for other health problems. It adopts a life cycle approach with services for all aspects of reproductive health rights. Although it fell short of demanding universal safe and legal abortion, it asked countries to deal with the public health consequences of unsafe abortion and to ensure that where abortion is legal it is safe (The Corner House and WGNRR 2004).

The Cairo programme of action is not binding but has proved a useful lobbying and advocacy tool. It has also been used more broadly as a platform

**10 Policy-makers are gradually acknowledging men's
household responsibilities.**

for women's rights because of its emphasis on gender equality and public
health and development, and its links to the Beijing platform of action (Fourth
World Conference on Women 1995). It was used to push for women's inclusion
in decision-making in Brazil; to fight for changes in property rights in Kenya;
and to lobby for human-centred health and development in the Philippines.
It persuaded the government of India to abandon targets and overt forms of
coercion. Governments now speak of reproductive rights, men's responsibility,
women's empowerment and women's rights instead of population control,
family planning methods and mother and child programmes. However, despite indications of success in reproductive health education, access to contraception, infant mortality and skilled care during childbirth, five- and ten-year
reviews show that the programme is still far from being implemented.

What is undermining Cairo?

Many macroeconomic factors undermine Cairo, linked to a growingly conservative environment and the predominance of World Bank policies. For
example, the Millennium Development Goals do not include the sexual and
reproductive rights agenda (Barton 2004, Harcourt 2004), a telling indication
of how much ground the Cairo agenda has lost. The goals exclude sexuality, reproductive rights and health as determinants of gender equality, and
focus on education for girls and maternal health and morbidity. This places
women and children's right to health within a purely biological framework.

'As feminists and women's rights activists we must continue to maintain a critical surveillance of the implementation of MDGs in order to protect our interests in equality and nondiscrimination,' warns Sunila Abeyeskera from Sri Lanka (ARROW 2004).

The goal to reduce maternal mortality is nevertheless important as more women are dying in childbirth and suffering from chronic ill health following complicated deliveries than 10 years ago. Maternal mortality remains a priority in Sub-Saharan Africa and south Asia in particular. However, the absence of other reproductive health and rights concerns reflects the UN's reluctance to recognize or take a strong stand on other sexual and reproductive health and rights issues in many arenas, particularly women's autonomy to choose, abortion and sexuality (DAWN 2004).

The universal rise of fundamentalism has fired a 'morality' debate with many examples of how these conservative approaches are undermining the sexual and reproductive health and rights agenda. One is the rule imposed by President Bush in 2001 prohibiting overseas NGOs from receiving US government aid if they promote or provide referrals for abortion. In 2002, the US government withheld US$ 34 million promised to UNFPA because it said it funded abortion in China. Meanwhile it is funding the anti-abortion lobby and promotion of abstinence overseas (using the ABC approach: Abstinence until marriage, Be faithful and Condoms where appropriate (Jacobson 2003)). The Vatican and conservative states consistently attack the sexual and reproductive health and rights agenda. Such strategies threaten many sexual and reproductive health and rights projects in the global South and are leading to increased unsafe abortion, closure of family planning clinics and shortages of contraceptive supplies.

Lack of donor funding is not the only obstacle. Broader underlying economic and political conditions are undermining women's health and their control over safe sex and childbearing. Health services are in decline and economically poor women in particular have little or no access to reproductive or other health services. Recent reports on poverty have tracked the deterioration of women's health, particularly those who are economically vulnerable. Global inequalities in income and health have been growing and hunger has increased despite falling population growth, as detailed in part D, chapter 3 (Yong et al. 2000, Desai 2004, Rao 2004).

Many activists are developing an alternative vision far more critical of the development establishment and globalization that goes beyond the Cairo consensus. They believe Cairo went along too readily with the neoliberal agenda that is proving so disastrous for the poor, the vast majority of whom are rural women and girl children. Structural adjustment and trade policies are leading to greater exploitation of women's time/work and sexuality (see, for example, Rao 2004, Antrobus 2004, Harcourt 2004, The Corner House and WGNRR 2004). Structural adjustment packages or privatization of health services, if and when they provide reproductive health care, offer a narrow family planning package mainly for women plus some treatment for sexually transmitted illnesses and child health. It is often provided only as emergency care with a user fee, or only in urban areas.

Cairo took a passive line and as a result could not guarantee women the basics they need to make reproductive health choices. It failed to take into account the power imbalances in economic and social structures among and between countries and between men and women. Some say its tendency to focus on abortion and reproductive rights marginalized the basic issues of primary health care, social security and investment in health systems. In reality women's health is largely determined by economic and social constraints – it is difficult to separate out reproductive rights and health from other economic and political rights and needs (such as land rights, food security and communal harmony) that impact on economically poor women's lives.

This more critical agenda proposes that the sexual and reproductive rights framework must be embedded in an understanding of both human rights and macroeconomic policies. In the years after Cairo many more women's groups began to make the links between trade and health and gender inequality, arguing that the increased violence against women and rise in fundamentalism is linked directly to market-oriented globalization. The fundamentalism of the market joins the fundamentalisms of ethnic, religious and moral right-wing groups in dismantling women's livelihoods, economic security and control over their lives and bodies. All this threatens women's hard-won health rights and access to resources that enable choices promoting health and well-being (UNFPA 2002).

Prejudice against poor women is so great that it amounts to a neo-Malthusian approach, some argue, embedded in US-led economic, development and migration policy that bolsters racism and fear. 'The programme of action has been one of the most controversial and challenged UN agreements in the last 50 years,' says Steven Sinding, director general of the International Planned Parenthood Federation. 'Sexual rights and reproductive health have become targets of new attacks from conservative and religious right forces. We need to identify and understand the main forces that are threatened by the Cairo consensus, and are working actively to undermine it' (Sinding 2004).

Activists must therefore work beyond the Cairo consensus and form alliances with a range of social movements striving for health, economic and social justice as part of the broader politics of social and economic transformation (see Box B4.1).

Box B4.1 Resources

ARROW, the Asian-Pacific Resource and Research Centre for Women, is an NGO committed to promoting and protecting women's health rights and needs, particularly in the areas of sexuality and reproductive health (http://www.arrow.org.my).

The Corner House carries out analyses, research and advocacy with the aim of linking issues, stimulating informed discussion and strategic thought on critical environmental and social concerns, and encouraging broad alliances to tackle them (http://www.thecornerhouse.org.uk./briefing/index.shtml).

The Center for Reproductive Rights is a nonprofit, legal advocacy organization that promotes and defends the reproductive rights of women worldwide (http://www.reproductiverights.org).

DAWN (Development Alternatives with Women for a New Era) is a network of women scholars and activists from the economic South who engage in feminist research and analysis of the global environment and are committed to working for economic justice, gender justice and democracy (http://www.dawn.org.fj/publications/DAWNInforms).

The International Planned Parenthood Federation (IPPF) is the largest voluntary organization in the world concerned with family planning and sexual and reproductive health. See in particular the score card system and the report of the Countdown 2015 Roundtable, London 2004 (http://www.ippf.org/resource/index.htm).

International Women's Health Coalition (IWHC) works to generate health and population policies, programmes, and funding that promote and protect the rights and health of girls and women worldwide. Its priorities are youth health and rights, safe abortion, sexual rights and gender equality, and HIV/AIDS and women (http://www.iwhc.org).

The UN Population Fund (UNFPA) is the world's largest international source

---

of funding for population and reproductive health programmes (http://www.unfpa.org).

UNIFEM, the UN women's fund, provides financial and technical assistance to innovative programmes and strategies that promote women's human rights, political participation and economic security (http://www.unifem.org).

Women's Global Network for Reproductive Rights (WGNRR) is an autonomous network of groups and individuals in every continent who aim to achieve and support reproductive rights for women (http://www.wgnrr.org/frameset.htm).

WHO Reproductive Health and Research comprises the UNDP/UNFPA/WHO/World Bank Special Programme of Research, Development and Research Training in Human Reproduction (HRP), and Programme Development in Reproductive Health (PDRH) (http://www.who.int/reproductive-health).

WICEJ is an international coalition representing organizations in all regions. It works to link gender with macroeconomic policy in international intergovernmental policy-making arenas from a human rights perspective (http://www.wicej.addr.com/publications.html).

Where are we now – the challenges

Progress is being made in some areas of sexual and reproductive health, despite vocal and organized opposition, setbacks and an increasingly hostile economic and political context. Governments around the world have adopted the Cairo framework and reaffirmed it in regional meetings in 2003–4. These reviews and other global meetings have also signalled some important new concerns.

Macroeconomic environment Health activists need to understand how macroeconomic trends are determining women's autonomy, sexual and reproductive rights and health. Sexual and reproductive health and rights activists need to join others working for broad social and economic transformation.

Fundamentalisms A concerted effort is needed to ensure that different forms of fundamentalism do not undermine the rights agenda. The politico-religious fundamentalisms are most prevalent, from Christianity to Islam and Hinduism. The rise of the fundamental political right in extremist movements across Asia, Latin America and the US is having a grim impact on women.

Poverty A major Cairo victory was to link poverty, development and population concerns to a range of social justice goals – gender equality, women's empowerment, and human rights. Today's agenda must recognize that this linkage requires a critique of the current development model, and public investments and resources to restore public health systems. Public health decision-making must be accountable to women, the poor, minorities, migrants, indigenous peoples and youth, enabling them to voice their own needs.

HIV/AIDS The pandemic has worsened dramatically since Cairo. Linkages should be made between HIV/AIDS and sexual and reproductive health, mainstreaming it in policies, programmes and practices. This requires reaching out to networks of HIV-positive people and affected communities, linking in terms of funding, advocacy and policy. Activists must also take into account the sexual and reproductive health rights and needs of youth, men who have sex with men, injecting drug users and sex workers. Practical measures are needed such as voluntary counselling and testing, condom promotion and access, programmes to prevent mother to child transmission, antiretroviral access and management and treatment of sexually transmitted illnesses. Social and cultural factors that define masculinity and their implications for their sexual partners, male and female, must also be addressed.

Abortion Unsafe illegal abortion is still a major cause of maternal death, particularly among young, poor and rural women. The Cairo discussion on abortion focused primarily on the public health impact of unsafe abortion. It also affirmed a woman's right to make decisions about her reproductive health and whether and when to have children. Many obstacles remain despite efforts in numerous countries to change laws and make safe services more accessible. Abortion must stay on the agenda. Making it safe, accessible and legal requires an alliance between many actors. Communication strategies are needed to influence public attitudes.

Sexuality Sexuality is now more openly discussed in policy debates, although sometimes in moralistic or victimizing terms in relation to women's sexuality and choices. It is important to ensure sexuality can be spoken about in relation to rights, equality, personhood, and freedom from shame and fear. The

141

debate on sexuality that Cairo stimulated needs to be continued among people of all ages in ways that address gender roles, power relationships, sexual diversity and sexual orientation. This is particularly important in the face of a re-emergence of the abstinence and virginity debates, continuing discrimination against gay men and women, and taboos against sexual pleasure.

Maternal health Reducing maternal mortality and morbidity demands more funding and attention. It should be understood as a complex political, socio-economic and cultural issue that requires major changes in health care and services, and cultural and political attitudes. The empowerment of women, families and communities and a shared sense of responsibility for pregnancy are needed so that women are in a position to ask for and receive access to good quality care. Functioning, well staffed health services are essential to prevent deaths from obstetric emergencies.

Women's rights and men's responsibilities Cairo shifted the focus from demographic targets to individual rights and needs, but women's rights are now under attack. Even if terms like gender, rights, sexuality and violence against women are on the mainstream health agenda, the challenge is to find the means to apply them in ways that will bring real change. Beyond the economic underpinnings there are also cultural and social needs to increase men's involvement and responsibilities through recognizing how masculinity operates in traditional power relations. More work and funding are needed to encourage men in non-violent behaviour, and to support women's rights and gender equity.

Youth rights and health Youth has become a much stronger issue since Cairo, in terms of both participation in the movement and their own needs and rights. It is now recognized as essential to respect and promote young people's human rights, including their sexual and reproductive rights. Youth – like women – is diverse, and rural youth, married adolescents, and out-of-school youth are especially likely to be marginalized. Health services should be youth-friendly, guaranteeing confidentiality, tolerance and understanding. Secular and religious education, the media and the Internet are all critical in promoting knowledge and honest and open discussion of sexual pleasure and identity, self-esteem and self-image. Involving youth in decision-making and policy formulation is vital.

Funding The estimated cost of universal access to sexual and reproductive health services is US$ 23 billion for 2005. Donors therefore have to triple their commitment. This is not just a question of activists lobbying governments on the basis of the promises made in Cairo; it requires governments, officials, parliamentarians and NGOs to work together to prove the economic and social benefits of sexual and reproductive health for all. Gender budgeting, introduced in the late 1990s and now practised in many countries, is a useful strategy to ensure that government resources are being spent on programmes and services that address women and men in an equal way and take gender needs into account. 'Gender budget analysis provides women with an indicator of government commitment to address women's specific needs and rights to health care, education and employment' (UNIFEM 2005).

Recommendations

Sexual and reproductive health and rights activists have two key strategies: to build on the Cairo consensus, and to join with others to change economic and political realities. The first approach assumes that empowerment is possible if current institutions and access to funding change, and if the UN systems and the rights framework deliver the Cairo and millennium goals. The second sees change as possible only with profound power shifts and radical social and economic change; it is not a question of negotiating with institutions or waiting to be empowered.

A mixed approach would be most effective. Only a reformist agenda negotiated with those in power may be possible for some groups, while for others a more pluralistic agenda working from the grass roots is possible, taking power while analysing the political and economic terrain. For example, joining forces with social movements to lobby for an end to debt will help release resources to create better conditions for poor women and men's health. In both cases

Sexual and reproductive health

the sexual and reproductive health and rights agenda has been well mapped out – the question now is how to convince others to understand those maps and strive to make the vital changes needed.

Strengthen the human rights framework Globally and nationally activists should work with human rights activists to ensure that human rights norms and standards, legal obligations and mechanisms of accountability for sexual and reproductive health are in place. Both groups need to strengthen capacity and understanding. The 2005 national, regional and global reviews of the Millennium Declaration and the Fourth World Conference on Women are important avenues for civil society to work with women's rights activists to ensure that the UN system continues to address violence against women and reproductive health and rights.

Work in alliances for economic and social justice Activists should develop strong links with women's groups working on economic and social justice issues to develop a framework based on macroeconomics, rights and gender justice that takes a holistic approach to women's livelihoods, health, and sexual and reproductive rights. They should build alliances with social movements engaged, for instance, in the World Social Forum, the People's Health Movement and peace movements.

Fight against fundamentalisms NGOs and governments should work together to counter the strategies of the fundamentalists and conservative right that are undermining the gender equality, sexuality and reproductive rights agenda. Activists should reach out to progressive religious voices and challenge those who distort religious teachings through violence, suppression, discrimination, shame and guilt.

Support policies for greater bodily integrity Activists should work with women's, youth and community organizations, policy-makers, trade unions, health and legal professionals, researchers and journalists to improve access to family planning services, and to establish, preserve and implement laws, norms and regulations that make safe, legal abortion accessible and available. These recommendations should be based on WHO guidance (WHO 1995) and implemented in line with principles of social justice and human rights.

Hold donors, governments and institutions to account Holding governments and key institutions accountable is critical – building on the work of many global networks. Sexual and reproductive health and rights must be strengthened in the Millennium Development Goals (see UNDP 2003 and IPPF and WGNRR newsletters).

Measure progress Better ways to measure and assess progress and thereby ensure more appropriate knowledge are needed. Measuring and assessing progress since Cairo has been led by WHO and Population Action International indicators and reports. Innovative approaches like the IPPF reproductive health report cards should be supported and extended to measure the contributions of different actors.

Produce better research Health and social science researchers should evaluate reproductive health successes and failures more accurately, working with health workers and NGOs to develop community-level data. Individual reproductive health and the quality and use of programme services at community and national level should be assessed. There is a need to understand links and causes as well as measuring multiple indicators. Governments and research institutes should produce gender-disaggregated data, and use more innovative research methods that draw on information from diverse sources.

References

ARROW (2004). Women's gender and rights perspectives in health, politics and programmes. *Arrows for Change,* 10:1, 1–2.

Antrobus P (2004). *The global women's movement.* London, Zed Books.

Bandarage A (1997). *Women, population and global crisis: a political-economic analysis.* London, Zed Books.

Barton C, ed. (2004). *Seeking accountability on women's human rights: women debate the millennium development goals.* New York, Women's Coalition for Economic Justice (http://www.siyanda.org/static/wcej_hrmdgs.htm, accessed 19 February 2005).

Correa S (in collaboration with Reichmann R) (1994). *Population and reproductive rights: feminist perspectives from the South.* London, Zed Books.

DAWN (2004). *Special supplement for the World Social Forum, Mumbai on the many faces of fundamentalism.* Mumbai (http://www.dawn.org.fj/publications/DAWN Informs/supplwsfjan04.pdf, accessed 19 February 2005).

Desai M (2004). Gender, health and globalization: a critical social movement perspective. *Development,* 47: 2, 36–42.

Fourth World Conference on Women (1995). *Beijing platform for action* (http://www. un.org/womenwatch/daw/beijing/platform/plat1.htm, accessed 25 January 2005).

Harcourt W (2004). *The road to the UN Millennium Development Goals. Some insights into the international debate.* Amsterdam (http://www.ipsnews.net/indepth/ MDGGoal5/wendyh.pdf, accessed 19 February 2005).

Harcourt W (forthcoming). The body politic in global development discourse: a WPP perspective. In: Harcourt W, Escobar A. *Women and the politics of place*. New York, Kumarian Press.

IRRAG (1998). *Negotiating reproductive rights: women's perspectives across countries and cultures*. London, Zed Books.

Jacobson J (2003). First global women's scorecard on Bush administration. *Women's Global Network for Reproductive Rights Newsletter*, 80, 12–19, November (http://www.wgnrr.org/frameset.htm, accessed 25 January 2005).

Lohmann L (2003). Re-imagining the population debate. *The Corner House Briefing*, 28, March.

Petchesky R (2003). *Global prescriptions: gendering health and human rights*. London, Zed Books.

Rao M (2004). *Malthusian arithmetic: from population control to reproductive health*. New Delhi, Sage.

Sen G, Barroso C (1996). *After Cairo: Challenges to women's organisations*. Presented at the workshop on reproductive health, rights and women's empowerment, New Delhi Centre for Development Studies, September.

Sinding S (2004). *Health, hope, rights and responsibilities*. Global Roundtable Action Agenda Summary, 2 September (http://www.countdown2015.org/Content Controller.aspx?ID=4835, accessed 20 February 2005).

The Corner House and WGNRR (2004). *A decade after Cairo: women's health in a free market economy*. Corner House Briefing, 31 June.

UNDP (2003). *Millennium Development Goals, national reports: a look through a gender lens*. New York, UNDP (http://www.siyanda.org/static/undp_mdgsgender.htm, accessed 20 February 2005).

UNFPA (2002). *State of world population 2002*. New York, UNFPA.

UNICPD (1994). *Programme of action of the UN International Conference on Population and Development* (http://www.iisd.ca/Cairo/program/p00000.html, accessed 19 February 2005).

UNIFEM (2005). *Gender responsive budgeting*. New York, UNDP (http://unifem.org/index.php?f_page_pid=19, accessed 20 February 2005).

WHO (1995). *Complications of abortion – technical and managerial guidelines for prevention and treatment*. Geneva, WHO.

Yong K, Millen J, Irwin A, Gershman J (2000). *Dying For growth: global inequality and the health of the poor*. Monroe, Maine, Common Courage Press.

B5 | Gene technology

Genohype: high hopes and poor returns?

High hopes were raised in the mid-1990s by the study of the genome – heralded as a revolution for humankind by scientists, industry and governments. The genetic makeup of human beings and of microbes and other life forms would be unravelled, paving the way for a host of improvements. Tests would establish each person's vulnerability to developing health problems such as a heart attack or a stroke, or to catching infections such as TB or HIV, and would also identify those who would respond to certain preventive measures, or to treatments with different kinds of drugs. It would allow the development of new vaccines, drugs and other treatments.

There has been significant progress in identifying and elucidating the sequences of genes from humans and other species. Much of the data is publicly and freely available, as on the website of the Sanger Institute, which benefits both publicly-funded scientists and for-profit companies in their quest for patentable inventions and process technologies.

Billions of dollars have been invested by governments, research institutes and industry. Governments of countries such as the US, Canada and China believed it was a key area for development and shaped their policies accordingly, driven not only by a genuine belief in the promises and prestige of genome technology, but also by the lure of new markets. Genome technology was seen as central to the European Commission's aim of becoming the most competitive and dynamic knowledge-based economy in the world (CEC 2001). On the whole, however, there is precious little return as yet in terms of diagnostics, preventative interventions and therapeutics that are clinically significant and of proven efficacy and safety (Sample 2004). Some even wonder whether the whole idea is a flop, prompting the British Broadcasting Corporation to air a radio programme called 'What's wrong with my genes? What went wrong with the human genome project' (BBC 2004). Others speak of 'genohype': the overblown expectations of the benefits genomics can bring to patient care and population health (Holtzman 1999).

This chapter will explore the positive and negative effects of the reorientation of health research towards genome technology. It begins by highlighting some illustrative key issues that emerged from the successful control of the SARS epidemic of 2002–2003. It assesses the economic importance of genome research. Finally it reviews the threat of further monopolization of knowledge and its commercial applications, and the implications for trust and trustworthiness in health care. It concludes with suggestions for action.

Questioning the 'genohype': some pertinent questions from the SARS epidemic

The microbial agent involved in the severe acute respiratory syndrome (SARS) epidemic of 2002–3 was swiftly identified and sequenced in a remarkable collaboration between otherwise highly competitive laboratories in Asia, Europe, and North America. These early exchanges, however, soon gave way to mutual wariness at the point when intellectual property claims were filed for the pathogen's sequences and other patentable findings with commercial potential. And regardless of the rapid success, the epidemic quickly subsided despite the absence of reliable diagnostics, vaccines or efficacious therapies – an outcome attributable to traditional institutional responses such as isolation and contact tracing, and possibly also to personal risk avoidance, the contributions of seasonality effects and cross-reacting immunity from related endemic microorganisms.

Most importantly, the economic and financial stakes involved ensured that SARS would not be a 'neglected disease' of the world's poor.

The case of SARS prompts a number of questions that could be asked of emerging biomedical technologies in general:

• How important are biomedical advances (including genomics) to population health and to patient care (distinguishing perhaps between knowledge-based practices and coping responses, as opposed to consumable commodities)?

• What is the relative significance of genetics in the etiology (and social ecology) of health and disease?

• What advances can genomics be realistically expected to contribute to disease control, diagnostic aids and treatment?

• What are the likely trajectories of genomics research and development, given the trends in funding of biomedical research, patent regimes, intellectual property rights and market-driven product development, and the unresolved problems of the neglected diseases?

• What environment would enable the useful potential of genomics to be realized – for an equitable harvest of benefits and a humane deployment of genomic technologies?

• What processes and institutions are needed to deal with these policy and ethical issues?

The social ecology of health and disease

The decline in mortality from infectious diseases in early industrializing countries in the 19th century owed little to medical science and its derived technologies (McKeown 1971). In England and Wales, for example, the mortality rate from respiratory tuberculosis, a major killer, declined by more than 85% between 1838 and 1945, well before the discovery and isolation of the antibiotic streptomycin in 1947 and also well before the widespread availability of BCG vaccination for protection against tuberculosis from the 1950s onwards. McKeown and others identified food intake and nutritional status, potable water supplies and environmental hygiene as the key factors in the decline of infectious mortality.

Mortality alone is an inadequate measure of population health. Nonetheless, recent efforts to devise more discriminating measures of disease burden that take into account morbidity, disability and functional capacities, and quality of life have not seriously undermined McKeown's thesis, notwithstanding the efficacy of some modern therapeutics and procedures in controlled, favourable circumstances. Biomedicine at best has contributed only modestly to improvements in population health. This is the context in which the future benefits of genomics must be evaluated.

The current focus on genome technology and the particular imagery around the human genome is unfortunately diverting attention from public health approaches to combating disease, ill health and poverty. Life is much more complex than the pattern of the molecules in our genes. It is also important to know why and when some genes in some people are switched on and why others are switched off. A major part is played by the microenvironment inside cells, but this is influenced by the macroenvironment, the body as a whole and the outside world. A host of physical and social factors play a role, and public health approaches, embedded in socioeconomic policies, will probably remain much more important than high-tech solutions in improving global health.

Justifiable exuberance or premature genohype?

Is genomics the panacea for human illness and infirmity? The director of the US National Human Genome Research Institute declared in 1999 that the benefits of mapping and sequencing the human genome 'would include a new understanding of genetic contributions to human disease and the development of rational strategies for minimizing or preventing disease phenotypes altogether'. There would be further prospects of 'genetic prediction of individual risks of disease and responsiveness to drugs...and the development of designer

Gene technology

149

drugs based on a genomic approach to targeting molecular pathways that [have] been disrupted in disease' (Collins 1999, Collins and McKusick, 2001).

Five years on, participants at a conference on genomics and health held by the US National Academy of Sciences (Institute of Medicine) reflected on the progress made in far more modest tones. Hopes had been high of dramatic advances in cancer treatment, but the media quoted prominent scientist Dr Gilbert Omenn as saying that despite an 'avalanche of genomic information... cancers remain a largely unsolved set of medical problems [for which] we continue to rely on highly toxic drugs' (Boyd 2004; see also Hernandez 2005).

One recent addition to the cancer armamentarium which has benefited from advances in molecular cancer biology is trastuzumab (Herceptin), used to treat HER2–positive metastatic breast cancer. It has been welcomed by clinicians but is not considered revolutionary. It extends lifetimes by a matter of months but does not avoid side-effects, is suitable for rather a small number of patients and is costly (Hedgecoe 2004). Gefitinib (Iressa), for non-small cell lung cancer, has been hailed as the next 'genetically targeted' treatment (Langreth 2004), but its manufacturer recently withdrew its application for European regulatory approval, following the release of clinical trial data that showed the drug did not increase lifespan (Tomlinson 2005). More generally, genomics had made little impact on clinical practice and outputs such as new treatments have failed to keep pace with increased research and development (R&D) spending (Nightingale and Martin 2004).

The relatively rare Mendelian disorders such as cystic fibrosis, phenylketonuria and Huntington's disease allow for relatively easy study of the associated molecular genetics because the risk of disease is dominated by mutations in a single gene. Prominent geneticists have pointed out that the overwhelming bulk of common chronic diseases (diabetes, coronary heart disease, cancers) have much more complex etiology that may include a familial component in addition to social, economic, psychological and biological factors. The relationship between genotype (DNA sequence at the gene locus of interest) and phenotype (manifest traits) therefore becomes correspondingly murky and contingent for those common diseases. The proportion of cases that can be attributed to susceptibility-conferring genotypes in a given population is typically small for common diseases such as breast cancer and colon cancer, making it both more difficult and less useful to identify the gene (ensembles) involved (Holtzman and Marteau 2000).

Even when the molecular genetics are tractable, knowledge of the molecular basis of a disease is not easily translatable into prevention or treatment. It took 70 years for streptomycin to become available for TB treatment from the

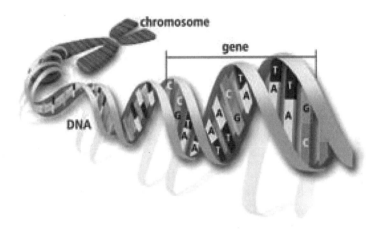

11 The human genome under threat of commercialization.

time Mycobacterium tuberculosis was identified as the agent involved. The molecular (genetic) basis of sickle-cell anemia was elucidated in the 1950s but palliative therapy has only recently become available. There has been little advance in the treatment of cystic fibrosis since the crucial gene was identified and cloned in 1989 and details of the molecular pathogenesis worked out. More encouragingly protease inhibitors, used in combination therapy along with reverse transcriptase inhibitors for treating HIV/AIDS patients, became available in the mid-1990s, about 10 years after the discovery of HIV-1.

Given that the success of gene-based therapies has so far been modest, with few promising candidates on the horizon, commercial interest is likely to shift towards genetic testing for 'disease susceptibility' – in line with a paradigm shift towards 'predictive medicine', or individual genetic profiling to assess the risk of future illnesses. This has the added attraction of mass markets, since genetic testing for disease susceptibility may be conducted routinely as part of well-person care and screening. Corporate R&D is seeking 'pills for the healthy ill' or worried well (Wallace 2002), to carve out new markets not just for screening tests but also for 'prophylactics' for those deemed to be at risk.

While busily seeking to create markets for its commodifiable biomedical outputs, market-driven R&D and its corporate sponsors will continue to ignore and bypass the diseases of the poor. This is also discussed at length in part B chapter 2 on medicines. Global spending on health research tripled from US$ 30 billion in 1990 to almost US$ 106 billion in 2001. It was split roughly between the public and private sectors, with the private nonprofit sector (including charities) playing a small but growing role. However, most R&D is still done by high-income countries in high-income countries to generate products tailored to those markets.

Complete figures are not available for spending on genomics. In 2000 the World Survey of Funding for Genomics estimated that private spending on R&D was around double the government and nonprofit spending, at US$ 1–2 billion. 'Even more than for medical research in general, the skew of research funding is heavily directed toward the developed economies with large pharmaceutical markets,' it concluded (Cook-Deegan et al. 2000). Research is mostly directed towards conditions affecting large populations in rich countries (see part E, chapter 7).

Even in rich countries, health research priorities do not reflect priority health needs. In the UK, for example, public research funds tend to follow the research investment strategies set by industry, rather than the needs of public health or health services. Research that is unlikely to be profitable or is of little scientific interest tends to be neglected (Harrison and New 2002) – including public health research, despite its enormous importance in reducing disease.

Genetics and the knowledge economy: who owns life?

Scientific effort leads to discoveries and inventions. Some harmful, such as weapons of mass destruction, but many useful. Until a decade ago most countries were free to define their laws governing the use of scientific knowledge, and it was felt to be beneficial to put such knowledge in the public domain for everyone to use. An ethos of scientific pride, and the respectability and honour from contributing to humanity's progress (and, more ominously, its military prowess) drove the mushrooming of discoveries and inventions in the 19th and 20th centuries. Funding by the public purse, industries and charities all played a role.

Lobbying by a few large companies and rich countries changed this. Its vehicle was the World Trade Organization (WTO) and its agreement on Trade Related Intellectual Property Rights (TRIPS), outlined in detail in part B, chapter 2 on medicines. The discourse moved away from the idea of scientific knowledge being publicly available towards the notion that private for-profit firms were well placed to create new knowledge and to translate that into useful products. It was argued that the discovery of molecules and other micro-aspects of life was painstaking and onerous, and it would be unfair if other countries could use this information freely.

This allowed the hitherto unthinkable idea of patenting discoveries, including life forms. Not everyone in the North agrees with this, of course: the Wellcome Trust continues to make newly discovered information freely available, while Cancer Research UK allows its patent on the breast cancer gene

BRCA2 to be used at no cost (Matthijs 2004). But the EU and its governments and the US shed long-held moral convictions in pursuit of competitive and technological advantage despite objections from UNESCO, European medical associations and WHO. The TRIPS agreement caused another sea change: patent-lifes were extended to 20 years (often 12 in the past) on highly contestable grounds (CIPR 2002). Patents are also now more likely to cover products as well as process technologies. This extraordinary expansion of monopolies in the knowledge economy is one of the defining paradoxes of modern times. It came about through a mixture of open debate and bullying behind the scenes (Elliott and Denny 2003, Jawara and Kwa 2003). It follows the rules of centuries-old mercantilism – the protection and expansion of one's own economy, usually at the expense of others – and contradicts the supposedly open spirit of competition and free trade.

Consumers are now expected to pay many times over, edging the poor and developing countries out of the buyers' market. They even dig in their pockets as taxpayers: many discoveries and inventions are based on freely accessible information generated by research financed by government institutions. Publicly funded researchers in biotechnology now have to negotiate their way through a maze of patents. The costs of this include paying licensing fees or having to send their specimens for tests to the laboratory of the monopoly holder of the licence, as well as the fees and opportunity costs of legal and administrative processes. This can lead to bizarre and unfair situations. In the US, families of patients with Canavan disease volunteered for gene research but found that its useful applications became commercialized and beyond their reach (AMA 2000). The patenting and licensing system slows down innovation (Matthijs 2004, AMA 2000), skews research towards the development of profitable products and offers no incentives for innovations which promote health for the poor. Moreover, the secrecy associated with commercial competition makes it more difficult to monitor and supervise the dangers and risks of manipulating and spreading life forms (Kimmelman 2005).

These developments disenfranchise developing countries. Alternative proposals include a global coalition to regain lost ground (Drahos and Braithwaite 2004) and alternatives to the patent regime (Love 2003, Baker 2004).

Owning your own genome: can you trust health care?

The implications of genetic screening dilemmas are problematic. Most of the tests on the market have not been approved by health care insurers, owing to their poor predictive value. It is quite unlikely that a person will develop a common illness such as Alzheimer's, coronary heart disease or diabetes, even when a test has shown they have a particular genetic makeup thought to be related to that disease. Nevertheless, a positive test result may cause anxiety and fear (Boseley 2004).

Insurers and some employers are keen on assessing medical information about their clients and employees, including genetic information. They also fear that people with bad risks could overinsure themselves for their own and their dependants' protection. In the marketplace, if one competitor demands information of a particular kind the others should do the same to maintain a level playing field. This was the case some 15 years ago in the developed world when HIV infection was, for most, a death sentence. It was in people's interests to know their HIV status, to be able to plan their future and protect their partners and children. At the same time, knowledge of your HIV status could ruin your prospects for decent housing, insurance or even a job, and expose you to other forms of discrimination.

In employment, however, there are no known situations where a genetic test appears fully justified. For example, genetic testing for sickle-cell disease was used on air crew in the US and UK who might be prone to blackouts when exposed to low atmospheric pressure. This policy, criticised as racist, has now been reversed: both countries recognized that it was unjustified because a pilot is extremely unlikely to develop the disease unnoticed and have a first blackout while flying a plane.

Most western countries have either banned or suspended the use of genetic test information for the purpose of risk selection. However, even in a highly regulated country such as the UK the voluntary system for limiting the use of genetic information has been ignored (Meek and Bachelor 2001). Some British insurers now demand the divulging of negative genetic test results, while requesting a huge amount of medical information from doctors. From there on, insurers will be able to analyse databases, develop actuarial tables and make informed guesses about applicants' genes. This could lead to the loading of premiums and if unchecked will open Pandora's box: with the further development of genetic profiling and sets of longitudinal data, risk assessment could eventually extend to applicants' children.

Trust and trustworthiness Most people do not question the collection of medical information, assuming that doctors and other health professionals act in their best interests (Fugelli 2001, O'Neill 2002). Few people, when baring body and soul, think that medical information may be used in evidence against them. Many volunteer to participate in medical research, often after advice or persuasion by their doctors, but few suspect that the spin-offs of that research may be commercialized, potentially blocking its use for poor, uninsured people and developing countries. Patients should be offered an informed choice including a warning of that possibility.

The current trend for doctors and nurses to initiate the collection of huge amounts of biomedical data about their patients is both scientifically and ethically wrong. Truly informed consent (Thornton 2003) and patient autonomy are often ignored and the medical benefits overstated (Getz et al. 2003). The negative effects on patients include anxiety about being at risk (Melzer and Zimmern 2002) and becoming one of the worried well. Issues include the conflict between acting as a truly confidential counsellor on potential genetic conditions and a collector of data for the purposes of the administration and control of health care, public health and risk selection.

Doctors may increasingly be asked to play a role in requests for selection of sex or other features of babies. Such requests may be used as conditions for marriage and lead to marginalization or exclusion and the further control and oppression of women and their reproductive rights. The eugenicist flavour of some of the proposed applications of genetic research, and their implications for people with disabilities, is a linked concern discussed in more detail in part C, chapter 2 on disability.

Trust in health professionals will not be greatly undermined by these developments in the short or medium term. Doctors and nurses come top in many countries' surveys of who is most trusted and respected, and this is unlikely to change. However, the commercialization of health care and commercial risk selection are progressing fast. Against this background, can health care, and can doctors and nurses, be trusted? Are they Trojan horses, whether they like it or not? How can they help ensure that patients' interests come first, individually and globally? Health professionals, their organizations and health-related NGOs need to respond to these questions.

Conclusions and proposals

The assumptions and activities of the scientific and commercial enterprises around biotechnology, especially genome technology, merit close scrutiny. A legal armamentarium has emerged to bring the human body and other life forms within the ambit of intellectual property, and present life as a commodity which can be patented, traded and made to yield a profit. The quest for competitive advantage and dominance in biotechnology has spurred governments and corporations to promote the privatization and commercialization of biotechnological knowledge. Current developments also threaten reproductive rights and undermine global and national equity. Governments, industry and scientists

Gene technology

are allowing a runaway agenda to shape new paradigms for the way we see life, health and health care, with global justice and equity on the losing end. To help restore the balance, the following proposals should be considered:

Democratization of the health research agenda. The national and international systems for setting the agenda for health research need to be overhauled. The relative importance of biotechnology research, including the study of the genome, should be weighed against research into diseases of poverty and the social ecology of health and disease. There should be genuine representation and participation of community groups in setting priorities and research design.

Global equity and justice first. Organizations focusing on health and equity should insist that genome technologies and their applications are guided by the core values of national and global equity, human rights including gender rights, and medical ethics (UN 1966 and 2001, WMA 1983, EFMA-WHO 2001, UNESCO 1997).

Health and equity impact and risk assessments. Civil society, and international groups of interested scientists, should demand that states and international organizations like WHO carry out health and equity impact assessments and risk assessments using such criteria as internationally agreed human rights in health and health care. They should be participatory, with genuine representation of civil society, and free from pressures arising from international economic and donor policies. Assessments should include the potential effects of different scenarios of genome applications on health and equity, nationally and internationally, in different social and health care systems. Expertise and experience on risk assessments and the precautionary principle can be drawn from environmental campaigns.

Equitable access to and use of knowledge. States and research funders should develop ways by which researchers give up or selectively forgo patent rights to help make useful inventions cheaply available for all.

Overhaul of regimes for intellectual property rights. This is needed to create a lasting solution to the crisis in the knowledge economy (see also part B, chapter 2). Solutions include reducing the length and coverage of patents, and liberal provisions for governments and UN institutions to buy patent rights from patent-holders if this is in the public interest, and/or arrangements for compulsory licensing (Love 2003, Baker 2004). Pressure on countries to accept deals unfavourable to their populations should be ended. There should be credible monitoring systems and sanctions. These improvements should be seen in the context of the need to establish a fair and equitable international trade system.

Monitor organizations. Organizations focusing on health and equity should monitor governments and international organizations such as WHO so that they do not lend legitimacy to the commercialization of human (and other) life and to 'genohype', which draws away resources and attention from addressing diseases of poverty and inequity.

Rethink the data collection role of health care providers. Confidentiality and human rights need to come first. Health professionals should rethink their role in collecting data that can be used for the purposes of insurances, risk selection for employment, health care administration and public health.

Ensure research meets priority needs. Health-related NGOs should explore the roles of individuals and groups who participate in biotechnology research (e.g. by allowing their samples to be used for genome research). NGOs could develop guidelines and a standard contract that stipulates that individuals will only participate in research if its eventual useful spin-offs are made available to poor users and poor countries at affordable prices. More fundamentally, citizens and NGOs should play a role in ensuring research projects make health needs, not market needs, the priority.

Risk selection and insurance in the public interest. The developments in human genomics confirm and strengthen arguments in favour of the establishment of inclusive non-discriminatory systems of health care and sickness insurance. NGOs should stress that such regulated or non-profit systems, characterized by cross-subsidization of the sick by the healthy and the poor by the rich, offer the only just approach to avoiding discrimination, inequity and exclusion whilst capturing the benefits of a humane and responsible development of genomics.

References

American Medical Association (AMA) (2000). *Report 9 of the Council of Scientific Affairs (I-oo): Patenting of genes and their mutations.* Chicago, AMA (http://www.ama-assn.org/ama/pub/category/13570.html, accessed 5 January 2005).

Baker D (2004). *Financing Drug research: What are the issues?* Center for Economic and Policy Research, Washington DC.

BBC (2004). What's wrong with my genes? What went wrong with the Human Genome Project? *BBC Radio 4*, 29 September 2100–2130 hr (UK time).

Boseley S (2004). Watchdog seeks controls on scary gene tests. Critics attack landmark decision on gene screening. *The Guardian*, September 9 (http://www.guardian.co.uk/uk_news/story/0,,1300119,00.html, accessed 14 March 2005).

Boyd R S (2004). Patients Have Yet to Benefit From Genome Research. *Miami Herald*, 12 October, pg 4A (http://www.miami.com/mld/miamiherald/2004/10/13/living/9895562.htm, accessed 14 March 2005).

Commission of the European Communities (CEC) (2001). *Towards a strategic vision of life sciences and biotechnology: consultation document.* Brussels (COM (2001) 454 final).

Commission on Intellectual Property Rights (CIPR) (2002). *Integrating intellectual property rights and development policy.* London, CIPR.

Collins FS (1999). Shattuck Lecture – Medical and Societal Consequences of the Human Genome Project. *New England Journal of Medicine,* 341:28–37.

Collins FS, McKusick VA (2001). Implications of the Human Genome Project for Medical Science. *Journal of the American Medical Association,* 285(5).

Cook-Deegan R, Chan C, Johnson A (2000). *World survey of funding for genomics research. Final report to the Global Forum for Health Research and WHO.* Washington, DC, Stanford-in-Washington Program (http://www.stanford.edu/class/siw198q/websites/genomics/finalrpt.pdf, accessed on 14 March 2004).

Drahos P, Braithwaite J (2004). *Who owns the knowledge economy? Political organising behind TRIPS* (Briefing 32). Dorset, The Corner House (http://www.thecornerhouse.org.uk/item.shtml?x=85821, accessed 14 March 2005).

European Forum of Medical Associations and World Health Organisation (EFMA-WHO) (2001). *Statement on the Human genome and International Patent Law.* Ljubljana, 9–11 March.

Elliott L, Denny C (2003). EU's secret plans hold poor countries to ransom. *The Guardian,* 25 February (http://www.guardian.co.uk/business/story/0,3604,902296,00.html, accessed on 14 March 2005).

Fugelli P (2001). Trust – in General Practice. *British Journal of General Practice* 5 1:575–9.

Getz L, Sigurdsson J, Hetlevik I (2003). Is opportunistic disease prevention in the consultation ethically justifiable? *British Medical Journal,* 327:498–500.

Harrison A, New B (2002). *Public interest, private decisions: health related research in the UK.* London, Kings Fund.

Hedgecoe A (2004). *The politics of personalised medicine: pharmacogenetics in the clinic.* Cambridge, Cambridge University Press.

Herandez L (ed.) (2005). *Implications of Genomics for Public Health: Workshop Summary.* Washington DC, The National Academies Press.

Holtzman NA (1999). Are genetic tests adequately regulated? [editorial]. *Science* 286(5439):409.

Holtzman NA and Marteau T (2000). Will genetics revolutionize medicine? *The New England Journal of Medicine,* 343:141–144.

Jawara F and Kwa A (2003). *Behind the scenes at the WTO. The real world of international trade negotiations.* London, Zed Books.

Kimmelman J (2005). Recent developments in gene transfer: risk and ethics. *British Medical Journal,* 330:79–82.

Langreth R (2004). Gene predicts cancer drug effectiveness. *Forbes Magazine,* 29 April.

Love J (2003). A new trade framework for global healthcare R&D. In: *Workshop on Access to Medicines and the Financing of Innovations in Health Care.* New York, NY, The Earth Institute at Columbia University and the Consumer Project on Technology (http://www.earthinstitute.columbia.edu/cgsd/documents/love_000.pdf, accessed 23 February 2005).

Matthijs G (2004). Patenting Genes. May slow down innovation and delay availability of cheaper genetic tests. *British Medical Journal,* 329:1358–60.

McKeown T (1971). A Historical Appraisal of the Medical Task. In: *Medical History and Medical Care*. London, Oxford University Press.

Meek J, Bachelor L (2001). Insurers 'broke code on gene information'. *The Guardian Weekly*, 10 May, p8 (http://www.guardian.co.uk/Archive/Article/0,4273,4179375,00. html accessed 14 March 2005).

Melzer D, Zimmern R (2002). Genetics and medicalisation. *British Medical Journal* 324:863–4.

Nightingale P, Martin P (2004). The myth of the biotech revolution. *Trends in Biotechnology*, 22:564–569.

O'Neill O (2002). *A question of Trust*. BBC Reith Lectures (http://www.bbc.co.uk/radio4/ reith2002/, accessed 23 February 2005).

Sample I (2004). The revolution is not won yet. *The Guardian,* 22 Jan (http://www. guardian.co.uk/life/feature/story/0,,1128145,00.html accessed 14 March 2005).

Thornton P (2003). Confidentiality: consent is not sufficient. *British Journal of General Practice,* 269–70.

Tomlinson H (2005). AstraZeneca withdraws application for cancer drug sale in EU. *The Guardian,* 5 Jan (http://www.guardian.co.uk/business/story/0,,1383338,00. html, accessed 14 March 2005).

UN (1966). *International Covenant on Economic, Social and Cultural Rights*. New York, NY, UN.

UN (2000). *The right to the highest attainable standard of health*. 11/08/2000. E/C.12/2000/4. (General Comments). Geneva, UN (http:// www.unhchr.ch/tbs/doc.nsf/385c2add1632f4a8c12565a9004dc311/ 40d009901358b0e2c1256915005090be?OpenDocument, accessed 15 March 2005).

UNESCO (1997). *Universal Declaration on the Human Genome and Human Rights*. Paris, UNESCO (http://portal.unesco.org/en/ev.php-URL_ID=13177&URL_DO=DO_ TOPIC&URL_SECTION=201.html, accessed 14 March 2005).

Wallace H (2002). *Genetics and 'Predictive Medicine': Selling Pills, Ignoring Causes*. Briefing Paper Number 18, May. Buxton, GeneWatch (http://www.genewatch.org/ Publications/Briefs/Brief18.pdf, accessed 14 March 2005).

World Medical Association (WMA) (1983). *International Code of Medical Ethics*. Ferney-Voltaire, WMA (http://www.wma.net/e/policy/c8.htm, accessed 14 March 2005).

Useful websites

http://www.genewatch.org

http://www.genetics-and-society.org

PART C | **Health of vulnerable groups**

Listening to and bringing forward the voices of the excluded and marginalized are key roles for civil society worldwide. This first *Global Health Watch* focuses on two groups of people – Indigenous peoples and people with disabilities – whose concerns are often marginalized and whose unfulfilled rights present fundamental challenges to health policymakers.

Discrimination against both sets of people runs extremely deep. Indigenous peoples are often seen as backward and even as a block on modernization and development. People with disabilities are often regarded as abnormal and denied full human rights as a result. The relationships of both these groups with health professionals have historically mirrored and reinforced the prejudices in the wider society. These chapters describe ways in which both groups have resisted and set their own agendas in the context of both health care and in society as a whole – but there is still a long way to go.

Campaigning can both provoke and be supported by legislative change at national and international levels – the current demands for an international convention on the rights of disabled people recognise this. But as a disabled man from the Congo points out, 'you cannot eat rights', while international policies and programmes sometimes seem irrelevant at the personal level. Moreover, as the experience of many Indigenous peoples illustrates, provision of health care in squalid 'resettlement camps' is not adequate recompense for the misappropriation of land and the denial of a lifestyle that is central to their concept of health and well being.

Rights need to be connected to broader agendas such as freedom from social marginalization, poverty, conflict and oppression – and the voices of groups such as people with disabilities and Indigenous peoples need to be heard in arenas where these issues are discussed.

C1 | Indigenous peoples

Introduction

Indigenous peoples account for an astonishing diversity of cultures, and have a vast and irreplaceable amount of knowledge, skills and ways to understand and relate to the world. They number over 350 million individuals in more than 70 countries and have more than 5,000 languages and cultures (International Work Group for Indigenous Affairs 2001).

Historically, many Indigenous peoples have suffered acts of genocide and lethal epidemics of diseases carried by colonialists and settlers from other countries. Oppression, land expropriation and environmental degradation continue to threaten the livelihoods of many Indigenous communities. Life for most is a struggle in the face of poverty, ill health and social disintegration, exacerbated by forced assimilation, consumerism, imposed modernization and institutional racism. Even in a country like Guatemala, where Indigenous peoples are the majority, the dominant minority views their culture as an obstacle to development.

The UN Committee on Economic, Social and Cultural Rights has been concerned about growing violations of rights to health, food and culture, particularly as a result of development-related activities. These often lead to the forced displacement of Indigenous peoples from their lands, denying them their sources of nutrition and breaking their symbiotic relationship with the land. At the extreme, systematic repression and deprivation threaten their survival. Ironically, exploitation of their land is often due to demand for the very resources they have carefully managed and protected for centuries – including

---

Box C1.1 The International Decade of the World's Indigenous Peoples: a failure?

'Despite the important institutional developments that have taken place in the framework of the Decade ... indigenous peoples in many countries continue to be among the poorest and most marginalized ... [T]he adoption of a declaration on the rights of indigenous peoples, one of the main objectives of the Decade, has not been achieved' (*Source*: United Nations Economic and Social Council 2004).

---

medicinal plants, timber and natural minerals (Barton 1994, King et al. 1996, Merson 2000).

In 1994, the UN declared an International Decade of the World's Indigenous Peoples, with the objective of 'strengthening international cooperation for the solution of problems faced by Indigenous people in such areas as human rights, the environment, development, education and health'. According to the UN Human Rights Commission, the decade saw little achievement (Box C1.1). Partly in recognition of this, the United Nations proclaimed a second International Decade of the World's Indigenous People, beginning in January 2005.

Who are Indigenous peoples?

Debate on the definition of the term 'Indigenous' has gone on for several decades. Different states and communities adopt different definitions. In some countries, the very existence of Indigenous people is denied altogether. The most widely used definitions are those used by the UN Working Group on Indigenous Populations and the International Labour Organization's (ILO) Convention Concerning Indigenous and Tribal peoples in Independent countries (1989). These set out the principle of 'self-identification as indigenous or tribal' as a fundamental criterion. Specifically, the ILO Convention applies the term to:

- Tribal peoples in independent countries whose social, cultural and economic conditions distinguish them from other sections of the national community, and whose status is regulated wholly or partially by their own customs or traditions or by special laws or regulations.
- Peoples in independent countries who are regarded as indigenous on account of their descent from the populations which inhabited the country, or a geographical region to which the country belongs, at the time of conquest or colonization or the establishment of present state boundaries and who, irrespective of their legal status, retain some or all of their own social, economic, cultural and political institutions.

The policy context

Human rights and recognition The human rights of Indigenous peoples are recognized in international laws and conventions. Over 150 states are party to the International Covenant on Civil and Political Rights (ICCPR) and the International Convention on the Elimination of All Forms of Racial Discrimination (ICERD). The ICCPR has explicit obligations to allow minorities to practise their cultures, religions and languages. The ICERD requires states to ensure that all people can access their human rights without discrimination. Other

12 Australian indigenous children in the desert exercise their rights to traditional methods of food gathering.

international standards oblige states to ensure that Indigenous peoples benefit equally and justly from development. These include the UN Declaration on the Rights of Persons Belonging to National or Ethnic, Religious and Linguistic Minorities (UNDM). Indigenous peoples also have 'the right to decide their own priorities for the process of development ... and shall participate in the formulation, implementation and evaluation of plans and programmes for national and regional development which may affect them directly,' according to the ILO Convention on Indigenous and Tribal Peoples (ILO 1989).

Indigenous peoples were also recognized at the 2002 World Summit on Sustainable Development in Johannesburg, which built on the recognition ten years earlier at the Rio de Janeiro UN Conference on Environment and Development, known as the Earth Summit. Agenda 21, a product of the Earth Summit, recognized that Indigenous peoples have a historical relationship with their lands and have developed a holistic knowledge of these lands and the natural environment. It recognised the inter-relationship between the environment and its sustainable development and the cultural, social, economic and physical well-being of Indigenous peoples.

Attempts to forge an international declaration dedicated specifically to the rights of Indigenous peoples have not yet succeeded. However, a draft declaration contains articles of particular relevance to the health sector – articles 23 and 24 establish Indigenous peoples' rights to traditional medicine and health practices and the protection of vital medicinal plants, animals and minerals; to determine, develop and administer health programmes affecting them; and to have access, without discrimination, to health services and medical care (UN High Commissioner for Human Rights 1994).

The continuing exploitation and oppression of Indigenous communities reveal dramatic failures by national and international institutions in upholding the rights of Indigenous peoples.

The Millennium Development Goals Inadequate attention to the health and development goals of Indigenous peoples is symptomatic of the failure of the MDG framework to address the issue of equity within and between countries. Indigenous peoples often constitute a minority and are among the poorest and least visible sections of society – unless there is a strong focus on equity and reaching the most vulnerable and marginalized peoples, actions to reach the MDG targets may exclude Indigenous peoples. According to the Inter-Agency Support Group for the UN Permanent Forum on Indigenous Issues (2004), Indigenous and tribal peoples are lagging behind other population groups in the achievement of the goals in most, if not all, countries; Indigenous and tribal women commonly face additional gender-based disadvantages and discrimination.

Land rights It is 'almost impossible to exaggerate the emotional, spiritual, and economic importance of land to Indigenous communities,' says an account of Brazil's Indian communities in the 20th century (Hemming 2003). In both industrialized and developing countries, dispossession from ancestral lands and the consequent disruption of community and culture have been key factors in marginalizing and impoverishing Indigenous peoples. From the San in Botswana to the Yora in Peru, from the Tampoen in Cambodia to the Jarawa of the Andaman Islands, from the Senoi in Malaysia to the Inuit of Canada and Aboriginal peoples of Australia, Indigenous peoples continue to face the threat of being dispossessed of their lands and livelihoods and resettled (see Boxes C1.2 and C1.3).

Indigenous peoples are under particular threat from multinational mining corporations seeking access to mineral deposits that lie on ancestral or tribal land. Although a number of NGOs and Indigenous peoples' groups try to protect the rights of Indigenous peoples, they often lose out to corporate power and pressure from governments and development agencies such as the World Bank, who argue that 'resettlement' is in the interest of both Indigenous peoples and the development of the country as a whole. The benefits of mining usually accrue to an elite; the environmental damage is suffered by the broader public; and the health and well-being of Indigenous peoples deteriorate under conditions of 'resettlement'.

Box C1.3 Sustainable systems of food production

Many of the ecologically sustainable food production and consumption systems of Indigenous peoples rely on access to land. The Mbya Guarani of Misiones, Argentina, for example, depend on access to the plants and fruits growing in thousands of hectares of the Paranaense rainforest. They do not own this land, but have traditionally lived off it in a non-exploitative and sustainable manner. However, the government of Misiones and a logging company have tried to pen them into an arbitrary parcel of 300 hectares. This represents not just a political conflict, but also a conflict between the 'modern' approach of short food chain ecosystems and fixed territories, and the Mbya Guarani approach of long food chain ecosystems and mobile territories.

Indigenous peoples

The health of Indigenous peoples

Health status According to WHO, the weak health and demographic information systems in most developing countries 'do not permit accurate, systematic and routine measurements and monitoring of demographic indicators or health trends and status of different population groups'. Information on populations in remote areas or informal settlements – where marginalized populations are often concentrated – is said to be 'particularly scant'. In those countries in which health data systems are better developed, there remain significant problems with the quality of data relating to the health and social outcomes of Indigenous people.

Racism and marginalization underlie the lack of commitment to collecting data on Indigenous communities who are often located in remote and inaccessible areas (Bourne 2003). Available data indicate that the health of Indigenous peoples is significantly poorer than other groups, with, for example, infant mortality rates up to three times higher (Basu 1994, Hudon 1999, Alessandri et al. 2001, Escobar et al. 2001, Hetzel 2001).

Many communities are overwhelmingly affected by communicable diseases and nutritional deficiencies. Loss of lands and environmental degradation underlie much loss of livelihoods and food security. Indigenous communities

---

Box C1.4 Abuse of Indigenous people's health and rights in Cambodia

Diang Phoeuk, Pao village elder, Taveng Krom commune, Rattanakiri Province, Cambodia, describes his community's experience:

'A few years ago a Cambodian mining company began excavating gold on land belonging to our village. Neither the company nor the district authorities had asked permission from the village elders. The mines were closely guarded day and night and we were strictly forbidden from entering the land on which the mining was taking place. Prior to the arrival of the miners we had seen little sickness in our village. Shortly after the mining started, villagers began to suffer from a range of health problems, which included diarrhoea, fever, headaches and coughing and vomiting with blood. The sickness mainly affected children but a small number of adults also were affected; 25–30 people became ill, of whom 13 eventually died. We feared that the village spirit had become angry, as outsiders were mining land, and this has been a taboo for a long time.' (*Source*: Bristow et al. 2003)

Box C1.5 Health status of Indigenous peoples in four countries

Australia is a rich country (per capita GDP of US$ 28,260 in 2002) with a high human development index (UNDP 2004). However, the health of its Aboriginal and Torres Strait Islander peoples – 460,140 people accounting for 2.4% of Australia's population (ABS 2002) – is significantly poorer than that of other Australians. Indigenous men are expected to live to the age of 56, some 21 years less than the national average (ABS 2003a). In 2001, the incidence of tuberculosis for Indigenous people was 10 times that of non-Indigenous Australians. Deaths from cardiovascular disease among Indigenous people aged 25–54 are up to 15 times higher than other Australians (ABS 2003b).

Bolivia is a very poor country (per capita GDP of US$ 2460 in 2002) with a low human development index (UNDP 2004). Unlike Australia, half the population is Indigenous – 4.2 million people from 37 distinct groups (Feiring and Minority Rights Group Partners 2003). However, 20% of Indigenous children die before they are one year old. Of those who survive the first 12 months, 14% die before reaching school age (Alderete 1999). The incidence of TB in Indigenous groups is five to eight times greater than the national average.

Cambodia is another very poor country (per capita GDP of US$ 2060 in 2002), with a low human development index (UNDP 2004). It has a small population of Indigenous people – around 100,000 in two provinces. More than 20% of children under five suffer from malnutrition and 52% are classified as underweight and stunted in growth (Health Unlimited 2002).

Uganda: In the near future, the Batwa pygmy tribe of Uganda (per capita GDP of US$ 1390 in 2002) may die out altogether. Only half the Batwa children born in Kisoro, Uganda, will reach their first birthday.

often depend on ecosystems that are rapidly deteriorating through no fault of their own (van Oostdam et al. 1999, Merson 2000, Powell and Steward 2001). In some instances, Indigenous peoples are exposed to environmental pollutants that have been prohibited in other parts of the world, such as the continuing use of DDT, Aldrin and Dieldrin in the western highlands of Guatemala.

Indigenous peoples often have higher rates of mental illness manifesting as alcoholism, substance abuse, depression and suicide: for instance,

Canadian Indigenous youth have 2–6 times greater risk than non-Indigenous youth (Single et al. 1999). These problems come in the wake of social disintegration caused by modernization and the destruction of traditional authority structures and autonomous decision-making. Ironically, improving access to modern health care is often used to help justify the forced resettlement of Indigenous peoples.

At best, the health situation of Indigenous peoples mirrors that of the world's very poorest, but is made worse by their social and cultural marginalization. There is no way of overestimating the urgency and gravity of the situation: political and cultural violence is a devastating reality for many communities who face 'serious difficulties such as the constant threat of territorial invasion and murder, the plundering of their resources, forced assimilation, cultural and legal discrimination, as well as a lack of recognition of their own institutions' (International Work Group for Indigenous Affairs 2004).

Concepts of health The concept of health embodied in many Indigenous peoples' cultures is wider and more ecological than the WHO definition. As with the WHO definition, health is considered as being more than the absence of illness. Factors such as the ability to work, the availability of work, and access to food and water are important. In addition, being in harmony with other people – family, neighbours and village – and with the environment is considered crucial (see Box C1.6). Their concept of health is typically one of collective well-being with other humans *and* other species.

Health services Indigenous peoples often have sophisticated and effective systems of traditional medicine (Crengle 2000, Hickman and Miller 2001, Fink 2002). Many traditional medicines have become targets of pharmaceutical companies seeking to establish patents on the active ingredients of these medicines (Mail et al. 1989, Trotti 2001). For example, in the early 1950s, using the knowledge of Indigenous healers in Madagascar, the pharmaceutical company Eli Lilly extracted two powerful cancer-fighting alkaloids from the rosy periwinkle plant – vinblastine and vincristine. Global sales of the two substances earned the company hundreds of millions of dollars. This phenomenon, termed 'biopiracy' to reflect the notion of the earth's natural resources and local knowledge being plundered for commercial profit, has become a new front in the struggle for Indigenous peoples' rights (Khor 2004).

At the same time, traditional health care systems have often been weakened, fragmented and undermined by 'western medicine' (Janes 1999, Chang 2001, Cook 2001). The loss of access to native 'pharmacies' is a major difficulty, often

'Well being means that my body and mind are happy and well and that I have a good appetite, that I eat and sleep well and have no problems in the family or in the village.' – Cham Heb, 20 years old, mother, Tampoeun ethnic group, Prak Village, Samaki commune, Rattanakiri Province, Cambodia.

'I think that well being in our house and home and also with our neighbours is when there is peace and happiness – and also when we love ourselves. It's like God says to us, you shouldn't only want your own well being, you should also think of your neighbours. You have to think of your neighbours, whether they have enough food to eat, or maybe they're suffering. It is important to think of them. You have to share the happiness that you may have with your brother.' – Juana Tzoy Quinillo, 55 years old, Traditional Birth Attendant and Curer, Pachojob', K´iche´ ethnic group, Santa Lucia la Reforma Municipality, Totonicapán Department, Guatemala.

'Well being is to live like other people and to fit in with them. Proper houses, water and nice clean clothes would make me happy and is what I need to be well.' – Jamba, traditional leader, San ethnic group, Uzera, Tsumkwe West, Namibia

'Well being, for me, is like the others have said, *utz'ilal*. It's when we're not fighting with our family, in the home. It also means peacefulness when we go to sleep.' – Irma Pu Tiu, Madre Vigilante, K´iche´ ethnic group, Gualtux, Santa Lucia la Reforma Municipality, Totonicapán Department, Guatemala.

(*Source*: Bristow et al. 2003)

caused by Indigenous people's evictions from their land or the degradation of their ecosystems.

Indigenous peoples recognize that they cannot address all their health problems through traditional medicine, especially as many communities face comparatively new diseases of which they have limited or no experience. Common causes of child mortality, such as diarrhoeal disease and acute respiratory disease, are relatively recent occurrences.

But Indigenous peoples often lack adequate access to basic allopathic health care when they need it (Pal et al. 2002, Simmons and Voyle 2003). Ac-

Box C1.7 Traditional birthing centre, Ayacucho, Peru

The following is the account of a young woman of the Occopecca Community giving birth at a government health facility:

'After walking very slowly for about two hours with my husband, I arrived at the health centre. I was in pain and very frightened about using the service for the first time, but as other women told me it was more safe for me and the baby, my husband and I decided to go there to deliver my baby. On arriving, the doctor, nurse and another man told me, 'only you can go inside, your husband will wait outside,' and told me to take off my clothes and to put on a very short robe that left my intimacy almost uncovered.

'I felt bad and humiliated and couldn't understand what they were talking about, as they were speaking Spanish and I only know a few words of that language. They forced me to lie down and, as you can imagine, how could I push if nobody was holding me, helping me to push? That is why I prefer my house. I am frightened of the health staff and how they treat you. They make you lie down and don't hold you and leave you alone suffering with your pain.

'After that we were asked to pay a penalty because I didn't go to my complete postnatal check ups. But we don't have money, and that is why they haven't given me my child's birth certificate. No, I prefer to avoid all this humiliation and suffering and will stay at home with my family next time.'

Not long after, Health Unlimited, a non-government organization, began to work together with the local community, traditional birth attendants and Ministry of Health personnel to design a birthing service that would be culturally appropriate. Health personnel were encouraged to be more sensitive to the needs of the Indigenous women. A new service combined the participation of traditional birth attendants and family members in the delivery, the use of a vertical delivery position, use of the traditional belt post-delivery, the possibility for women to wear their own clothes when giving birth, and the avoidance of enemas and shaving. Family members were also allowed to receive the placenta so that they could bury it according to their beliefs. (*Source*: Bristow et al. 2003)

cess is constrained by financial, geographic and cultural barriers. Indigenous peoples are low on governments' priority lists, especially when they live in remote areas where services may be difficult to provide, and population density is lower. Where services are available, Indigenous peoples are often reluctant or afraid to use them because staff can be insensitive, discriminatory and un-friendly (Escobar et al. 2001, Palafox et al. 2001). Many communities have little information on their rights and entitlement to health care.

What is often required is a combination of improved access to modern, allo-pathic health care combined with revitalizing certain elements of traditional health care. There has been some progress in valuing traditional health prac-tices as a complement to allopathic medicine. In the north-eastern tribal area of India, for example, allopathic health workers have been asked to regard local traditional healers as allies, not rivals. The case study in Box C1.7 describes a successful marriage of modern obstetric care with important socio-cultural dimensions of childbirth in an Indigenous community in Peru.

Recommendations

A global health community committed to health for all must act urgently to promote and protect the health of Indigenous peoples. This requires placing health in the context of Indigenous peoples' social, cultural and land rights. Oppression, prejudice and institutionalized racism must be challenged as a key step to the fulfilment of health rights. The following proposals aim to alert the global health community to ways of rising to these challenges.

Governments, health and development agencies Health professionals can help to demonstrate the public health wisdom in many Indigenous peoples' cultures. Health workers and international health agencies should also sup-port the work, including legal action, of Indigenous peoples and NGOs cam-paigning for political and land rights that underpin the struggle for better health.

In recognition of the general failure of the first Decade of the World's In-digenous Peoples to strengthen international cooperation in solving problems faced by Indigenous people, civil society and international health agencies should pay closer attention to developments during the second Decade of the World's Indigenous Peoples, and the voluntary fund created to encour-age progress in improving the health and fulfilling the rights of Indigenous peoples. The UN Permanent Forum could serve as a focal point for Indigenous peoples to raise issues, but it needs to be less bureaucratic and to set up mechanisms to ensure that the voices of Indigenous communities and organ-izations, particularly those of isolated communities in developing countries and unstable areas, are heard. Ensuring that provision is made for the use of Indigenous languages in the Permanent Forum and other sites of discussion is critical.

Box C1.8 Indigenous organizations and networks

Asian Indigenous and Tribal Peoples Network (AITPN), India <http://www.aitpn.org>

Indigenous Peoples Alliance of the Archipelago (AMAN), Jl. B No. 4, RT/RW 001/006, Kompleks Rawa Bambu I, Pasar Minggu, Jakarta Selatan 12520, Indonesia

Cooperative Research Centre for Aboriginal Health, Australia <http://www.crcah.org.au>

Coordinadora de las Organizaciones Indigenas de la Cuenca Amazonica (COICA), Ecuador <http://www.coica.org>

Foundation for Aboriginal and Islander Research Action (FAIRA), Australia <http://www.faira.org.au>

Forest Peoples Programme, United Kingdom <http://www.forestpeoples.gn.apc.org>

Health Unlimited, United Kingdom <http://www.healthunlimited.org>

Innu Nation, Canada <http://www.innu.ca>

International Alliance of the Indigenous and Tribal Peoples of the Tropical Forests, Thailand <http://www.international-alliance.org>

Minority Rights Group, United Kingdom <http://www.minorityrights.org>

Russian Association of Indigenous Peoples of the North, Russia <http://www.raipon.org>

Survival International, United Kingdom <http://www.survival-international.org>

(*Source*: Bristow et al. 2003)

WHO should give greater priority to the health of Indigenous peoples. Its focus on this at WHO headquarters lies with the Health and Human Rights Team in the Department of Ethics, Trade, Human Rights and Health Law, but it requires a bigger budget and higher profile. There should be a dedicated department and programme of work for the protection and promotion of Indigenous peoples' health, and for fostering links between traditional and allopathic health systems. It should also protect traditional healers from exploitation by large pharmaceutical companies seeking to patent traditional medicines and knowledge.

Similarly, donors need a far stronger commitment to ensuring that the health needs of Indigenous peoples are included in their development plans, and should do more to assist the participation of Indigenous peoples in the implementation and evaluation of donor funded projects. More thorough study is needed of the design and effect of donor health programmes in countries with Indigenous peoples. To what extent are they appropriate to the needs and culture of Indigenous peoples, and how are they being monitored and evaluated?

The participation of Indigenous peoples in civil society and NGO consultations must also improve. It is essential to accommodate their particular needs and cultures. The process of participation must be equitable, informed and transparent. Indigenous communities and organizations must be invited and supported to participate in policy and programme design, implementation and evaluation. Information and meetings should be available in their languages, and marginalized groups within minority and Indigenous communities, such as women, older people, and people with disabilities, should also be heard.

Health services Health services need to be organized and tailored to enhance and collaborate with Indigenous cultures and traditional health systems. A commitment to empowering Indigenous people to make their own decisions about the nature of health services should lie at the core of health systems development, as discussed in part B, chapter 1.

One of the challenges in doing this is that Indigenous peoples' groups are heterogeneous, with varying degrees of assimilation into modern society and connection with traditional ways of life. Different groups also have different views about the right path for future development. There is therefore no blueprint health service for Indigenous peoples. The design of services requires careful planning in the light of historical and socio-economic factors and peoples' right to self-determination. NGOs can help ministries of health to develop appropriate and sensitive programmes, especially organizations staffed and run by Indigenous peoples with extensive experience in the development of culturally and socially appropriate health services.

In countries with Indigenous populations, health professional associations should make much more effort to understand the health systems and beliefs of Indigenous peoples. National associations should use membership funding and seek government funding to set up special programmes of work aimed at educating themselves and the broader health professional community, and at countering ignorance and prejudice in their societies.

Research There is a widely-acknowledged lack of data on the health status of Indigenous peoples. Indigenous communities and organizations are calling for more research to assess or measure the impact of interventions to reduce inequalities and to inform their own ideas about the health challenges they

> *Box C1.9 National Indigenous health research as a catalyst for development*
>
> Canada has a research institute dedicated to supporting and funding aboriginal health research and capacity building – the Institute of Aboriginal Peoples' Health (http://www.cihr-irsc.gc.ca/e/8668.html). Some of its aims are to support ethical and innovative research that is responsive to Indigenous health priorities; to support research that contributes to the improvement of the health of vulnerable populations worldwide; to engage with the general public about the challenges of improving Indigenous health; and to accelerate the transfer of research within and between communities.

face. Research is crucial to support advocacy for the development of more appropriate and effective health services for Indigenous peoples. It can be used to support advocacy on land and civil rights, and to mobilize people towards community empowerment and organization.

References

ABS (2002). *Population distribution, Aboriginal and Torres Strait Islander Australians, 2001.* Canberra, Australian Bureau of Statistics (http://www.healthinfonet.ecu.edu.au/frames.htm, accessed 25 February 2005).

ABS (2003a). *Deaths Australia 2002.* Canberra, Australian Bureau of Statistics (http://www.healthinfonet.ecu.edu.au/frames.htm, accessed 25 February 2005).

ABS (2003b). *The health and welfare of Australia's Aboriginal and Torres Strait Islander peoples.* Canberra, Australian Bureau of Statistics (http://www.healthinfonet.ecu.edu.au/frames.htm, accessed 25 February 2005).

Alderete E (1999). *The Health of Indigenous People.* Geneva. WHO (http://whqlibdoc.who.int/hq/1999/WHO_SDE_HSD_99.1.pdf, accessed 16 March 2005).

Alessandri L et al. (2001). Perinatal and post-neonatal mortality among Indigenous and non-Indigenous infants born in Western Australia, 1980–1998. *Medical Journal of Australia*, 175(4): 185–9.

Barton J (1994). Ethnobotany and intellectual property rights. *Ciba Foundation Symposium*, 185: 214–21.

Basu S (1994). *A health profile of tribal India.* Health Millions 2(2): 12–4.

Bourne R (2003). *Invisible lives. Undercounted, underrepresented and underneath: the socio-economic plight of indigenous peoples in the Commonwealth.* London, Commonwealth Studies Unit.

Bristow F et al. eds. (2003). *Utz Wachil: health and wellbeing among indigenous peoples.* London, Health Unlimited/ London School of Hygiene and Tropical Medicine.

Chang H (2001). Hawaiian health practitioners in contemporary society. *Pacific Health Dialog*, 8(2): 260–73.

Cook B (2001). A call for respect and equality for indigenous scholarship in Hawaiian health. *Pacific Health Dialog*, 8(2): 368–74.

Crengle S (2000). The development of Maori primary care services. *Pacific Health Dialog*, 7(1): 48–53.

Escobar A et al. (2001). Tuberculosis among indigenous populations in Rondonia, Amazonia, Brazil. *Cad Saude Publica*, 17(2): 285–98.

Feiring B, Minority Rights Group Partners (2003). *Indigenous peoples and poverty: the cases of Bolivia, Guatemala, Honduras and Nicaragua.* London (http://www.minorityrights.org/Dev/mrg_dev_title12_LatinAmerica/mrg_dev_title12_Latin America_index.htm, accessed 25 February 2005).

Fink S (2002). International efforts spotlight traditional, complementary, and alternative medicine. *American Journal of Public Health*, 92(11): 1734–9.

Health Unlimited (2002). *Ratanakiri and Preah Vihear: primary health care projects.* London (http://www.healthunlimited.org/cambodia/index.htm, accessed 25 February 2005).

Hemming J (2003). *Die if you must: Brazilian Indians in the twentieth century.* London, Macmillan.

Hetzel D (2001). Death, disease and diversity in Australia, 1951 to 2000. *Medical Journal of Australia*, 174(1): 21–4.

Hickman M, Miller D (2001*).* Indigenous ways of healing guinea worm by the Sonninke culture in Mauritania, West Africa. *Hawaii Medical Journal,* 60(4): 95–8.

Hudon S (1999). Demographic situation of the Innus of Quebec, 1973 to 1993. *Cahiers Québécois de Démographie,* 28(1–2): 237–69.

Inter-Agency Support Group for the UN Permanent Forum on Indigenous Issues (2004). *Statement of the Inter-Agency Support group on Indigenous Issues regarding Indigenous Peoples and the Millennium Development Goals. UN Permanent Forum on Indigenous Issues, 30 September and 1 October.* Geneva (http://www.un.org/esa/socdev/unpfii/links_unsystem/inter_agency_statement.htm, accessed 15 March 2005).

International Labour Organisation (1989). Convention No. 169 concerning indigenous and tribal peoples in independent countries. In: *International labour conventions and recommendations 1919–1991*, 1436–47. Volume 2 (1963–1991). Geneva, International Labour Office.

International Work Group for Indigenous Affairs (2001). *The indigenous world 2000/2001.* Copenhagen, International Work Group for Indigenous Affairs.

International Work Group for Indigenous Affairs (2004). *Indigenous issues.* Copenhagen, International Work Group for Indigenous Affairs.

Janes C (1999). The health transition, global modernity and the crisis of traditional medicine: the Tibetan case. *Social Science and Medicine,* 48(12): 1803–20.

Khor M (2004). *A worldwide fight against biopiracy and patents on life.* Penang (http://www.twnside.org.sg/title/pat-ch.htm, accessed 6 March 2005).

King SR, Carlson TJ, Moran K (1996). Biological diversity, indigenous knowledge, drug discovery and intellectual property rights: creating reciprocity and maintaining relationships. *Journal of Ethnopharmacology*, 51(1–3): 45–57.

Mail P et al. (1989). Expanding practice horizons: learning from American Indian patients. *Patient Education & Counselling*, 13(2): 91–102.

Merson J (2000). Bio-prospecting or bio-piracy: intellectual property rights and biodiversity in a colonial and postcolonial context. *Osiris*, 15: 282–96.

Indigenous peoples

Pal D et al. (2002). Help-seeking patterns for children with epilepsy in rural India: implications for service delivery. *Epilepsia,* 43(8): 904–11.

Palafox N et al. (2001). Cultural competence: a proposal for physicians reaching out to Native Hawaiian patients. *Pacific Health Dialog,* 8(2): 388–92.

Powell D, Stewart D (2001). Children: the unwitting target of environmental injustices. *Pediatric Clinics of North America,* 48(5): 1291–305.

Simmons D, Voyle J (2003). Reaching hard-to-reach, high-risk populations: piloting a health promotion and diabetes disease prevention programme on an urban marae in New Zealand. *Health Promotion International,* 18(1): 41–50.

Single E et al. (1999). *Canadian Profile: Alcohol, Tobacco and Other Drugs.* Ottawa, Canadian Centre on Substance Abuse and the Centre for Addiction and Mental Health.

The Missionaries of Africa (2005). *Protest assassination of Sister Dorothy Stang* (http://www.africamission-mafr.org/sisterdorothy.htm, accessed 15 March 2005).

Trotti J (2001). Compensation versus colonization: a common heritage approach to the use of indigenous medicine in developing Western pharmaceuticals. *Food Drug Law Journal,* 56(3): 367–83.

UNDP [online database] (2004). *Human Development Report 2004.* Geneva, UNDP (http://hdr.undp.org/statistics, accessed 25 February 2005).

United Nations Economic and Social Council (2004). *Report of the Secretary-General on the preliminary review by the Coordinator of the International Decade of the World's Indigenous People on the activities of the United Nations system in relation to the Decade.* New York, UN.

United Nations High Commissioner for Human Rights (UNHCHR) (1994). *Draft United Nations Declaration on the Rights of Indigenous Peoples.* Geneva, UNHCHR.

Van Oostdam J, et al. (1999). Human health implications of environmental contaminants in Arctic Canada: a review. *Science of the Total Environment,* 230(1–3): 1–82.

C2 | Disabled people

Disability must first be defined as it is experienced by all disabled people, regardless of age and gender, including those with sensory, physical and intellectual impairment and mental health difficulties. Then, with this shared understanding, an assessment can be made of how well disabled people are being supported within mainstream agendas for health and well-being, the fight against global poverty and the human rights agenda. The chapter then shows how disabled people are taking control over their lives, changing their environments and demanding their right to full participation in society and to equality in freedom and dignity, despite massive violations of their rights and lack of visibility on mainstream development agendas.

Context

Twenty years ago WHO reported that despite some efforts in the areas of rehabilitation and prevention, disabled people were being denied inclusion in their communities and self-determination. Not enough steps were being taken to eliminate the barriers to their full participation in society (WHO 1985). A target was set to be achieved by 2000: 'Disabled people should have the physical and economic opportunities that allow at least for a socially and economically fulfilling and mentally creative life'. This could be achieved if societies 'developed positive attitudes towards disabled people and set up programmes aimed at providing appropriate physical, social and economic opportunities for them to develop their capacities to lead a healthy life'.

Some progress has been made since 1985. A report from the UN Human Rights Commission, on the current use and future potential of UN human rights instruments in the context of disability, says a long overdue and imperfect reform process is under way throughout the world. However, it also notes that the process is slow and uneven, in some places almost non-existent (Quinn and Degener 2003).

Disabled people not only form 20% of the world's poorest people, but poverty also increases the chances of disability – through vitamin A and iodine deficiencies, poor nutrition, bad working conditions, poor sanitation, environmental pollution and lack of health care (Sen and Wolfensohn 2003). Disabled people require higher incomes than non-disabled people to maintain the same living standard because of the social barriers, yet most have lower incomes.

Box C2.1 The facts about disability

Only 2% of disabled children in the developing world receive any education or rehabilitation.

Most public buildings and transport systems throughout the world are inaccessible to the majority of disabled people.

Disabled people of working age in developed and developing countries are three times more like to be unemployed and live in real poverty (65% of disabled people in the UK live below the poverty line).

Disabled people are subjected to appalling abuse. For example:

A family in Spain kept a disabled woman in a stinking six-foot hole for 40 years (1998).

An 18–month-old girl in the UK was refused use of a ventilator or antibiotics because of a legal and medical judgement on the quality of her life (1997).

An 11–year-old boy living at home with his family in Japan was murdered by his brother because 'he was mentally handicapped and had no future' (2000).

Disabled children were starved to death in a Kiev hospital, Ukraine, because staff stole their food (1995).

A man with multiple impairments died in the US after being beaten and stuffed in a dustbin. Authorities called it a 'cruel prank' (1994).

Two people pleading guilty to the killing of disabled family members in the UK were given non-custodial sentences (2000). (*Source*: DAA 2002)

These expenses do not diminish when they are in employment because they are paid disproportionately low wages.

The definition of disability The reasons why progress is so slow and health and well-being systematically denied to disabled people are rooted in the definition of disability. Traditionally, they have been seen as people who are impaired, functionally limited and unable to do things. It was believed that the duty of society was to change the impaired individual to conform to community norms – through cure, treatment or rehabilitation. Disabled people were the commodity of health professionals, and as such a source of power and resources for the professionals, not people in their own right with the same rights to life, participation and personal autonomy as everyone else. Problems that arose around disability could be solved by excluding them in special institutions, by community-based service provision which emphasized them as recipients of care and special treatment, or simply by neglect because their needs were deemed to be too expensive or not met by mainstream services. To put it bluntly, it was seen as socially unproductive and unsustainable for a developing country to provide resources to support disabled people in their communities. In the developed world, which did not have the excuse of lack of resources, the solutions were to exclude them from the mainstream and to build hierarchical, urban-based systems and services that allocated resources to the professionals rather than the service users.

These social, medical and individual attitudes to disability were embodied in the International Classification of Impairment, Disability and Handicap (ICIDH) formulated in 1980 by WHO as part of the International Classification of Diseases, the international standard diagnostic classification used for all general epidemiological and many health management purposes. The experts brought together to formulate this classification used a causal, linear approach, with its roots in disease and impairment and the outcomes in a person's inability to participate like everyone else in society. The expert group had no members from the disability rights movement – it was not seen as an issue in 1980 that disabled people had rights, including the right to a voice in policies and programmes that directly affected them.

The disability rights movement By that time, however, disabled leaders world-wide had arrived at a clear shared analysis of the situation and a definition of disability. They understood the wide range of social and environmental factors – services, systems, the personal context and environment – that contributed to erecting the disabling barriers that prevented the full and equal participation of disabled people in their societies and communities. This 'social model' of disability proposed that it was not the individual that had to change, but society that should make radical changes through systems, services and attitudes. Above all, disabled people had to be recognized as people – as human beings with equal rights.

This understanding of the social model of disability and the right to protection against exclusion and degrading and inhuman treatment was the catalyst in building a coherent and democratic movement of disabled people. It aimed to ensure that disabled people could be heard in political debate and that future systems and services would mainstream them and acknowledge their humanity. Growing out of a world where disability organizations were either large charitable institutions or single-impairment groups fighting for services, Disabled Peoples' International (DPI) was formed in 1981 to be the international voice of disabled people.

DPI has always included all disabled people regardless of impairment. At its inception, the 44 countries originally involved agreed the principle that all people are equal – and that includes disabled people. 'The principle of equality implies that the needs of each and every individual are of equal importance, that these needs must be made the basis for the planning of our societies and that all available resources must be employed in such a way as to ensure equal participation for each and every individual. Policies of concern to disabled people, therefore, very often involve the distribution of resources in society and as such are political issues' (DPI 1981).

One of its first steps was to apply to the UN for consultative status and to have a substantial input into the UN World Programme of Action Concerning Disabled Persons, agreed by all member states at the 1983 general assembly as the recommendations to support the Decade of Disabled Persons (1983–1992) and to implement the full and equal participation of disabled people in society. This programme of action became a very important lobbying tool for all disabled people's organizations and was elaborated by the UN Standard Rules on the Equalization of Opportunities of People with Disabilities to mark the end of the decade. A panel of experts was set up to advise the UN special rapporteur to monitor these rules, including DPI, Inclusion International (for families and people with intellectual impairments), World Blind Union, World Federation of the Deaf, World Network of Users of the Psychiatric System and Rehabilitation International. With the addition of the World Federation of Deaf/Blind, these organizations have provided a much wider and stronger body of influence, particularly on the formulation of a convention on the rights of disabled people that started in 2002.

Revising the definition and assessing progress

Another important step for the now burgeoning disability rights movement was to call for revision of the ICIDH to reflect the social definition of disability. Using the argument that WHO saw health as a human rights issue, it said disabled people were human beings and therefore disability could no longer be seen as part of the continuum of disease and incapacity. WHO took rather a long time to respond and eventually started the revision process in the early 1990s; the final new International Classification of Functioning, Disability and Health (ICF) was agreed by the WHO general assembly in 2001. WHO has said this relates to all people, that participation is not a consequence of impairment or functioning but a description of components of health, and that the list of environmental factors (including systems, services, policies and attitudes) describes the context in which people live (WHO 2001).

13 A disabled man driving his own home made buggy/taxi with another disabled man as passenger in Nairobi, Kenya

These factors also highlight the disabling effects of poverty, malnutrition, lack of micronutrients, poor sanitation and lack of immunization and show that improved nutrition, food security, access to health care, education, clean water, sanitation and immunization empower people, as do access to transport systems and safer working and living environments. By using the environmental factors in relation to personal factors, the classification can be used to see how wars and armed conflict can cause disabling impairments.

WHO also considers that its family of classifications provides a useful tool to describe and compare population health internationally, going beyond the traditional use of infant and maternal mortality as the key indicator. Unfortunately there is little indication that this is happening. The supporters of QALYs (quality adjusted life years) and DALYs (disability adjusted life years) argue that these relatively similar systems give a better idea of a country's use of its resources and development. The resulting tables seem to suggest, however, that the more disabled people a country has, the lower its status. Using mortality rates as an assessment of a country's development sends out messages ascribing causality to lack of health care, poverty, malnutrition and other factors, but disability-adjusted evidence implies that it is disabled people themselves who are the problem. It is to be hoped that future assessments will shift away from QALYs and DALYs to the more real context of the ICF.

183

> ### Box C2.2 A disabled man from Congo speaks out
>
> 'I am 35 years old now and have never tasted all these facilities I am reading in the Standard Rules. They are a dream! We don't have any rights other that the right of receiving pity words, which we don't need! We cannot make any change to our rights when we are still in the dust asking for cents in the streets, but by improving ourselves through education. There is no encouragement from the government or society.' (*Source*: DAA 2003)

Development According to the man from the Congo (Box C2.2) and many others, you cannot eat rights, nor do international policies and programmes seem relevant at the personal level. Disabled people at the grassroots are systematically ignored in disaster situations and relief aid – if for no other reason than that they cannot get access to that aid – and are rendered particularly vulnerable in times of armed conflict, being deliberately annihilated by warring parties, often hundreds at a time (DAA 2002).

Leaving disabled people off the development agenda has also been a major barrier. It will be impossible to cut poverty in half by 2015 unless disabled people are brought into the development mainstream, says former World Bank president James Wolfensohn. Disabled delegates from 15 developing countries got together in 2003 to discuss why they were left off the agenda and to put forward suggestions for reform. Mainstreaming would mean the expansion of possibilities, establishment of new partners, mutual support and solidarity, said delegate Alexander Phiri, a disabled rights activist from Zimbabwe. 'Instead of proving that we are 10% of any given population and 20% of the world's poorest, we must convince society that we are an irreplaceable part of 100%. If the idea behind mainstreaming is to create a society for all, we need to agree, for example, that no development funds, loans and grants should be spent on projects that are not accessed by all people, including disabled people' (International Service 2003). All agreed that the way forward was through their united, loud and strong voice lobbying governments, policy-makers and funders to recognize the importance and value of that voice and resource it to be mainstreamed at all levels in political and development processes.

Finding solutions

Disabled people's organizations are increasingly realizing that to ensure sustainability, social change based on equality and rights is just as important as fulfilling individual needs, if not more so. Disabled people may be given the tools to run their own small business – but unless their community accepts them as an equal or the bank gives them a small loan on the same basis as non-disabled entrepreneurs, they will not be able to operate. There is no point in providing a hearing aid if the battery cannot be renewed or charged locally. There is no point in governments announcing 'free education for all' if this does not include disabled children. Disabled people, using their own experience to stimulate strategies and actions, have come up with some fine solutions to ensure their rights to equality and participation.

In the North, 'independent living' was disabled people's solution to freeing themselves from the domination of the medical and charitable professionals and disempowering services. From the late 1970s on, starting in the US and quickly spreading to Canada, the UK, Sweden, Finland and Japan and now to most of Europe and Australia, the principles of self-determination have been implemented by disabled people's organizations through local, non-residential centres of enablement, providing the support and services to lead full and equal lives.

Each organization responded to the principles of independent living in its own way and as appropriate to its local environment. Most have focused on personal support systems, advocacy, housing, transport, access to public facilities, education, employment and working with political and social systems to ensure local, social change. The key is that disabled people must be in control of their own organizations and lives. The result of this activism has been a new generation of disabled people whose expectations of self-determination, inclusion and participation are equal to those of their non-disabled peers – even if those expectations are not actively met. Those organizations also produced a cadre of leaders who, using their experience at the grass roots, were and still are active nationally, regionally and internationally in the struggle for justice. Disabled people in the South have also implemented their own form of independent living in policies and programmes (Box C2.3).

This growth of respect and equality of opportunity has to be enforced through non-discrimination legislation. People's attitudes cannot be changed overnight – legislation is needed to change behaviour. Antidiscrimination legislation for disabled people is increasingly appearing on statute books but is useless without an enforcement procedure. The UN Standard Rules have provided good guidance but have not, in the main, been implemented because there has been no monitoring or exposure of the monitoring mechanisms of the international human rights instruments. Part of disability invisibility is that disabled people are not specifically mentioned in human rights instru-

> ## Box C2.3 The independent living movement in the South – some examples
>
> *Self-Help Association of Paraplegics (SHAP) in Soweto, South Africa.* When it started in 1981, disabled people had little chance of survival in such an inaccessible and hostile environment, let alone a decent standard of living (Fletcher and Hurst 1995). It started as a factory employing only disabled people sub-contracted to provide components for industry. It expanded to include transport, education, personal support, sports and a choir. And as with the independent living movement in the North, the leaders of this and other similar initiatives in the developing world became active in building a democratic, political movement of disabled people's organizations.
>
> Another good example of a form of independent living is the *disability component of the Andhra Pradesh rural poverty reduction programme* in which disabled people play a leading role, including initial planning and survey. They set up *sangams* (common interest self-help groups) at village level so that disabled people could work together to improve their situation socially and economically. They define their own needs and barriers and take action collectively. They organize demand for their entitlements and legal certification (many disabled children and adults are never registered). They work to get disabled children into schools and for them to obtain the necessary health care and assistive devices. One of their biggest accomplishments is to be treated with respect. 'Now people don't call us "the lame boy" or "the blind girl" but address us by our real names' (Werner 2002).

ments, except the Convention on the Rights of the Child. Nor do the monitoring bodies take disabled people into account when scrutinizing country reports. This is why it is important to have a convention supporting the rights of disabled people – though monitoring it must have appropriate status, not just another report to the UN general assembly that can be agreed and then ignored.

Bioethics and a healthy nation Recognition of disabled people's rights has undoubtedly begun – even though implementation seems a long way off. However, in the last ten years or so a barrier has arisen that is currently unbreachable: the eugenic attitudes underpinning much of the rhetoric and policies around the new genetic sciences (discussed in more detail in part B, chapter 5). Many disabled people are only alive today because of scientific progress generally and new medical techniques in particular, as the DPI Europe position statement on bioethics says: 'Of course we wish to promote and sustain such advances where these lead to benefits for everyone. But we want to see research directed at improving the quality of our lives, not denying us the opportunity to live. The genetic goal of the prevention of disease and impairment by the prevention of lives judged not to be "normal" is a threat to human diversity. It is a potential Nagasaki for everyone, not just disabled people. The threat is powerful and imminent' (DPI/Europe 2000).

Like everyone else, disabled people want scientific advances that alleviate pain and help them to participate more fully in their lives. What must be contested are scientific advances that ignore the intrinsic humanity of disabled people – that see impaired genes only of use if they can be enhanced. Many modern scientists define eugenics as promoting a healthy nation, and advocate the right of choice. But the whole notion of 'healthy' in this context raises many concerns.

China advocated a healthy nation by enforcing a one-child only families policy. Then, when it discovered that this practice disturbed the balance of the population and endangered sustainability, it introduced a law to guarantee the health of mothers and infants and to improve the quality of born children. It tried to prevent abnormal births by sterilization, banning the marriage of disabled people, and aborting disabled foetuses. It did, however, stop short of euthanasia of children born with disabling impairments (Xinhua 1994). New draft amendments to the Family Code of Albania bar marriage to people with certain mental and physical disabilities (Amnesty International 2004). The Netherlands is discussing extending legal euthanasia to people incapable of deciding for themselves, including disabled children, and such procedures have already been carried out (Sterling 2004).

Until very recently national bioethics committees have mostly been established in developed countries, where the need to make decisions and introduce legislation to control scientific advances has been most necessary. But now such committees are springing up all over the world – the latest in Pakistan – illustrating the seriousness with which they are taking these advances. The influence of the new genetic sciences is becoming increasingly important to everyone, and is also bringing increased power to the transnational pharmaceutical corporations through research and higher profits. Like some non-disabled people, disabled people are often used for research, often without their permission. Global health statistics based on QALYs, and the achievement of a 'healthy' nation through scientific advances to eliminate disabled genes, combine to encourage governments to see genetics as a solution for health for all. The debates do not consider that people born with

187

disabilities are less than 2% of the disability population and that the majority of disabling impairments are caused by poverty and exclusion. Throughout the world, power and economics prevail in the war against the weak.

Recommendations

- Listen to the voices of the excluded. Promote and support the voice and status of disabled people.
- Understand the nature of exclusion – establish longitudinal data sets based on environmental impacts to monitor disabled people's lives.
- Look for solutions through equality, inclusion and rights. Society has to change, as well as routine daily behaviour.
- Ensure the disability dimension is included in all agendas – especially poverty and development.
- Build alliances to make a difference.
- Include disabled people in the monitoring of all human rights instruments and promote an international convention on the rights of disabled people.
- Above all, recognize the intrinsic humanity of each disabled person, regardless of impairment.

References

Amnesty International (2004). *Albania: disability and the right to marry.* Press release, 11 November.

Disability Awareness in Action (DAA) (2002). *A Real Horror Story: The Abuse of Disabled People's Human Rights.* DAA Human Rights Database report. London, DAA.

DAA (2003). *Testimony concerning human rights abuse against disabled people.* Submission to the UN Human Rights Commission. London, DAA.

Disabled Peoples' International/Europe (2000). *Disabled people speak on the new genetics.* Position statement on bioethics and human rights. London, DPI/Europe.

Disabled Peoples' International (1981). *Proceedings of the first world congress.* Singapore, DPI.

Fletcher A, Hurst R (1995). *Overcoming obstacles to the integration of disabled people.* Report for the World Summit on Social Development, London, DAA.

International Service (2003). *Left off the agenda? Mainstreaming disability in development.* Conference report (http://www.internationalservice.org.uk/conference.html, accessed 26 January 2005).

Quinn G, Degener T (2003). *A study on the current use and future potential of the UN human rights instruments in the context of disability.* Geneva, UN Human Rights Commission.

Sen A, Wolfensohn J (2003). Helping disabled people to come out of the shadows. *Global Viewpoint* (http://www.worldbank.org.cn/English/content/382b63052692. shtml, accessed 26 January 2005).

Sterling T (2004). *Netherlands Hospital Euthanizes Babies* (http://apnews.myway.com/article/20041130/D86MEAA80.html, accessed 26 February 2005).

Werner D (2002). The role of disabled persons in overcoming rural poverty in Andhra Pradesh, India. *Newsletter from the Sierra Madre*, 48, Palo Alto, Healthwrights.

World Health Organisation (1985) *Targets for Health for All*. Copenhagen, WHO Regional Office for Europe.

WHO (2001). *International classification of functioning, disability and health*. Short version. Geneva, WHO.

Xinhua [anonymous] (1994). News agency domestic service report, Beijing, Xinhua, 27 October.

The 1978 Alma Ata Declaration recognized that the goal of 'Health for All' would be achieved only by addressing the underlying social, economic and environmental determinants of health. Simply improving health care services would not be enough on their own, but health care professionals and health care systems could facilitate and promote action for health in a wide range of different sectors.

Part D of the *Global Health Watch* demonstrates why this approach is needed by discussing the profound health impacts of lack of access to water and education, conflict, food insecurity and environmental degradation, particularly climate change.

Despite the diversity of topics covered, there are several points of convergence. For instance, it is invariably the health of poorer and more vulnerable groups that is worst affected by changes in people's external environments or in services that sustain health. Rapid climate change will hit the poorest hardest; conflict damages the fragile coping strategies of vulnerable households; and the privatization of water and education services increases poverty.

The need to reduce inequities through a strong public sector response in health-sustaining services mirrors that required in the health care sector itself. Key services around the world have been affected by constraints put on public expenditure.

The growing power of the corporate sector is evident in the chapters on food security and climate change – the activities of unregulated and uncontrolled big business threaten to ruin still further the environments and diets of whole countries. Once again, stronger international and national regulation of markets is urgently and desperately needed.

Policy dilemmas thrown up by the informal and formal commercialization of water and education services are similar. All the chapters cite the need to challenge the attempts of big corporations to capture lucrative markets, concerns that are common to many issues explored in Section B of this report. These similarities suggest that NGOs, civil society movements (and policymakers) involved in all these different fields need to work together more.

What kind of world lets the desire for profit undermine the very possibility of human existence itself? The kind of world that lets conflicts large and small continue to claim so many lives. Many governments and businesses in both North and South are complicit in diverting money, people and materials towards building arsenals of nuclear, chemical and biological weapons that could obliterate the world and all life many times over. The chapter on conflict, however, is not despairing: it calls for a 'culture of peace' and suggests that promoting health and equity is key to reducing conflict worldwide.

In recent years, the annual World Social Forums have been gatherings of a multitude of NGOs from different sectors with wide-ranging campaigns. The relevance and rationale of bringing such groups together is apparent when looking at the different sectors through a health lens – they all share a common agenda of democratizing the global political economy; redistributing wealth and power; strengthening the role and accountability of governments; and reining in the excesses of corporate activity.

D1 | Climate change

Introduction

Environmental degradation in general, and climate change in particular, represent one of the biggest threats to human health, particularly the health of younger people in the future and that of future generations. Yet repairing the damage and preventing further harm to the environment are nowhere near priorities of local, national and international public health strategies.

Environmental degradation can have both direct and indirect impacts on health. Pollutants in air, water and soil can have a direct toxic effect on human health or they can aggravate pre-existing conditions. Air pollution, for instance, can cause inflammation of the lungs, increase the risk of coronary artery disease and lung cancer, and aggravate pre-existing asthma and Chronic Obstructive Pulmonary Disease (COPD).

Stratospheric ozone depletion, meanwhile, caused by the release of chlorofluorocarbons (once widely used as refrigerants, insulating foams and solvents), methyl bromide (used as a pesticide), halons (used in fire extinguishers) and methyl chloroform (used as an industrial solvent) has an indirect effect on human health. When these various pollutants reach the stratosphere, they break apart, releasing their constituent chlorine or bromine atoms, which cause ozone molecules to break up and disintegrate. With less of the protective ozone layer around the earth, more ultraviolet B radiation reaches the earth's surface, increasing rates of skin cancer.

Indirect effects of environmental degradation on health include aggravated levels of poverty, reduced levels of biodiversity and a changing climate. This chapter focuses on the causes, effects and challenges related to climate change as well as the contribution of transport to climate change and health.

Dramatic climate change

The impact of human activity on the earth's climate system – whether this impact is called climate change, global warming or the greenhouse effect – is often cited as the world's most serious environmental challenge. It is a 'greater threat than global terrorism', according to the UK government's chief scientific adviser (King 2004).

The relatively stable climate on which human communities depend is already changing. The average temperature of the earth's surface has risen by

0.6 °C since the late 18th century, an unprecedented increase since historical records began. The period from 1995 to 2004 included nine of the ten warmest years on record (WMO 2004), and climate-related extreme weather events – hurricanes, tropical storms, flooding, drought and heat waves – now occur with increased frequency around the world.

More worryingly, the average temperature of the earth's surface is expected to rise by between 1.4°C to 5.8 °C by the year 2100. Even the minimum predicted increase (1.4°C) within this time frame will be faster and larger than any century-long temperature trend in the last 10,000 years. Many scientists believe that an average temperature increase of 2°C by 2100 is the threshold of 'dangerous climate change' (Parry et al. 2001, IPCC 2001 a). The task required to prevent such a rise is enormous.

The Intergovernmental Panel on Climate Change (IPCC), the global body of scientists convened by the UN to study the causes, impacts and responses to climate change, is in no doubt that humanity faces a grave threat. Furthermore, they conclude that '(t)he impacts of climate change will fall disproportionately upon developing countries and the poor persons within all countries, thereby exacerbating inequities in health status and access to adequate food, clean water and other resources' (IPCC 2001 b). Cruelly, these communities are also the least responsible for damage to the climate.

What is climate change and what are the prime drivers of human influence on the climate?

The global climate system is driven and maintained by a complex set of interactions involving solar energy, and the effects of clouds and the oceans. Added to these interactions are a variety of effects resulting from human activity, in particular industrialization, agriculture, urbanization and deforestation.

The main reasons for the increase in global temperatures are: the previous 150 years of burning ever-greater quantities of fossil fuels (oil, petrol and coal); deforestation; and certain farming methods. Transport and travel are particularly major causes of climate change through the burning of fossil fuels (see Box D1.1). These activities have increased the amount of 'greenhouse gases' in the atmosphere – in particular, carbon dioxide, methane and nitrous oxide. Concentrations of carbon dioxide are now about one third higher than in pre-industrial times (IPCCc).

Greenhouse gases occur naturally and are critical for life on earth. They keep some of the sun's warmth from reflecting back into space; without them, the earth would be a significantly colder and less hospitable place. But their increasing quantities are now causing global warming and dramatic climate change (IPCC 2001a).

Rapid climate change will manifest itself in different ways in different parts of the world. It will include more frequent severe weather events; changes in rainfall patterns, including more frequent occurrences in drought; severe heat waves; and in some places, more severe winters.

Box D1.1   The effect of transport on climate change and health

Transport has become a growing public health issue. Transport and travel are major causes of climate change – their share of world greenhouse gas emissions increased from 19% in 1971 to 23% in 1997 (IEA 1999c, IPCC 2001b). Transport energy use in 2000 was 25% higher than in 1990 and is expected to grow by nearly 90% between 2000 and 2030 because of the increasing movement of goods and people (IEA 2004).

Air travel is the least energy efficient form of transport, followed by cars and trucks. Aviation now causes 3.5% of human-generated global warming and could rise to 15% by 2050 (IPCC 2001d). In 2003, 1.6 billion passengers flew by plane, a figure that could exceed 2.3 billion by 2010. The industry predicts a rise in the number of miles flown by passengers and freight as well.

Current transport and travel patterns also harm human health directly. Globally, road crashes kill 1.2 million people and injure another 50 million each year (WHO 2004). By 2020, road injuries may be the third largest cause of disability-adjusted life years lost (Murray 1996). The populations of the rapidly expanding megacities in Asia, Africa and Latin America are increasingly exposed to levels of ambient air pollution that are often worse than those experienced in industrialized countries in the first half of the 20th century. Air pollution contributes to a higher prevalence of cancers of the trachea, bronchus and lung, and various cardio-respiratory diseases.

Modes of travel (in particular the use of cars) also negatively affect health by promoting unhealthy lifestyles. The car has reduced or denied opportunities for walking and cycling, thereby encouraging obesity and cardiovascular disease. A third of car trips in Europe cover under 3 kilometres and half less than 5 kilometres, distances that can be covered by bicycle in 15–20 minutes or by brisk walking in 30–50 minutes (WHO 2004). Some cities have even banned or discouraged cycling because there are too many cars on the road (Barter 2003). Roads and traffic can also disintegrate and

---

fragment communities; create stress; and consume land that could be used for agriculture or recreation.

The health effects of pollution, injuries and community severance all fall more heavily on the economically disadvantaged, children and the elderly. The unequal effect on the poor occurs both within and between countries.

The public health problems related to transport and travel show considerable inter-country difference. For example, walking and cycling is 4-5 times greater in Europe than in US and Canada, and public transport use 4-6 times greater (Pucher 1996). In Santiago 30% of people cycle or walk to work, while in Brasilia the figure is 2%; in Copenhagen it is 32% compared to 0.3% in Atlanta, 22% in Tokyo and 6% in Sydney (Newman 1999).

Across the world, car numbers and distances travelled are still rising. In OECD countries, the number of motor vehicles is expected to increase by up to 62% between 2003-2012. These countries are also leading the trend towards larger and less fuel-efficient vehicles – in spite of over two decades of serious concern over global warming. Sports utility vehicle purchases now account for more than half the market in the US, while the average Ford car is less fuel-efficient today than the Model T was over 80 years ago (Reuters 2003).

Vehicle numbers are also expanding across the world. In Thailand, the number of registered motor vehicles more than tripled from 4.9 million in 1987 to 17.7 million in 1997. In China, the number quadrupled between 1990 and 2002 to more than 55 million. If China reached Japan's level of car ownership, it would require 13 million hectares of land – equivalent to over half China's current rice cropland (Whitelegg 2003).

Impact of climate change

Since the first IPCC report in 1990, there has been a dramatic improvement in awareness of the impacts of climate change on health. The World Health Organization (WHO), the World Meteorological Organization (WMO) and the UN Environment Programme (UNEP) have published an extensive overview of these impacts (McMichael et al. 2003). Their review also points to several uncertainties and caveats including: a) the complexity of climate systems and measuring related health outcomes; b) the uncertainty in the range of assumptions linked to making an assessment; and c) the differential vulnerability of communities due to differences in population density, level of economic development, local availability food, local environmental conditions and pre-existing health status (Woodward et al. 2000).

Nonetheless, the effects of climate change will be extensive:

- Droughts and changes in rainfall patterns will damage agricultural systems, threaten the food security of millions of people and worsen the existing food insecurity of millions of others, especially in Sub-Saharan Africa.
- The loss of habitats will result in the loss of biodiversity – up to one third of plant and animal species could disappear by 2050 in the absence of serious efforts to reduce the pollution that is causing climate change (Thomas 2004).
- Global sea levels, which rose on average by 10-20 centimetres during the 20th century, are expected to rise by a further 9 to 88 centimetres by the year 2100. If the higher end of the predicted rise in temperature is reached (5.8°C), the sea could inundate the heavily populated coastlines of countries like Bangladesh; cause the disappearance of nations like the Maldives; and destroy freshwater supplies for billions of people (for a full overview, see IPCC 2001b).
- As climate change provokes poverty and mass migrations, some social responses may compound the problem with human rights abuses – those forced to leave their homes and lands because of the effects of climate change ('climate change refugees') may be met with violence, racism and unsanitary refugee camps. It is estimated that there could be 150 million environmental refugees by 2050, an increase of 125 million from the current figure of 25 million, the majority of them in developing countries.
- An increase in the frequency of extreme weather events will result in more frequent humanitarian emergencies, particularly affecting populations in high-risk areas such as coastal zones and cities in developing countries.
- As water sources are threatened, the prospect of more conflicts over scarce water resources could rise.
- The number of excess deaths caused by thermal extremes (of heat or of cold) will rise particularly in vulnerable groups: those already suffering from cardiovascular and respiratory disease; the very young; and the elderly and frail.
- Climate change will also lead to increased rates of infectious disease, including various vector-borne and water-related diseases. Changes in temperature and surface water can affect the life-cycle of mosquitoes. As a consequence, diseases such as malaria and dengue fever, currently largely confined to tropical or subtropical regions, may spread to countries in

temperate climates (Bouma and Kaay 1995). Diarrhoeal diseases, including cholera, cryptosporidium, giardia, shigellosis and typhoid, may increase as a result of more frequent and severe floods and drought (McMichael et al. 2003).

- Climate change is also expected to increase rates of rodent-borne disease (because of a warmer climate changing habitats that will allow rodents to move into new areas), including leptospirosis, tularaemia, viral haemorrhagic diseases, lyme disease, tick-borne encephalitis and hantavirus pulmonary syndrome.

The economic and societal costs of these impacts are estimated to be huge (Parry et al. 2001), and will overwhelm even the most optimistic projections for economic growth in vulnerable regions. An increase of 2°C by the 2050s could result in:

- 228 million more people at risk from malaria;
- 12 million more at risk from hunger as crop yields fall;
- 2240 million more at risk from water shortages, particularly in the subtropics;
- 20 million more at risk from coastal flooding.

An increase of 4°C could by the 2080s result in:

- 334 million more people at risk from malaria;
- 128 million more at risk from hunger as crop yields fall;
- 3500 million more at risk from water shortages, particularly in the subtropics;
- 108 million more at risk from coastal flooding.

The institutional and political response to climate change

Just two years after the publication of the first IPCC report, the UN Framework Convention on Climate Change (UNFCCC) was agreed and signed at the 1992 UN Conference on Environment and Development (the 'Earth Summit') held in Rio de Janeiro. Some 189 countries, including the United States, have now ratified the Convention. This calls on Parties to:

'Protect the climate system for the benefit of present and future generations of humankind, on the basis of equity and in accordance with their common but differentiated responsibilities and respective capabilities. Accordingly, the developed country Parties should take the lead in combating climate change and the adverse affects thereof.'

However, the Convention created non-binding targets for industrialized

14 Droughts threaten the food security of millions in the developing world.

countries to bring their greenhouse gas emissions back to 1990 levels by the year 2000. In 1995, the Parties to the Convention established 'as a matter of urgency' a process to negotiate a new protocol, one with binding targets and timeframes. The result was the Kyoto Protocol, agreed in 1997, whose aim is for developed countries only to reduce their 1990 levels of emissions by a minimum of 5% by 2008-2012. Some 129 countries have since acceded to or ratified the protocol, although it 'entered into force' and became legally binding only in 2005, eight years after it was drafted.

Although it is a step in the right direction, the Kyoto Protocol offers little reassurance. To start with, the level of reduction in emissions that it requires is totally inadequate. The IPCC estimates that, in order to avoid catastrophic destabilization of the climate, global greenhouse gas emissions need to be halved by 2050. Allowing for economic development in non-industrialized (Southern) countries, emissions from the North will need to be reduced by 60-80% in the same time frame – ten times greater than the reductions called for by Kyoto.

Secondly, the biggest polluter in the world, the United States, withdrew from the Kyoto Protocol in 2001. The US, with 4% of the global population, is responsible for 25% of global carbon dioxide emissions. Another country that has failed to support the Kyoto Protocol is Australia.

Thirdly, some observers think that the reporting and accountability mechanisms are too weak. There is widespread concern that the Kyoto Protocol will 'leak', failing to deliver the carbon dioxide emission reductions it requires. A lack of institutional capacity may mean that it will be impossible to verify the reductions claimed, especially by means of the flexible mechanisms (see Box D1.2).

Fourthly, others object to the inclusion of 'carbon sinks' – the planting of trees to absorb or 'offset' carbon emissions – as carbon stored in the tree will eventually find its way back into the atmosphere, meaning that the burden of reducing emissions is simply shifted to future generations. Sinks can also divert political and financial resources away from the primary task: to reduce carbon dioxide emissions.

Finally, there are concerns about the appropriateness of some of the flexible mechanisms (see Box D1.2) in the Kyoto protocol. These mechanisms are based on the premise that the global atmosphere can be 'commodified' for trading within a market system. Developed countries that have ratified the

---

Box D1.2 The flexible mechanisms of the Kyoto Protocol

There are two flexible mechanisms for countries to meet their Kyoto Protocol targets – the Clean Development Mechanism (CDM) and Joint Implementation.

The CDM is designed to generate emissions reductions credits for developed countries that finance emissions-reducing projects in developing countries. For example, Canada is financing an energy efficiency project in China. By helping to reduce emissions in China, Canada will gain additional credits to increase its own level of emissions. These projects must be approved by the CDM executive board and are intended to contribute to sustainable development in the developing country partners.

Joint Implementation is the means by which industrialized countries cooperate with each other in meeting emissions reduction targets. For example, a German-financed energy efficiency project in the Russian Federation, or Norwegian-financed renewable energy projects in Hungary that reduce emissions, can be credited to the country that financed the project. In theory, this is an efficient means of generating the same overall emissions reductions for industrialized countries. In practice, however, the 'reductions' could be 'theoretical' as well because the emissions baselines in the cooperating countries are not always accurate and are often inflated estimates of future emissions (hot air).

Protocol can meet their targets by reducing their own domestic emissions or by trading in various ways for 'emissions reductions credits' – countries may buy or sell their 'right' to emit greenhouse gases. Such trading does not recognize the rights of those who lack the funds to participate in the market.

Getting to the root of the problem

Critics point out that the Kyoto Protocol characterizes the problem of climate change and the production of greenhouse gases without addressing the institutions and power imbalances that have resulted in both the overuse and unequal use of the atmosphere (Lohmann 2001). Understanding the political dimensions to the problem of climate change is vital if there is to be any hope of addressing the public health emergency that will ensue.

The forces shaping many of the socio-economic and health inequalities between poor and rich countries are also driving climate change. The growth of corporate globalization and market liberalization, which has created unprecedented wealth for a significant minority of the world's population, does not just result in the social costs described in part A, but also has environmental costs. The expansion in global trade, which has increased carbon emissions because of the increased movement in goods, services and people, has benefited millions of consumers in richer countries, and the profit margins of a relatively small number of corporations, most of them based in industrialized countries. Particularly notable is the increase in the movement of food, both within and between countries, which has been accompanied by corresponding increases in obesity but no significant reductions in malnutrition (see part D chapter 3). Several billions of poorer people in developing countries have seen their lands and livelihoods turned into environmentally-damaging agricultural systems that produce food and commodities for higher income countries. These people not only receive little, if any, benefit from such agriculture; they are also the ones who bear the brunt of the costs associated with environmental degradation.

Serious political commitment and widespread social mobilization are needed to change the current patterns and forms of economic globalization, and to overcome the disproportionate and unaccountable power of large corporations and financial institutions, many of which are reluctant for people to become better informed and educated about the consequences of rapid climate change. Such commitment and mobilization are also needed to ensure action to prevent further climate change and to tackle the consequences of the change that will undoubtedly take place.

Corporations and institutions rooted in the oil, automobile and transport-related industries particularly stand to lose out from an effective response to climate change unless they themselves change. Using attractive advertising campaigns, some large oil companies such as Shell and BP promote themselves as 'green' industries and emphasize their involvement in renewable energies while still continuing, if not expanding, their search for oil. Exxon Mobil has run an advertising campaign in the US press extensively criticising the Kyoto Protocol and dismissing the widely accepted consensus on the science of climate change. Oil companies have also spent $12 million since 1997 in funding 'think-tanks' and lobby groups that question climate change and oppose efforts to address it, yet individuals from these groups often appear in the media as 'independent experts'.

Powerful institutions with vested interests, and the governments of the major industrialized countries, are clearly at the root of the lack of progress in implementing an effective response to the climate problem facing everyone. There is neither the commitment nor leadership required to address the problem. For example, in the last 10 years, although the World Bank Group distributed approximately $1.5 billion for renewable energy projects around the world, it made approximately $27.6 billion available to the extractive industries (oil, coal and gas exploration) and the fossil-fuelled power sector. Expenditure on fossil fuels and the energy sector relative to renewable energy currently exists at a ratio of 18:1. And while the UK is making an effort to raise the issue of climate change for discussion, UK Prime Minister Tony Blair told the World Economic Forum in 2005 that any action requiring cuts in economic growth would not succeed.

Citizens around the world are slowly beginning to realize and respond to the climate change crisis. But the nature of that citizen response must become more robust. Individual consumer action will not be enough. In the medium- to long-term, economic growth and climate protection are not compatible. The viability and emulation of Western lifestyles and consumption patterns needs to be examined and alternatives developed.

Recommendations

If the political obstacles can be overcome, the IPCC suggests that it would be possible to surpass the Kyoto targets with existing technology at relatively modest costs (IPCC 2001b). Even relatively conventional economic analysts, such as the former head of the Confederation of British Industry Adair Turner, have suggested that meeting the challenge of climate change could be achieved without crippling expense. As a member of the International Climate Task Force, Turner said that it would even be possible to meet the more pressing

15 Transport and travel are major drivers of climate change.

need of staying under the 2°C increase threshold by spending around 0.05% per year of global GDP on actions that can prevent dangerous climate change. In other words, delaying the economic growth that would have occurred by 2050 to spring 2051 (International Climate Change Taskforce 2005). It is certainly possible and imperative to help the most vulnerable countries and communities to adapt to climate change.

What is required is a social mobilization that insists on:

- Cuts in greenhouse gas emissions by industrialized countries in the order of 60-80% (relative to 1990 levels) by the middle of this century – far beyond the targets of the Kyoto Protocol.
- Funds and other resources for poorer countries to adapt to irreversible climate change, bearing in mind that richer country subsidies to their domestic fossil fuel industries stood at US$ 73 billion per year in the late 1990s (see Box D1.3).

Climate change

Box D1.3 Adaptation to climate change and equity

It is becoming increasingly clear that the adverse impacts of climate change in the near term (over the next decade or so) are almost impossible to prevent, even with the most drastic cuts in emissions. Hence adaptation to climate change in addition to reduced emissions is vital.

The seventh Conference of Parties to the UN Framework Convention on Climate Change in Morocco in 2001 created several new funds (as part of the 'Marrakesh Accords') to help developing countries adapt to the impacts of climate change. However, contributions to these funds are purely voluntary and have attracted only small amounts from a few rich countries.

- The widespread implementation of small-scale renewable energy projects that can simultaneously tackle poverty and reduce climate change. This will require political commitment, new funds from governments in all countries, and a major shift in the priorities of the World Bank and other development bodies.

The World Health Organization and UNICEF need to be lending their weight to the campaign, using their mandate to protect the health of current and future generations.

Health professional associations, especially public health associations (particularly within developed countries), should be calling for local health impact assessments on climate change of trade and economic activities as well as of health care services. Doctors and other health professionals need to communicate the threats of climate change to health as a public health emergency, and to publicize ways of tackling that emergency and minimizing further climate change. As with many other topics in this report , the health community as a whole needs to take up a more independent and assertive position in relation to the policy agendas set in the trade and industrial sectors.

Recommendations on transport Reducing transport's contribution to climate change requires reversing the trend for greater car and truck numbers and longer journeys (see Box D1.1). Although technology can improve efficiency, more vehicles, larger vehicles and longer journeys can negate these improvements.

The core objectives must be to:

- Redesign trade rules. Governments must prioritize implementing national and international measures aimed at 'internalizing' social and environmental costs – the 'polluter pays' principle.
- Promote land use policies that aim to meet needs for access to jobs, goods, services and leisure locally by encouraging walking, cycling and public transport.
- Promote walking and cycling as the least polluting, healthiest and most equitable modes of transport, in particular by reducing the danger faced by walkers and cyclists from more harmful means of transport.
- Stop subsidizing harmful transport and travel, whether through road building, grants to car manufacturers, low tax on aviation fuel, or World Bank subsidies for fossil fuel production.

Resources

Climate change related resources

BP's Environment Policies <http://www.bp.com/genericsection.do?categoryId=931&contentId=2016995>.

Linkages is provided by the International Institute for Sustainable Development. It is designed to be an electronic clearing-house for information on past and upcoming international meetings related to environment and development policy <http://www.iisd.ca/>.

The Global Commons Institute (GCI) is an independent group concerned with the protection of the global commons <http://www.gci.org.uk/>.

United Nations Framework Convention on Climate Change (UNFCCC) and the Kyoto protocol <http://unfccc.int>.

Transport related resources

carfree.com: website with detailed ideas how to design car free cities <http://www.carfree.com>.

Transport and Health study group: this is a network of health and transport professionals in the UK involved in understanding and addressing the links between transport and health. Involved in promoting Green Travel Plans for health services <http://www.stockport.nhs.uk/thsg>.

Victoria Transport Policy Institute: provides free on-line a wide range of papers on transport. These include the economic costs, the health effects, and how to introduce change <http://www.vtpio>.

References

Barter P (2003). Southeast Asian Urban Transport: A Kaleidoscope of Challenges and Choices. In: Whitelegg, J and Haq, G (eds) (2003). *The Earthscan Reader in World Transport Policy and Practice*. Earthscan, London.

Bouma M, van der Kaay H (1995). Epidemic malaria in India's Thar desert. *The Lancet*, 373, 132–3.

International Energy Association (IEA) (2004). *World Energy Outlook*. Paris, IEA.

Intergovernmental Panel on Climate Change (IPCC) (2001a). *Climate change 2001: the scientific basis.* Cambridge, Cambridge University Press.

IPCC (2001b). *Climate change 2001: impacts, adaptation, and vulnerability.* Cambridge, Cambridge University Press.

IPCC (2001c). *Climate change 2001: synthesis report. A contribution to Working Groups I, II and III to the Third Assessment Report of the Intergovernmental Panel on Climate Change.* [Watson RT and the Core writing team (eds.)]. Cambridge and New York, Cambridge University Press.

IPCC (2001d). *Climate change 2001: mitigation.* Cambridge, Cambridge University Press.

International Climate Change Taskforce (2005). *Meeting the climate challenge: recommendations of the international climate task force.* London, Washington DC and Canberra, Institute for Public Policy Research, The Center for American Progress, The Australia Institute.

King D (2004). Climate change science: adapt, mitigate or ignore. *Science*, 303:176–7.

Lohmann L (2001). *Corner House Briefing 24: Democracy or carbocracy? Intellectual corruption and the future of the climate debate.* London, The Corner House.

McMichael AJ et al. eds. (2003). *Climate change and human health: risks and responses.* Geneva, WHO.

Murray CJL, Lopez AD, eds (1996). *The global burden of disease: a comprehensive assessment of mortality and disability from diseases, injuries, and risk factors in 1990 and projected to 2020.* Cambridge (MA), Harvard University Press.

Newman P and Kenworthy J (1999). *Sustainability and cities: overcoming automobile dependence.* Island Press, Washington DC.

Parry M et al (2001). Millions at risk. Global Environment Change. *Tiempo*, Issue 44/45, September (www.cru.uea.ac.uk/tiempo/floor0/archive/issue4445/t4445a7.htm, accessed 21 March 2005).

Pucher J, Lefevere C (1996). *The urban transport crisis in Europe and North America.* London, Macmillan Press.

Reuters (2003). Sierra Club Challenges Ford's Fuel Economy at 100. *Reuters,* 5 June.

Schwela D and Zali O eds (1999). *Urban traffic pollution.* New York, WHO.

Thomas CD et al. (2004). Extinction risk from climate change. *Nature*, 427, 145–8.

Whitelegg J and Haq G (2003). The Global Transport Problem: Same Issues but a Different Place. In: Whitelegg J and Haq G eds. *The Earthscan Reader in World Transport Policy and Practice.* Earthscan, London.

WHO (2003). *Climate change and human health – risks and responses: summary.* Geneva, WHO.

WHO (2004). *World report on road traffic injury prevention.* Geneva, WHO.

Woodward A et al. (2000). Protecting human health in a changing world: the role of social and economic development. *Bulletin of the World Health Organization,* 78 (9):1148-1155.

World Meteorological Organization (WMO) (2004). *WMO Statement on the Status of the Global Climate in 2004: Global Temperature Fourth Warmest.* Geneva, WMO.

D2 | Water

Access to enough clean water, taken for granted by most people in developed countries, is a matter of life and death for millions (see Box D2.1). The daily grind of searching for and collecting water is also part of a state of poverty that affects dignity, self-respect and other aspects of well-being that transcend the notion of 'basic' needs (Jarmon 1997).

Water scarcity should also be framed as an environmental and political issue. Climate change could account for 20% of the projected increase in global water scarcity, while continuing deforestation and the destruction of wetlands would also reduce freshwater access to many communities. Freshwater resources are further reduced by environmental pollution – for example, two million tons of industrial wastes and chemicals, human waste, agricultural fertilizers, pesticides and pesticide residues are disposed of in receiving waters every day (UN/WWAP 2003). As ever, the poor are the worst affected, with half the population of developing countries exposed to polluted water sources.

This chapter focuses on one particular aspect of the global water crisis – the privatization and commodification of water and water services. UN agencies and governments often refer to the essential human right to adequate access to water, its special cultural and religious value and the requirement for the governance of water to be democratic, just, transparent and accountable: 'Water should be treated as a social and cultural good, and not primarily as an economic commodity' (United Nations Economic and Social Council 2002). However, increasing privatization suggests a gap between the rhetoric of human rights and the treatment of water as a commodity governed by market forces.

Access to water and sanitation

An estimated 2.6 billion people – about 40% of humanity – lack adequate sanitation and 1.1 billion lack access to 'improved' water sources (WHO/UNICEF 2002). The lowest drinking water coverage rates are in Sub-Saharan Africa (58%) and in the Pacific (52%), but the largest numbers of unserved people are in Asia. India and China have nearly 1.5 billion people without adequate sanitation. The number of people without access to adequate sanitation rose between 1990 and 2000 (WHO 2002) and none of the regions with inadequate sanitation are on track for meeting the MDG sanitation target. A growing

Box D2.1 The importance of water to health

A child dies every 15 seconds from water-related diseases. This amounts to nearly 6000 deaths every day, the equivalent of 20 Jumbo jets crashing. In 2000, the estimated deaths due to diarrhoea and other diseases associated with water, sanitation and hygiene were 2,213,000.

The ingestion of contaminated water can lead to a variety of illnesses including cholera, typhoid and dysentery. Up to 2.1 million deaths a year due to diarrhoeal diseases are attributable to the 'water, sanitation and hygiene' risk factor, 90% in children under five. The malnutrition that accompanies diarrhoeal disease places millions more at greater susceptibility to death from other diseases.

Waterborne diseases also cause illness. For example, more than 200 million people worldwide are infected by schistosomiasis, causing 20,000 deaths a year; 88 million children under 15 are infected each year with schistosomes (bilharzia).

The supply of adequate quantities of water is important for household and personal hygiene. Disease can be spread through contaminated food and person-to-person contact. For example, trachoma is spread by flies, fingers and clothing coming into contact with infected eyes, especially among young children. It is common in areas that are hot, dry and dusty and where there is not enough water for people to wash regularly. It is the main cause of preventable blindness in the developing world, with six million people already permanently blinded. (*Source*: WHO and UNICEF 2000)

proportion of people without access to adequate water and sanitation live in the fast-growing peri-urban slums of third world cities.

There has been some improvement in access to an improved source of water since the 1990s, defined as access to a household connection, public standpipe, borehole, protected dug well, protected spring or rainwater collection tanks. It does not mean regular, easy and reliable access and the figures under-represent the extent of water insecurity. For example, water services to hundreds of thousands of families with a household connection or access to a public standpipe are often interrupted. People may also have their supply disconnected when they cannot pay municipal or private sector bills, and the use of automatic disconnection devices such as prepaid water meters is growing.

Since 1950 total water consumption has increased six-fold while the world population has doubled, indicating a highly skewed distribution of global water consumption worldwide. Each person in the US uses 250–300 litres of water a day, while the average person in the developing world uses only 10 litres for drinking, washing and cooking. Furthermore, the price of water relative to income shows huge differences from one country to another. In the UK a family of four spends 0.22% of its income on water, while a family of six in Ghana spends 20%, as well as the time spent queuing at a communal tap and taking the water home.

At the same time some consumers have become adept at capturing more of the state's water supplies at discounted rates. Large water consumers such as the corporate industrial and agricultural sectors and parts of the leisure industry pay less for consuming more – like golf tourism in Thailand, Indonesia, Malaysia and South Africa, which induces water 'scarcity' and groundwater pollution.

Commodification and privatization

'Commodification' refers to processes that reduce water to a private good to be traded and priced according to market signals. The metering and volumetric pricing of water is often advocated as a mechanism to reduce overconsumption and encourage conservation, and a rationale for the establishment of a market model in which the price of water and a 'willingness to pay' determines how water is produced, allocated, distributed and consumed (McDonald and Ruiters 2005).

Pricing water has been a crucial part of neoliberal and 'new public management reforms' allowing the 'true' cost of managing and supplying water to be recovered directly from consumers, and shifting the management and financing of public water services to private firms. Privatization includes selling public assets, tendering water concessions and awarding management contracts to private companies, usually to manage the supply and cost-recovery of water services, with the capital assets remaining in public ownership. They may also receive public subsidies to help them ensure coverage of the poor. Such arrangements, typically described as public-private partnerships, are sometimes structured to provide a public guarantee of private profits. For millions of people in peri-urban slums and informal settlements, privatization takes the form of an informal and unregulated market supplied by providers such as street vendors; even here, self-help schemes may be encouraged by governments as another way of shifting responsibility to communities.

The major private water companies supply water to only about 5% of the world's population, but their activities are crucial to the water question more generally. The biggest four had a total combined revenue of over US$ 25 billion in 2001 (Table D2.1). The profitability of the control and supply of water is evident not just in the revenue, but also in the vast sums spent on promoting privatization. The European Commission, and in particular the UK and French governments, have also supported the global liberalization of the water sector in support of the big corporations. Meanwhile for much of the past decade French magistrates have been investigating allegations of corruption against Suez and Vivendi, and convicted senior executives of paying bribes to obtain water contracts (Friends of the Earth 2003).

Most of the commodification and privatization of the water sector in developing countries has been undertaken at the bidding of the World Bank and IMF (McDonald and Ruiters 2005). Twelve of the 40 Fund loans to different countries in 2000 included conditions on water sector policy reforms that included increased cost recovery and privatization. Nearly 90% of Bank water and sanitation sector loans approved in 2001 contained cost recovery conditions and 86% contained privatization conditions. In 2002 and 2003 all loans promoted privatization. Cost recovery was promoted with 91% of funds in 2002 and 99% in 2003 (Grusky and Fiil-Flynn 2004). Some of the poorest countries, including Mozambique, Benin, Niger, Rwanda, Tanzania, Cameroon and Kenya, have privatized their water supply under pressure from the Fund and the Bank.

Various global forums foster the commodification of water. The Global Water Partnership is funded by several government aid agencies, the World Bank, UNDP and other organizations like the Ford Foundation. The World Water Council (WWC) was established to provide decision-makers with advice and assistance. Both institutions portray themselves as committed to human development, but are heavily influenced by the for-profit sector. Because the concept of water as a commodity is still unpopular and politically unacceptable, they provide a vehicle for the major water companies and multilateral banks to influence UN agencies and NGOs, and to disguise their commercial motives as public interest (Friends of the Earth 2003). This is especially apparent at the triennial World Water Forum, which resembles a UN global convention with thousands of participants and a concurrent meeting of senior politicians and bureaucrats who produce a ministerial statement.

The second forum in 2000 endorsed a large role for the for-profit sector while rejecting the principle that water be considered a fundamental human right. There was little reference to debt relief, overconsumption, community empowerment, land reform or corporate regulation, despite their importance in resolving water crises worldwide. The views of civil society organizations could only be presented from the floor or in their own press conferences. There was a much bigger media and civil society presence at the third forum

TABLE D2.1 Top corporate players in the world water industry

Corporation	Water subsidiary	Country base	Total revenue 2001 ($bn)	Total profits 2001 ($bn)	Water revenue 2001 ($bn)
Vivendi Universal	Vivendi Water	France	51.7	-1.02	11.90
Suez	ONDEO	France	37.2	1.8	8.84
RWE	Thames	Germany	55.5	1.11	2.8 (1 yr projected)
Bouygues	SAUR	France	17.9	0.301	2.18
United Utilities	United Utilities Water	UK	2.7	0.467	1.35
Severn Trent		UK	2.6	0.307	1.28
AWG plc	Anglian Water	UK	2.6	0.195	1.03
Kelda	Yorkshire Water	UK	1.1	0.231	0.8
Bechtel	International Water	US/UK	15.1 (2000 figures)	n/a	n/a

Source: Polaris Institute 2003

in 2003, but it was again used to promote policy proposals in favour of the corporate sector.

Trade agreements also seek to reduce government control over domestic water supplies. Under the General Agreement for Trade and Services (GATS), discussed in more detail in part A, WTO member states, under pressure from the EC in particular, are agreeing to liberalize their public water services and open the water sector to corporate investment. GATS also allows federal, state and local water regulations to be challenged as barriers to trade, and makes it extremely difficult to reverse failed privatization experiments.

Social, public health and environmental considerations clash with the imperatives of trade and commerce. That is why 146 NGOs from all over the world issued the Evian Challenge at a G8 summit, calling on the EU to withdraw its water requests of other WTO members immediately and to withdraw its proposal to bring 'water for human use' into the current GATS negotiations (Public Citizen 2003a).

Corporations have already started to sue governments to gain access to domestic water sources. For example, the US company Sun Belt is suing the government of Canada under the North American Free Trade Agreement because British Columbia banned water exports several years ago. The company says this law violates several NAFTA-based investor rights and is claiming US$ 220 million in compensation for lost profits (International Forum on Globalization 2005).

Under cover of these international trade agreements, companies are setting their sights on the mass transport of bulk water, for example by towing icebergs, diverting rivers and transporting water in super-tankers, and developing technology to tow huge sealed bags of fresh water across the ocean for sale. The US Global Water Corporation, a Canadian company, has signed an agreement with Sitka, Alaska, to export 18 billion gallons of glacier water a year to China, where it will be bottled in 'free trade' zones to take advantage of cheap labour (see part A, and Barlow and Clarke 2002). The company brochure entices investors 'to harvest the accelerating opportunity...as traditional sources of water around the world become progressively depleted and degraded'.

Commodification and privatization in practice

Given the importance of water to health, and the reshaping of relationships between government, business and civil society in the water sector, the commodification and privatization of water naturally cause concern in civil society worldwide – but have received surprising little attention in health policy circles.

16 Protesting against the privatization of water in Cochabamba, Bolivia.

WHO says governments hold the 'primary responsibility' for ensuring the realization of water rights (WHO 2003). Yet government bureaucracies are being shrunk to make way for private sector ownership and control, and responsibility for ensuring access to water is being transferred to individual

---

Box D2.2 *The public sector can do it just as well*

Porto Alegre City in Brazil has developed one of the best water utilities in Latin America. Porto Alegre's civil servants campaigned to bring the leftist Worker's Party to power in the city in 1989 and set up what is now cited by the UN as a model for local governance – participatory budgeting processes that allowed the new administration to raise taxes and invest them wisely and rationally for the city's overall prosperity. In ten years Porto Alegre improved water coverage to 99.5% of residents, and reduced infant mortality to 13.8 deaths per 1000 births compared to a national average of 65.

---

households. This is highlighted by the growing use of self-disconnecting pre-paid water meters in countries such as Brazil, the US, the Philippines, Namibia, Swaziland, Tanzania, Brazil, Nigeria and Curacao. Banned in the UK in 1999 because they were considered a health threat and an affront to the notion of citizenship, an international civil society campaign is under way against them (see Resources).

The transition from old to new roles and from old to new rules in this re-arrangement of relationships has not been altogether successful (Gutierrez et al. 2003). Granted, the private sector can fill the gap and provide a better service when governments are corrupt and inefficient. The non-profit independent sector has demonstrated its ability to improve access to water, particularly to the poor. But even well-intentioned private efforts cannot be sustained without a democratic, accountable state. There is no evidence of the intrinsic superiority of the private sector over the public (1997), and many examples of public sector effectiveness and efficiency (Box D2.2) and private sector collapses.

Furthermore, profit-maximizing companies tend to abuse their natural monopolies, underinvest, overcharge consumers, cut off supplies to those who cannot pay, neglect the environment, and shift pollution costs to the public. 'The rising level of private investment in water services has been accompanied by an alarming number of incidents involving corporate malfeasance and irresponsibility and rising charges that effectively exclude the poor' (Friends of the Earth 2003).

The capacity for effective regulation is often weak, in low and middle-income countries owing to an absolute lack of human and financial resources, while even strong regulation, as in the UK, can be costly and sometimes ineffective (Box D2.3). Countries that have seen privatization accompanied by cuts in public sector budgets are particularly susceptible to regulatory capture or failure.

> **Box D2.3 Regulating private water companies in the UK**
>
> Water privatization in England and Wales is sometimes cited as a positive model that dramatically reduced financial burdens on taxpayers, mobilized billions in private capital, improved water quality standards, and increased efficiency in water and sanitation services.
>
> The supposed success is partly ascribed to an effective regulatory framework with three sets of regulators – economic, environmental and quality. Various rules and rights have emerged, including price-setting by the economic regulator and a system of penalties and fines for contractual breaches and environmental offences. Private companies cannot disconnect any user and prepaid meters are outlawed.
>
> Nevertheless there is evidence of regulatory and market failure despite this robust regulatory framework, active consumer groups and an open media. Water companies continue to breach environmental standards and underinvest in infrastructure. The system tolerates high levels of leakage because it is considered more cost-effective to increase desalination capacity than to conserve water. Although profit margins and profits have recently decreased, it remains questionable whether the public and the environment are better served by privatization (Lobina and Hall 2001, Hall 2004).

Indeed, a major indictment of the thrust to privatize the water sector, especially in developing countries, has been the simultaneous insistence on downsizing governments and failing to invest in empowering civil society to hold government and the private sector accountable to social and environmental standards. In some countries, deregulation and privatization are actively supported by government officials and local elites who may benefit personally (Box D2.4).

Many governments are also being coaxed to 'decentralize' – dismantle central government water services and create smaller local structures – while changing their role from direct provider to stakeholder, facilitator or enabler of services. With no accompanying capacity development of the decentralized structures, this weakens regulatory capacity. Case studies from Accra, Dar es Salaam and Kathmandu reveal the power imbalance between poorly paid local civil servants, with insufficient information and staff support, having to oversee and negotiate with highly paid, well-connected and well-informed lawyers from multinational companies (Gutierrez et al. 2003).

Public sector failure is rarely improved by the introduction of for-profit companies. Communities can find their interests and views further marginal-

Water

Box D2.4 Water privatization hits the poor in the Philippines

With the support and advice of the World Bank, Manila agreed to one of the world's biggest water privatizations in 1997, when 25-year rights to operate and expand water and sewerage services were granted to Manila Water (co-owned by Bechtel and the Ayala family from the Philippines) and Maynilad Water (co-owned by Ondeo/Suez and the Lopez family from the Philippines).

Suez promised to lower rates and expand the infrastructure for the 7.5 million households covered by the concession. While the government promised a price freeze until 2007, the contract had several mechanisms permitting 'extraordinary price adjustments'. Other promises included 100% infrastructure coverage by 2007 and US$ 7.5 billion of new investments over 25 years. Unaccounted water would fall to 32% in 2007 and the city would save US$4 billion over 25 years.

Maynilad asked for the first rate increase only a year into the contract. The Asian Labor Network calculated that an ordinary Filipino family would therefore have to forgo 87–147 pesos a month, effectively depriving them of three full meals or three kilos of rice. The ordinary householder now has to spend a day's income on water.

Shortly before Maynilad took control almost 2000 workers were retired to lower costs. Six months into the contract, a further 750 were laid off. But it continued to seek contract renegotiations, including rate increases and postponement of obligations to meet investment targets. This should have caused it to forfeit its performance bond, but the company used legal action to block it.

The most controversial contract renegotiation involved passing foreign exchange losses on to consumers. This ensured that Suez could continue to use its major foreign corporate suppliers and consultants (rather than local sources) while billing consumers to cover for the effects of peso devaluation. However, this demand was refused by the government. The companies threatened to terminate their contract when, after six previous rate increases, they were unable to persuade the regulator to approve another one. (*Source*: Public Citizen 2003b)

ized where services or water projects have been defined by contracts between governments and for-profit contractors. When problems arise, blame is shifted to and fro between governments and contractors.

The private sector overestimates the cost of expanding water services. Investment needs to rise from an annual US$ 75 million to US$ 180 billion to achieve the MDG targets (Winpenny 2003), but the International Rivers Network says the targets could be met with an additional US$ 10 billion a year if more cost-effective and appropriate approaches were used, while Women in Europe for a Common Future agrees that much less money is needed if the technology is right (European Public Health Alliance 2003). A socially oriented approach to water services is often cheaper and politically more sustainable. Donor focus should therefore shift to other key players – government officials, NGOs, small-scale and micro enterprises and civil society organizations.

Finally, the argument that privatization fills the public financing gap (it

---

Box D2.5 Civil society fights back

In 1999, at the insistence of the World Bank, the Bolivian government awarded a concession to a private company to manage and supply water in Cochabamba. The local press reported that foreign investors acquired the city water system, worth millions of dollars, for less than US$ 20,000 of up-front capital in a sale in which they were the only bidder.

The government had promised no more than a 10% rise in prices as a result of the privatization, but Aguas del Tunari, a subsidiary of the Bechtel Corporation, implemented massive hikes up to three times higher. Families earning a minimum wage of US$ 60 a month suddenly faced water bills of US$ 20 a month.

Cochabamba residents shut down their city for four straight days in 2000, with a general strike led by a new alliance of labour community leaders and academics. The government was forced to agree to a price cut. When nothing happened, the residents took to the streets again. In response, the government declared martial law, arrested protest leaders and shut down radio stations. Protesters were shot at and even killed. But finally the government conceded and agreed to every demand. Bechtel's contract was cancelled and replaced with a community-controlled water system that is providing water more equitably and universally than before. Bechtel responded with an unsuccessful US$ 25 million lawsuit for lost profits.

Five years later a new privatization scheme was attempted in the city of El Alto, again with the full backing of the World Bank. Civil society fought back and once again won the battle through mass mobilizations (*Source*: Public Citizen 2003b).

Box D2.6 Two flushes a day

The government of South Africa, armed with World Bank policy advice, has promoted water commodification, cost recovery and privatization. Trade unions and other civil society groups initiated a campaign against the privatization of essential municipal services in 1997. A cholera outbreak affecting more than 150,000 people in KwaZulu-Natal province was triggered when municipal governments cut off the water supply. The government then revised its policy to include the provision of up to 6000 litres of free water per household per month, after which charges would be levied. A number of settlements had prepaid self-disconnection water meters installed, to ensure effective and efficient cost recovery. The 6000 litres are inadequate for many households, representing only two toilet flushes a day per person for a household of eight, for those lucky enough to have flush toilets. Secondly, the price of consumption over 6000 litres is unaffordable for many: to receive sufficient quantities for dignified living, poor households spend up to a quarter of their available income on water. The response by organized communities is often to reconnect disconnected systems illegally.

---

is better to have private sector investment than no investment) has begun to unravel. Less than 1% of total private investment in the water and sanitation sector has occurred in Sub-Saharan Africa, the region with the greatest need. Furthermore, private sector investment in developing countries has often been accompanied by financial losses and social protests in response to water cut-offs and rising prices. There is growing awareness that the private sector is unable to establish a model that combines profits and service to the poor. Transnational water companies are treading more softly, having found the profit potential is not quite what they expected in the developing world. They are more reluctant to manage the supply of water services to poor communities without financial guarantees from governments.

In some cases where profit has not reached targets or losses have been suffered, companies have used the World Bank's international arbitration court, the International Centre for the Settlement of Investment Disputes, or other mechanisms to transfer losses to the state or development budgets. They seek to drain the coffers of the Bank and other multilateral and bilateral aid agencies, including export credit agencies and local pension funds, to guarantee their own profits. The Camdessus report from the World Panel on Financing

Box D2.7 US citizens told to boil their water

In 1998 the city of Atlanta, Georgia, US, signed a 20-year US$ 428 million contract with United Water, a subsidiary of Suez. The company vastly overstated the amount of money it could save the city and vastly underestimated the work needed to maintain and operate the system. Almost immediately after signing the contract, it started asking for more money. When the city refused, it came back with a bill of US$ 80 million for additional expenditures. Again, the city refused to approve the payments.

Meanwhile United Water was improperly charging the city for work it did not do. It billed an extra US$ 37.6 million for additional service authorizations, capital repair and maintenance, of which the city paid nearly US$ 16 million. Pay was withheld for the rest because the work was either incomplete or had not been started. Routine maintenance was billed as 'capital repairs' and much-needed infrastructure rehabilitation was neglected. Trust in the company eroded to the point that the city spent US$1 million to hire inspectors to verify United Water's reports.

Desperate to cut costs, United Water reduced the number of employees from 700 to 300. The much-vaunted privatization savings still did not materialize, and the promise that a consumer rate hike could be averted through savings was broken. Sewer bill rates rose about 12% annually.

The deputy water commissioner admitted that people had lost confidence in the water itself due to the number of warnings to boil water before consumption and the frequency of discoloured water coming from their taps. Officials finally concluded it was time to end the relationship. Now they face the daunting task of taking back their water system and performing the needed upgrades neglected during United Water's tenure. (*Source*: Public Citizen 2003b)

Water Infrastructure (Winpenny 2003) clarified the intention of the Bank, the global water corporations and their lobby organizations to restructure international institutional and financial frameworks to reduce corporate liability and risk, and suggest new financial mechanisms to provide public financial guarantees and political risk insurance to the private sector.

The role of WHO and UNICEF

WHO and UNICEF have a long history of promoting access to water as an essential part of the right to health. However, their role and relevance in the water sector have diminished. In the face of influence from the World Bank, IMF, EC, WTO and corporate sector, they are not at the forefront of influencing the policy agenda – but they should be.

A joint WHO/UNICEF monitoring programme tracks progress towards the MDG targets related to water supply and sanitation. Its interim report lists the major obstacles to improving access in Sub-Saharan Africa as conflict and political instability, high rates of population growth and the low priority given to water and sanitation. Among the approaches shown to be effective in speeding up progress, it says, are 'decentralizing responsibility and ownership and providing a choice of service levels to communities, based on their ability and willingness to pay' (WHO/UNICEF 2004). These statements, which essentially endorse privatization and public sector fragmentation, could just as well have been found in a World Bank or WWC-inspired document.

Furthermore, the report's discussion of disparities in water coverage was entirely limited to intracountry disparities between urban and rural populations, between income quintiles and between men and women. Disparities between regions and countries were completely ignored. This is an inadequate analytical framework for an increasingly integrated world, and gives the false impression that unsustainably high consumption levels in rich countries have nothing to do with water problems in poor countries.

Right to Water, published by WHO and developed with UNHCR, made strong reference to the central role of government in instituting comprehensive regulatory measures with respect to pollution, disconnection of water supplies, land use and access to water supplies (WHO 2003). It says countries should adopt 'comprehensive and integrated strategies and programmes to ensure there is sufficient and safe water for present and future generations'. Such strategies and programmes may include reducing depletion of water resources; reducing and eliminating contamination of watersheds and water-related ecosystems; increasing the efficient use of water by end-users; and reducing water wastage in its distribution.

As the report notes, this requires a strong and central role for government, and one where individual and corporate freedom might need to be curtailed to ensure public benefits. Furthermore, where water services have been devolved, national governments must ensure that local authorities 'have at their disposal sufficient resources to maintain and extend the necessary water services and facilities'. Yet it falls short of identifying the factors that undermine the capacity of governments to fulfil their responsibilities, and the capacity of civil society to ensure they are held accountable. Meanwhile it says citizens may have to contribute financially and in other ways to ensure the realization of their rights to water. Worse still, it does this while accentuating the human rights obligations of government and downplaying those of the private sector.

The health sector response

Many civil society groups say water policy should be governed through democratic structures; the right to water should be a fundamental responsibility of governments; and comprehensive regulatory measures are needed on environmental protection and land use. There is less agreement on the role of the private sector. For example, the People's World Water Forum says water services must be provided by the public sector; where there are failures, they should be addressed directly rather than privatizing the sector. Others have no ideological opposition to public-private partnerships, especially when the public sector can be undemocratic and unaccountable. Some argue that public-private partnerships of the right kind can be beneficial, including partnerships with and improved government regulation of the many informal small-scale vendors in middle and low-income countries. They want clearer distinctions between profit-maximizing private companies and other private sector actors, and between the supply and pricing of water on market-based principles as opposed to social and environmental criteria.

Whether or not civil society agrees there should be a role for the private sector, it can unite on a number of positions. There is a re-emergence of highly politicized civil society activism in the water and health sectors. Health professionals' organizations cannot be expected to monitor water sector reform closely, but they can endorse, publicize and support nongovernmental networks, policy recommendations and position papers – see Resources for further information.

Recommendations

Strengthen the public sector The public sector needs to be strengthened, in low and middle-income countries in particular, to finance and manage the delivery of services and to regulate the private sector. This requires an institutional framework that promotes accountable and ethical government. Meanwhile, the recommendations of the Camdessus report should be rejected, at least until there are clear criteria and plans for establishing transparent, efficient and accountable statutory and non-statutory systems and procedures for regulating for-profit operations in the water sector.

Resist pro-privatization reforms Pro-privatization reforms promoted by the World Bank and certain donors (often under the cloak of the WWC, GWP,

Water

WWF and trade agreements, and with the backing of the corporate sector) should be resisted. Where significant public sector failures and corruption are found, donors should put greater emphasis on helping the non-profit private sector to develop skills, experience and aptitude to implement better water projects.

Increase overall investment in the water sector Increased private sector investment has not materialized or has resulted in problems, while development assistance is inadequate. When overall levels of aid began to rise again in 2001–2 (see part E, chapter 5), aid for water continued to decline. The bilateral water sector share dropped from 9% in 1999–2000 to 6% in 2001–2 (Manning 2003).

Stronger support for Water for All WHO and other agencies should adopt a bolder and more progressive position. They should research, monitor and challenge the effects of neoliberal water sector policy, and promote Water for All.

Resources

The Water Manifesto, developed by a group of officials, academics and civil society representatives, aims to establish fundamental principles to guide public policy on water management and supply. 'Water is a common good, it is the trust of humanity, and belongs to all of us. Water is a citizen's business. Water policy implies a high degree of democracy at local, national, continental and world levels,' it says (Global Initiators Committee for the Water Contract 1998, Petrella 2001).

The People's World Water Forum, based on feeder social movements from rural and urban areas across the world, calls for the decommodification of water. Its founding statement declares: 'Water is a human right... corporations have no business profiting from peoples' need for water... governments are failing in their responsibilities to their citizens and nature' (People's World Water Forum 2004).

The European Federation of Public Service Unions, which represents 8 million public service workers and works with a wide coalition of NGOs, also opposes privatization, citing evidence that public water systems give quantifiably better results on quality, cost, and accessibility (http://www.epsu.org).

For details of the campaign against prepaid water meters, including *Eleven reasons to oppose prepaid water meters*, see (<http://www.citizen.org/documents/opposeppm.pdf>) and Public Citizen (http://www.citizen.org).

References

Barlow M, Clarke T (2002*). Blue Gold. The fight to stop the corporate theft of the world's water.* New York, The New Press.

European Public Health Alliance (2003). *Civil society unites on water.* Brussels (http:// www.epha.org/a/701, accessed 15 March 2005).

Friends of the Earth International (2003). *Water justice for all: global and local resistance to the control and commodification of water.* Amsterdam, Friends of the Earth International.

Global Initiators Committee for the Water Contract (1998). *The Water Manifesto, The Right to Life.* Lisbon.

Grusky S and Fiil-Flynn M (2004). *Will the World Bank Back Down? Water Privatization in a Climate of Global Protest.* Washington DC, Public Citizen.

Gutierrez E et al. (2003). New Rules, New Roles: Does PSP Benefit the Poor? Synthesis Report. London, WaterAid and Tearfund.

Hall D (2004). [Personal Communication].

International Forum on Globalization (2005). *The free trade area of the Americas and the threat to water.* San Francisco (http://www.ifg.org/programs/ftaawater.htm, accessed 3 February 2005).

Jarmon, J (1997). Water Supply and Sanitation. In: Beall J ed. *A City for All: Valuing Difference and Working with Diversity.* London, Zed Books

Lobina E and Hall D (2001). UK water privatization – a briefing. London, PSIRU (http:// www.psiru.org/reports/2001-02-W-UK-over.doc, accessed 16 March 2005).

Manning, R (2003). *Development Cooperation 2003 Report – Efforts and Policies of the Members of the Development Assistance Committee.* Paris, OECD.

McDonald D and Ruiters G (2005). *The Age of Commodity, Water privatization in Southern Africa.* London, Earthscan.

Petrella R (2001). *The water manifesto: Arguments for a world water contract.* London, Zed Books.

People's World Water Forum (2004). Declaration of the People's World Water Movement (http://www.citizen.org/cmep/Water/conferences/articles.cfm?ID=11053, accessed 15 March 2005).

Polaris Institute (2003). *Global Water Grab: How Corporations are planning to take control of Local Water Services.* Ottawa (http://www.polarisinstitute.org/pubs/pubs_ pdfs/gwg_english.pdf, accessed 3 February 2005).

Public Citizen (2003a). *The Evian Challenge: a civil society call for the EU to withdraw its GATS water requests.* Washington DC (http://www.citizen.org/documents/ evianchallenge.pdf, accessed 3 February 2005).

Public Citizen (2003b). *Water Privatization Fiascos: Broken Promises and Social Turmoil.* Washington DC, Public Citizen.

United Nations Economic and Social Council (2002). *The right to water : 20/01/2003, E/C.12/2002/11. (General Comment No. 15).* New York, UN.

WHO (2002). *World Health Report 2002 – Reducing Risks, Promoting Healthy Life.* Geneva, WHO.

— (2003). *Right to water. Health and human rights publication series no. 3.* Geneva, WHO.

WHO/UNICEF (2002). *Global Water Supply and Sanitation Assessment 2000 Report.* Geneva, WHO.

Water

WHO/UNICEF (2004). *Joint Monitoring Programme for Water Supply and Sanitation, 2004. Meeting the MDG drinking water and sanitation target: a mid-term assessment of progress.* New York and Geneva, WHO and UNICEF.

Winpenny J (2003). *Financing water for all: Report of the World Panel on Financing Water Infrastructure.* Marseilles, World Water Council and Global Water Partnership.

D3 | Food

Undernutrition is by far the most important single cause of illness and death globally, accounting for 12% of all deaths and 16% of disability-adjusted life years lost. Low weight for age is associated with more than half of all deaths in young children, accounting for more than six million children a year (Pelletier et al. 1995). Babies who survive the early disadvantages of low birth weight are far more likely to develop obesity, diabetes and hypertension in adulthood. The costs of undernutrition in terms of lost development and productivity are enormous. Even mild to moderate undernutrition in the womb reduces future cognitive development. Thus nutrition plays a crucial role in the reproduction of poverty from one generation to the next, and must be tackled to meet the Millennium Development Goals (Box D3.1).

The number of people suffering from food insecurity and hunger is grow-

---

Box D3.1 How nutrition underpins the Millennium Development Goals

Goal 1: Eradicate extreme poverty and hunger Malnutrition erodes human capital, reduces resilience to shocks and reduces productivity (impaired physical and mental capacity).

Goal 2: Achieve universal primary education Malnutrition reduces mental capacity and school performance. Malnourished children are less likely to enrol in school, and more likely to enrol later.

Goal 3: Promote gender equality and empower women Better-nourished girls are more likely to stay in school and to have more control over future choices.

Goal 4: Reduce child mortality Malnutrition is directly or indirectly associated with more than half of all child mortality.

Goal 5: Improve maternal health Malnutrition, in particular iron deficiency and vitamin A deficiency, increases the risk of maternal mortality.

Goal 6: Combat HIV/AIDS, TB, malaria, and other diseases Malnutrition hastens the onset of AIDS among HIV-positive people, and generally increases susceptibility to infectious diseases.

(*Source*: SCN 2004)

---

ing – even though food production has doubled in the past 40 years, as has production per head, while food prices are at an all-time low. This chapter aims to explain why malnutrition exists in so many regions and countries when there is enough food; why hunger and food insecurity have grown in spite of declining food prices; why the distribution of available food is heavily skewed toward the rich; and how the increased concentration of power in the hands of a small number of vast corporations has resulted in the accumulation of huge profits on the one hand and chronic food insecurity for millions of people on the other.

Figures, trends and causes

Every day 799 million people in developing countries – about 18% of the world's population – go hungry. In South Asia one person in four goes hungry, and in Sub-Saharan Africa the share is as high as one in three. There were reductions in the number of chronically hungry people in the first half of the 1990s, but the number increased by over 18 million between 1995 and 1997 (Food and Agricultural Organization 2003).

The situation regarding the proportion and numbers of people who are undernourished is even bleaker. The number of undernourished people actually increased by 4.5 million a year in the late 1990s. Twenty-six countries, most already with a large proportion of their population undernourished,

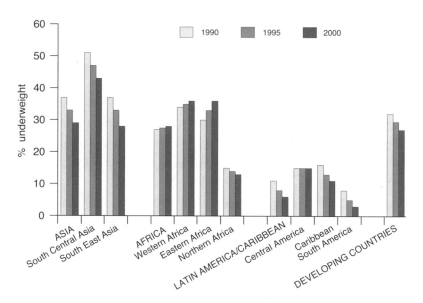

Figure D3.1 Trends in child malnutrition in developing countries, 1990–2000 (*Source:* SCN 2004)

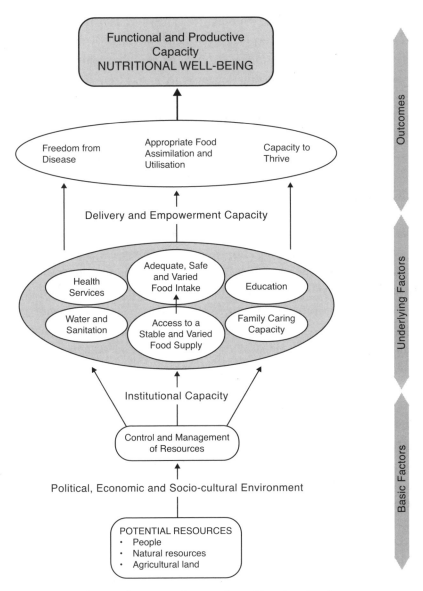

Figure D3.2 Determinants of nutritional well-being
(*Source*: **UNICEF 1994**)

experienced increases: between 1992 and 2000, the number of hungry people went up by almost 60 million (Food and Agricultural Organization 2003). Only three of the 10 African countries with maternal nutrition data showed a decline in the last decade in the prevalence of severe maternal undernutrition (defined as a body mass index of less than 16) (Standing Committee on Nutrition 2004).

Around 175 million children under five are estimated to be underweight, a third of preschool children are stunted, 16% of newborn babies weigh less than 2.5 kg, and 243 million adults are severely malnourished. Two billion women and children are anaemic (James et al. 2001), 250 million children suffer from vitamin A deficiency and two billion people are at risk from iodine deficiency (Micronutrient Initiative 1998). The proportion and absolute number of malnourished children has increased in Sub-Saharan Africa (see Figure D3.1).

Malnutrition has different levels of causation, as indicated by UNICEF's conceptual model. This illustrates not only immediate biological causes such as illness and inadequate food and nutrients, but also what underlies them, such as price, availability, and economic and political factors (UNICEF 1994) (Figure D3.2). It is strongly linked with poverty: poor children are more likely to be underweight at birth (Gillespie et al. 2003) and less likely to receive energy-rich complementary food (Brown et al. 1998) and iodized salt (UNICEF 1998). At least they are more likely to be breastfed, and for longer, in poorer countries (Butz et al. 1984), although HIV is now eroding this advantage. Poorer children live in environments that predispose them to illness and death (Esrey 1996), are less likely to live in households with safe water or sanitation (Huttly et al. 1997) and more likely to be exposed to indoor air pollution from coal and biomass fuel such as wood or animal dung used for cooking and heating, coupled with inadequate ventilation (Bruce et al. 2000).

The food production and supply system

The global value of trading in food grew from US$ 224 billion in 1972 to US$ 438 billion in 1998. The globalization of food systems is nothing new, but the current pace and scale of change are unprecedented. Food now constitutes 11% of global trade in terms of value, a higher percentage than fuel (Pinstrup-Andersen and Babinard 2001). This increase has been accompanied throughout the food chain by the consolidation of agricultural and food companies into large transnational corporations, whose growth has allowed them astounding control in key sectors such as meat, cereal, processing and retail (Table D3.1). In 1994, 50% of US farm products came from 2% of the farms (Lehman and Krebs 1996). In the agrochemical sector ten companies control 81% of the US$ 29 billion global market. This dominance is increasing with the aggressive marketing of genetically modified seeds (Box D3.2).

The corporations have developed global brand names and global marketing strategies, albeit adapted to local tastes. They are defined by the global sourcing of their supplies; the centralization of strategic assets, resources and decision-making; and the maintenance of operations in several countries to serve a more unified global market. The rise of the meat industry exemplifies

TABLE D3.1 Corporate control of US food sectors

Sector	Concentration ratio (%)	Companies involved
Beef packers	81	Tyson (IBP), ConAgra Beef Cos, Cargill (Excel), Farmland National Beef Pkg Co
Pork packers	59	Smithfield, Tyson (IBP), ConAgra (Swift), Cargill (Excel)
Pork production	46	Smithfield Foods, Premium Standard Farms (ContiGroup), Seaboard Corp, Triumph Pork Group (Farmland Managed)
Broilers	50	Tyson Foods, Gold Kist, Pilgrim's Pride, ConAgra
Turkeys	45	Hormel (Jennie-O Turkeys), Butterball (ConAgra), Cargill's Turkeys, Pilgrim's Pride
Animal feed plants	25	Land O'Lakes Farmland Feed LLC Purina Mills, Cargill Animal Nutrition (Nutrena), ADM (Moorman's), JD, Heiskell & Co
Terminal grain handling facilities	60	Cargill, Cenex Harvest States, ADM, General Mills
Corn exports	81	Cargill-Continental Grain, ADM, Zen Noh
Soybean exports	65	Cargill-Continental Grain, ADM, Zen Noh
Flour milling	61	ADM Milling, ConAgra, Cargill, General Mills
Soybean crushing	80	ADM, Cargill, Bunge, AGP
Ethanol production	49	ADM, Minnesota Corn Producers (ADM has 50% equity stake), Williams Energy Services, Cargill
Dairy processors	n/a	Dean Foods (Suiza Foods Corp), Kraft Foods (Philip Morris), Dairy Farmers of America, Land O'Lakes
Food retailing	38	Kroger, Albertson's, Safeway, Wal-Mart, Ahold

Source: Lang 1999

many of the processes at play in the new food system. Meat production has increased five-fold over the last 50 years and has doubled since 1997, facilitated by a massive increase in the production of animal feeds. Since the early 1960s, livestock has increased from three billion to more than five billion, and fowl from four billion to 16 billion. Producing meat requires large amounts of grain, and most of the corn and soya beans harvested worldwide are used to fatten livestock.

A globalized sector has emerged, with global sourcing of feed inputs and global marketing of meat-related commodities. Sanderson (1986) used the

Food

> ## Box D3.2 *Genetic engineering and nutrition*
>
> The claim that this technology will lead to the development of highly nutritious cereals that could contribute to the fight against malnutrition is an important justification for the investment in genetically engineered seeds and crops. However, miracles like 'golden rice' and 'protein potatoes' will not solve the problem of vitamin A deficiency and protein malnutrition.
>
> Golden rice is a genetically engineered rice which is supposed to produce 30µg/100gm of beta carotene, or vitamin A, after development. The levels of beta carotene are actually much lower, while farmers' varieties such as Himalayan red rice have much higher levels of vitamin A. Food crops and edible plants such as amaranth leaves, coriander leaves and curry leaves have 1000 – 1400 µg of vitamin A, 70 times more than 'golden rice'. Golden rice will thus reduce vitamin A availability and hence increase vitamin A deficiency and blindness.
>
> While not producing more nutrition, genetic engineering creates new public health risks. Its promoters say it is no different from conventional breeding, and hence poses no new health or ecological risks – but conventional breeding does not transfer genes from bacteria and animals to plants. It does not put fish genes into potatoes or scorpion genes into cabbage. It does not put antibiotic resistance markers and viral promoters in plants. These pose new public health risks.
>
> We are in danger of creating a food and health system in which biodiversity and biotechnology are owned and controlled by one or two gene giants who deny citizens freedom to choose independent science, and enclose the 'commons' of biodiversity and knowledge through patents and intellectual property rights. In South Africa, for example, Monsanto completely controls the national market for genetically modified seed, 60% of the hybrid maize market and 90% of the wheat market. Three companies (Cargill, Pioneer and CP-DeKalb) control almost 70% of the Asian seed market, supplying hybrid seed for 25% of the total corn area. Four corporations now own nearly 45% of all patents for staple crops such as rice, maize, wheat and potatoes. (*Source*: Shiva 2004)

term 'world steer' to capture the global production of beef: 'Regardless of nationality of ownership, the world steer reorganizes beef production to meet international standards through expensive feeds and medicines, concentrated feedlots and centralized slaughtering. The displacement of traditional marketing and processing means that small sideline producers lose access to markets...As a result they lose milk and meat.'

The system is a web of contractual relationships turning the farmer into a contractor, who provides the labour and often some capital but never owns the product as it moves through the supply chain. Fewer and fewer households can subsist on herding, fishing or forestry. Every other hungry person is living in a farm household, on marginal lands where environmental degradation and exclusion threaten agricultural production. Poor fishers are seeing their catches reduced by commercial fishing, and foresters are losing their rights as logging companies move in under government concessions. The average land holding per head among rural farmers in developing countries declined from 3.6 hectares in 1972 to 0.26 hectares in 1992 – and continues to fall. If the poor are to benefit from the livestock revolution they must forsake mixed farming and become contract farmers for food corporations, in precarious dependence on distant markets and prices (McMichael 2001).

A right or a commodity?

Food not only fulfils a fundamental need but also has great symbolic and social value. Legitimization of the erosion of control of such an important commodity by communities and nations has required the hijacking and redefinition of basic terms such as development and food security. More specifically the idea of food security has been reconstructed as a global market function based on the presence of a free market and governed by corporate rather than social criteria. This position was boldly stated by a senior US official at the 1986 Uruguay Round, which laid the foundations of the WTO Agreement on Agriculture: 'The idea that developing countries should feed themselves is an anachronism from a bygone era. They could better ensure their food security by relying on US agricultural products, which are available in most cases at much lower cost' (quoted in Bello 2000).

The North American Free Trade Agreement between the US, Canada and Mexico is an early example of this new model (discussed in more detail in Part A). The overproduction of food supported by massive subsidies in the US and Europe in particular has led to the 'dumping' of food on developing countries. US subsidies result in major crops being put on the international market at well below their production costs: wheat by an average of 43% below cost of production; rice 35%; soya beans 25%; and cotton 61% (Institute for Agriculture and Trade Policy 2004). This depression of commodity prices has a devastating effect on farmers in developing countries. Subsidies to farming in the OECD countries, which totalled US\$ 311 billion in 2001 (US\$ 850 million

Food

17 Market, Ethiopia. Third World producers are under threat from heavily-subsidized EU and US farmers.

a day) displace farming in the developing countries, costing the world's poor countries about US$ 24 billion a year in lost agricultural and agroindustrial income (International Food Policy Research Institute 2004).

There has also been a decline in agricultural and rural investment in many developing countries, resulting in falling agricultural productivity. Only about 4.2% of land under cultivation in Africa is irrigated; fertilizer application is 15% lower today than in 1980; the number of tractors per worker is 25% lower than in 1980 and the lowest in the world (World Bank 2002). Agricultural productivity per worker has fallen by about 12% since the early 1980s, while yields have been level or falling for many crops in many countries. Cereal yields average 1120 kg per hectare, compared with 2067 kg per hectare for the world as a whole. Yields of the most important staple food grains, tubers and legumes (maize, millet, sorghum, yams, cassava, groundnuts) in most African countries are no higher today than in 1980. Africa's share of world agricultural trade fell from 8% in 1965 to 3% in 1996 (Stevens and Kennan 2001).

The story is similar in nearly all developing countries. For example, the average Indian family of four reduced consumption of foodgrains by 76 kg between 1998 and 2003 – to levels last seen just after Independence (Patnaik 2004). This dramatic fall can be traced to the collapse in rural employment and incomes resulting from liberalization of the agricultural sector.

The shift away from national food sufficiency has increased drastically across developing countries – world cereal, wheat and rice imports have grown from 80, 46 and 6.5 million metric tonnes respectively in 1961 to 278, 120 and 27 million metric tonnes in 2001. The fastest growth of food imports has occurred in Africa, which accounted for 18% of world imports in 2001, up from 8% 15 years earlier (FAO 2004). Governments are often powerless to reverse this as policies imposed by the IMF/World Bank, such as removing subsidies for fertilizer or charging user fees for dipping cattle, directly affect the cost of agricultural inputs.

It is too late to reverse the demise of the agricultural sector in many of these countries. Moreover, especially in urban settings, people now want to eat imported foodstuffs such as wheat and rice. Reliance on the export of selected agricultural products to a few key markets makes many developing countries especially vulnerable to policy changes in these markets. For example, the European Union accounts for about half the exports to African countries and about 41% of imports. Ironically the least food-secure countries are most reliant on agricultural exports and therefore most vulnerable to policy and market changes.

Women are bearing the brunt of globalization, trade liberalization and HIV/AIDS. They are responsible for 80% of food production in Africa, including the most labour-intensive work such as planting, fertilizing, irrigating, weeding, harvesting and marketing. They achieve this despite unequal access to land (less than 1% of land is owned by women), to inputs such as improved seeds, fertilizer, information and credit (less than 10% of credit provided to small farmers goes to women). Their work also extends to food preparation, as well as nurturing activities. There is convincing evidence that women with similar inputs are more efficient farmers than men (Carloni 1987).

In summary, the current wave of liberalization is occurring in the context of massive concentration and control of the food system by corporations based in developed countries. Liberalization of agricultural trade has therefore further strengthened and consolidated an international division of labour in agriculture. In 1990, the OECD countries controlled 90% of the global seed market. From 1970–1996, the OECD share of the volume of world cereal exports rose from 73% to 82%; the US remained the world's major exporter of commercial crops such as maize, soya bean and wheat; and the share of Africa, Latin

Food

America and Asia in world cereal imports increased to nearly 60% (Pistorius and van Wijk 1999). Liberalization has, on the whole, contributed to increasing inequalities within both developed and developing countries.

Globalization and diet

The globalization of the food chain and the concomitant concentration of power and control by transnational corporations are also changing diets rapidly, such as the sharp rise in meat consumption among urbanized populations in developing countries. This shift is accelerating as the corporations seek new markets. McDonalds and other similar chains are taking full advantage of the opportunities: by 1994 a third of McDonalds restaurants were outside the US, accounting for half of its profits, and four out of every five new ones are overseas. Many developing countries have their own versions of McDonalds. Within a comparatively short time from their introduction in China, a poll found that two in three Chinese people recognized the brand name of Coca Cola, 42% recognized Pepsi and 40% recognized Nestle.

The global marketing and systematic moulding of taste is a central feature of the new globalization of the food industry (Barnett and Cavanagh 1994). In Vietnam, 'international branded ice cream is better funded and has the advantage of up-market foreign cachet, both expanding the market in dairy products (in a low dairy consumption country) and their market share' (Lang 2001). In the US alone the food industry spends over US$ 30 billion on direct advertising and promotions – more than any other industry. In 1998, promotion costs for popular sweet bars were US$ 10–50 million, for soft drinks up to US$ 115.5 million and McDonald's just over a billion (Nestle and Jacobsen 2001). Food advertising expenditures in the developing countries are lower but growing fast as incomes increase. In south east Asia, for example, food advertising expenditures tripled between 1984 and 1990, from US$ 2 billion to 6 billion. Mexicans now drink more Coca Cola than milk (Jacobsen 2000).

The uptake of a high-fat, high-sugar diet is especially pervasive among newly urbanized populations. Between 1989 and 1993 the number of rich urban Chinese households consuming a low-fat diet (less than 10% of calories from fat) fell from 7% to 0.3% and those consuming a high-fat diet (more than 30% of calories from fat) rose from 23% to 67% (Popkin 2001). Transitions in diet that took more than 50 years in Japan have occurred in less than two in China. The savings in preparation time, the convenience and sometimes the value for money of street and fast foods are important factors, but the dietary transition has also been explicitly encouraged through investments such as the World

Bank's US$ 93.5 million loan to China for 130 feedlots and five beef processing centres for its nascent beef industry and the entry of large food multinationals and food retailers (McMichael 2004).

Muted responses

Developing countries cannot afford these epidemics of under- and over-nutrition. The direct medical costs of obesity are estimated at US$ 40 billion per year in the US alone. Prevention is the only feasible solution for developing countries. However, in the face of the monumental global changes in production, marketing and retail driving these epidemics, the present dominant focus on individual lifestyle changes (eat less fat, cut down on salt intake etc) is clearly not sufficient. This ignores repeated and expensive failures in attempts to change diets through improving knowledge alone. As Nestle et al. (1998) point out when discussing the North American diet: 'Despite two decades of recommendations for fat reduction and the introduction of nearly 6000 new fat-modified foods within the last five years, the population as a whole does not appear to be reducing its absolute intake of dietary fat.'

In summary, diets across the globe are being shaped by a concentrated and global food industry that is continually battling to increase demand and sales. Public health attempts to restrict this are being resisted fiercely (Chopra and Darnton-Hill 2004). Moreover, the international agencies are under great pressure from big business. The privatization of public health, one aspect of economic globalization, is impoverishing and commercializing the UN agencies concerned with nutrition, food policy and public health. This is the context for the 'private-public-people-partnerships', such as GAIN (Global Action and Information on Nutrition) instituted by the Gates Foundation, that are said to be a way of delivering health more effectively and efficiently. But these partnerships have the potential to increase market penetration by the transnational food and drug industry. The WHO/FAO technical report on diet, nutrition and the prevention of chronic disease (2002) is a recent example of the food industry creating a smokescreen of apparently conflicting scientific data to subvert WHO's response to the overnutrition epidemic (Cannon 2004). The experience of the Codex Alimentarius Commission provides another example (see Box D3.3).

Multilateral collective strategies, at least the development of international standards and national legislation, are essential to protect and promote national food security and public health (Chopra et al. 2002) and require strong leadership from international agencies. Civil society will have to play a more active role. The concept of food security must be recaptured and reframed in

Food

Box D3.3 Regulating the food industry

The Codex Alimentarius Commission is an important body jointly established by FAO and WHO to develop food standards, guidelines and related texts such as codes of practice. These aim to protect consumers' health, ensure fair practices in the food trade, and promote coordination of all food standards work undertaken by international and governmental bodies and NGOs.

The Codex has assumed much greater power since the establishment of the WTO, which will use Codex standards in trade disputes. A 1993 review found it had 26 representatives from public interest groups compared with 662 industry representatives. Nestlé, one of the largest food companies in the world, sent over 30 representatives, more than most countries. Only 7% and 10% of representatives came from Africa and Latin America respectively, compared to over 60% from Europe and North America. Nearly 40% of the participants on the working group on standards for food additives and contaminants represented transnational corporations of industry federations, including 61 representatives from the world's largest food and agrochemical companies (Avery et al. 1993). Despite agreement to address these imbalances, 71% of developed countries were represented at a key meeting in 2002 but only 18% of developing countries. There were 95 government delegates (43% of participants) and 90 industry delegates, and the majority of industry delegates were on government delegations.

---

public health and environmental terms. A corporate model of monoculture and standardized processed foods expands the distance between producers and consumers, appropriates increasingly scarce land in the global south for export agriculture, accelerates adverse climatic effects, and concentrates inordinate power in the hands of a few transnational corporations to determine who gets to eat what. Reversing this process requires coordinated action on many fronts to restore food to the status of a human right as well as a cultural right, where ecological and cultural diversity is respected and sustained, and food is once again recognized as more than just another commodity.

References

ACC/SCN (2004). *Fifth Report on the World Nutrition Situation: Nutrition for Improved Development Outcomes*. Geneva, ACC/SCN.

Avery N, Drake M, Lang T (1993). *Cracking the codex: a report on the Codex Alimentarius Commission*. London, National Food Alliance.

Barnett R, Cavanagh J (1994). *Global dreams: Imperial corporations and new world order*. New York, NY, Simon & Schuster.

Bello W (2000). Does world trade need World Trade Organization? *Businessworld*, 11 January.

Brown K, Dewey K, Allen L (1998). *Complementary feeding of young children in developing countries: A review of the literature*. Geneva, World Health Organization.

Bruce N, Perez-Padilla R, Albalak R (2000). Indoor air pollution in developing countries: A major environmental and public health challenge. *Bulletin of the World Health Organization*, 78:1078–92.

Butz WP, Habicht JP, DaVanzo J (1984). Environmental factors in the relationship between breastfeeding and infant mortality: The role of sanitation and water in Malaysia. *American Journal of Epidemiology*, 119:516–25.

Cannon G (2004). Why the Bush administration and the global sugar industry are determined to demolish the 2004 WHO global strategy on diet, physical activity and health. *Public Health Nutrition*, 7:369–380.

Carloni A, ed. (1987). *Women in development: A.I.D.'s experience, 1973–1985, Vol. 1. Synthesis paper*. Washington, DC, United States Agency for International Development.

Chopra M, Darnton-Hill I (2004). Diet and Tobacco: Not so different after all? *British Medical Journal*, 328:1558–1560.

Chopra M, Galbraith S, Darnton-Hill I (2002). A global response to a global problem: the epidemic of overnutrition. *Bulletin of the World Health Organization*, 80:952–8.

Esrey SA (1996). Water, waste, and well-being: A multicountry study. *American Journal of Epidemiology*, 143:608–23.

Food and Agriculture Organization (2003). *World Hunger Report*. Rome, FAO.

Gillespie S, McLachlan M, Shrimpton R (2003). *Combating malnutrition. Time to act*. Washington, DC, The World Bank Group.

Huttly SR, Morris SS, Pisani V (1997). Prevention of diarrhoea in young children in developing countries. *Bulletin of the World Health Organization*, 75:163–74.

Institute for Agriculture and Trade Policy (2004). *US dumping on world agricultural markets*. IATP, Minnesota (http://www.iatp.org, accessed 23rd August 2004).

International Food and Policy Research Institute (2004). *How much does it hurt? Impact of agricultural polices on developing countries*. Washington DC, IFPRI (http: www.ifpri.org, accessed 14th August 2004).

Jacobsen MF (2000). *Liquid candy: How soft drinks are harming Americans' health*. Washington, DC, Center for Science in the Public Interest.

James P (2001). Ending malnutrition by 2020: An agenda for change in the Millenium. *Food and Nutrition Bulletin Supplement*. August 2001.

Lang T (1999). Food and Nutrition. In: Weil O, McKee M, Brodin M, Oberle D, eds. *Priorities for public health actions in the European Union*. Paris, Société français de santé publique.

Lang T (2001). Trade, public health and food. In: McKee M, Garner P, Stott R, eds. *International Co-operation in Health*. Oxford, Oxford University Press.

Lehman K, Krebs A (1996). Control of the world's food supply. In: Mander J, Goldsmith E, eds. *The case against the global economy*. San Francisco, CA, Sierra Club Books.

Food

McMichael P (2001). The impact of globalisation, free trade and technology on food and nutrition in the new millennium. *The Proceedings of the Nutrition Society*, 60:215–20.

— (2004). *Development and social change: A global perspective*, 3rd ed. London, Sage Press.

Micronutrient Initiative (1998). *Fighting the hidden hunger*. Ottawa, MI Publications.

Nestle M, Jacobsen MF (2001). Halting the obesity epidemic: A public health approach. *Public Health Reports*, 115:12–21.

Patnaik U (2004). External trade, domestic employment and food security: Recent outcomes of trade liberalisation and neo-liberal economic reforms in Inda. at: *International Workshop on Policies against Hunger III*. Berlin, German Federal Ministry of Consumer Protection, Food and Agriculture, 20–22 October.

Pelletier D, et al. (1995). The effects of malnutrition on child mortality in developing countries. *Bulletin of the World Health Organization*, 73:443–8.

Pinstrup-Andersen P, Babinard J (2001). Globalisation and human nutrition: Opportunities and risks for the poor in developing countries. *African Journal of Food and Nutritional Sciences*, 1:9–18.

Pistorius R, van Wijk J (1999). *The exploitation of plant genetic information. Political strategies in crop development*. Oxon, CABI Publishing.

Popkin BM (2001). Nutrition in transition: the changing global nutrition challenge. *Asia Pacific Journal of Clinical Nutrition*, 10(Suppl):S13–8.

Sanderson S (1986). Emergence of the 'World Steer': Internationalisation and foreign domination in Latin American cattle production. In: Tullis FH, Hollist WL, eds. *Food, the State and international political economy*. Lincoln, University of Nebraska Press.

Standing Committee on Nutrition (SCN) (2004). *Fifth report on the world nutrition situation: Nutrition for improved development outcomes*. Geneva, UN Standing Committee on Nutrition.

Shiva V (2004) (personal communication).

Stevens C, Kennan J (2001). Food aid and trade. In: Devereux S, Maxwell S, eds. *Food security in Sub-Saharan Africa*. Pietermaritzburg, University of Natal Press.

UNICEF (1994). *State of the World's Children*. New York, NY, UNICEF.

UNICEF (1998). *State of the World's Children*. New York, NY, UNICEF.

WHO (2002). *Diet, nutrition and the prevention of chronic diseases. Report of the joint WHO/FAO expert consultation*. Geneva, World Health Organization (WHO Technical Report Series, No. 916).

World Bank (2002). *From Action to Impact: the Africa Region's Rural Strategy*. Washington, DC, World Bank, Rural Development Operations, the Africa Region.

D4 | Education

Some 135 million children between the ages of 7 and 18 in the developing world have never been to school (Gordon 2003). Globally, over 100 million children aged 6–12 are not enrolled in primary school, while 137 million young people will begin their adult lives lacking the basic tools of literacy and numeracy (UNESCO 2004). The burden of illiteracy, like the burden of disease, falls overwhelmingly on those who are female, poor and rural. This chapter discusses why all this should concern health sector policy-makers and activists, and suggests how education and health activists could together address the common causes of inequality in health and education.

Education as a determinant of health outcomes

Education – particularly for girls and women – improves health outcomes. Even a few years of basic education is correlated with greater use of health services, increased social status and decision-making power for women, and better health outcomes. For example, education levels are strongly predictive of better knowledge, safer behaviour and reduced HIV infection rates – so much so that education has been described as 'the single most effective preventive weapon against HIV/AIDS' (UNAIDS 2002, World Bank 2002) (see Box D4.1).

Education improves health outcomes for two main reasons. It provides some protection from such shocks as ill health and disability, price and credit swings, and natural and environmental disasters by enabling more secure employment, higher incomes, and better access to economic assets and credit. Even among those with similar incomes, the educated are generally healthier than the uneducated (Pritchett and Summers 1996), because:

- education equips them to understand, evaluate and apply facts;
- it increases the ability to acquire and use health-related information and services (World Bank 1993, WHO 2003);
- it gives greater bargaining power in household decisions and personal relationships – particularly important for women, as it often translates into increased allocation of household resources to child health, schooling and nutrition (Thomas 1990, Herz and Sperling 2004); and
- it increases social status.

Child and maternal mortality Each extra year of maternal education in the

> ### Box D4.1 Education as a determinant of health outcomes: the example of HIV/AIDS
>
> Research on the social determinants of HIV/AIDS has shown education levels to be strongly predictive of better knowledge, safer behaviour and, most importantly, reduced infection rates – so much so that education has been described as the 'social vaccine' and 'the single most effective preventive weapon against HIV/AIDS' (UNAIDS 2002, World Bank 2002).
>
> Young people's risk of contracting HIV in Uganda appears to halve when they have a complete primary school education, even without specific AIDS education (DeWalque 2004, Global Campaign for Education 2004a). This finding, echoed by similar research in other countries, provides strong evidence of the positive impact of primary school completion on actual HIV outcomes.
>
> One reason that schooling reduces HIV risk is that it increases knowledge of the disease and is correlated with changes in sexual behaviour. Literate women are three times more likely than illiterate women to know that a healthy-looking person can have HIV, and four times more likely to know the main ways to avoid AIDS, according to a 32–country study (Vandemoortele and Delamonica 2000). Evidence from 17 countries in Africa and four in Latin America shows that better educated girls delay sexual activity longer, and are more likely to require their partners to use condoms (UNAIDS and WHO 2000). Education also accelerates behaviour change among young men, making them more receptive to prevention messages and more likely to adopt condom use.

developing world reduces under-five child mortality by 5–10% (UNICEF 2004). Women's educational attainment explained more than 80% of the decline in infant mortality from 1983–1999 in five Indian states, and was a far more powerful explanatory variable than public spending on health services or changes in household income (Bhalla et al. 2003). In Africa, children born to mothers with five years of primary education are 40% more likely to survive to age five (Summers 1994). Interestingly, child mortality is influenced by the extent of inequality between men's and women's education levels, and not just the absolute level of women's education (Abu-Ghaida and Klasen 2004).

Women who have been to school are less likely to die during childbirth. Every additional year of education will prevent two maternal deaths in every 1000 women. Education also improves maternal health by increasing knowledge about health-care practices and the use of health services during pregnancy and birth; improving nutrition; and increasing birth spacing. For example, in Bangladesh – where women typically eat last and least – women with at least a fifth-grade education are more likely to eat more in pregnancy, improving chances for a healthy outcome for themselves as well as their infants (Karim et al. 2002).

Malnutrition Improvements in women's education explained nearly half the decline in child malnutrition in 63 developing countries between 1970 and 1990, with increased food availability a distant second. 'Partly because a mother uses her new knowledge and the additional income she earns from it to improve diets, care, and sanitation for her children, female education is probably the strongest instrument we have for reducing infant mortality and child malnutrition' (Smith and Haddad 1999). These results are echoed in other studies.

Entitlement and empowerment As mentioned above, educated women are more likely to make use of health services, including those that effectively prevent childhood disease (Sandiford et al. 1995). Globally, educated mothers are about 50% more likely to immunize their children than are uneducated mothers (Herz and Sperling 2004). They tend to be able to exercise greater autonomy in personal and sexual relationships, which allows them to delay first sexual activity, marry later, begin childbearing later, have fewer children, and resist practices such as female genital cutting, domestic violence and early marriage for their own daughters (see Box D4.2) (Jejeebhoy 1998, Sen 1999, Herz and Sperling 2004). Doubling the proportion of women with a secondary education would reduce average fertility rates from 5.3 to 3.9 children per woman, according to a 65–country analysis of fertility and secondary school attainment (Subbarao and Raney 1995). But it is not just the level of women's education that matters: the lower the gap between men's and women's education, the lower the fertility rate (Klasen 1999).

The impact of health on education Of course, ill health also has a significant negative impact on education outcomes. Diseases such as malaria, tuberculosis, and HIV/AIDS keep millions of children – and teachers – away from the classroom temporarily or permanently. Millions more turn up at school every day suffering from problems like malnutrition, gastroenteritis and parasite infection, which impair their concentration and can diminish cognitive abilities in the long term. A school-based health and nutrition programme that provided

Box D4.2 Education and women's health

Educated women are less likely to have their daughters subjected to female genital cutting, and educated girls are less likely to undergo it, studies suggest. In Ivory Coast 55% of women with no education had undergone it, while the prevalence was 24% among those with a primary education or more (WHO 1998).

The increased earning capacity and social standing, later age of marriage, and access to information and health services that come along with education may help women resist domestic violence. Women with some formal schooling are more likely to leave abusive relationships than women with no schooling (Herz and Sperling 2004). Controlling for other influences, education does deter violence. Studies in India show that women's education can affect the probability of being beaten; having had schooling can result in better physical outcomes (Sen 1999, Jejeebhoy 1998).

PROGRESA (*Programa Nacional de Educación, Salud y Alimentación*) has educated Mexican women on health and nutrition issues, provided new spaces in which to communicate with other women, educated girls to improve their position in the future, and increased self-confidence and self-esteem. It began in 1997 as a countrywide effort to fight extreme poverty in rural areas. With a budget of US$ 500 million, it provides monetary assistance, nutritional supplements, educational grants and a basic health package to poor families. One of its innovations is to provide money directly to women.

deworming, micronutrient supplementation, latrines and clean water, and health education resulted in a 20% increase in school attendance in Burkina Faso, as well as significant improvements in pupil health (UNESCO 2004).

Is universal education attainable?

The MDGs set two targets for education: gender parity in primary and secondary enrolments, preferably by 2005, and universal completion of primary education by 2015. Although they are described as the most attainable of the MDGs, the world is not on track to achieve either.

Gender parity 2005 will earn a particularly shameful place in history as the year when the world missed the first of all the MDG targets: a large majority of countries will not achieve gender parity in primary and secondary education in

2005, and on present trends about 40% will not even make it by 2015 (UNESCO 2004). Failure to achieve it will cost the lives of over a million children under five in 2005 alone (Abu-Ghaida and Klasen 2004).

South Asia, Sub-Saharan Africa, the Middle East and North Africa all made progress on reducing these disparities in 1975–1999. South Asia remains the most educationally unequal region in the world; women average only about half as many years of education as men, and female secondary level enrolment rates are only two thirds of male rates. In Sub-Saharan Africa, the increases in equality in primary enrolment in 1980–1990 often tended to reflect absolute declines in boys' enrolment rather than improvements in girls'.

Universal primary completion Between 104 and 121 million children are estimated to be out of school, the majority girls. Their numbers are declining only slowly (by about a million a year) and at current rates not only will the target be missed, but neither universal primary completion nor gender parity will be attained over the next decade (UNICEF 2004, UNESCO 2004), and Africa will not get all its children into school until 2130 at the earliest.

Spending per primary pupil is typically about US$ 110 per year across the developing world, much less in the poorest countries (Devarajan et al. 2002). Pupil-teacher ratios are high, hours of instruction insufficient, and learning achievements low. More than half the countries in Sub-Saharan Africa had more than 44 pupils per teacher in 2001, a significant deterioration on the 1990 figure of 40:1. More than half the countries of south Asia have ratios of more than 40:1 (UNESCO 2004).

Making education a right for all The current distribution of education, heavily skewed against girls and the poor, reinforces rather than counteracts the skewed distribution of other assets, including health. This represents an enormous loss of human potential, as well as a denial of fundamental rights.

The burden of illiteracy, like the burden of disease, is concentrated not just among girls and women, but also among the poor, ethnic minorities and those in rural areas. There are only a few developing countries in which the rich have not already achieved universal primary education; but in many countries children from the poorest households receive little or no schooling. A more equitable distribution of educational opportunities could be achieved through increased investment in basic education, abolishing fees and charges, and affirmative action budgets giving priority to girls and the poorest. This would create new assets for the poor without making anyone else worse off (see the Mexican example in Box D4.2). Simply abolishing fees and other charges for primary education is a very effective way to redistribute educational assets to the poor and women, as shown in Uganda, Malawi, Tanzania, Zambia and Kenya.

Education is unequally distributed not only within, but between countries. The average person in an OECD country receives about 15 years' schooling. In South Asia and Sub-Saharan Africa the average is less than three years for women, four for African men and five for south Asian men (Abu-Ghaida and Klasen 2004). Research strongly suggests that countries may be unable to make the leap from a low-returns economy to a high-skill, high-growth path until the population averages more than six years' schooling (Azariadis and Drazen 1990).

Rich countries and the international community must be held accountable for their promises to achieve Education for All by 2015. This, while only a starting point, is also essential to break the South's continuing dependency on the North. It would only cost about US$ 100 per child per year to achieve universal completion of primary school (Devarajan et al. 2002).

The classroom as a site of socialization

The classroom is the place where most children first learn to interact with external authority; it transmits attitudes and assumptions that will last for a lifetime. At school, they may learn that they, and others like them, are stupid, lazy and worthless. Activists in South Asia express deep concern about the role of schools in promoting patriarchy and caste prejudice. In India's public schools, for example, children from poor and lower caste backgrounds are beaten and verbally abused more often than other children (GCE 2003). Sexual abuse of girl pupils is a problem in many African, Asian and Latin American countries.

On the other hand, the very fact of attending school, mastering new knowledge, and being recognized by adults can give children a sense of agency and achievement that defies their subordinate circumstances in the world outside. Sangeeta, a 16-year-old from India, says: 'I didn't go to school because I had so much work at home. Here at school, I am learning so much. I am learning to think well of myself. I want to become a teacher, so that I can make others feel like me now' (GCE 2003). There are many encouraging examples of the deliberate use of classrooms and other structured learning spaces to develop positive self-awareness and empower learners to take charge of their own bodies and health (see Boxes D4.3 and D4.4).

Socialization at school has acquired new urgency and importance in the context of HIV/AIDS. The self-image and psychological well-being of AIDS orphans in Zambia strongly depends on their ability to keep attending school,

Box D4.3 Programmes that aim to empower

Mahila Samakhya, the Education for Women's Equality programme in Bihar, India, aims to change not only women's and girls' ideas about themselves, but also society's notions about their traditional role. When the project was launched Bihar had the lowest female literacy rate in the country at 23%. There are now over 2000 local women's groups with more than 50,000 members. As well as demanding adult literacy provision for themselves and getting hundreds of women elected to local government bodies, they have taken an active role in ensuring educational opportunities for their daughters. The centres offer girls a fast track not only to education but to empowerment. Girls learn how to take decisions, assume leadership and develop collective strategies to change their lives (GCE 2003).

The REFLECT and Stepping Stones programmes for adolescents and adults, now being implemented by NGOs in many countries, emphasize inspiring learners to take greater control over their lives and their communities (Renton 2004). They use simple participatory tools to help learners analyse concerns such as the causes and seasonality of common diseases, male and female workloads, and domestic violence.

Lok Jumbish, a participatory community-driven education initiative in India, soon realized that adolescent girls needed a lot more than reading, writing and arithmetic. Building their self-esteem and confidence, giving them information about their body, health and hygiene, and letting them discover the joys of childhood, was also important (GCE 2003).

not only for status reasons, but also because it is the only place where they experience positive affirmation from adults (USAID 2002).

Life skills education Spurred by the AIDS crisis, donors have invested significantly in the development of 'life skills' programmes and learning materials for schools. A recent UN survey of 71 countries found that 85% had established or were developing such programmes. The aim is to exploit the socializing power of the classroom to help children develop negotiation skills, critical thinking and self-esteem, so they are more likely to make decisions that reduce their HIV risk. However, a forthcoming 17–country study (GCE 2005) shows that implementation of such programmes has been quite patchy. Even where implementation has been attempted, lack of adequate training and support to educators has undermined success.

Education

> ### Box D4.4 Promoting life skills and better health through education
>
> *Focusing Resources on Effective School Health (FRESH)* is a partnership that seeks to promote comprehensive policies for health in national education systems. The FRESH framework includes health-related school policies, provision of safe water and adequate sanitation in schools, skills-based health education, and school-based health and nutrition services. The aim is to put these components together in every school to create an environment that promotes learning and attendance. Students acquire skills needed for positive behavioural change, including interpersonal communication, value clarification, decision-making, negotiation, goal-setting, self-assertion, and stress management (FRESH 2003).
>
> *Students Partnership Worldwide*, working in partnership with education ministries and focusing on rural schools, is running youth-driven school health programmes in Zimbabwe, Tanzania, Uganda and South Africa – delivered by trained volunteers just a few years older than the students. The programmes are described as affirmative; uncontroversial; high profile; highly participatory; locally and community owned; holistic, and integrated with health services outside schools; and clearly targeted, with measurable outcomes (World Bank 2001).

However, evaluations show that behaviour change through school-based life skills education can be effective (Kirby et al. 1994, Bollinger et al. 2004). In Peru, for example, a skills-based education programme on sexuality and HIV/AIDS prevention in secondary school was found to have a significant effect on knowledge, sexuality, acceptance of contraception, tolerance of people with AIDS, and prevention-oriented behaviour (Caceres et al. 1994).

The politics of public services: Time for new alliances?

The trends currently threatening equitable provision of public health and education often have similar structural and political causes, as discussed in detail in part A. In some countries, public schools, like public clinics and hospitals, are fast becoming a ghetto for the poor. In others, many communities do not have access to any schools or clinics at all.

Often underlying a crisis of access and quality are some of the following trends:

- per capita public spending falling behind increases in demand;
- disproportionate spending on services primarily used by affluent urban groups (universities and hospitals);
- gradual withdrawal of public support from schools (or clinics), and the introduction or escalation of user fees;
- private sector provision encouraged through hidden or explicit subsidies;
- failure to maintain infrastructure and supplies, so that public facilities can barely function (schools without books or chalk, clinics without drugs or electricity);
- replacement of trained professionals on permanent contracts with low-paid temporary workers, and/or gradual erosion of public sector wages.

While these trends may be deplorable, they are not unpredictable. Like public health services, public schools consume a relatively large share of government budgets, and create rationing issues (universal primary education, for example, fuels demand for free secondary education). The poor – typically the least organized and influential voters – have the most to gain from public spending on primary health care and primary and basic education. It is tempting to politicians to cut these services first and deepest when budgets are under strain – whether from an unsustainable debt burden, slow growth or high military spending. And embattled governments will undoubtedly find their load lessened if the public gradually stops expecting a right to quality health care and education from the state, and gets used to paying for private services instead.

In response to these political realities, stronger alliances are needed at the national level to pressure governments for more and better spending on basic services. NGOs, social movements, unions and faith-based organizations need to come together in a far more concerted and strategic effort to mobilize the public and gain politicians' interest and support, particularly ahead of key moments such as elections.

However, while the main responsibility for achieving education and health for all rests with national governments, in some cases the actions (or lack of action) of the international financial institutions and donor community have left national governments without the means to finance and staff such services. Joined-up advocacy and campaigning – linking national and global levels, and bridging sectoral divides – are essential to change this balance of forces.

The rest of this chapter looks at policy issues needing urgent attention in both the health and education sectors.

18 Children in China at school. Literacy can play a key role in achieving health for all.

Opposing wage caps and user fees Rather than competing for a share of the same tightly constrained and inadequate budget, health and education activists should join forces to advocate universal and free provision of basic services, and to help find sustainable ways to finance such services.

After determined campaigning by civil society, the World Bank recently reversed its policy on user fees in primary education, and is now pledged to oppose education fees actively and work with governments to dismantle them. Under similar pressure from national civil society, a string of developing country governments have abolished primary education fees following Uganda's pioneering example in 1996, with the result that enrolments have gone up by 50–250% and government spending on education has increased.

However, there is an urgent need for further pressure on donors to cancel debt and increase aid, so that governments can afford to expand services and personnel adequately in response to the massive increases in demand that follow removal of fees.

Macro-economic conditionalities imposed by international financial institutions are also an issue of concern, as they sometimes restrict badly-need investment in health and education provision. One very direct way in which IFI conditionalities impinge on public services is through caps on the public sector wage bill, a favourite IFI recipe for cutting deficits and restraining inflation. In practice this means either a freeze on hiring, a freeze on wages or both; Zambia's IMF-recommended wage cap, for example, meant it was unable to recruit 9000 badly needed primary teachers or to implement long-overdue salary increases (GCE 2004b). Such policies have proven particularly disastrous in countries facing high rates of AIDS-related attrition, and may also contribute to an outflow of teachers and nurses from the public sector to better paid jobs elsewhere.

Recommendations

Mobilize the public around the right to free, good quality services for all. Doctors, nurses, and teachers can participate in local actions organized by health and education networks. Examples include Global Action Week and the White Band Days (see Resources). They can also talk with teachers' organizations and education NGOs to explore possible cross-sectoral programmes such as school-based health, nutrition and life skills interventions, or education programmes for adolescents and adults that also empower them to make better health choices.

Build a common voice on issues of shared concern. At national level, health sector groups should make links with education coalitions to tackle issues like user fees, privatization, donor and lender policies affecting the public sector workforce, and lack of participation and transparency in national budgetary processes or donor/government negotiations.

Challenge governments to put quality public services for poverty eradication at the top of the international agenda, and ensure that health and education are a major focus of the upcoming UN five-year review of progress on the MDGs in September. At regional level, health networks can collaborate with education networks, other networks and trade unions on joint events, press statements, research reports launched just before key meetings, and campaign actions.

Internationally, major campaigns, networks, faith-based organizations and trade unions are coming together in the Global Call to Action Against Poverty to demand debt cancellation, fair trade, more and better aid, and national government policies and budgets giving priority to the eradication of poverty and fair trade. By rallying tens of millions of people in support of a single bold message, it is possible to create a noise too big for politicians to ignore. The costs of silence are too great to contemplate.

Resources

The *Global Campaign for Education* brings together teachers' unions, Southern NGO networks, international NGOs and civil society coalitions on the right to education (see www.campaignforeducation.org for a list of national contacts). Its annual Global Action Week on the right to education, held every

249

April, mobilizes millions of people at school and community level (see www. campaignforeducation.org/action or e-mail actionweek@campaignforeducation.org).

The *White Band Days* being organized by the Global Call to Action Against Poverty involve wearing a simple white band to show your support for debt cancellation, more aid and fair trade (see www.whiteband.org).

Monitoring state budgets and tracking expenditure on health, education and other services has proven a very effective advocacy tool in many countries (see www.internationalbudget.org for case studies and how-to guides).

References

Abu-Ghaida D, Klasen S (2004). *The economic and human development costs of missing the millennium development goal on gender equity.* Washington, DC, World Bank (Discussion Paper No. 29710).

Azariadis C, Drazen A (1990). Threshold externalities in economic development. *Quarterly Journal of Economics*, 105(2): 501–26.

Bhalla S, Saigal S, Basu N (2003). *Girls' education is it – nothing else matters (much).* New Delhi, Oxus Research & Investments (Background paper for World Development Report 2003/04).

Bollinger L, Cooper-Arnold K, Stover J (2004). Where are the gaps? The effects of HIV-prevention interventions on behavioral change. *Studies in Family Planning,* 35(1):27–38.

Caceres C et al. (1994). Evaluating a school-based intervention for STD/AIDS prevention in Peru. *Journal of Adolescent Health*, 15:582–591.

De Walque, D (2004). *How does the impact of an HIV/AIDS information campaign vary with educational attainment? Evidence from rural Uganda.* Washington, DC, World Bank Development Research Group, 2004 (Working Paper).

Devarajan S, Miller M, Swanson E (2002). *Goals for development: history, prospects and costs.* Washington, DC (Working Paper) (http://econ.worldbank.org/files/13269_wps2819.pdf, accessed 25 February 2005).

FRESH (2003). *The FRESH school health tool kit.* Paris, UNESCO (http://portal.unesco.org/education/en/ev.php-URL_ID=34993&URL_DO=DO_TOPIC&URL_SECTION=201.html, accessed 20 December 2004).

Global Campaign for Education (2003). *A fair chance: attaining gender equality in basic education by 2005.* Brussels, GCE.

Global Campaign for Education (2004a). *Learning to survive: how education for all would save millions of young people from HIV/AIDS.* Brussels (http://www.campaignforeducation.org/resources/Apr2004/Learning%20to%20Survive%20final%202604.doc, accessed 25 February 2005).

Global Campaign for Education (2004b). *Undervaluing teachers: how IMF policies squeeze Zambia's education system.* Brussels (http://www.campaignforeducation.org/resources/resources_latest.php, accessed 25 February 2005).

Global Campaign for Education (2005) (forthcoming). *Deadly inertia: a cross-country study of ministry of education policy responses to HIV/AIDS.* Brussels, Global Campaign for Education, 2005.

Gordon D et al. (2003). *The distribution of child poverty in the developing world: report to UNICEF (final draft)*. Bristol, University of Bristol Centre for International Poverty Research.

Herz B, Sperling G (2004). *What works in girls' education*. Washington, DC, Center for Foreign Relations.

Jejeebhoy S (1998). Wife-beating in rural India: a husband's right? Evidence from survey data. *Economic and Political Weekly*, 23(15):855–62.

Karim R et al. (2002). *Determinants of food consumption during pregnancy in rural Bangladesh: examination of evaluative data from the Bangladesh Integrated Nutrition Project*. Boston, Tufts University Food Policy and Applied Nutrition Programme (Discussion Paper No. 11).

Kirby D et al. (1994). School-based programs to reduce risk behaviors: A review of effectiveness. *Public Health Reports*, 1994, 109:339–61.

Klasen S (1999). *Does gender inequality reduce growth and development? Evidence from cross-country regressions*. Washington, DC, World Bank (Policy Research Report on Gender and Development Working Paper No. 7).

Pritchett L, Summers L (1996). Wealthier is healthier. *Journal of Human Resources*, 1996, 31:841–868.

Renton, L (2004). Empowering communities in the face of HIV/AIDS through STAR (Stepping Stones and Reflect). (http://www.healthcomms.org/pdf/STARsummary.pdf, accessed 18/2/05).

Sandiford P et al (1995). The impact of women's literacy on child health and its interaction with access to health services. *Population Studies*, 49:5–17.

Sen P (1999). Enhancing women's choices in responding to domestic violence in Calcutta: a comparison of employment and education. *European Journal of Development Research*, 11(2):65–86.

Smith L, Haddad L (1999). *Explaining Child Malnutrition in Developing Countries*. Washington DC, International Food Policy Research Institute (Research Report No. 111).

Subbarao K, Raney L (1995). Social gains from female education. *Economic Development and Cultural Change*, 44(1):105–28.

Summers L (1994). *Investing in All the People: Educating Women in Developing Countries*. Washington, DC, World Bank (EDI Seminar Paper No. 45).

Thomas D (1990). Intrahousehold resource allocation: an inferential approach. *Journal of Human Resources*, 25:634–64.

UNAIDS (2002). *HIV/AIDS and education: a strategic approach*. Geneva, UNAIDS.

UNAIDS and WHO (2000). *Report on the Global HIV/AIDS Epidemic*. Geneva, UNAIDS.

UNESCO (2004). *EFA Global Monitoring Report 2004/5. The Quality Imperative*. Paris, UNESCO.

UNICEF (2004). *State of the World's Children Report*. New York (http://www.unicef.org/sowc04/, accessed 18 February 2005).

USAID (2002). *Results of the Orphans and Vulnerable Children Head of Household Baseline Survey in Four Districts in Zambia*. Zambia, USAID, SCOPE-OVC, and Family Health International.

Vandemoortele J, Delamonica E (2000). Education 'vaccine' against HIV/AIDS. *Current Issues in Comparative Education*, 3(1).

World Bank (1993). *World Development Report*. New York, Oxford University Press.

Education

World Bank (2001). *Engendering Development: Through Gender Equality in Rights, Resources, and Voice.* Washington, DC, World Bank and Oxford University Press.

World Bank (2002). *Education and HIV/AIDS: A Window of Hope.* Washington, DC, World Bank.

World Health Organization (1998). *Female Genital Mutilation.* Geneva, World Health Organization.

World Health Organization (2003). *The World Health Report 2003: Shaping the Future.* Geneva, World Health Organization.

D5 | War

War has an enormous and tragic impact on people's lives. It accounts for more death and disability than many major diseases; destroys families, communities, and sometimes entire nations and cultures; diverts limited resources from health and other human services and damages the infrastructure that supports them; and violates human rights. The mindset of war – that violence is the best way to resolve conflicts – contributes to domestic violence, street crime, and many other kinds of violence. War damages the environment. In sum, it threatens not only health but also the very fabric of our civilization (Levy and Sidel 1997).

The impact of war on health

Some of the impacts of war on health are obvious, some are not (WHO 2002). The direct impact on mortality and morbidity is apparent. An estimated 191 million people died directly or indirectly as a result of conflict during the 20th century, more than half of them civilians (Rummel 1994). The exact figures are unknowable because of generally poor record-keeping in many countries and its disruption in times of conflict (Zwi, Ugalde and Richards 1999). Active armed conflicts – primarily civil wars – continue in many parts of the world: 21 major armed conflicts occurred in 19 different locations during 2002. During the post-Cold War period of 1990–2001 there were 57 major armed conflicts in 45 locations, all internal except those between Iraq and Kuwait, India and Pakistan, and Ethiopia and Eritrea, although in 15 of them other states contributed regular military troops. Conflicts concerning government became slightly more frequent during that period than those concerning territory (Eriksson et al. 2003).

These civil wars exert a huge toll in human suffering. For example, at least three million civilians probably died in the civil war in the Democratic Republic of Congo (Roberts et al. 2001). Over 30 years of civil war in Ethiopia have led to the deaths of a million people, about half of them civilians (Kloos 1992). Civilians, particularly women and children, bear a disproportionate share of these casualties (Ahlstram 1991).

Many people survive wars only to be physically scarred for life. Millions of survivors are chronically disabled from injuries sustained during wars or their immediate aftermath. Landmines are a particular threat. For example, one in

236 people in Cambodia is an amputee as a result of a landmine explosion (Stover et al. 1994). Around a third of the soldiers who survived the civil war in Ethiopia were injured or disabled and at least 40,000 people lost one or more limbs during the war.

Millions more people are psychologically impaired from wars during which they were physically or sexually assaulted; were forced to serve as soldiers; witnessed the death of family members; or experienced the destruction of their communities or even nations. Psychological trauma may be demonstrated in disturbed and antisocial behaviour such as aggression toward others, including family members. Many combatants suffer from post-traumatic stress disorder on return from military action (Kanter 2005).

Rape has been used as a weapon in many wars – in Algeria, Bangladesh, India, Indonesia, Korea, Liberia, Rwanda, Uganda, the former Yugoslavia and elsewhere. Soldiers rape the families of their enemies as acts of humiliation and revenge; during the war in Bosnia and Herzegovina military personnel raped at least 10,000 women (Ashford and Huet-Vaughn 1997). The social chaos brought about by war also creates situations and conditions for sexual violence (Mann et al. 1994).

Children are particularly vulnerable during and after wars. Many die as a result of malnutrition, disease or military attacks; many are physically or psychologically injured; some are forced to become soldiers or sexual slaves to military officers. Their health suffers in many other ways, as reflected by increased mortality and decreased immunization (Machel 1996).

The health-supporting infrastructure, which in many countries is in poor condition before war begins, may be destroyed – including health-care facilities, electricity-generating plants, food-supply systems, water-treatment and sanitation facilities, and transport and communication systems. This deprives civilians of access to food, clean water and health services. For example, during Gulf War I in 1991 and the ensuing 12 years of economic sanctions against Iraq, an estimated 350,000 to 500,000 children died, mostly owing to inadequate nutrition, contaminated water and shortages of medicines, all related to destruction of the infrastructure. The 2003 attack on Iraq led by the US and UK devastated much of its infrastructure, leading again to numerous civilian deaths (summarized in Medact 2003 & 2004).

Armed conflict, or the threat of it, accounts for most of the refugees and internally displaced persons in the world today. Refugees and internally displaced persons are vulnerable to malnutrition, infectious diseases, injuries, and criminal and military attacks. At the start of 2002, there were an estimated 19.8 million worldwide. Twelve million were officially recognized as refugees by the

19 Chechnya destroyed. War has wide ranging implications for people's health.

United Nations High Commissioner for Refugees (this excluded three million Palestinians). Donor governments and international organizations have generally failed to provide adequate financial support for refugees and internally displaced persons. In 2002, there were 20–25 million internally displaced persons, many living in more extreme conditions than those who received refugee assistance – only 5.3 million of them received UNHCR aid in 2002 (Hampton 1998, Cranna 1994, Macrae and Zwi 1994, WorldWatch Institute 2003).

In addition to its direct effects, war and preparation for war have indirect and less obvious impacts on health that fall into three categories: diversion of resources; domestic and community violence; and damage to the environment. First, war and the preparation for war divert huge resources from health and human services and other productive societal endeavours. These are detailed in the discussion of militarism below.

Second, war often creates a circle of violence, increasing domestic and community violence in countries engaged in war. It teaches people that violence is an acceptable method for settling conflicts, including children and adolescents. Men, sometimes former military servicemen who have been trained to use violence, commit more acts of violence against women. The return home of servicemen and women can damage health and well-being, through separations, divorces, dysfunctional family interactions and other forms of post-traumatic stress (Kanter 2005).

> ### Box D5.1 The disastrous impact of war on the environment
>
> Destruction of urban environments by aerial carpet bombing of cities in Europe and Japan during World War II.
>
> Over 600 oil well fires in Kuwait, ignited by retreating Iraqi troops in 1991, had a devastating effect on the affected areas' ecology and caused acute respiratory symptoms among people exposed, sometimes far away.
>
> Destruction of environmental resources, such as the destruction of mangrove forests by Agent Orange (a herbicide widely used by the US) and bombs during the Vietnam war.
>
> Contamination of rivers, streams, and groundwater supplies, such as occurs with chemical leakage from rusting metal containers at military storage sites.

Finally, war and the preparation for war have profound impacts on the environment. Military activities consume huge quantities of non-renewable resources, such as fuels to power aircraft and ships, and rare metals used in the production of equipment and weapons (Sidel and Shahi 1997). More profoundly, military activities contribute to widespread pollution and environmental contamination (see examples in Box D5.1) (Levy et al. 2000). Less obvious are the environmental impacts of preparation for war, such as the huge amounts of non-renewable fossil fuels used by the military before (as well as during and after) wars and the environmental hazards of toxic and radioactive wastes, which can contaminate air, soil, and both surface water and groundwater (Renner 1997).

The changing nature of war Overall, war takes an increasing toll on civilians, both by direct attack on them or by 'collateral damage' caused by weapons directed at military targets. During some wars in the 1990s, approximately 90% of the people killed were noncombatants (Garfield and Neugut 2000). Many were innocent bystanders caught in the crossfire of opposing armies; others were specifically targeted civilians. The changing nature of war includes use of new weapons, drone (unmanned) aircraft and high-altitude bombers, and the increasing use of suicide or homicide bombers in guerrilla warfare and what is termed 'terrorism'.

The US has claimed the right to conduct a 'preventive' or 'pre-emptive' war against nations that it perceives as posing a threat to its security and has initiated a 'war on terrorism'. In addition, its 2002 nuclear policy says it may choose to use nuclear weapons not only in response to a nuclear attack but also against attack by other weapons of mass destruction (US Department of State 2002). The pre-emptive strike against Iraq by the governments of the US and UK may lead to abandonment of the rules and procedures of law and diplomacy that have prevented many wars.

Underlying causes of conflict and militarism

The underlying causes of armed conflict and militarism include poverty, social inequities, adverse effects of globalization, and shame and humiliation. Some of the underlying causes of war are becoming more prevalent or worsening, including the persistence of socioeconomic disparities and other forms of social injustice. The rich-poor divide is growing, as documented in part A. Abundant resources, such as oil, minerals, metals, gemstones, drug crops and timber, have also fuelled many wars in developing countries. Globalization, also discussed in part A, may be among the causes of violence and war if it leads to exploitation of people, of the environment and of other resources (Cornia and Court 2001, Zwi et al. 2002).

The Carnegie Commission on Preventing Deadly Conflict (1997) has identified factors that put nations at risk of violent conflict. These include:

- lack of democratic processes and unequal access to power, particularly where power arises from religious or ethnic identity, and leaders are repressive or abusive of human rights;
- social inequality characterized by markedly unequal distribution of resources and access to them, especially where the economy is in decline and there is, as a result, more social inequality and more competition for resources;
- control by one group of valuable natural resources such as oil, timber, drugs or gems; and
- demographic changes that outstrip the nation's capacity to provide basic necessary services and opportunities for employment.

The commission might also have noted that the consequences of colonialism are still felt in many countries. Colonialism destroyed political systems, replaced them with new ones unrelated to the population's cultural values and created commercial dependence. Neocolonialism, through multilateral agencies, transnational corporations and international organizations, and in some instances with the use of the military, is responsible for social inequality, control of natural resources, and lack of democratic processes. In many countries, the US has systematically opposed political processes that would have resolved some of the problems identified by the commission, often with invasions, assassinations and violence.

What has been called 'terrorism' is another important form of armed conflict. Levy and Sidel (2003) define it as politically motivated violence or the threat of violence, especially against civilians, with the intent to induce fear. Its causes include exploitation and dominance by a power that is considered illegitimate, exacerbated nationalism, religious fanaticism, and shame and humiliation of people. The US definition of terrorism excludes acts by nation-states, which it considers to be a part of 'war', but many analysts define such acts as the carpet-bombing of cities during World War II or the use of napalm in Vietnam as terrorism. The US and other nations must increase funding for humanitarian and sustainable development programmes to address the root causes of terrorism and political violence such as hunger, illiteracy and unemployment.

Militarism in developing countries Militarism is the subordination of the ideals or policies of a nation's government or of its civil society to military goals or policies. It has two major components, ideological and financial. In 2003, nations spent US$ 956 billion on war and the preparation for war; the US spent almost half of that. World military spending that year increased by about 11% from 2002, mostly due to spiralling US military spending (Stockholm International Peace Research Institute 2004a).

Expenditures for war and the preparation for war divert huge human, financial, and other resources from health and human services and other productive endeavours. In the US, for example, as military expenditures soar, there have been ongoing and substantial cutbacks in government-operated and financed health and human services. This problem is often more acute in less developed countries affected by armed conflict or the threat of it. Their populations have high rates of death and disease and relatively short life expectancy, but many spend much more on military activities than on public health. Governments in some developing countries annually spend US$ 10–20 per capita on military purposes, but only $1 on health.

The disarmament agenda

Prevention of war and, if war is initiated, lessening of its health consequences require not only the measures discussed above but also the reduction or elimination of weapons. The main types of weapons are described below:

Nuclear weapons The nuclear bombs detonated over Japan in 1945 each had an explosive force equivalent to about 15,000 tons of TNT. Each killed or fatally wounded about 100,000 people and caused additional thousands of injuries and illnesses from the blast, heat, and radiation (Yokoro and Kamada 1997). During the 1950s, the US and the USSR developed thermonuclear weapons (hydrogen bombs) with an explosive force of up to 20 million tons of TNT each. They could cause millions of casualties, catastrophic global health problems and 'nuclear winter' (Sidel et al. 1962). The nations known to possess stockpiles of nuclear weapons are the US, Russian Federation, China, UK, France, India, Pakistan and Israel. There are still approximately 34,000 nuclear weapons in these eight stockpiles combined, with an estimated explosive yield of 650,000 Hiroshima-sized bombs. Five thousand of these weapons are ready to fire at a few minutes' notice (Forrow and Sidel 1998). The United States is developing 'usable' nuclear weapons (Sidel et al. 2003)

There is no comprehensive treaty banning the use or mandating the destruction of nuclear weapons. The US should set an example for the rest of the world by renouncing the first use of nuclear weapons and the development of new nuclear weapons, and work with the Russian Federation to dismantle nuclear warheads and increase funding for programmes to secure nuclear materials so they will not fall into others' hands.

Radiological weapons Depleted uranium, a toxic and radioactive material, has been used as a shell casing in recent years because of its density and pyrophoric qualities (igniting spontaneously on contact with air). It was used by the US in Gulf War I and the wars in the Balkans and Afghanistan, and by both US and UK in Gulf War II. An estimated 320–1000 metric tons of DU remain in Iraq, Kuwait and Saudi Arabia. Its use arguably constitutes a violation of the Hague Convention (which bans use of 'poison or poisoned weapons'), the Geneva Conventions, and the UN Charter (Depleted Uranium Education Project 1997).

Chemical weapons The serious toxic effects of chemical weapons can include permanent disability and death. In 1994 and 1995, terrorist attacks using sarin gas in the underground railways of two Japanese cities caused 19 deaths and many serious injuries (Lifton 1999). Destruction of these weapons is taking place, but stockpiles remain in several countries (Spanjaard and Khabib 2003).

The Chemical Weapons Convention (CWC), which entered into effect in 1997, is the first multilateral disarmament agreement that provides for the elimination of an entire category of weapons of mass destruction. It prohibits all development, production, acquisition, stockpiling, transfer, and use of chemical weapons. The US should work to reduce the threat, stop the spread, and hasten the destruction of chemical weapons by strengthening the inspection regime and by accelerating the safe disposal of its own chemical weapons.

Biological weapons Biological weapons are composed of living microorganisms, such as bacteria and viruses, and products of microorganisms, such as toxins. They are designed to cause disease, disability, and death in humans or animals. Some diseases, such as smallpox, can be spread from one infected person to another; others, such as anthrax, cannot. Toxins such as botulinum are viewed as both biological and chemical weapons. Biological weapons have rarely been effectively used (Carus 2000) but the release of anthrax spores in the US in 2001 and allegations that some nations have stockpiles of smallpox virus have caused concern (Cohen et al. 2004).

The 1975 Biological Weapons Convention (BWC) prohibits the development, production, stockpiling, retention, and acquisition of biological agents or toxins of any type or quantity that do not have protective, medical, or other peaceful purposes, and of any weapons or means of delivery for them. The US and other nations need to strengthen it to include a stringent verification protocol by enactment of enabling legislation by all nations, and by suspension of ambiguous 'defensive' research (Arms Control Association 2004).

Anti-personnel landmines Anti-personnel landmines have been called 'weapons of mass destruction, one person at a time'. Civilians are the most likely to be injured or killed by landmines, which have been inserted into the ground of many nations (Stover et al.1997). Since the entry into force of the Anti-Personnel Landmine Convention in 1997, production has markedly dropped, 20 million stockpiled mines have been destroyed, and four million have been cleared. It has been signed by 144 countries, but the US, Russian Federation, South Korea, India, Pakistan and China, which between them have stockpiles of more than 180 million anti-personnel mines, have not ratified it (*The Lancet* 2004). Many mines are still buried, and enormous resources are required to continue unearthing and destroying them; an additional 20,000 people will probably be injured by mines during 2005, most in poor areas with limited access to health care and rehabilitation.

Small arms and light weapons 'Conventional weapons' such as explosives, incendiaries, and small arms cause the vast majority of casualties in current wars. Much can be done to improve control over legal small arms to decrease the risk of their misuse and diversion into illegal arms markets. International agreements at global and regional level that are designed to prevent or decrease illicit small arms trade need to be promoted and strengthened. Measures to reduce proliferation and misuse include adoption and enforcement of stronger gun-control laws, strengthening of export and import licence authorizations, and better record-keeping on arms production, possession and transfer. The UN Small Arms Action Plan needs to be supported.

Legal and illegal arms sales are the source of most of the small arms and light weapons used in ongoing armed conflicts. The US is the world leader in supplying conventional weapons to other countries: 43 companies sold US$ 94.6 billion in arms in 2000, representing 60% of total arms sales of the top 100 arms-producing companies.

The previous downward trend in major arms transfers appears to have been reversed – more major weapons were delivered in 2001 and 2003 (Stockholm International Peace Research Institute 2004). The major suppliers of conventional weapons in 1999–2003 were the US (34%) and the Russian Federation (30%), which supplied more arms than all other countries combined. The leading recipients of major conventional weapons in the same period were China and India, followed by Greece, Turkey, the UK, Egypt, Taiwan and South Korea, together accounting for nearly half.

The health sector response

The health sector should play an important role in leading efforts by civil society to recapture government from the corporate sector and particularly from the military-industrial complex. These efforts must include controlling weapons, preventing armed violence, promoting multilateralism, ending poverty and social injustice, and creating a culture of peace. While support of these efforts requires action from many sectors, health workers and their organizations have major responsibilities, as follows:

Controlling weapons People in the health sector are already playing a major role in action to prevent war, control weapons and outlaw weapons of mass destruction. For example, International Physicians for the Prevention of Nuclear War was awarded the 1985 Nobel Peace Prize for work to prevent use of nuclear weapons and ban their production, testing, and transfer. Health professionals and others have made similar efforts to strengthen the conventions on biological and chemical weapons.

Preventing armed violence Acts of violence by individuals and non-state

War

> ## Box D5.2 Military spending and the UN: whose priorities?
>
> One year's world military expenditure of US$ 880 billion would fund the entire UN system for more than 70 years.
>
> The entire UN system (excluding the World Bank and IMF) spends US$12 billion a year. The annual budget for its core functions is US$ 1.25 billion. This is equivalent to only 4% of New York City's annual budget – and nearly US$1 billion less than the yearly cost of Tokyo's fire department.

groups and by nation states must be prevented by strengthening international institutions, rejecting unilateral pre-emptive war as a means of resolving international conflict, and increasing support for the UN and other cooperative security programmes. Specifically, the US must change priorities to reflect real security needs, by eliminating military spending for wasteful Pentagon programmes and investing those resources in urgent domestic needs for health care, education, and jobs; by providing new investments in renewable energy alternatives to reduce dependence on foreign oil; and by providing adequate peacekeeping funding to secure peace and stability.

Promoting multilateralism Since its foundation in 1946 the UN has attempted to live up to the goal in its charter, 'to save succeeding generations from the scourge of war'. Its mandate also includes protecting human rights, promoting international justice, and helping people achieve a sustainable standard of living. Its programmes and agencies have made an enormous difference to people's lives. Yet the resources allocated by its member states are grossly inadequate (see Box D5.2).

The UN has no army and no police, but relies on the contribution of troops and other personnel to halt conflicts. The US and other members of the Security Council, and not the secretary-general, decide when and where to deploy peacekeeping troops. Long-term conflicts fester, such as those in the Sudan and Kashmir and the Israeli-Palestinian conflict, while conflicting national priorities deadlock the UN's ability to act. In fact if stymied by the veto, the organization has little power beyond the bully pulpit. The US and the UK severely weakened the UN by their illegal invasion of Iraq in 2003. The US has also failed to support the International War Crimes Tribunal through signature and ratification of the Statute of the International Criminal Court.

Ending poverty and social injustice Poverty and other manifestations of social injustice contribute to conditions that lead to armed conflict. Growing socio-economic and other disparities between the rich and the poor within countries, and between rich and poor nations, also contribute to the likelihood of armed conflict. Rich countries can help to address these underlying conditions through policies and programmes that redistribute wealth within and among nations, and by providing financial and technical assistance to less developed nations.

Creating a culture of peace The Hague Appeal for Peace Civil Society Conference was held on the centenary of the 1899 Hague Peace Conference, which explored ways of making war more humane. The 1999 conference, attended by 1000 individuals and representatives of civil society organizations, was devoted to finding methods to prevent war and to establish a culture of peace (see Box D5.3).

People in the health sector can do much to promote a culture of peace in which nonviolent means are used to settle conflicts. A culture of peace is based on the values, attitudes, and behaviours that form the deep roots of peace. They are in some ways the opposite of the values, attitudes, and behaviours that reflect and inspire war and violence, but should not be equated with just the absence of war. A culture of peace can exist at the level of the relationship,

War

family, workplace, school and community as well as at the level of the state and in international relations.

References

Arms Control Association (2004). *Fact Sheet: The Biological Weapons Convention at a Glance*. Washington DC (http://www.armscontrol.org/factsheets/bwcataglance.asp, accessed 21 February 2005).

Ashford M-W, Huet-Vaughn Y (1997). The Impact of War on Women. In: Levy BS, Sidel VW, eds. *War and Public Health*. New York, Oxford University Press.

Carnegie Commission on Preventing Deadly Conflict (1997). *Preventing deadly conflict: final report*. New York, Carnegie Corporation.

Carus WS, (2000). The Rajneeshees. In: J.B. Tucker, ed. *Toxic Terror: Assessing Terrorist Use of Chemical and Biological Weapons*. Cambridge, Mass, MIT Press.

Cohen HW, Gould RM, Sidel VW (2004). The Pitfalls of Bioterrorism Preparedness: The Anthrax and Smallpox Experiences. *American Journal of Public Health*, 94:1667–1671.

Cornia GA, Court J (2001). *Inequality, Growth and Poverty in the Era of Liberalization and Globalization*. Helsinki, UNU World Institute for Development Economics Research.

Cranna M (1994). *The True Cost of Conflict*. London, Earthscan.

Depleted Uranium Educatation Project (1997). *Metal of Dishonor: Depleted Uranium*. New York, International Action Center.

Eriksson M, Sollenberg M, Wallensteen P (2003). Patterns of major armed conflicts, 1990–2002. In: Stockholm International Peace Research Institute. *SIPRI Yearbook 2003: Armaments, Disarmament and International Security*. Oxford, Oxford University Press.

Forrow L, Sidel VW (1998). Medicine and nuclear war: from Hiroshima to mutual assured destruction to Abolition 2000. *Journal of the American Medical Association*, 1998, 280: 456–461.

Garfield RM, Neugut AI (2000). The human consequences of war. In: BS Levy, VW Sidel, eds. *War and Public Health*. Washington DC, American Puiblic Health Association.

Hague Appeal for Peace (1998). *Hague Agenda for Peace and Justice for the 21st Century*. New York (http://www.haguepeace.org, accessed 21 February 2005).

Hampton J (1998). *Internally displaced people: a global survey*. London, Earthscan.

Kanter E (2005). Post-traumatic stress disorders. In: BS Levy, et al. *Preventing Occupational Disease and Injury*, 2nd ed. Washington DC, American Public Health Association.

Kloos H (1992). Health Impacts of War in Ethiopia. *Disasters*, 16:347–354.

Levy BS, Sidel VW (1997). *War and Public Health*. New York, Oxford University Press.

Levy BS, Sidel VW (2003). Challenges that Terrorism Poses to Public Health. In: BS Levy, VW Sidel, eds. *Terrorism and Public Health*. New York, Oxford University Press.

Levy BS et al. (2000). The environmental consequences of war. In: BS Levy, VW Sidel, eds. *War and Public Health*. New York, Oxford University Press.

Lifton RJ, 1999. *Destroying the World In Order to Save It: Aum Shinrikyo, Apocalyptic Violence, and the New Global Terrorism*. New York, Henry Holt.

Machel G (1996). *Impact of Armed Conflict on Children*. New York, UNICEF.

Macrae J, Zwi A (1994). Famine, complex emergencies and international policy in Africa: an overview. In: J Macrae and A Zwi, eds. *War and hunger: rethinking international responses to complex emergencies*. London, Zed Books.

Mann J et al. (1994). Bosnia: The War Against Public Health. *Medicine and Global Survival,* 1:130–146.

Medact (2003). *Continuing Collateral Damage: The health and environmental costs of war on Iraq 2003*. London, Medact.

Medact (2004). *Enduring effects of war: health in Iraq 2004*. London, Medact.

Renner M (1997). Environmental and health effects of weapons production, testing, and maintenance. In: BS Levy, VW Sidel eds. *War and Public Health*. New York, Oxford University Press.

Roberts L, Hale C, Belyakdoumi F, et al. (2001). *Mortality in Eastern Democratic Republic of Congo: Results from Eleven Mortality Surveys*. New York, International Rescue Committee.

Rummel RJ (1994). *Death by Government: Genocide and Mass Murder since 1900*. New Brunswick NJ, and London, Transaction Publications.

Sidel VW, Geiger HJ, Lown B (1962). The medical consequences of thermonuclear war. The physician's role in the post-attack period. *New England Journal of Medicine,* 266: 1137–1145.

Sidel VW, Shahi G (1997). The impact of military activities on development, environment, and health. In: GS Shahi, et al. eds. *International Perspectives on Environment, Development, and Health: Towards a Sustainable World*. New York, Springer.

Sidel VW et al. (2003). *The Threat of Low-yield Earth-penetrating Nuclear Weapons to Civilian Populations: Nuclear Bunker Busters and their Medical Consequences*. Cambridge, Mass, International Physicians for the Prevention of Nuclear War.

Spanjaard H and Khabib O (2003). Chemical Weapons. In: Levy B and Sidel V eds., *Terrorism and Public Health*. New York, Oxford University Press.

Stockholm International Peace Research Institute (2004). *SIPRI Yearbook 2004: Armaments, Disarmament, and International Security*. Stockholm, SIPRI.

Stockholm International Peace Research Institute (2004). *Recent trends in military expenditure*. Stockholm (http://www.sipri.org/contents/milap/milex/mex_trends.html/view?searchterm=Recent%20trends%20in%20military%20expenditure, accessed 20 February 2005).

Stover E, Cobey JC, Fine J (1997). The Public Health Effects of Land Mines. In: Levy BS, Sidel VW, eds. *War and Public Health*. New York, Oxford University Press.

Stover E et al. (1994). The Medical and Social Consequences of Land Mines in Cambodia. *Journal of the American Medical Association,* 272 : 331–336.

The Lancet (2004). Landmines and their victims remain priorities. *The Lancet,* 364:2070.

US Department of State (2002). *Nuclear Posture Review*. Washington DC, US Department of State.

WHO (2002). *World Report on Violence and Health*. Geneva, WHO.

WorldWatch Institute (2003). *Vital Signs*. Washington DC, WorldWatch Institute.

Yokoro K and Kamada N (1997). The Public Health Effects of the Use of Nuclear Weapons. In: BS Levy, VW Sidel, eds. *War and Public Health*. New York, Oxford University Press.

Zwi AB, Fustukian S, Sethi D (2002). Conflict and the humanitarian response. In: K Lee, K Buse, S Fustukian, ed. *Health Policy in a Globalizing World*. Cambridge, Cambridge University Press.

Zwi A, Ugalde A, and Richards P (1999). The Effects of War and Political Violence on Health Services. In: Kurtz L, ed. *Encyclopedia of Violence, Peace and Conflict*. San Diego, Academic Press.

PART E | Holding to account: global institutions, transnational corporations and rich nations

Although positioned near the end, this section of the *Global Health Watch* is its central component. Here the *Watch* goes beyond other annual reports on aspects of world health to reflect on the performance of global institutions, governments and corporations.

The monitoring component of the *Watch* is diverse, combining short and long pieces on these different actors. But again, common themes emerge. First amongst these is meanness. The chapter on aid reveals how much richer the developed nations have got over the last forty years, but how they spend nearly exactly the same now on aid to the developing world as they did in the 1960s. Despite repayments worth hundreds of millions of dollars, developing nations are still paying through the nose for mistakes made both by them-selves *and* rich nations during the lending frenzy of the 1970s. Or rather, it is the poor in the developing world today who unfairly pay for the past mistakes of governments and institutions long gone or from distant lands.

The second common theme is lack of democracy. The chapters on the international institutions – WHO, Unicef, the World Bank and the Inter-national Monetary Fund, as well as analysis of the World Trade Organization in part A of the *Watch* – reveal a crisis of governance provoked by the attempts of rich nations to make the international order in their own image. The recent US-driven appointments of Paul Wolfowitz and Ann Veneman to head the World Bank and Unicef respectively are symptoms of the crisis. The chap-ters suggest reforms to re-balance the scales of influence.

A third theme is misuse of power. Mismanagement and distorted priorities are a common factor in the despair felt by many working in and around the health-promoting international institutions. A deliberately long chapter on WHO concentrates not only the harsh external environment the organization faces, but the internal management problems which lead to organizational paralysis. But, as the chapter shows, change from within is possible.

Finally, health is a field where the effects of corporate decisions are keenly felt. Two case studies on tobacco control and the marketing of breastmilk substitutes show both how business can be regulated by international regulatory intervention, and the success of international advocacy by citizens' groups; although they also show the continuing attempts by corporations to undermine these regulations. Overall, the environment for business couldn't be friendlier, with massive falls registered in taxes on profits in the developed world as another case study shows. The case study suggests that we need to fight a campaign for increased tax or risk the withering away of the state and our public services.

E1 | World Health Organization

The strategic importance of the WHO as the UN's specialist health agency, its many influential programmes and policies at global, regional and national and community levels, and perhaps above all, its humanitarian mission, earn it worldwide authority and guarantee it a central place in this report.

While it may be seen as the leading global health organization, it does not have the greatest impact on health. As many sections of this report illustrate, transnational corporations and other global institutions – particularly the World Bank and International Monetary Fund – have a growing influence on population health that outweighs WHO's. Furthermore, some of these institutions, the Bank in particular, now operate in direct competition with WHO as the leading influence on health sector policy. The rise of neoliberal economics and the accompanying attacks on multilateralism led by the US have created a new, difficult context for WHO's work to which the organization, starved of resources and sometimes poorly led and managed, is failing to find an effective response.

The purpose of this chapter is to explore this decline in WHO's fortunes from the perspective of a critical friend, and suggest how it might begin to be reversed. The problems of global health and global health governance are beyond the reach of any entity working in isolation, requiring WHO leaders and staff, governments, health professionals and civil society to work together in new alliances. A new shared vision of WHO for the 21st century must draw on its strengths, but be reshaped for the modern world, as part of a broader vision of global governance. And then we have to make it reality. The Health for All movement partly succeeded in moving from vision to action: this time round, as inequalities widen and the health of many of the world's poorest people worsens, we have to do even better, because failure will be catastrophic.

A complex organization

Entering the Geneva headquarters of WHO is an awe-inspiring, even intimidating experience. Having made your way there past a series of imposing buildings occupied by a range of famous organizations, including the United Nations and the International Red Cross, and admiring the distant views of the Swiss Alps, you finally reach a huge 1960s block set in a grassy campus. Its interior, gleaming with glass and marble, seems designed to impress rather

20 Health ministers gather at the World Health Assembly.

than befriend. Besuited bureaucrats and smart secretaries rub shoulders with visitors from every corner of the globe, and the enormous restaurant offers an exotic menu to match. Upstairs, rather less smart corridors of small cubicles house hundreds of health professionals from all over the world.

The calm, hushed atmosphere is a far cry from the simple bush hut where WHO consultants are encouraging midwives to help new mothers feed their babies from the breast rather than a bottle. It is a long way from the WHO office in a country in conflict where staff operate under conditions of physical danger. Yet all these settings are part of the same organization, the UN's specialized agency for health and the world's leading health body. The immense range of what WHO does and where it does it, the complexity and regional differences in its structures, and the infinite variety of people who work for it and with it, make generalizations about it both difficult and dangerous. Inevitably, too, such a large and diffuse organization provokes strong feelings, from optimism and inspiration to frustration, anger and despair.

This chapter cannot do justice to the full range of WHO activity and the many criticisms and reform proposals. Issues of global health policy are discussed elsewhere in this report. Rather, it will present a brief report card on WHO as an institution. In reviewing recent major criticisms and reforms, it is noted that the critics are long on description but short on solutions. The final part of the chapter therefore focuses on three major drivers of WHO performance – resources, the internal environment of WHO, and the attitudes of member states – and how they need to change.

The sources consulted worldwide in making this assessment include literature written by academics, development agencies, policy analysts, present and
former WHO staff members and health journalists. The official views of some
member states were reviewed selectively in literature from individual countries
and major donor networks. Interviews were conducted with past and present
WHO staff members, consultants and advisers, and other observers. The staff
members included people working at global, regional and country levels in
a range of specialties and fields, at different levels of seniority and from different national backgrounds, some newly arrived in the organization, others
long-serving. Many WHO informants felt anxious about speaking openly, and
all were interviewed on the basis that they would not be identifiable. The views
described here represent an aggregate rather than those of any individual.

Some background

WHO came into formal existence in 1948 as the UN specialist agency for
health, incorporating several existing organizations that represented a long
history of international health cooperation. WHO's objective is the attainment by all peoples of the highest possible level of health, defined as a state
of complete physical, mental and social well-being and not merely the absence
of disease or infirmity. Its constitution also asserts that health is a fundamental human right and that governments are responsible for the health of their
peoples – bold statements treated warily by governments who equated social
equity and socialized medicine with 'the Communist threat' (Lee 1998). Thus
politics and health were inseparable even at WHO's birth.

The importance of health to the global political agenda of the day was reflected in the decision to give WHO its own funding system and a governing
body of all member states that is still unique among UN specialist agencies.
Its basic composition and overall organizational structure have changed little
since 1948. Like other UN non-subsidiary specialist agencies its governing body
makes its own decisions, but reports annually to the UN. All UN member states
and others may join it. Through the World Health Assembly, its 192 member
states approve the programme of work and budget and decide major policy. A
32–strong executive board with rotating membership, selected on the basis of
personal expertise rather than country representation (although a geographical
balance is maintained), oversees implementation of assembly decisions (WHO
global website, 2005). Its accountability to its annual global and regional as-
semblies of delegations from all member states is unique in the UN system, and
offers developing countries unparalleled opportunities to exert influence.

The Secretariat is the administrative and technical organ responsible for implementing the activities. It has around 3500 staff on fixed-term or career-service appointments, and several thousand more on short-term contracts and secondments, working either at headquarters, in the six regional offices and their outposts and specialist centres, or in WHO offices in around 140 countries. The balance of power and resources between these three main operational levels has been a matter of debate and disagreement since 1948.

A third of the staff are 'professional', among whom the vast majority are medical doctors and two thirds are men, with the proportion of women decreasing at senior levels. The other two thirds are 'general' staff, ie working in administrative and support services, with women disproportionately over-represented. A quota system is meant to ensure a fair distribution of staff from all regions, but in practice is often ignored to recruit a favoured candidate, especially when a very specialized set of skills/experience is required.

As well as these directly appointed staff, a huge variety and number of people worldwide work on projects or in centres funded or supported by WHO. Many different institutions have evolved in partnership with WHO to meet particular needs, with an infinite variety of funding and governance arrangements. Hundreds of designated WHO Collaborating Centres conduct jointly agreed programmes of work, sometimes strongly supported with funds and secondments from member states. No organogram could successfully capture the range and complexity of the WHO family, a fact that highlights the many challenges of achieving good overall governance.

Milestones A look at some of WHO's major historical milestones (Lee 1998) illustrates the magnitude of its challenges, the complexity of the environment in which it operates, and some of its successes. It also shows the longevity of its leadership, with only six directors-general (DG) in nearly 60 years. Each has led or at least presided over significant change. Best remembered is Dr Halfdan Mahler, DG from 1973–1988, whose term of office is often spoken of as a golden age of WHO and perhaps of global health in general. He established WHO as a global 'health conscience', challenging the commercial practices of transnational corporations in the pharmaceutical and food industries. He initiated or endorsed such key initiatives as the expanded programme on immunization, the model list of essential drugs, the international code on breast milk substitutes, and – the jewel in the crown – the Alma Ata declaration (discussed in detail in part B, chapter 1).

Mahler's visionary and inspirational leadership was always going to be a hard act to follow. It was the misfortune of his successor Dr Hiroshi Nakajima not only to lack those qualities but also to take office at a time when neoliberal

Box E1.1 Milestones in WHO history

1948 WHO established as the UN's specialist agency for health. April 7, when its constitution approved, becomes World Health Day. First World Health Assembly (WHA) attended by 53 member states. Mass treatment programmes begun for syphilis.

1951 WHO member states adopt the International Sanitary Regulations (later renamed the International Health Regulations, they are the only binding rules governing international health).

1955 Intensified malaria eradication programme launched.

1959 WHA commits to global eradication of smallpox (lack of funds means programme not started till 1967). First *World health situation report.*

1964 WHA withdraws South Africa's voting rights in protest against apartheid. South Africa leaves WHO.

1965 WHO puts forward the basic health services model.

1973–88 Dr Halfdan Mahler is third director-general.

1974 Expanded programme on immunization created.

1977 WHA proposes Health for All by the Year 2000. Publishes model list of essential drugs. Last natural case of smallpox identified.

1978 Alma Ata declaration on primary health care signed by 134 countries.

1981 WHA adopts international code on the marketing of breast-milk substitutes.

1982 Consultative meeting on AIDS in Geneva.

1986 Ottawa charter for health promotion signed.

1988–98 Dr Hiroshi Nakajima is fourth DG.

1995 First WHO *World health report* published.

1998–2003 Dr Gro Harlem Brundtland is fifth DG.

2000 Commission on Macroeconomics and Health established; *World Health Report* on health systems.

2003 Dr Lee Jong-wook is sixth DG. Launches 3 by 5 initiative. WHO Framework Convention on Tobacco Control.

2005 Commission on Social Determinants of Health established.

(*Source*: most data drawn from Lee 1998)

health policies were beginning to supersede the social justice model of health for all. The backdrop was a global ideological shift to the right, accompanied by economic recession, oil crises and rising debt. WHO's core funding remained static while new actors entered the health field and challenged its leadership role. Even those who did not much like what the World Bank said about the route to better health nevertheless felt obliged to accept its large loans conditional on implementing market-oriented health sector reforms.

At the same time, new health threats demanded urgent responses – arising from AIDS and other newly emerging diseases, from complex emergencies combining armed conflict with human or natural disasters and social disintegration, and from demographic and social shifts (Lee 1998, Buse and Walt 2002). Nakajima struggled and ultimately failed to come up with convincing responses to these challenges, also alienating WHO staff and partners through his management style, high-profile disagreements and communication failures. Few lamented his departure.

The election in 1998 of Dr Gro Harlem Brundtland, who combined a medical background with national and international political experience, was widely welcomed. She set about pushing health higher up the international development agenda, through initiatives like the Commission on Macroeconomics and Health that explored the relationship between economic growth and health. Her most acclaimed achievements included putting health on the agenda at the summit where the UN Millennium Development Goals were agreed, and persuading all member states to endorse the 2003 WHO Framework Convention on Tobacco Control, the world's first public health treaty (see part E, chapter 4). There are mixed views about her tenure, during which WHO also strengthened its organizational and ideological relationship with the World Bank and encouraged and pursued controversial public-private partnership initiatives (Buse and Walt 2002).

Meanwhile Brundtland introduced sweeping internal reforms aiming to make WHO more businesslike and results-oriented. New top managers were appointed and large numbers of staff redeployed in a major restructuring that gradually eroded the internal optimism generated by her appointment (Lerer and Matzopoulos 2001). Many staff felt that it was just change for change's sake, or for the sake of promoting people who were in favour not necessarily for the right reasons, and the organizational climate was uncomfortable. At the end of her five-year term WHO remained centralized and top-heavy, still dominated by white men from developed countries (Yamey 2002).

The appointment of her successor Dr Lee Jong-wook was likewise initially greeted enthusiastically by many staff who felt that an insider would handle internal matters more sensitively – he has worked in WHO since 1983 – though others were concerned that his experience was too strongly rooted in vertical programmes, and that he was susceptible to US influence. Hopes were further raised by his attempts to revitalize WHO's commitment to Health for All, in contrast to Brundtland's more neoliberal focus.

After 18 months in post (at the time of writing) it is too early to pass definitive judgement. Lee's flagship initiative to treat three million people with AIDS with antiretroviral therapy by the year 2005 (known as 3 by 5) demonstrates a passionate, high-risk approach that has divided staff and partners, arousing both support and opposition. The influence of private foundations (e.g. Gates) and public-private partnerships (e.g. GFATM, GAVI) continues to grow and the question of WHO's place in this emerging configuration is still unresolved. Meanwhile the new Commission on Social Determinants of Health could represent an important advance.

Many of these shifts in WHO policy and management over the decades were reflected in the six WHO regional offices, though their locally elected regional directors (RDs) exercise considerable autonomy from headquarters. The changes gradually filter down through the regional offices to the WHO country offices they administer, although these too may enjoy much independence from a distant regional centre that sometimes has only limited knowledge of what is going on in the field. Seen by many as the most important focus of WHO activity, and promised a stronger role in the Lee reforms, most of the country offices remain attached to low-prestige ministries of health, and are weak and inadequately resourced in comparison with the country-based offices of other international organizations and government development agencies.

Current context: recent successes

Even the harshest critics admit that WHO can claim many important achievements since 1948. Many are highlighted elsewhere in this report. In disease prevention and control WHO led the global eradication of smallpox. It is making good progress towards eradication of poliomyelitis, leprosy and dracunculiasis, and ongoing efforts to tackle malaria, cholera, tuberculosis and HIV/AIDS (albeit inadequately funded and unlikely to reach the desired targets). Its leadership role in collecting, analyzing and disseminating health evidence is unrivalled. It is the leading global authority preparing guidelines and standards on numerous issues, and the foremost source of scientific and technical knowledge in health.

In many countries it remains the best trusted source of objective, evidence-based, ethically sound guidance and support on health. Since Lee's appointment as DG it has regained some of its reputation as the world's health conscience, and facilitation of an effective global response to the severe acute respiratory syndrome (SARS) outbreak has underlined its critical public health

275

role. 'It is for all (this) work that the world recognises the need for WHO as a cornerstone of international relations' (Lee 1998).

Many formal and informal evaluations and commentaries on WHO mention its traditional strengths (for example Godlee 1997, Lee 1998, Lerer and Matzopoulos 2001, Wibulpolprasert and Tangcharoensathien 2001, Buse and Walt 2002, DFID 2002, Minelli 2003, Selbervik and Jerve 2003, Kickbusch 2004, Murray et al. 2004, interviews and personal communications). These include:

- advocacy for marginalized population groups such as the poor, people with AIDS and people with mental illness;
- performing important global communicable disease surveillance and control functions, as with SARS;
- production of authoritative guidelines and standards that support excellent practice;
- global, regional and national health reports and cross-country studies providing an evidence base for policy, practice and advocacy;
- excellent staff whose technical expertise and international health experience are unsurpassed;
- provision of effective technical support in some countries, within tight resource constraints;
- promotion of agendas that are value-based, knowledge-based and support health, rather than ideologically driven or politically motivated;
- innovative intersectoral programmes such as Healthy Cities.

There is also praise for recent work, some of which builds on these traditional strengths, and some of which is taking WHO into new areas of work:

- returning health to the international development agenda;
- good practical and analytical work on key areas such as violence and health and complex emergencies;
- the gradual renaissance of primary health care and health promotion, including challenges to commercial interests that damage health;
- interagency alliances such as the Partnership for Safe Motherhood and Newborn Health;
- active support for a greater investment in relevant and applied health systems research;
- emerging innovative approaches to knowledge management using new technology;
- more active and transparent engagement in WHO reform processes with some influential member states, such as the Multilateral Organizations Performance Assessment Network of eight leading donor countries;

- stronger internal focus on performance management and results;
- better training of WHO staff, for example on human rights;
- effective advocacy for global tobacco control and access to medicines.

A controversial review of its partnership with WHO by the UK Department for International Development pronounced it 'an improving organization' (DFID 2002), while others note how WHO has begun to 'refashion and reposition itself as the coordinator, strategic planner, and leader of "global health" initiatives' (Brown et al. 2004). Much of this praise, however, has a ritual air, run through rapidly as an appetiser to the main dish – strong criticism.

Current context: major criticisms

The often contradictory accusations and criticisms of WHO reflect the existence of a wide range of critics, with different agendas. A number of criticisms emanate from interests that want to weaken WHO's mandate and capacity to tackle urgent global health problems, especially poverty, or to challenge the hazard merchants (commercial enterprises profiting from products that damage health). Other criticisms reflect frustration over WHO's lack of political will and strength to tackle the drivers of poverty and health inequity, and its inefficiencies. Of the latter group, the following bullet points represent a selection of the more common criticisms:

- WHO's 'vertical', single-focus disease control programmes, reflecting the continued domination of biomedical thinking, are said to lack impact or sustainability and to hinder systemic, intersectoral approaches.
- The balance between normative, global standard-setting activities and technical cooperation with countries is said to be wrong.
- Its priorities are constantly skewed by intense political pressure from member states.
- Its multiple and sometimes conflicting roles as advocate, technical adviser, monitor and evaluator limits its ability to discharge functions such as independent global reporting.
- It has not built effective partnerships with civil society.
- Its relations with other major international agencies, such as the Global Fund for AIDS, TB and Malaria, are dogged by turf wars.
- It is said to be compromising on values and moral principles by entering into public-private partnerships with business interests whose activities it should be condemning rather than courting.
- Its leadership is accused of being ineffective and is beset by rumours of corruption and nepotism.

- Its management is top-heavy, hierarchical, overpaid and centralized, ruling autocratically over an entrenched, bureaucratic subculture.
- Its staff are dominated by professionals from developed countries with insufficient experience of poor countries.

These criticisms and others appear in hundreds of books, articles and speeches and their range and scope is enormous. They may appear unbalanced simply because of the tendency to focus on bad news rather than good news. Some are diametrically opposed. Some reveal a tendency to use WHO as a scapegoat and a desire for quick-fix solutions. Strong critiques come from member states, often off the record, who then vote differently in WHO fora, act in ways that undermine or manipulate the organization, and fail to support the progressives within. The criticisms made by WHO staff and consultants are usually at least as tough as those of external academic observers, but also more rounded as their experience perhaps makes them more aware of the positives.

The problems laid at WHO's door are not just many, but are often way beyond its control. It is tempting to underestimate the complexity of the challenges, or to view the problem as the failures of an individual organization rather than a collective global one. Moreover, similar criticisms are being levelled at other international agencies in the prevailing mood of widespread discontent with the UN system and weak international governance (see the other chapters in part E). A recent survey commissioned by leading donor countries found the performance of WHO, UNICEF and the World Bank perceived to be broadly similar by its informants (Selbervik and Jerve 2003).

Finally, and perhaps crucially, the critiques are long on description and accusation, and short on practical solutions. There is little consensus about what needs to be done beyond indisputable statements about tackling poverty and inequality. The most powerful group of commentaries call for stronger global health governance. According to Buse and Walt (2002), globalization requires novel arrangements for health governance in which partners work together – international organizations; nation states; and global and local private, for-profit and civil society organizations. They ask how the present patchwork of alliances and partnerships in health can move towards a system of good global governance without losing their energy and creativity. Kickbusch (2004) says this means strengthening WHO and giving it a new and stronger mandate, including ensuring 'transparency and accountability in global health governance through a new kind of reporting system that is requested of all international health actors', even taking countries to an international court for crimes against humanity if they refuse to take action based on the best public health evidence and knowledge.

21 WHO – up in the clouds?

Reactions have been mixed to this idea of WHO as a 'world policeman' but director-general Lee at least agrees that 'business as usual' will not do. He promises a return to the aims and ethical commitments of Health for All – scale-up of health systems, guided by the principles and practice of primary health care, adapted to a rapidly changing health landscape and delivered through synergizing swift responses to health emergencies with long-term strengthening of health infrastructure. Asserting that a world torn by gross health inequalities is in serious trouble, he asks whether WHO and its partners are up to the challenge, and gives his answer: 'We have to be' (Lee 2003).

Yet can WHO make the enormous internal shifts in culture and practice and develop the leadership capacity essential at all levels to turn Dr Lee's rhetoric into reality – to drive good global health governance, secure the necessary resources and deliver effective programmes? And can the other global health leaders sink their differences to support WHO and each other in a new spirit of co-operation and commitment? The prospects for WHO reform will now be considered with reference to its resources, internal environment and political context.

Inadequate resources

Standing in the marble halls of WHO headquarters in Geneva, or seeing a WHO official check in to fly business class to a distant location, it is hard to imagine that the organization is in a long-running funding crisis. But appearances can be deceptive. The global WHO biennial budget of US$ 2,223 million for 2002 and 2003 was woefully inadequate for its purpose. It is a tiny fraction of the health spending of any high-income member state: equivalent, for example, to just over 0.5% of the approximate budget spent on England's national health service at the same time (Department of Health 2004).

WHO's core budget was US$ 843 million for those two years. The ratio of core funds to extrabudgetary funds (voluntary donations from all sources) is therefore approximately 1:2.6. Each member state's contribution to the regular budget is determined by a complex formula that takes the size of its economy into account, so the percentage to be contributed (though it is not always paid) ranges from 0.001% to 25% of WHO's core funding (the latter from the US). Since the early 1980s WHO, along with other UN agencies, has had zero growth in its regular budget, whose value in real terms has diminished dramatically. Some countries fail to pay their dues on time, whether through indolence or policy. The US only pays 80% of its levy because of its dissatisfaction with WHO (and other UN agencies). The amounts are in any case modest. For example, the UK contributes only US$ 22 million a year to the WHO regular budget (DFID 2002) – just 0.02% of England's national health service budget in 2004 – though it gives much more in extrabudgetary funds.

It is often mistakenly assumed that WHO is a donor agency. When hoping to start a new training programme for nurses, say, or an advocacy campaign on destigmatizing mental illness, people often say, 'Let's ask WHO for money.' In fact, in order to function, WHO itself has to take its begging bowl to countries, other agencies and charitable foundations and is increasingly turning to public-private partnerships (Buse and Walt 2002). The rich countries prefer to exert greater control over their money by giving WHO extrabudgetary funds earmarked for specific projects, rather than more core funding. Competition for such money is cut-throat and requires excellent internal coordination, as well as intensive input from professionals whose sole function is fundraising. Both are lacking in WHO so much time and effort is wasted. Programmes compete against each other for funds, internally and externally, while staff hired for their technical knowledge reluctantly find themselves fundraising. Thus the donors help to sustain an incentive system by which WHO must compete with itself, and with other organizations, for scarce funds, resulting in inefficiency and waste of human resources.

The most important negative consequence, however, is that health priorities are distorted and even neglected to conform with the desires of donors and the requirement to demonstrate quick results to them and their political paymasters. WHO has felt obliged to sideline the primary health care approach in favour of so-called 'vertical' programmes that focus on controlling specific diseases to specific targets – 'a case of the tail wagging the dog so vigorously as to make it almost dysfunctional and disoriented' (Banerji 2004). This epidemic of donor-driven programmes is not cost-effective, not sustainable, and may damage health system infrastructures. WHO cannot fairly be blamed for it, since it is so often undermined by big global health initiatives, the focus of major donors on NGOs, and the policies of government donors and huge foundations like Gates; but it does stand accused of not fighting hard enough against the trend.

Other problems arise from the trend towards public-private partnerships: first, the way in which WHO's ability to safeguard the public interest is potentially compromised by greater interaction with the commercial sector. Programmes jointly funded and implemented by a consortium of public and private partners may, if care is not taken, inappropriately benefit the private partners rather than the target populations. Yet safeguards against conflicts of interest are underdeveloped in WHO. Second, there has been little consideration of whether it would be better to find alternatives to partnerships with business, given the fragmentation caused by adding further institutional partners to the international health aid mix (Richter 2004).

Most WHO programmes and departments have to spend their budget allocation on salaries and overheads rather than programme activities. This has far-reaching negative implications in the absence of adequate programme funding, or good coordination between or even within departments, or properly resourced central functions (for example, translation, interpretation and publishing). In one important and fairly typical HQ department, the biennial cost of employing over 30 staff runs into several millions of dollars while the regular programme budget is only US\$ 500,000, supplemented by very few extrabudgetary funds. Thus staff run essentially separate programmes that are barely funded from the regular budget, and in some cases barely funded at all.

All this has a strong impact on the organizational climate and staff development. While some motivated staff move elsewhere, many of those who remain for many years, often described as 'dead wood', have few other attractive options. Too many are stuck in a honey trap – they cannot afford to leave as similar employment back home may not pay so well, especially in developing countries. WHO staff members in professional grades in headquarters and regional offices have tax-free salaries, an excellent pension scheme and many other benefits, although they often also pay for two residences, one at home and one in their duty station, and other expenses such as school fees.

World Health Organization

The hundreds of staff who work for long periods in WHO offices on a series of rolling short-term contracts are by contrast poorly paid and have few benefits. This saves the organization money and gives it greater power to hire and fire, but it damages the security and often productiveness of the individual worker, while undermining the effectiveness and sustainability of many programmes.

The internal environment: Jurassic Park or Changing History?

New posters appeared all over WHO headquarters early in 2004 promoting its latest world health report (WHO 2004). No-one disagreed with its main message, a call for a comprehensive HIV/AIDS strategy, but its title caused tongues to wag furiously. *Changing History* was doubtless chosen to inspire WHO staff and partners to redouble their efforts in the battle against the pandemic. Many people, however, did not see it that way. It seemed to them just another example of the WHO leaders' delusions of grandeur: believing that WHO can change history when it cannot apparently even change itself.

This lack of capacity in management and leadership is just one of a formidable array of hindering forces that compound the funding problems described above. It receives special attention here for three main reasons. First, whatever changes occur in its external environment, WHO will not be able to improve without better leadership and management. Second, the policy analysts, academics and public health specialists who are the biggest group of published commentators on WHO pay it little attention beyond repeating the criticism. Third, reform from within is directly within WHO's grasp, unlike many of the other challenges it faces, and is therefore a good starting point.

In the interviews conducted for this chapter, a pattern of apathy, anger, cynicism and despair emerged. The positive talk mostly comes from the successful people at the top or from the idealistic newcomers, but not from the vast majority in the middle. People often like complaining about their bosses, but this is of a different order and the pervasively depressed but frantic mood inside WHO is a cause for huge concern. Neither is it new: the atmosphere changes so little over the years that when long-term WHO-watchers and workers return after an absence they feel they are in a time warp.

It is not only low morale that contributes to the time warp feeling. Most programmes continue to lack the human and financial resources needed to achieve their ambitious goals. Most staff still work extremely hard to achieve the impossible, though a few escape into endless, pointless duty travel or hide away in front of a computer producing the 10th or 20th draft of a paper that few will ever read, still less act on. People feel unsupported and unable to speak openly, while bullying and sexual harassment are swept under the carpet. Despite the efforts of dedicated individual staff members, there are too few effective functioning mechanisms to give staff a collective voice or handle grievances well, let alone a robust, independent personnel department to lead much-needed improvements.

What happens to turn people motivated by altruism, full of ideas and expertise, and determined to make a difference, into tyrannical, cynical or fearful bureaucrats? The obvious answers are lack of leadership and poor management. Few staff have the necessary management skills when they start work in WHO, and little is done to develop them. Most senior WHO leaders are promoted from within, so they know their own system extremely well but may have had little exposure to different and better ways of doing things. Moreover, an overwhelming majority of the professional staff are doctors – an extraordinarily archaic feature given that teamwork, collaboration and intersectoral, interdisciplinary approaches are such frequent WHO buzzwords. Where are the nurses, social scientists, psychologists and action researchers? The doctors may have important medical knowledge but their training and professional socialization on the lone hero model rarely teaches them how to be effective managers or interdependent team members (Davies 1995).

The WHO regional offices have been scrutinized to a varying degree, depending on the openness of the regional directors. They tend to be elected on reform platforms, yet the politically charged environment, the corrosive effects of power and status, and their desire to ensure they are re-elected can gradually dampen their zeal. For example, in 1994 growing dissatisfaction with European regional director Dr Jo Eirik Asvall led to an unprecedented open letter from a significant number of programme managers, asking member states for active help with reform. Their pessimism contrasted with the upbeat earlier years under Asvall and his predecessor Dr Leo Kaprio (RD from 1967–1985), when Health for All guided and inspired the values, structure and programmes of the regional office.

The open letter changed little, and Asvall was re-elected in 1995. When he retired in 2000 hopes were high that his successor Dr Marc Danzon, who did not sign the letter but had seemed sympathetic to its messages, would provide a fresh approach. Yet his reaction to an external evaluation of WHO health care reform programmes in 2002 highlighted how such expectations had largely been dashed. Although pressure from member states ensured the report was presented to the next regional committee, there was no sense that it was ever taken seriously.

An internally commissioned programme review from the same period

283

found that the organizational culture of the European regional office was characterized by 'scarcity affecting competition and creating a prevailing climate of insecurity and protectionism that stands as a fundamental barrier to integrated working' (Panch 2002). It noted programme managers' limited experience of multiagency working, and a pervasive lack of communication between programmes. The regional office was considered a peripheral presence in member states and its support of health systems development was described as incoherent, inward-looking, and reluctant to relinquish its historical ascendancy. Its lack of management capacity was also noted. All these shortcomings were reported by staff themselves and their sense of frustration was palpable.

These problems are not peculiar to the European regional office, which is considered by no means the worst performer of the six regional offices. The African regional office in particular has been strongly criticized in recent years (*The Lancet* 2004), along with most of the African country offices, including charges of inefficiency, nepotism and corruption.

The political context: power games

Member states A third set of forces interacts with and compounds the funding and capacity problems described above: the attitude of member states. Their influence on the organization through the World Health Assembly, regional committees and collaborative country agreements, combined with their role in electing the DG and RDs, helps create an intensely political environment in which power games can easily supersede health goals.

In the race for top positions, both elected and appointed, support from the candidate's own country may be decisive. Improper pressure may be exerted to ensure a particular appointment or secure votes from weaker countries. Getting your own national elected – regardless of suitability for the role – is the overriding concern in the crude arena of global politics. Thus the Japanese government manoeuvred strongly for the re-election of Dr Nakajima even though his first term showed no progress and support for him was waning. Furthermore, incumbent candidates are tempted into making pre-election promises to countries to attract their vote, promises that are not necessarily in line with agreed organizational priorities or health needs. These are familiar problems with electoral politics, and perhaps the surprise is that senior WHO staff are still regarded as technocrats first and politicians second, rather than the other way round.

Many member states, particularly developing countries, would like WHO to play a stronger stewardship role in bringing together and helping coordinate the role of international and bilateral agencies and international NGOs to develop a unified, purposeful health strategy and activities to implement it. They see WHO as the natural international leader here, a trusted, independent and honest broker with strong humanitarian values that advocates adherence to key principles and international agreements.

Strengthening WHO's presence in countries technically, financially and politically could be a means of helping countries to develop a policy framework for better health that enables them to decide what donor assistance they want and to control it effectively. The senior WHO post in a country should be held by a highly qualified senior expert with director status, supported by an able team of national staff and rotated staff from elsewhere in WHO. A greater country focus, as promised by Dr Lee (and his predecessors, without very visible results), could counterbalance the centralized bureaucracy in HQ and regional offices – while recognizing that good intercountry work, including setting global and regional norms and standards, grows from and synergizes the bottom-up, intersectoral, collaborative approach to planning and implementation in countries.

The countries that are most in need of WHO support are usually, however, those with the least power and influence. The US and other OECD countries exert tight control over WHO, not least because of their control of funding. Recent public discussions have shown how the US in particular continually pressurizes WHO to steer clear of 'macroeconomics' and 'trade issues' that it says are outside its scope, and to avoid such terminology as 'the right to health'. The lack of consensus among member states about WHO's mandate naturally reflects the conflicts within the international order.

Civil society One way of circumventing inappropriate pressure from member states and other global institutions is to promote transparency and greater accountability to civil society. However, civil society's role in WHO is quite restricted. Around 200 civil society organizations are in 'formal' relations, meaning they can participate in WHO meetings, including those of the governing bodies (the Assembly and the executive board) where they have a right to make a statement – although not a vote. Another 500 organizations have no formal rights but 'informal' relationships with WHO, mostly through contacts made on work programmes. Both private for-profit and private nonprofit NGOs are included in the WHO definition of civil society, raising controversy about conflicts of interest and highlighting the need for policy-makers to distinguish between public-benefit and private-benefit organizations.

Perhaps mindful of her battles with member states during the row over the 2000 *World Health Report*, the higher profile of CSOs in securing access

Box E1.2 WHO and the People's Health Movement

The idea of a People's Health Assembly emerged in the early 1990s when it was realized that WHO's World Health Assembly was unable to hear the people's voices. A new forum was required. The first People's Health Assembly in Bangladesh in 2000 attracted 1500 people – health professionals and activists from 75 countries. A common concern was the sidelining by governments and international agencies of the goals of Health for All. The dialogue led to a consensus People's Charter for Health, the manifesto of a nascent People's Health Movement, which is now a growing coalition of people's organizations, civil society organizations, NGOs, social activists, health professionals, academics and researchers . Its goal is to re-establish health and equitable development as top priorities in local, national and international policy-making, with comprehensive primary health care as the strategy to achieve these priorities.

The assembly agreed that the institutional mechanisms needed to implement comprehensive primary health care had been neglected. The dominant technical approach – medically driven, vertical and top-down – was reflected in the organizational structure of many ministries of health and of WHO itself. Since then, the links between the Movement and WHO have grown stronger, boosted by the interest of incoming director-general Dr Lee.

'Grassroots movements are enormously important, especially in the health field,' Dr Lee told PHM representatives at a meeting in 2003. 'These movements bring the views, feelings, and expressions of those who really know. It seems almost hypocritical for WHO people here in Geneva to be talking about poverty – here, as we pay $2 for a cup of coffee, while millions struggle to survive and sustain their families on $1 a day. For this very reason, we urgently need your input. We need to hear the voices of the communities you represent. It is vital for WHO to listen to you and your communities.'

Since 2000, PHM has called for a radical transformation of WHO so that it responds to health challenges in a manner which benefits the poor, avoids vertical approaches, ensures intersectoral work, involves people's organizations in the World Health Assembly, and ensures independence from corporate interests. It has made a wide-ranging series of recommendations to WHO, summarized in the Charter and available at <www.phmovement.org>.

to medicines, and the mobilizing role of the first People's Health Assembly in 2000, Brundtland tried to raise the civil society profile, notably through the establishment of the Civil Society Initiative. These attempts have been hampered by member states and no new policy on the issue has been agreed, although meetings between Dr Lee and the People's Health Movement have been positive (Box E1.2). Greater openness to CSO involvement would bring many benefits, including closer scrutiny of policy and an institutionalized challenge to the ability of member states and corporate interests to bully WHO. It would also increase the political challenges of the environment in which WHO works, while CSOs would have to be accountable and differentiated on a public-interest basis.

Relations with other international agencies The diminished power of WHO in relation to the World Bank has been noted elsewhere in this report. The controversial nature of the Bank's policy advice to developing countries has barely been challenged in public by WHO, and for a period in the 1990s they often sang from the same hymn sheet. At other times WHO has been forced to take a weakened position: for example, its guide to the health implications of multilateral trade agreements was watered down under pressure from the World Trade Organization (Jawara and Kwa 2003). At country level WHO officials often find themselves in competition with the Bank: while the World Bank has a mandate that also includes influencing and interacting with the more powerful trade and financial ministries, WHO's mandate tends to be restricted to the health sector.

There have recently been signs of a change, with WHO making statements about restrictions on health spending imposed by the Bank and the International Monetary Fund. However, it is woefully lacking in social policy specialists, economists, and trade and intellectual property lawyers who could help create an alternative agenda. The headquarters department of health and development which should be responsible for these efforts has been reorganized twice in three years. Yet WHO's understanding of health and health systems must be rooted in a strong analytical framework in which social, economic, cultural and political determinants are taken into account. The present techno-managerial analysis, predominantly biomedical rather than social, is inadequate and leads to weak or skewed solutions.

Some ways forward

Woefully inadequate resources, poor management and leadership practices, and the power games of international politics are just some of the forces hindering sustainable change in WHO. The obstacles to change are powerful and in many ways are similar to the difficulties of achieving lasting change in the international order or in successfully reforming health care systems.

The revival of the Primary Health Care Approach (part B, chapter 1) is advocated by Dr Lee and supported by many internally. But an organization that does not listen to its own staff, punishes candour, rewards conformity and does not know how to co-operate with external partners is poorly placed to advocate those principles. An organization that does not practise what it preaches, and displays such a striking dissonance between its espoused values and its actual ways of working, lacks expertise as well as credibility and is in no shape to lead or support change internally or externally.

People who are not themselves empowered and constantly developing cannot empower or develop others. WHO cannot provide serious support to such initiatives as long as its own staff have so little understanding of change management and the ingredients of effective management practices and leadership. Ironically, these practices, drawn from researched experience and present in every successful change process, are embodied in the philosophy of Health for All.

Many organizations have successfully reinvented themselves and there is no reason why this cannot happen in WHO, but difficult choices will have to be made. WHO has neither the resources nor the authority to be all things to all people; its tendency to do too many things with too few resources is increasingly unsustainable. Member states must recognize this and work with WHO to develop a new and more focused action agenda based on its strengths and unique 'comparative advantage', with no exceptions made because of special pleading or donor demands. Some major roles for WHO that have been reiterated in the interviews and literature consulted in writing this chapter are noted in the recommendations as a starting point for discussion.

Dialogue with key actors can clarify and re-energize WHO's specific contribution to global health improvement and governance. Ways must be found to overcome the barriers of competitive rivalry that are destabilizing efforts to tackle the world's health problems. There is more than enough for everyone to do without wasting time and resources in turf wars. Links with civil society must be strengthened so that the top table round which the rich and powerful gather becomes an open, democratic, global decision-making forum where all can meet, speak their minds, listen and be heard. That will move us closer to WHO's noble objective, as set out in its constitution – 'the attainment by all peoples of the highest possible level of health'.

Recommendations

WHO's core purpose   Below are proposals for WHO's core roles derived from our literature review and interviews, which can be debated and fleshed out in the future:

- Acting as the world's health conscience, promoting a moral framework for health and development policy, and asserting the human right to health.
- Promoting the principles of the Alma Ata declaration on Health for All.
- Establishing, maintaining and monitoring global norms and standards on health and health care.
- Strengthening its role as an informed and trusted repository and disseminator of health information and experience.
- Conducting, commissioning and synthesizing health and health systems research, including research on the health impact of economic activities.
- Promoting and protecting the global commons, including the creation of transnational goods such as research and development capacity, and control of transnational externalities such as spread of pathogens.
- Providing a mechanism for coordinating transnational/cross-boundary threats to health.
- Strengthening WHO's presence in countries to play a stronger stewardship role in coordinating and bringing together international and bilateral agencies and international NGOs to develop a unified, purposeful multisectoral health strategy and activities to implement it.

Democratization/ governance

- Take measures to position WHO as an organization of the people as well as of governments. This involves representation of broader groups of interests including civil society, and processes that ensure a wide range of voices is heard and heeded.
- Support and expand the Civil Society Initiative at WHO. Southern civil society organizations need support to have a more direct voice. Public-interest organizations must be differentiated from those representing commercial interests, including front organizations funded by transnational corporations.
- The politicized nature of the elections of the director-general and regional directors needs to be tempered. Possible solutions include a wider franchise, perhaps with an electoral college of international public health experts to complement the member states' votes, including representatives from civil society organizations. Candidates should be required to publish a manifesto and WHO should facilitate widespread debate about them, with

World Health Organization

open selection criteria that reflect the roles' leadership and management requirements.

- There should be a strategic assessment of where WHO should be influential in the interests of health in relation to other multilateral bodies, and the existing liaison mechanisms between WHO and the international trade and financial institutions.

Funding and programming

- Donors should strive to increase their overall donations towards an agreed target.
- Donors should shift a proportion of their funding of extrabudgetary programmes into the regular budget. The aim should be a roughly equal apportioning of funding between the two arms of the budget, without any corresponding decline in the total budget.
- WHO should work on fewer priorities and ask donors to match their resources to them, to shift the balance between staff costs and activities and avoid 'project-chasing'; these priorities should be followed through in collaborative agreements with member states.
- Programmes (and the organization's structure) should be organized around the Primary Health Care Approach, resulting in the strengthening of systems-oriented units and divisions.
- Extrabudgetary donations should follow agreed overall priorities – donors should avoid tying them too tightly to specific programmes and outputs.
- Explicit resource allocation formulae should be developed to encourage better balances between core/extrabudgetary and staff/programme costs.
- The benefits, risks and costs of global public-private partnerships in health should be openly debated and compared to alternatives.
- WHO should develop strong safeguards against conflicts of interest in funding, priority-setting and partnerships.

Leadership and management Actions that WHO leaders can take to change the culture and improve their management and leadership:

- Revisit WHO's mission with all staff to renew their collective ownership and commitment: clarify priorities, agree comparative advantages, and from that develop a strategy, allocate funds and stick to it, including sufficient funding for core infrastructure functions.
- Recruit more diverse staff from different backgrounds and cultures, including more women, more people from the South, more people who are not

doctors, and more people with experience in a variety of settings in developing countries, intersectoral action and project management.

- Require proof of effective leadership and management experience as a criterion for staff recruitment, especially at senior levels.
- Make WHO a learning organization with a culture committed to continuous improvement, through giving all staff excellent continuing professional development opportunities; high-level management training for all senior staff; learning from good practice and sharing ideas, approaches and information; and regular, meaningful, non-blaming collective and individual performance review.
- Introduce regular rotation of staff to avoid stagnation and gain experience at global, regional and country levels.
- End casualization of the workforce, including reducing number of staff employed for long periods on a series of short-term contracts.
- Stop unstructured consultancies, internships and secondments that have little benefit for the individual, WHO or countries.
- Make better use of the expertise of senior WHO-friendly practitioners, academics, policy-makers and researchers, including short-term secondments.
- Review and streamline administrative processes and procedures.
- Strengthen the capacity and independence of WHO personnel departments, and introduce/enforce robust personnel policies with mechanisms for rapid response and staff support, and zero tolerance of corruption, nepotism and abuse of staff.
- Strengthen mechanisms to represent staff interests, including a staff association organized on trade union principles with collective bargaining powers and a properly resourced secretariat.

References

Banerji D (2004). *Contribution to WHO Bulletin roundtable on donor funding and national allocations on health.* Unpublished paper.

Brown T, Cueto M, Fee E (2004). *The World Health Organization and the Transition from 'International' to 'Global' Public Health.* Joint Learning Initiative Paper 1–1. Harvard, MA., Global Health Trust (http://www.globalhealthtrust.org/doc/abstracts/WG1/FeeBrownCuetoPAPER.pdf, accessed 29 March 2005).

Buse K, Walt G (2002). The World Health Organization and global public-private health partnerships: in search of 'good' global health governance. In: Reich M, ed. *Public-private partnerships for public health*, Harvard series on population and international health. Cambridge, Ma, Harvard University Press.

Davies C (1995). *Gender and the professional predicament in nursing.* Milton Keynes, Open University Press.

Department for International Development (2002). *Working in partnership with the World Health Organization.* Institutional Strategy Paper. London, DFID.

Department of Health (2004). *Departmental report (summary report).* London, Department of Health (http://www.dh.gov.uk).

Godlee F (1997). WHO reform and global health. *British Medical Journal*, 314:1359, May 10.

Jawara F and Kwa A (2003). *Behind the scenes at the WTO.* London, Zed Books.

Kickbusch I (2004). *The end of public health as we know it: constructing global health in the 21st century.* Hugh R Leavell Lecture, April (www.ilonakickbusch.com, accessed 26 February 2005).

Lee JW (2003). Global health improvement and WHO: shaping the future. *The Lancet*, 362:2083–88, December 20/27.

Lee K (1998). *Historical dictionary of the World Health Organization.* Historical Dictionaries of International Organizations, No 15. Lanham, Md, and London, The Scarecrow Press.

Lerer L, Matzopoulos R (2001). 'The worst of the both worlds': the management reform of the World Health Organization. *International Journal of Health Services* 31:421.

Minelli E (2003). *WHO: the mandate of a specialized agency of the United Nations.* Geneva Foundation for Medical Education and Research (www.gfmer.ch).

Murray C, Lopez A, Wibulpolprasert S (2004). Monitoring global health: time for new solutions. *British Medical Journal,* 329:1096–1100, November 6.

Panch T (2002). *WHO EURO and health systems development.* Health Systems Development programme, Copenhagen, WHO Regional Office for Europe internal document.

Richter, J (2004). *Elements for Discussion: Public-private partnerships and international health policy-making. How can public interests be safeguarded?* Helsinki: Finnish Ministry for Foreign Affairs (http://global.finland.fi/julkaisut/pdf/public_private2004.pdf, accessed 29 March 2005).

Selbervik H, Jerve A (2003). *MOPAN: report from the 2003 pilot exercise.* Bergen, Chr Michelsen Institute (www.cmi.no, accessed 10 March 2005).

The Lancet (2004). WHO's African regional office must evolve or die. Unsigned editorial, 364:475–6, August 7.

WHO (2004). *The world health report 2004: changing history.* Geneva, WHO.

Wibulpolprasert S, Tangcharoensathien V (2001). Health systems performance – what's next? *Bulletin of the World Health Organization*, 79(6), 489.

Yamey G (2002). WHO's management: struggling to transform a 'fossilised bureaucracy'. *British Medical Journal*, 325:1170–1173, November 16.

Information about WHO, many important documents, and links to its regional office websites and other health organizations are available at its global web site www.who.int.

E2 | UNICEF

In 2005, Carol Bellamy, UNICEF's executive director, stepped down from a position she had occupied for 10 years as the world's most senior advocate for child health. She left at a critical time. The fourth Millennium Development Goal – reducing the under-five mortality rate by two thirds between 1990 and 2015 – will not be met in many countries. 'Progress against child mortality has so far been so slow that no sub-Saharan country in Africa is on target to reach that MDG' (World Bank 2004).

More than 10 million children die every year (Black et al. 2003). Over 60% of those deaths were and remain preventable. Under-nutrition contributes to the deaths of over half of all children. Cost-effective interventions are available for all major causes of child mortality, but coverage levels are appallingly low in the 42 countries that account for 90% of child deaths: 80% of children do not receive oral rehydration therapy when they need it, 61% of children under six months are not exclusively breastfed, 60% do not receive treatment for acute respiratory infections, and 45% do not receive vitamin A supplements. The gap in survival between the richest and poorest children is increasing.

Box E2.1 UNICEF

UNICEF was created in 1946 as the UN International Children's Emergency Fund to tackle the threats posed to children in Europe from disease and famine after World War II. It became a permanent part of the UN in 1953. Health has become an increasingly central part of its work over the decades. At present, UNICEF has five priorities embedded within its programmes: girls' education; immunisation; HIV/AIDS; early childhood development; and child protection.

Its income in 2003 was US$1.6 billion, 64% of which came as a result of contributions made directly by member governments. It has 7000 staff working in 157 countries. Nearly 90% of its staff works outside of the agency's headquarters, making it one of the most decentralized UN agencies. The organization is governed by a 36-member executive board made up of government representatives elected by the UN Economic and Social Council. (*Source*: http://www.unicef.org)

Box E2.2 Who is Ann Veneman, the new head of UNICEF?

Ann Veneman is the outgoing US Agriculture Secretary, making her a senior member of the Bush administration.

Her recent round of speeches accepting the position as head of UNICEF suggest a conservative line on family planning, raising concern amongst NGOs who work in the field of reproductive health (Illingworth 2005).

Her close connection with the corporate agribusiness sector (Nichols 2001; Mattera 2004) raises concerns that she will not address many of the root problems of household food insecurity, but may even support and foster the increasing control of food production and processing systems by a small number of major agribusiness corporations.

Veneman joined the US Department of Agriculture in 1986, serving as Associate Administrator until 1989. During this time she helped negotiate the Uruguay round talks for the General Agreement on Tariffs and Trade. She subsequently served as Deputy Undersecretary of Agriculture for International Affairs and Commodity Programs. From 1991 to 1993, she served as the second in command at the Department of Agriculture.

At this point Veneman took a break from government and went to work with the high-powered law firm and lobby group, Patton Boggs, as well as serving on the Board of Directors of Calgene – the first company to market genetically-engineered food. (Calgene was eventually bought out by Monsanto – the country's leading biotech company, which in turn, became part of pharmaceutical company Pharmacia in 2000.) Veneman also served on the International Policy Council on Agriculture, Food and Trade, a lobby group funded by Cargill, Nestle, Kraft, and Archer Daniels Midland.

In 1995 she went back to government, when she was appointed Secretary of the California Department of Food and Agriculture. In 1999 she once again passed through the revolving door between the government and corporate sectors, and worked as an attorney with Nossaman, Guthner, Knox and Elliott before being appointed by Bush as Secretary of State for Agriculture in 2001.

During her tenure, she is said to have advanced the interests of food production and processing conglomerates, allowed policies that led to the displacement of family farms by large industrial farms, supported the genetic modification of food and defended biotech experimentation with agriculture (Flanders and Stauber 2004; Nichols 2001).

In sum, for almost a decade, children and child health have failed to get the attention they deserve.

Given this failure of children, the appointment of Bellamy's successor should have generated widespread professional and public discussion. Yet there was only private lobbying and public silence; the entire appointment process was shrouded in secrecy. The announcement in January 2005 that Ann Veneman would become UNICEF's fifth executive director, continuing an unbroken line of Americans at the helm since it was founded, has been greeted with anxiety and despair (PHM 2005). She has no track record in child health (see Box E2.2).

Experts in international child health consulted by *The Lancet* in 2004 thought that UNICEF needed to be led by an energetic and inspirational person who was ambitious for the future of the world's children, with political integrity, a willingness to speak with a strong voice against power, and a proven interest in the well-being and health of children (Horton 2004). Ms Veneman is not even a near fit.

The selection of Veneman was made by Kofi Annan, who chose to make a politically motivated appointment that would be favourable to the UN's largest funder – the US government. This thoroughly discredited process of selection damages the integrity of the UN system and may prove disastrous for the future of child health. Veneman can serve no more than two five-year terms. But UNICEF and children deserve better.

Before the end of her first five-year term, the world must agree on a new process of selection for the sixth head of UNICEF to take office in 2010. Nominations should be placed on the public record and not be limited to US citizens. Each shortlisted nominee should appear and be questioned before a specially appointed UN intergovernmental committee, with balanced representation between high, middle, and low income countries – including those nations that bear the greatest burden of child mortality. In this way, selection would be more transparent, fair and meritocratic.

The challenge to UNICEF

The fact that 10.8 million children die every year prompted a recent discussion in *The Lancet* (Horton 2004) about the role and effectiveness of UNICEF. While there is unanimity about the importance of an effective UN agency dedicated to promoting the survival, health and rights of children, there are clearly differences of opinion about the appropriate role and functions of UNICEF.

According to the *Lancet* article, UNICEF lost its way during Bellamy's 10-year term when it shifted attention away from the child survival programmes of her predecessor, the late James Grant. Others, on the other hand, point to a positive legacy of Bellamy which saw UNICEF promote a greater recognition of the rights of children, including the right to protection from violence, abuse, exploitation and discrimination; and the importance of girls' education and early childhood development.

These differing perceptions reflect a tension between those who advocate a selective approach to reducing mortality as the ultimate priority (particularly of young children, and usually involving health care interventions) with those who see UNICEF's vision as being broader and more developmental.

In our view, this tension does not reflect a choice between mutually incompatible approaches, but the need for strategic balance. It would be harmful and counter-productive for UNICEF to revert back to a narrow 'child survival' agenda, as it did in the 1980s under the leadership of James Grant when UNICEF focused on the delivery of life-saving technology in the absence of a more comprehensive agenda for child development and rights. In the words of one *Lancet* respondent, 'we do not want to return to the days when we could not discuss children's quality of life, so intensely were we focused on body counts' (McCann 2005).

On the other hand, child survival clearly needs to be at the heart of UNICEF. But the appropriate response to the unacceptable levels of child deaths cannot be seen solely in terms of UNICEF. It is a challenge for many agencies, in particular WHO. The delivery of essential child health care interventions should form a central part of WHO's mission, with WHO (and not UNICEF) taking the lead in developing the strategies and systems to enable the delivery of essential health care, including immunizations, and the clinical management of diarrhoeal disease and ARIs.

It should be within the ambit of WHO, together with other health systems stakeholders, in particular, ministries of health, to determine the most appropriate way to balance dedicated child health programmes within comprehensive health systems development. The challenge for UNICEF is to develop a working relationship with WHO that supports this mission, rather than to act in parallel. This could entail UNICEF continuing to do much of its excellent programmatic work, but within the framework of a comprehensive health systems agenda.

UNICEF should also bring to bear its mandate to protect children upon the various public policy reforms that undermine the capacity of governments to ensure adequate safety nets for the vulnerable and marginalized sections of society, including children. This would build on UNICEF's landmark study (Cornia, Jolly and Stewart 1987), *Adjustment with a Human Face*, which prompted a global debate on how to protect children and women from the effects of economic reform. Today, UNICEF should be asking similarly searching questions about the effect of neoliberal policy reform and privatization on the health of children.

What about addressing the inadequate lack of access to education, the exploitation and trafficking of children in an unregulated global economy and the need for family planning? Should such issues form a part of UNICEF's core priorities? Undoubtedly so – the organization's mission to protect, nourish and cherish children cannot be reduced to the mere delivery of life-saving technologies within the health sector. It should be UNICEF's mission to place the well-being of children at the centre of the UN, and at the centre of globalization.

In doing so, UNICEF, as with other UN agencies, must address its internal weakneses and address the frequent media reports of waste, nepotism, cronyism, discrimination, and harassment with better management and effective action (Hackbarth 2004). However, the clarity of vision around UNICEF's role and priorities, and any improvement of its own performance, may ultimately amount to nothing if the organization is headed up, not by a friend of children in poor countries, but by a friend of corporate America.

It will be essential for the global health community to keep its eyes firmly trained on UNICEF in the coming years.

References

Black R, Morris S, Bryce J (2003). Where and why are 10 million children dying every year? *The Lancet*, 361: 2226–2234.

Cornia G, Jolly R and Stewart F (1987*). Adjustment with a human face.* Oxford, Oxford University Press.

Flanders and Stauber (2004). *Agriculture Secretary Veneman's Tenure Marked by Anthrax Scare, Trade Disputes and Mad Cow Disease* (http://www.democracynow.org/article.pl?sid=04/11/16/1611229 , accessed 18 March 2005).

Hackbarth S (2005). Unicef: Suggestions for change. *Lancet*, 365: 290–1.

Horton R (2004). UNICEF leadership 2005–2015: a call for strategic change. *Lancet* 2004; 364: 2071–74.

Illingworth B (2005). *Who is Ann Veneman.* Planned Parenthood Federation of America (http://www.plannedparenthood.org/pp2/portal/files/portal/webzine/globaldispatch/gd-050209-veneman.xml, accessed 18 March 2005).

Mattera P (2004). *USDA Inc: How Agribusiness has Hijacked Regulatory Policy at the US Department of Agriculture,* Corporate Research Project of Good Jobs First (http://www.agribusinessaccountability.org/pdfs//289_USDA%20Inc..pdf, accessed 15 March 2005).

McCann M (2005). Unicef: Suggestions for change. *Lancet*, 365: 292.

Nichols J (2001). *Meet Ann Veneman – Perhaps Bush's Most Dangerous Cabinet Pick* (http://www.commondreams.org/views01/0115-04.htm, accessed 18 March 2005).

Peoples Health Movement (2005). *Defend UNICEF's mission to defend children!* PHM (http://www.saveunicef.org, accessed 14 March 2005).

World Bank (2004). *Rising to the challenges: the Millennium Development Goals for Health.* Washington, World Bank.

E3 | The World Bank and the International Monetary Fund

The World Bank and the International Monetary Fund were set up at a meeting of 43 countries in Bretton Woods, New Hampshire, US in July 1944. The reform of these 'Bretton Woods institutions' and the establishment of systems to hold them accountable to civil society are vital public health challenges. This chapter describes how they are managed and governed, within the broader political and economic context detailed in part A, and proposes reforms.

What are the Bretton Woods institutions?

The World Bank Group is the second largest public development institution in the world, lending around US$25 billion a year to reduce poverty and facilitate economic growth in developing countries. (Only the European Investment Bank is larger, but much of its lending is to European Union countries.) The World Bank was initially established to improve the capacity of countries to trade by lending money to war-ravaged countries for long-term reconstruction and development projects. It now exerts the single largest influence over policy-making through the conditions attached to its loans, and the research and advice it provides to governments. It has become a much bigger influence than the WHO in the health sector.

The IMF also influences the health sector through its ability to dictate countries' macroeconomic and fiscal policies. It was established to create a stable climate for international trade by harmonizing its country members' monetary policies and maintaining exchange-rate stability. It was designed to provide temporary financial assistance to countries encountering difficulties with their balance of payments.

Governance of the World Bank Group The World Bank Group comprises five institutions. The original institution was the International Bank for Reconstruction and Development, often simply known as the World Bank. Led by a president appointed by the US government, it employs nearly 10,000 staff including 4000 in its country offices. Its board of governors is largely ceremonial, while its executive directors are appointed civil servants who meet regularly in Washington, using voting power based on one dollar, one vote. The US holds 17% of the vote, giving it a veto over any decisions requiring a super-majority of

85%, and is represented by its own director. In contrast, 47 sub-Saharan African countries have only two directors (out of 24) and 7% of the vote.

According to a now outdated formula, each member country is assigned a capital quota of which it pays in 2% in hard currency (gold or US dollars) and 18% in national currency. The remaining 80% is kept callable (to be paid in the event of unusually high demands placed on the Bank's lending capacity). This guarantee acts as a form of collateral allowing the Bank (or more precisely the IBRD) to raise most of its loan money through the sale of bonds to private investors. In contrast, funding for the interest-free loans and grants of the International Development Association (the World Bank Group's public-sector lending facility) is raised from the rich countries every three years.

Loans were originally supposed to be given to specific projects – usually infrastructure projects such as the construction of highways, dams and telecommunications facilities. Many of these loans contributed to the debt crisis that emerged in the 1980s. Developing countries were encouraged to borrow heavily to invest in infrastructure when interest rates were low, but corruption, poor project design and a sharp rise in interest rates played havoc with their ability to repay. Today, approximately 15% of the debt of the poorest, most heavily indebted countries is held by the Bank and the Fund. Estimates vary as to how much of this is 'odious' debt, i.e. funds knowingly lent to regimes where the probability of misuse was high – perhaps as much as US$ 100 billion.

In 1980, the Bank began to do more than just lend money and introduced structural adjustment programmes (SAP), long-term loans to countries experiencing recurrent balance of payments problems. These came with a variety of conditions aimed at restructuring their economies so they could earn the foreign currency needed to repay outstanding loans. Restructuring consisted of reducing public expenditure; liberalizing trade, investment and capital controls; deregulation; and the privatization of state-owned enterprises. The priority was debt repayment – often at the cost of people's lives and health.

Governance of the IMF When countries join the Fund, they deposit a quota subscription that determines both how much they can withdraw in a crisis, and voting rights. The Fund employs about 2700 staff, virtually all in Washington. Like the Bank's structural adjustment lending, it lends money to countries with balance of payments problems for short-term measures to restore financial health. Borrowers must implement a set of economic reforms. Loans are disbursed in instalments, each tied to compliance with structural adjustment policies. They are granted to low-income countries at a concessional interest rate while others are provided at market rates. Typically, member countries

22 World Bank: the centre of world health policy?

are allowed to borrow over a period of 1–4 years to support macroeconomic stabilization programmes, and repayments are made in 3–10 years. Less often countries can access very short-term financing in an economic crisis, requiring repayment in 1–2 years with a heavier surcharge.

The influence of Bretton Woods

'The belief that the Bank forces its agenda on developing countries is consistent and overwhelming in all regions and virtually all countries,' according to a survey of 2600 opinion leaders in 48 countries (World Bank 2003). The Bank and Fund can influence government policy choices in a surprising number of ways, most obviously through 'hard' conditions – certain policy reforms which must be implemented before any funds are handed over. This type of conditionality reached its peak in the late 1990s: the average number of Fund structural conditions rose from three in 1988 to 16 in 1998, while the average Bank loan was accompanied by dozens of conditions.

In 2000 the Bank renamed its deeply unpopular structural adjustment programmes. Poverty Reduction Support Credits are supposed to emphasize recipient country ownership and fund programmes identified in Poverty Reduction Strategy Papers developed by governments. There is widespread dissatisfaction that major economic decisions remain in the hands of finance ministry officials in consultation with Bank and Fund economists (Stewart and Wang 2003). A review of African PRSPs concluded that their elements of policy were strikingly similar to those pursued under structural adjustment (UNCTAD 2002).

A second type of influence is the 'signalling' function to other donors. The Fund sits at the top of the donors' pecking order. A country cannot borrow from the Bank if it does not have a Fund programme, and no Fund and Bank programme means no bilateral donor will lend. This power over the on-off switch is being consolidated through efforts towards donor harmonization, which, although intended to provide relief from the procedural burden of maintaining multiple donor relationships, risks giving the Bank and Fund more influence over aid and debt relief (Bretton Woods Project 2003a).

Bank economists use the Country Policy and Institutional Assessment to rank the policy performance of low-income countries to determine the amount of lending they may receive. This score is then used by the Bank and other donors in making decisions on aid allocation and debt sustainability. Some of the 16 indicators are subjective and highly politicized (CNES 2004), while the data used are not available to the public or governments. What is obvious to governments is the policy mix that will score high and therefore turn on the donor tap.

A third way of influencing government policy is the provision of 'analytical, advisory and assessment' services. Since 1996 the Bank's president has emphasized its role as a 'knowledge bank', framing development debates and influencing civil servants' thinking.

Criticisms of the Bank and Fund

Effects of structural adjustment The package of liberalization, deregulation and privatization, known as the Washington Consensus, has failed to achieve the promised economic growth (SAPRIN 2004). Imposition of these conditions has often led to the destruction of entire sectors of the economy and severely undermined social services. Many countries have experienced 'IMF riots' after conditions requiring wage freezes or the removal of price controls pushed vulnerable citizens over the edge (Kruse 2003).

The use of explicit conditions tied to specific loans is simply ineffective (see, for example, Killick et al. 1998). They are often imposed without regard to the country's historical, social, economic and institutional characteristics. They undermine the accountability of policy-makers to their citizens and erode the sustainability of the reforms and the institutions that implement them. The approach to conditionality is being softened in response to pressure: the Bank has acknowledged the need to understand the impacts of policy changes on the most vulnerable *before* the policies are implemented. A 2003 Fund review resulted in a reduction in the number of overt conditions, while the Bank's use of conditionality is to be reviewed in 2005.

Impact of mega-projects The types of development project funded by the Group are a cause for concern. Many infrastructure projects have negative social and environmental consequences. Bank-funded construction of hydro-electric dams has resulted in the displacement of Indigenous peoples without proper compensation and destroyed fragile ecosystems. There is particular concern over continued support for oil, gas and mining projects, and the conflict between Bank rhetoric on climate change and the reality of its lending programmes. The Bank has yet to provide evidence that support for extractive industries fulfils its mandate to reduce poverty; local people subjected to the pollution of their air, land, and drinking water enjoy few – if any – of the benefits.

Undermining state provision The Bank, working in partnership with the private sector, is accused of undermining the role of the state as the primary provider of essential goods and services. Corporate pressure exerted via major shareholding countries has resulted in an ideological bias towards privatization, and maintains support for loans to transnational corporations that amount to little more than corporate welfare (see part A, and part D, chapter 2 for example).

Shrinking the Bank and shunning the Fund

Reform is long overdue. However, the most influential players are the finance ministers of the G7 countries, above all the US Treasury which sees no need for reform. Their financial support of the Bank and Fund fails to generate debate in parliament, leaving key decisions in the hands of civil servants. Similarly, investors in World Bank bonds floated to finance the IBRD have yet to really make their presence felt: a new campaign, the World Bank Bonds Boycott, is attempting to change this. The citizens of rich countries have little opportunity to debate, let alone influence their actions. The greatest impact of civil society has been through direct action – protests in the streets of borrower countries under austerity programmes; decades-long battles against ineffective and unjust projects; long campaigns against the privatization of services.

The reform agenda

Many critics say the Bank and Fund are unreformable. Those who advocate reform call for different kinds of actions from many sections of civil society: activists generating pressure for change in the streets; academics providing evidence; public servants defending the right to essential services; parliamentarians reclaiming national sovereignty over policy-making; and NGOs carrying all these messages to governments and the institutions. Reform should address a number of issues, as follows:

Organizational structure The Bank must be governed and managed by directors and senior staff appointed through open and meritocratic rules. The composition and voting power of the boards must reflect fairer representation of the recipient countries, rather than the rich countries' influence and corporate interests. The staff of the Bank and the Fund must become more diverse.

Decision-making and transparency Voting procedures on the board must become transparent and formalized and key documents published. Final authority for national development strategies must rest with sovereign parliaments, not with the board (Bretton Woods Project 2004).

Public accountability Greater powers must be given to independent evaluation bodies. The Bank and the Fund must become subject to international law.

Reform measures specific to the Fund include:

Mandate Create regional monetary funds to encourage a tailored response to financial imbalances; eliminate loan conditions other than those relating to repayment and transparency.

Lending Return to original mandate to provide short-term finance to address short-term crises; remove the 'seal of approval' function.

Surveillance and monitoring The same discipline should apply to all member countries, including powerful actors; surveillance should be exercised by independent evaluators, not Fund staff.

Reform measures specific to the Bank include:

Mandate Roll back the Bank's 'mission creep' into national policy-making and issue areas for which other specialized agencies have a mandate, e.g. health.

Projects The repayment terms of credit instruments should be suited to the revenue-generating potential of the project funded. Social and environmental policies should explicitly refer to international standards and the Bank should respond to judgements by international treaty bodies. Private sector arms should not subsidize transnational corporations and instead should assist small and medium enterprises from developing countries. Independent arbitration should ensure that when Bank projects fail because of poor design, the costs are shared with the borrower government.

Structural adjustment Eliminate all conditions except those relating to transparency and the prevention of corruption in public spending. Introduce peer review mechanisms for countries. Respond to the analysis of UN specialized agencies on broader governance issues, rather than conduct such analysis.

Knowledge End role as global think-tank on all development policy issues; subject all Bank research to peer review; end pretensions to leadership on global public goods; and stop training and capacity-building of journalists, parliamentarians etc.

Resources and further information

The *Bretton Woods Project* is a UK-based watchdog of the World Bank and IMF (http://www.brettonwoodsproject.org).

IFIwatchnet connects organizations worldwide monitoring the international financial institutions (http://www.ifiwatchnet.org).

World Bank Bonds Boycott (http://www.worldbankboycott.org).

References

Bretton Woods Project (2003a). Harmonisation and coherence: white knights or Trojan horses? (http://www.brettonwoodsproject.org/article.shtml?cmd%5B126%5D=x-126–16735, accessed 25 February 2005).

Bretton Woods Project (2003b). US, Europeans trade blows over lack of progress on Bank, Fund governance reform (http://www.brettonwoodsproject.org/article.shtml?cmd[126]=x-126–16567, accessed 25 February 2005).

Bretton Woods Project (2004). Parliaments reign in IFIs: international campaign gains momentum (http://www.brettonwoodsproject.org/article.shtml?cmd[126]=x-126-72225, accessed 25 February 2005).

CNES (2004). Judge and jury: the World Bank's scorecard for borrowing governments. Citizen's Network for Essential Services (http://www.servicesforall.org, accessed 28 February 2005).

Killick T, Gunatilaka R, Marr A (1998). *Aid and the political economy of political change*. London and New York, Routledge.

Kruse T (2003). *The IMF and the Bolivian crisis* (http://www.ifiwatchnet.org/doc/bolivi-aimf.pdf, accessed 26 February 2005).

Stewart F, Wang M (2003). *Do PRSPs empower poor countries and disempower the World Bank, or is it the other way round?* Working paper 108, May, Queen Elizabeth

House, University of Oxford (http://www.eurodad.org/uploadstore/cms/docs/WbevalMay03.pdf).

Structural Adjustment Participatory Review Initiative Network (SAPRIN) (2004). *Structural adjustment: the policy roots of economic crisis, poverty and inequality.* London, Zed Books.

UNCTAD (2002). *Economic development in Africa: from adjustment to poverty reduction, what is new?* Geneva, UNCTAD.

World Bank (2003). *The Global Poll: multinational survey of opinion leaders 2002.* Washington DC, World Bank.

E4 | Big business

This chapter deals with the regulation of big business in the interests of health through legal restrictions and financial taxation.

Corporate power is growing – of the 100 largest economic entities in the world, 51 are corporations. The combined sales of the top 200 businesses are 18 times that of the combined income of the poorest quarter of the world's population (Anderson and Cavanagh 2000). Assessing their impact on health, and trying to prevent negative consequences, is therefore an urgent public health responsibility.

The case studies below suggest ways in which successful regulation can occur and where more action is needed. The examples of control of tobacco and breast-milk substitutes are described as positive instances of global regulatory arrangements which support health. It is important to learn lessons from these successes and to note the continuing battles that need to be fought. A third case study looks at the declining tax burden on corporations and suggests that a global campaign needs to be fought to defend taxation as a key source of public expenditure for health and health-sustaining services.

Case study 1: The Global Tobacco Treaty

Irresponsible and dangerous corporate actions threaten people's lives around the world every day. With so much at stake, people from many backgrounds are coming together to use a range of strategies to challenge corporate abuses, and working together toward a world where major decisions affecting people and the environment are based on the public interest, not on maximizing corporate profits.

Corporations often cause and get away with serious damage to people and the environment because of their political influence. They typically use this influence to block or eliminate proposed public protections, and to promote and enact policies and regulations that benefit their bottom line at the expense of the public good. As part A of the *Watch* showed, they are assisted by a variety of trade-related agreements and rules that reduce government power to regulate and protect public health and the environment. Transnational corporations in particular operate globally with few limits on their power and influence or strong, enforceable standards.

This section looks at the global challenge to Big Tobacco, one of the most powerful and deadly industries in the world. The WHO Framework Convention on Tobacco Control (FCTC) is a critical tool for protecting and promoting public health and corporate accountability and its implementation would help to end the global tobacco epidemic. Its history to date provides lessons that may be applicable when challenging other industries that threaten health, environmental and human rights. This was recognized in a 2003 issue of *Tobacco Reporter*, a prominent industry journal: 'Tobacco executives caution other industries about allowing WHO to assume such control over their global market. BAT pointed out that as the world's first international health agreement, the tobacco control treaty sets a precedent that could affect many other industries' (*Tobacco Reporter* 2003).

Overview of the FCTC The FCTC is a milestone in the history of corporate accountability and public health. As an international agreement adopted by the 192 member states of WHO, it could change the way tobacco giants like Philip Morris (now Altria), British American Tobacco (BAT) and Japan Tobacco International (JTI) operate. Between the first negotiating session in 2000, and February 2005 when the treaty took effect as international law, at least 20 million people died from tobacco-related illnesses. If current trends continue, these illnesses will become the world's leading cause of death by 2030, with 70% of the deaths occurring in the global South.

The World Health Assembly had called in 1996 for development of the world's first public health treaty to control the spread of tobacco addiction, and set the negotiating process in motion in 1999. Director-general Gro Harlem Brundtland put it on a fast track with the goal of adoption by 2003. WHO and member states convened working groups to prepare the draft elements and an inter-governmental negotiating body began talks. The 192 countries of the WHA adopted the treaty unanimously on 21 May 2003.

From the beginning of the process developing countries pushed for effective measures to reverse the global tobacco epidemic and hold tobacco transnationals accountable for their abuses. India, Iran, Jamaica, Palau, Senegal, South Africa and Thailand played key leadership roles during the negotiations. Early in the treaty's development, evidence from once-secret corporate documents showed that the tobacco industry had operated for years with the expressed intention of subverting the role of governments and WHO in implementing health policies. The WHA responded in 2001 with a precedent-setting resolution, WHA54.18, calling on WHO to monitor the global impact of the tobacco industry's political activities and urging governments to ensure the integrity of health policy development. This paved the way for the treaty

23 The Marlboro Man was described by his creator as 'the right image to capture the youth market's fancy ... a perfect symbol of independence and individualistic rebellion'. The advertising icon made Marlboro the favourite cigarette among US teenagers and the world's leading cigarette brand.

to include provisions protecting public health policies from interference by tobacco corporations, their subsidiaries and affiliates.

Well over 200 NGOs were active on the treaty, including 26 public interest NGOs in official relations with WHO. The Network for Accountability of Tobacco Transnationals (NATT) comprises more than 100 consumer, human rights, environmental, faith-based and corporate accountability organizations in over 50 countries, while the Framework Convention Alliance has 187 members including major international tobacco control and public health organizations. These NGOs provided technical assistance to government delegates, monitored and exposed tobacco industry abuses such as interference in public health policy, generated direct pressure on the transnationals, increased visibility of tobacco control issues in the media, and raised public awareness of the treaty. Corporate Accountability International's consumer boycott targeting Kraft Foods, owned by Philip Morris/Altria, raised public awareness of abuses like the Marlboro Man, an advertising icon that helped make Marlboro the world's leading cigarette brand (see Illustration 23). It exposed the truth behind its corporate image, and reduced its economic and political influence.

These shifts in the public and political climate helped provide WHO and member states with the political will and momentum to pursue the treaty, which opened for signature in 2003. Within a year there were 168 signatories, making it one of the most rapidly embraced UN treaties ever. Over 40 countries had ratified it through their domestic processes by late 2004, triggering its entry into force on 27 February 2005 in the ratifying countries. The 40th ratification makes it the first international, legally binding public health treaty under the auspices of WHO.

Key provisions of the FCTC The treaty includes a range of provisions that will change business as usual for Big Tobacco. Some of the key provisions from a corporate accountability perspective are discussed below:

ADVERTISING, PROMOTION AND SPONSORSHIP [article 13] The treaty includes a comprehensive ban on tobacco advertising, promotion and sponsorship.

PUBLIC HEALTH VS. TRADE IN TOBACCO [Preamble] The treaty gives governments the right to put the health of their citizens above trade and commercial interests. The first line of the treaty, establishing that parties to this convention are 'determined to give priority to their right to protect public health', will provide interpretive guidance if tobacco control measures based on the treaty are attacked under trade or investment agreements.

PROTECTING PUBLIC HEALTH POLICY FROM TOBACCO INDUSTRY INTERFERENCE [Articles 5.3, 12(e) and 20.4(c)] The treaty obligates parties to protect public health policies from commercial and other vested interests of the tobacco industry, and calls for exchange of information on 'the activities of the tobacco industry which have an impact on the Convention or national tobacco control activities'. The inclusion of this language will help empower countries to curtail the tobacco industry's involvement in and influence over public health policy.

LIABILITY AND COMPENSATION FOR HARMS CAUSED BY TOBACCO [Articles 4.5 and 19] Unfortunately the treaty does not include a clear statement of the industry's responsibility for harms caused by its products. It does, however, encourage international cooperation to hold tobacco corporations liable for the harms they cause. The inclusion of an article on liability in a framework convention is a significant step toward holding the transnationals accountable.

TREATY MECHANISMS AND INSTITUTIONS [Articles 23–26 and 30] No reservations are allowed to this convention, which means countries cannot sign it and then opt out of certain obligations such as the ban on tobacco advertising, promotion and sponsorship.

DEDICATED FUNDING [Articles 5.6 and 26] The final text recognizes the importance of dedicated funding for the treaty. Many decisions on financing have been deferred to the Conference of the Parties, restricting participation to countries that have demonstrated their commitment ratifying the treaty.

A country can ratify the treaty when it can implement and enforce it within its borders. Now that 40 countries have done so it enters into force, or becomes legally binding on those countries that are parties to it. A violation of the treaty is a violation of international law and will be dealt with accordingly (as defined by the treaty after it is entered into force) by the countries that are parties. However, as there is no regulating body but rather name-and-shame type enforcement, civil society and health organizations will need to play a critical role in monitoring enforcement, supporting implementation and trying to strengthen the treaty through campaigning and lobbying.

Within a few years drivers in Mexico should no longer see the Marlboro Man on passing billboards, Ghanaian television stations will refrain from televising hip-hop contests sponsored by BAT, and Benson and Hedges will cease giving away free phones, lighters, and hats to promote their cigarettes in Sri Lanka. Fewer children will become addicted to tobacco: there has already been a dramatic drop in youth addiction in countries where the majority of tobacco advertisements, promotions and sponsorships are prohibited as part of a comprehensive tobacco control programme. The treaty will also make it easier for governments to pass tobacco control legislation, since it will make lobbying and other activities of the tobacco transnationals more transparent. International cooperation in legal matters pertaining to tobacco will make it far more likely that the tobacco transnationals begin to pay the true costs of their deadly business.

They will not give up without a fight, however. Tobacco transnationals and their investors in countries including the US, Japan, Germany, China, Turkey, Zimbabwe and Pakistan have the most to gain from delaying implementation. Internal Philip Morris/Altria documents released through litigation indicate this is a key corporate strategy, as recommended by the Washington-based firm Mongoven, Biscoe & Duchin. 'The first alternative to an onerous convention is to delay its crafting and adoption . . . Any pressures to delay the finalisation of the convention would require the combined efforts of several individuals or coalitions of countries and various NGOs,' it said, advising that WHA meetings were key intervention points to delay or strongly influence movements in negotiations. It also recommended focusing on the treaty by regions, and having a central corporate-wide strategy. (During Corporate Accountability International's campaign on the infant formula industry in the late 1970s and early 1980s, this company advised Nestlé on how to fight the boycott and the WHO code on marketing breast-milk substitutes.)

Setting a precedent The treaty is a milestone in the history of public health and corporate accountability. Its implementation will be a dramatic change from the voluntary standards or codes industry proposes, which are non-binding, lack independent oversight and are often ineffective. Here are some of the ways it breaks new ground:

BAN ON ADVERTISING, PROMOTION AND SPONSORSHIP [Article 13] The treaty requires parties to implement a comprehensive ban or restrictions on tobacco advertising, promotion and sponsorship – the first time a treaty calls for such a ban on an otherwise legal product.

EXCLUSION OF THE TOBACCO INDUSTRY [Articles 5.3, 12(e)] The treaty includes strong, binding language which bars the tobacco industry from involvement in public health policy-making and calls on governments to be alert to attempts to undermine such policies. These provisions represent an important evolution in the global community's response to corporate influence on public policy-making.

PUBLIC DISCLOSURE OF INFORMATION [Articles 4.1, 10, 20] The treaty establishes the principle that every person should be informed about the dangers of tobacco. Earlier agreements required the disclosure of information but did not call for it to be shared with the public. This provision represents an exciting expansion of international right-to-know law. It establishes a precedent for other industries to make available relevant information such as ingredients and nutritional value of food products, dangers of oil development and extraction, and health effects of pharmaceutical products.

PARTICIPATION OF CIVIL SOCIETY [Preamble, Articles 4.7, 12(e)] The treaty strongly establishes the principle that civil society participation is essential in achieving the objectives of the treaty and its protocols, while explicitly excluding NGOs affiliated with the tobacco industry from involvement in tobacco control strategies. This is the first time the operative text of an international agreement has affirmed the vital role of civil society.

A story of hope The story of the treaty inspires hope: the developing world, led by a block of all 46 African nations and supported by dozens of civil society organizations, united to prevent the spread of tobacco addiction, disease and death. One key element is the involvement of people at the grass roots in building government support, despite staunch US opposition throughout and aggressive attempts by the tobacco giants to derail it. Thousands of people took action globally in support of the FCTC through International Weeks of Resistance to Tobacco Transnationals and other vehicles.

Continued opposition to the treaty is expected from the tobacco industry and its government allies, but it has the necessary momentum from governments, backed by broad-based civil society support, to be implemented effectively in a growing number of countries. Civil society and health professionals are more important than ever to support ratification and implementation at country level. Monitoring and exposing ongoing tobacco industry interference in public policy is also vital. With continued support from citizens throughout the world, this treaty could save millions of lives.

Useful resources

Corporate Accountability International, formerly Infact, is a membership organization that wages and wins campaigns challenging irresponsible and dangerous corporate actions around the world. For over 25 years it has forced corporations like Nestlé, General Electric and Philip Morris/Altria to stop abusive actions. It is an NGO in official relations with WHO. For more information visit http://www.stopcorporateabuse.org.

The Network for Accountability of Tobacco Transnationals (*NATT*), launched by Corporate Accountability International in 1999, includes more than 100 NGOs from over 50 countries working to enforce the Framework Convention on Tobacco Control.

References

Anderson S and Cavanagh J (2000). *Top 200: the Rise of Global Corporate Power.* Washington DC, Institute for Policy Studies (http://www.ips-dc.org/reports/top200.htm, accessed on 16 March 2005).

Tobacco Reporter (2003). Who's in control? Just how binding will the FCTC be? July (http://www.tobaccoreporter.com/backissues/Jul2003/story1.asp, accessed on 16 March 2005).

The full text of the global tobacco treaty is available on the internet at: http://www. who.int/tobacco/fctc/text/final

Philip Morris/Altria documents can be obtained at: http://www.pmdocs.com

Case study 2: Breastmilk substitutes

The health benefits associated with exclusive breastfeeding for the first six months of life have been well documented: it is good for children in all countries and at all levels of socioeconomic development. It is often a matter of life or death in poor countries, yet is continually under threat from the promotion of breastmilk substitutes. Civil society, public health practitioners and NGOs fought to curb these harmful marketing practices in the 1970s and 1980s, and the International Code of Marketing of Breastmilk Substitutes was adopted by the World Health Assembly in 1981 (WHO 1981), and strengthened and clarified in a subsequent series of assembly resolutions. The code was particularly important in establishing a precedent for regulating the harmful practices of transnational corporations. Although adherence to the code has been patchy, it has helped to improve breastfeeding rates, and thereby reduce child mortality

Two important civil society networks are encouraging compliance: the International Baby Food Action Network (IBFAN) and the World Alliance for Breast-feeding Action (WABA). Both play a crucial role in upholding its principles and the regulatory function of governments, identifying non-adherence and pressing for action. Nevertheless baby milk companies continue to use health facilities to influence mothers and staff with their promotional material, especially in countries that have not implemented or fully applied the code and subsequent resolutions. Free supplies and samples of formula remain a major problem, with companies competing to receive equal and sometimes exclusive treatment by hospitals. Distribution and display of company materials is widespread, and more prevalent in countries where consumer purchasing power is high, such as Hong Kong, Singapore and the United Arab Emirates (IBFAN 2004).

Companies also exploit weaknesses in the code. For example, since direct marketing to mothers is restricted, companies mark promotional material as 'information for health professionals' and supply it in bulk to health facilities where mothers are the intended audience. Nestlé even states that material for health professionals is intended for distribution to mothers.

Advertising is designed to give the impression that infant formula gives babies an added advantage, even suggesting that formula supplemented with fatty acids provides 'intelligence in a bottle'. Not only is there no proof that such supplementation has a beneficial effect, the fact that it is not superior to breastmilk is not mentioned. Companies also suggest that other added ingredients bring a product 'closer to breastmilk', boosting immunity to disease and promoting healthy growth – misleading claims that are promotional in nature and prohibited by the code. Many companies wrongly claim that the code applies only to infant formula, not to 'other products marketed or represented as breastmilk substitutes'.

The promotion of breastmilk substitutes by health services may act as an endorsement of the product and undermine public health messages that promote exclusive breastfeeding. An increasing number of health professionals are becoming addicted to company donations and sponsorship. The impact

24 A pack of Cerelac cereal food purchased in Bulgaria on 2 June 2003, labelled for use from 4 months. Campaigners found that nearly ten years after it was required to stop labelling complementary foods for use from before 6 months of age, Nestlé was still doing so.

315

on professional integrity of handouts, gifts and grants from industry is far-reaching (see also part B, chapter 2 on handouts from drug companies).

But what of the other key actors? This section presents a first attempt to develop a scorecard of the past and present performance of some of them. The scores are not based on a structured appraisal but have been compiled through a consensus process, involving a number of people from academia, IBFAN and WABA centrally involved in the promotion of breastfeeding and protection of public health. They are presented here as an example of one possible approach to monitoring of performance of key global health institutions. More rigorous assessment of performance is of course needed: this is just a starting point.

Indicator 1: Overall promotion of breastfeeding and support for the code
Under political pressure, WHO has not played a strong leadership role in ensuring compliance with the code. It came under significant pressure from the US administration to water down its promotion of the code. Much of its effort to promote the code has been weak, and leadership on the issue in Geneva has been poor – thus losing extrabudgetary support from two bilateral donors during the 1980s and early 1990s.

UNICEF has played a more significant role in promoting breastfeeding. It started talking about the importance of breastfeeding in the early 1980s, did a lot of work on the code in the 1980s and began to fund programmes by around 1990, despite threats from the US government to withdraw funding if it took too strong a line against the unethical marketing practices of the baby food companies. Without its intervention, the support of the Swedish and Dutch aid agencies and the lobbying of international NGOs, the code could have suffered an early demise. UNICEF also deserves much of the credit for the Baby-Friendly Hospital Initiative, widely successful in increasing exclusive breastfeeding in the early weeks of life.

However, along with other UN agencies' work on breastfeeding, this work greatly declined after 1997 as a result of the diversion of staff time and funding to the new UN policy on HIV and infant feeding. UNICEF's pro-breastfeeding talk has recently returned to early 1980s levels, but the funding is not yet back to the levels seen in the 1990s. After years of depending on extrabudgetary funds for a post for legal work on the code, UNICEF has recently incorporated the post into its core budget, signalling a commitment to continue its support for implementation of the code. However, WHO's recent performance is considered less positive. Staff in the nutrition department with responsibility for the code are considered to have done too little to promote it and have at times even undermined it in public meetings.

USAID has also funded work on breastfeeding, mainly through NGOs like WELSTART and LINKAGES. The Canadian International Development Agency has also begun to take an interest. The work of all these agencies should likewise be monitored.

Promotion of breastfeeding scorecard

UNICEF: B + (requires more funding to reach an A grade)
WHO: C +
Swedish and Dutch aid agencies: A
Other Scandinavian bilaterals: B+
USAID and CIDA: B -

Support of the code scorecard

UNICEF: A+
Swedish and Dutch aid agencies: A
WHO: C

Indicator 2: Promoting HIV-free survival in infants born to HIV-positive mothers In 1997, UNICEF joined WHO and UNAIDS in changing UN agency recommendations on the feeding of infants born to HIV-positive mothers in low-income settings, in response to political pressure. This was done with little consultation or involvement of child health and breastfeeding experts. Part of the motivation for the change was that breastfeeding reduced the overall impact of short-course AZT (an antiretroviral drug) in reducing vertical HIV transmission. However, the initial enthusiasm to reduce mother-to-child transmission did not consider carefully enough the trade-off between HIV transmission and the impact of breastmilk substitution on infant survival.

In addition, UNICEF programmes and other programmes began to subsidize and provide free infant formula to HIV-positive mothers. In 1998 UNAIDS, UNICEF and WHO announced they were giving free formula to 30,000 babies born to low-income mothers at 11 pilot sites. Concerns that this would lead to unsafe feeding or mixed feeding (which might result in a higher rate of HIV transmission from breastmilk) were not addressed. It was commonly explained that informed choice on how to feed was a human right, and that the provision of free formula helped women to fulfil their right.

Amazingly, these pilot sites were only evaluated in relation to logistical issues, and not in relation to child health outcomes. Given the failure to evaluate child health outcomes and the difficulty of keeping an infant alive without breastmilk in low-income settings, it is impossible to know whether this new policy has led to any increase in HIV-free survival of infants born to HIV-positive mothers – but it seems doubtful. This had led to dissatisfaction within UNICEF and criticism from some child health and breastfeeding experts.

Matters have improved since, largely because there is greater recognition of the dangers associated with the promotion of formula feeding in poor communities. In 2002 UNICEF decided to stop funding the free supply of breastmilk substitutes, although this was criticized in the press and by some 'HIV activist' groups. It has engaged constructively with WABA and co-hosted a meeting that brought the HIV and breastfeeding scientific communities together, in Arusha in 2002. It now says that since 90% of HIV-positive mothers do not know their HIV status, the best way to reduce overall postnatal transmission is to promote exclusive breastfeeding as a social norm.

Appropriate policy on breastmilk substitutes for HIV positive mothers scorecard:

UNICEF: A (having been a C between 1997 to 2000)

Other UN Agencies (including WHO): C

References

WHO (1981). *International Code of Marketing of Breast-milk Substitutes.* Geneva, WHO (http://www.who.int/nut/documents/code_english.PDF, accessed on 16 March 2005).

IBFAN (2004). *Breaking the rules, stretching the rules 2004: evidence of violations of the International Code of Marketing of Breastmilk Substitutes and subsequent resolutions.* Geneva, IBFAN (http://www.ibfan.org/english/codewatch/btr04/btr04contents.html, accessed on 16 March 2005).

Case study 3: Tax and corporate evasion

Tax is the lifeblood of any society. The reason is simple: it pays for most of the things we take for granted. Society cannot exist without government and governments cannot exist without tax. So tax is a vital constituent to make a society work. It is essential for addressing the global health issues presented in this report, and it is appropriate and urgent that we declare 'tax justice' as a key global public health issue.

Tax justice means everyone paying 'fair' tax and 'affordable' tax. In the countries where most people live on less than US$2 a day it is hard to conceive of any level of tax that would be affordable – most people live in absolute poverty. Any additional burden would be intolerable. The only just tax for them would be no tax. In contrast, in rich countries where many people earn in excess of US$75,000 a year, people can afford to pay quite reasonable amounts of tax and not suffer real hardship.

Tax justice implies a system where those who have more absolute income (from whatever its source, and however it is technically defined) pay both more tax in absolute terms *and* more in proportion to that income. This is not a new idea. Progressive taxation has been part of the social agenda for a very long time.

Changes in the pattern of tax within countries Over the last decade or so, the global trend has been towards a lowering of the tax burden of the rich and a narrowing of the difference in the tax rate between the rich and the poor. In particular, there has been a steady decline in the taxation of corporate profits.

In Brazil, between 1995 and 2001, employee's income tax rates rose by 14% and social security contributions by 75%. Tax on profits, however, was reduced by 8% over the same period. This shift from tax on those with the ability to pay to those without such ability has been exacerbated by an increasing VAT burden in Brazil. Value Added Tax is a tax on spending, and the poor spend all their income to survive, but the rich don't need to as they save. The result is that in Brazil lower income households pay approximately 26.5% of their after-tax income on VAT whilst high income households pay only 7.3% on VAT.

In the UK, the tax burden shouldered by individuals had risen to 73.5% in 2004, from 62.4% in 1997. During the same period, the taxes paid on profits by UK companies fell from £34.3 billion in 1999/2000 to £28.1 billion in 2003/04 and are expected to be no more than £24 billion in 2004/05. At the same time, data from the UK reveals that in 2002 in the UK all income groups bar the lowest 10% paid between 30% and 35% of their income in all taxes. However, the lowest 10% of income earners paid over 50% in tax when indirect taxes were taken into account (Hills 2004). Modern society is imposing flat rate and regressive taxes, not progressive ones.

The situation is even more extreme in the USA. Eighty-two of America's largest and most profitable corporations paid no federal income tax in at least one year during the first three years of the George W. Bush administration, a period when federal corporate tax collections fell to their lowest sustained level in six decades (Citizens for Tax Justice USA 2004). At the same time, the US administration is suggesting a national sales tax to replace most current federal income taxes. Such taxes always mean the poor pay proportionately more than the rich.

At least these cases illustrate that tax is still being paid. In the USA, for example, the overall tax burden according to the OECD (OECD 2004) was 25.4% in 2003, compared with 25.6% in 1975. In the UK the overall burden in the same two years was exactly the same at 35.3%. However, the overall contribution made by companies to that tax burden has fallen. So too has the burden of the rich, as indicated by substantial falling tax rates over the years so that rates of up to 98% in the UK in the 1970s are now compared with a maximum income tax rate of 40%. Overall, there has been a fall in average tax rates on company profits from 37.5% to under 31% between 1996 and 2003 (see Figure E4.1) (KPMG 2003).

Globalization and tax avoidance The trends in the pattern of taxation within countries have not happened by chance. This shift in the tax burden has been the result of big business, and their accountants and lawyers influencing government. Furthermore, the deregulation of the financial services sector and exchange controls now means that money can flow much more freely around the world. The manifestations have been:

- a massive increase in the use of tax havens by individuals and companies to avoid their obligations to pay tax. The result is that the Cayman Islands are now the fifth largest banking centre in the world even though no real economic activity actually takes place there. Varying estimates suggest that between a quarter and a half of all world trade is routed through such havens. Offshore companies are being formed at the rate of about 150,000 per year, and are now numbered in the millions. It is estimated that about US$11 trillion is held in offshore bank accounts;
- a professional culture in which lawyers and accountants blatantly seek to manipulate and avoid any regulation designed to stop the abuse of the tax system.

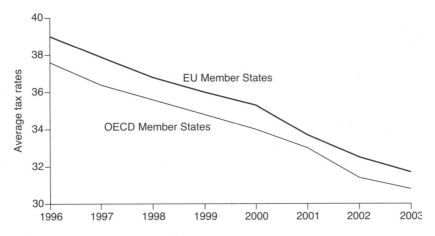

Figure E4.1 Average company tax rates in the EU and OECD, 1996–2003 (%)
(*Source*: KPMG 2003)

These trends in taxation are underpinning the slow disintegration in the capacity of governments not just to ensure the fulfilment of human rights, but to ensure the social cohesion of societies. Activists need to:

- reclaim the language of tax, so it is seen as a contribution to society, not a cost to be minimized as most businesses claim it is now;
- make tax payment the core test of the corporate social responsibility of a company. Charitable works are not enough;
- transform accounting so that international companies have to declare how much tax they are paying, and where, which they do not do now;
- suggest the creation of 'general anti avoidance provisions' in tax law so that courts have greater power to strike down schemes promoted solely to avoid tax;
- work with the UN and others to promote a world tax authority with the ability to create fair global taxation for global companies;
- promote the idea that sustainable development requires a country to have a sustainable tax system, and suggest that aid assistance needs to be given to create these systems which are a prerequisite of sustainable health systems;
- continue to highlight the harm that tax havens cause to the well being of the world;
- illustrate the malpractice of large firms of lawyers and accountants who promote aggressive tax avoidance schemes.

This is an ambitious programme that can be helped by publicizing the issue in journals and newspapers; lobbying the UN tax conference and creating dialogue with other international and national agencies on tax; advocating for health NGOs to make tax a public health issue; and embarrassing professional firms into changing their ways.

References

Citizens for Tax Justice (2004). *Bush Policies Drive Surge in Corporate Tax Freeloading.* Washington DC, Citizens for Tax Justice (http://www.ctj.org/corpfed04pr.pdf, accessed October 2004).

Hills J (2004). *Inequality and the State.* Oxford, Oxford University Press.

KPMG (2003). *Corporate Tax Rate Survey – January 2003.* KPMG International (http://www.us.kpmg.com/microsite/global_tax/ctr_survey/2003CorprorateTaxSurveyFINAL.pdf, accessed on 18 March 2005).

OECD (2004) . *Tax payments rose in some OECD countries in 2003, but fell in others.* Paris, OECD (http://www.oecd.org/document/21/0,2340,en_2649_201185_33808789_1_1_1_1,00.html, accessed 12 October 2004).

E5 | Aid

Official development assistance (otherwise known as aid or ODA) consists of grants, loans and technical cooperation from governments and international bodies, with the objectives of promoting economic development and welfare (OECD 2005). Much aid is channelled through bilateral agreements between donor and recipient governments, some to multilateral agencies such as WHO and the World Bank, and much of the rest to NGOs and independent organizations such as the Global Fund to fight AIDS, TB and Malaria.

This chapter describes three key aspects of aid: its volume and distribution and its use in support of the political agendas of rich countries, most notably the 'war on terror' and privatization. Many other debates about aid are not discussed here, such as the effects of aid on political institutions in developing countries (Wangwe 2004). Some are raised elsewhere in this report, including the coordination of donors and the fragmenting impact of aid on health systems (part B, chapter 1); inappropriate conditions placed on recipient countries by donors; and the effects of aid on economic growth in poor countries.

Global aid trends – volume

From 1960 there was a steady rise in volume aid peaking in 1992, the year of the Earth Summit, when donors pledged further modest increases. In fact aid

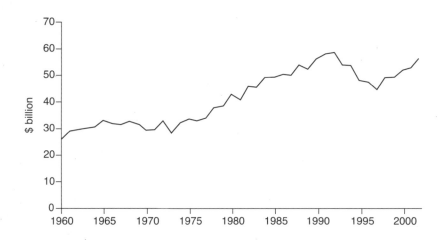

Figure E5.1 The long-term trend in ODA from DAC donors – in $ billions real terms (2001 prices) (*Source*: Randel et al. 2004)

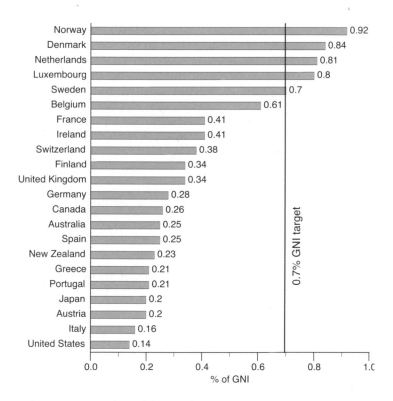

Figure E5.2 Provisional figures for ODA as a percentage of GNI from DAC donors in 2003

then fell by 24% in real terms between 1992 and 1997 (Figure E5.1). The last few years have seen a reversal in the decline, but the increases fall far short of the additional US$ 50 billion a year needed to reach the Millennium Development Goals. Only five rich countries (Norway, Denmark, the Netherlands, Luxembourg and Sweden) met the UN aid target of 0.7% GNI in 2003 (see Figure E5.2). Meanwhile the Bush administration has requested more than US$ 565 billion from Congress for military purposes and its 'war on terror' (Randel et al. 2004). (These figures and those in the next section were provided by Judith Randel and Tony German of Development Initiatives, based on research on OECD Donor Assistance Committee statistics.)

The volume of aid in 2003 was 3.9% more than in 2002 in real terms. This follows a 7.2% real terms increase in 2001–2. Provisional figures suggest that the total from donor countries rose from US$ 58.3 billion in 2002 to US$ 68.5 billion in 2003. Substantial increases from some of the largest (G8) donors – the US (up by 17%), the UK (12%) and France (10%) – outweighed big falls in aid from Japan (down 9%) and Italy (17%). In terms of actual amounts the US contributes most, followed by Japan, France, Germany and the UK; but

Aid

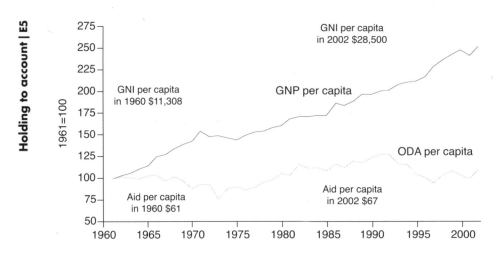

Figure E5.3 The growing gap: aid from rich nations has not kept pace with their wealth (*Source*: Randel et al. 2004)

although it is the biggest donor, the US is not the most generous – when the amount given is compared to each country's national wealth, it comes last.

Although aid more than doubled in real terms over a 40–year period, this does not mean donor countries are more generous – they became much richer over the same period. Figure E5.3 shows how the growth in aid per person from donor countries compares with how much richer people in those countries have become. While wealth in donor countries has gone up by 152%, from US\$ 11,303 per person to US\$ 28,500, aid per person has risen by less than 10%, from US\$ 61 to US\$ 67.

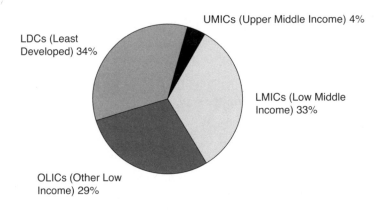

Figure E5.4 Share of aid to poorer countries 2002 (*Source*: Randel et al. 2004)

Global aid trends – allocation

Where is aid allocated? In 2002, a third of global aid went to the 49 least developed countries, while 29% went to other low-income countries including India, China, Ghana, Indonesia, Pakistan, Nigeria and Zimbabwe. Lower middle-income countries received a third, including Bolivia, Bosnia and Herzegovina, Egypt, Fiji, Iraq, Morocco, Palestine, Papua New Guinea, Peru, the Philippines and Yugoslavia. Upper middle-income countries received 4% (see Figure E5.4).

Aid has shifted to different regions. In 1992–2002 the major changes were a 5% fall in aid to east Asia and a 5% rise in aid to south and central Asia. The share of aid to Sub-Saharan Africa rose from 33% to 36% and Europe's share more than doubled from 5% to 11%.

Aid for political purposes

Aid is used and spent on many different things. The amount spent on basic health and other social programmes is surprisingly small (see Figure E5.5). It is easily diverted to projects to support export promotion and win geopolitical influence. Two key trends are the use of aid to bolster the 'war on terror', and the vigorous promotion of the privatization of industry and public services in poor countries.

Aid and the war on terror Official development assistance has always reflected donors' geopolitical imperatives. The growing priority now appears to be their security interests. In 2003 the OECD released a controversial policy statement. 'Development co-operation has an important role to play in helping to de-

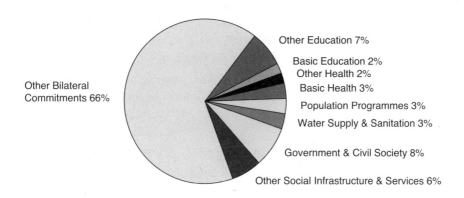

Figure E5.5 Shares of bilateral aid to basic needs
(*Source:* Randel et al. 2004)

prive terrorists of popular support and addressing the conditions that terrorist leaders feed on and exploit,' it said. There was a suggestion that donors may need to 'calibrate' current aid approaches and allocations to take account of terrorism prevention (OECD 2003). This opens up the possibility not only of making terrorism prevention a goal of development cooperation, but of giving it precedence over existing, internationally agreed development goals (BOND 2003a). The impact on aid allocations and the nature of donor cooperation with developing countries is only just beginning to be seen.

The US, the world's biggest donor measured by volume, increasingly allocates bilateral aid according to concerns related to the 'war on terror': countries with large Muslim populations and insurgency movements are automatic priorities. After 11 September, Washington made substantial increases in foreign aid to Pakistan, India, the Philippines and Indonesia – foci of the Bush administration's anti-terrorism efforts in Asia. One example is increased military funding to Indonesia (Lum 2002), the world's largest Muslim country, which plays a strategic role in world geopolitics. US military intelligence claims that the Java-based Jemaah Islamiyah is active in Al Qaeda. Soon after 11 September the US began to loosen restrictions on military aid despite Indonesia's record of human rights abuses in East Timor, Aceh province and West Papua (Hallinan 2002). US bilateral assistance in south and east Asia generally shows a growing emphasis on military aid:

- US aid to east Asia grew by 47% in 2000–2003, while the US economic support fund (ESF) doubled. These rises are dwarfed by huge increases in military-related aid. Expenditure through the US foreign military fund (FMF) in east Asia, for example, grew by 1614%. Expenditure on US international military education and training (IMET) grew by 4575% and it is now the largest US aid programme in east Asia.
- US aid to south Asia grew by 85% in 2000–2003. This pales in comparison with the large expansion in IMET, which grew by 593%. The largest increase was in the ESF, from zero to US$ 242 million, jumping to 40% of US bilateral assistance in the region in 2003 and now the largest US aid programme, followed by development assistance with 36% (Lum 2002).

US military and security-related aid to Africa has also increased since 11 September. Countries that have hitherto been of little importance to the US have garnered new funding via the war on terror, like Djibouti, which received US$ 31 million for allowing the US to set up a permanent military base. Under the Pan-Sahelian Initiative, established in 2002, US military advisers provide weapons, vehicles and military training to anti-terrorism squads in Mali, Niger, Chad and Mauritania (BOND 2003b).

US involvement in Iraq and Afghanistan threatens to undercut other US development initiatives. With the US budget stretched by expenditure in Iraq, the government announced that it would not meet President Bush's earlier promises of US$ 15 billion over 5 years to combat HIV/AIDS. The much-heralded US 'Millennium Challenge Account' (MCA) was also only allocated US$ 1 billion over financial years 2002–2004.

Overall, there are concerns that the recent increases in aid from the developed world are being lost to new donor-driven priorities relating to the War on Terror. A substantial proportion of these ODA rises have been directed to reconstruction and stabilization in Iraq, Afghanistan and Pakistan. Nearly half of all the funds in 2002 to the UN's twenty-five humanitarian appeals went to just one country, Afghanistan. More recently, donor interest in Afghanistan has waned. Of the US$ 1352 million committed for March 2003 to March 2004, much of it emergency assistance, only US$ 536 million was actually disbursed. Much of the immediate post-conflict stabilization costs have been financed from short-term allocations from military budgets (Woods et al. 2004). Meanwhile, the October 2003 donor conference on Iraq pledged US$ 33 billion for the period 2003–07. This compares with annual ODA to Sub-Saharan Africa of US$ 11 billion.

Aid and privatization Multilateral and bilateral agencies use aid money to fund the privatization of public services and boost the profits of private sector companies. This highlights the need for civil society to monitor how tax contributions are used under the guise of overseas development. All information in this section is obtained from War on Want (2004).

Conditionality attached to World Bank lending during the 1980s and 1990s provided the impetus for privatization of public services in developing countries, as highlighted frequently in this report. Its lending directive for this period (Operational Directive 8.60) specified privatization as a reform goal, and country after country was instructed to start a national privatization programme. Its 2002 private sector development strategy called on all parts of the Bank group to promote privatization of infrastructure and social services in developing countries, with particular emphasis on 'frontier' sectors such as water, energy, health care and education.

Donor governments play an important supporting role, particularly the UK's department for international development, which has positioned itself as a champion of privatization and taken the lead in a number of new initiatives.

Aid

Box E5.1 Key privatization advisers

The consulting arms of the Big Four accountancy firms take the lion's share of privatization consultancy contracts in developing countries:

- PricewaterhouseCoopers
- KPMG
- Deloitte Touche Tohmatsu
- Ernst & Young.

Arthur Andersen, the fifth of the Big Five before its fall from grace over the Enron scandal in 2001, has also been engaged in numerous privatizations in developing countries. Its consulting arm split from the parent company in 2000, renaming itself Accenture.

Other key players come from the financial sector, with many of the world's largest banks now also involved in privatization consultancy in developing countries:

- ABN AMRO
- NM Rothschild
- Credit Suisse First Boston
- Dresdner Kleinwort Wasserstein
- Morgan Stanley
- HSBC
- Citigroup.

Consultancies such as the UK's Adam Smith International and the US' Louis Berger Group have also established themselves as leading players in privatization. Individual sectors also have their own specialist consultants, such as Mott MacDonald and Stone & Webster in the water and energy sectors, IPA Energy Consulting in the power sector, and Canadian consultancy CPCS Transcom in transport. Other companies provide specialist services, such as legal consultants CMS Cameron McKenna and Baker & McKenzie. (*Source*: War on Want 2004)

For example, in 2002 it created the Emerging Africa Infrastructure Fund with backing from Sweden, Switzerland, the Netherlands and private financiers Barclays and the Standard Bank Group. This is designed to mobilize up to US$ 450 million of private sector investment finance in the privatization of public services in African countries and to fund new infrastructure projects, with particular emphasis on energy, telecommunications, transport and water.

TABLE E5.1 Value (in £) of new DFID contracts awarded to Big Five consultants, 1997–2002

	1997–8	1998–9	1999–2000	2000–1	2001–2
PwC	5,575,135	11,193,643	13,405,142	19,018,515	3,075,210
Ernst and Young	445,792	838,429	286,800	11,610	43,023
Deloitte Touche	4,185	269,070	749,262	8,478,352	633,884
KPMG	7,104,728	2,548,237	12,773,757	4,700,110	2,185,931
Arthur Andersen	-	24,558,244	27,724	83,721	114,162
Total	13,129,840	39,407,623	27,242,685	32,292,308	6,052,210

Source: War on Want 2004

It is open only to private companies and will not finance public sector investment.

UK Department for International Development (DFID) has also taken a lead in the creation of new global institutions to advance privatization. One of the most influential is the Public Private Infrastructure Advisory Facility, launched in 1999 in collaboration with the Bank and the government of Japan, a 'technical assistance' facility to advise developing countries how to 'tap the full potential of private involvement in infrastructure'. Working from the Bank's headquarters, its main focus is promoting the increased involvement of private sector service companies in water and sanitation, energy, transport and telecommunications, and advising on multisector issues such as utilities regulation. It has also been engaged in the ongoing battle for hearts and minds in developing countries, running workshops, study tours and public awareness campaigns such as the 'knowledge programme' for journalists from nine African countries that aimed to counter public scepticism over water privatization by encouraging more positive media coverage.

Both the Bank and DFID have developed strong partnerships with consultants from private companies (see Box E5.1), whose 'technical assistance' to developing countries has recently become an integral part of the reform process; governments are often required to accept them as advisers as part of the financial support package on offer. In the first five years of the Labour government (1997–2002) DFID agreed new contracts worth over US$ 220 million in consultancy fees to the Big Five accountancy firms (see Table E5.1). India, the largest recipient of UK aid, provides a good example of this use of privatization consultants. In addition to huge sums paid to consultants advising on Orissa's electricity privatization, DFID engaged Andersen Consulting and PricewaterhouseCoopers for the initial phase of the Haryana State Electricity

Aid

Board privatization, and reportedly paid around US$ 50 million to consultants advising on the first phase of power privatization in Andhra Pradesh.

Adam Smith International, the consultancy arm of the Adam Smith Institute, has been awarded around US$ 1.4 million by DFID to assist the privatization programme of the government of Tanzania, including US$ 812,000 to support a public relations unit. Its outputs include a pop video broadcast on local television, a series of short dramas by Tanzania's top comedian, and an open Privatization Day at Dar es Salaam's Royal Palm Hotel. Tanzania's upbeat Privatization Song is even available internationally via the website of the Parastatal Sector Reform Commission.

Recommendations

- All donors must establish and be accountable to a realistic timetable to fulfil their longstanding commitment to spend 0.7% of their gross national income on official development assistance.

- aid must remain clearly and unequivocally dedicated to achieving existing development goals. Increases must not be used to justify spending it on other priorities. Northern governments should find the necessary resources in appropriate non-ODA budget lines to respond to terrorism in a manner that is proportional and coherent with human rights and democratic norms (BOND 2003b);

- donors must not insist on the privatization of public services as a condition of development assistance to developing countries, nor on any requirement that their governments must engage privatization consultants to qualify for aid.

References

BOND (2003a). Joint statement by members of the International Global Security and Development Network on the Development Assistance Committee policy statement and reference document. *A development co-operation lens on Terrorism prevention: key entry points for action.* British Overseas NGOs for Development (http://www.bond.org.uk/advocacy/gsd/gsdjoint.htm, accessed 18 October 2004).

BOND (2003b). *Global security and development September update.* British Overseas NGOs for Development (http://www.bond.org.uk/advocacy/globalsecurity.htm, accessed 15 March 2005).

Hallinan C (2002). Supporting Indonesia's military bad idea – again. *Asia Times Online* (http://www.atimes.com/se-asia/DF14Ae01.html, accessed 14 June 2004).

Lum T (2002). *US foreign aid to east and south Asia: selected recipients.* Washington DC, Congressional Research Service Report for Congress.

OECD (2003). *A development cooperation lens on terrorism prevention: key entry points of action.* Development Assistance Committee, OECD (http://www.oecd.org/dataoecd/17/4/16085708.pdf, accessed 16 February 2005).

OECD (2005). *Development Co-operation Directorate (DAC) glossary* (http://www.
oecd.org/glossary/0,2586,en_2649_33721_1965693_1_1_1_1,00.html#1965422,
accessed 16 February 2005).

Randel J, German T, Ewing D eds. (2004). *The Reality of Aid.* London, Zed Books.

Wangwe S (2004). The politics of autonomy and sovereignty: Tanzania's aid relationship. In: Bromley S, Mackintosh M, Brown W, Wuyts M eds. *Making the international: economic interdependence and political order.* London and Milton Keynes,
Pluto Press and the Open University.

War on Want (2004). *Profiting from Poverty: Privatization Consultants, DFID and Public
Services.* London, War on Want.

Woods N et al. (2004). *Reconciling effective aid and global security: implications for the
emerging international development architecture.* Oxford, Global Economic Governance Programme (http://users.ox.ac.uk/~ntwoods/IDAFinalDraft2(26Nov2004).pdf,
accessed 1 March 2005).

Aid

E6 | Debt relief

'Since 2000, the developing world has been a net exporter of capital to the advanced economies' – World Bank 2004.

'The largest international flow of fixed-income debt today takes the form of borrowing by the world's richest nations at (probably) negative real interest rates from countries with very large numbers of poor' – Larry Summers, Harvard University, 2004.

The global economy today appears to be approaching a 'tipping point' – a point at which the vast imbalances that characterize the international financial system may well tip over into recession, or even worse into a period of debt-deflation not unlike that faced by Japan in 1990. These imbalances, and in particular rich country debts, eclipse the debts of poor countries.

The instability caused by these huge debts and other imbalances is partly a result of the lack of G7 coordination and cooperation in the management of trade, exchange rate volatility, rising levels of debt and climate change. This failure is leading to global political tensions, a collapse of multilateralism, and growing calls for higher subsidies and protection from unfair competition. It is exacerbated by the decision of the US central bank and government to do nothing to arrest the decline in the value of the dollar, which has depreciated by 30% since 2002, increasing trade tensions and causing the Japanese central bank to borrow massively to manage the dollar/yen relationship (in effect Japanese central bankers are managing trading relationships). It is one of the factors, along with falling supplies and rising demand, that provoked oil producers to raise prices, further exacerbating existing imbalances.

Another major cause of global instability is the historically unprecedented foreign deficit built up by the US, the most indebted nation on earth. The net foreign indebtedness of the US is in excess of US$ 3 trillion, compared with US$ 176 billion owed by 42 heavily indebted poor countries. The US trade deficit – just one part of its net foreign indebtedness – soared to yet another record in 2004, reaching 5.3% of GDP, or US$ 617.7 billion – US$ 121.2 billion higher than in 2003. It was driven by an extraordinary rise in imports, which grew by 16.3% in 2004. Exports also grew at a healthy 12.3%.

The US deficit arises from a consumption boom largely financed by low-

25 Breaking the chains of debt: protestors at Sikh temple, Birmingham, UK.

income countries. As the World Bank notes (2004), 'financing the US current account deficit has been shouldered by official institutions in developing countries that have invested reserves accumulated through good trade performance, effective exchange-rate management, and the strengthening in capital flows. Inflows of foreign official assets to the US amounted to US$ 208 billion during 2003, compared with US$ 95 billion for 2002, *financing almost 40% of the US current account deficit*' (our italics).

Neoliberal economists assure us that in a deregulated world capital flows from where it is plentiful to where it is scarce – but the reverse is happening today. Capital is being sucked out of low-income countries with large numbers of poor people, and moved to high-income countries with large numbers of the very rich. The injustice of transfers from the poor to the rich through debt repayments, unfair terms of trade and excessive consumption of natural resources has been widely explored in development literature. However, insufficient attention has been paid to financial transfers that enable rich countries to live off poor countries.

The poor finance the rich

The structural changes central to globalization that have created this situation occurred in 1971, when President Nixon unilaterally broke up the dollar-gold standard, and introduced the Treasury bill standard instead. These changes mean that in the absence of gold as a reserve currency, low-income countries are required to hold as their reserves low-cost loans (Treasury bills) lent to the US. In other words, poor countries hold US Treasury bills in order to prove they have 'money in the bank', for example to pay for exports. They need to offer low-cost loans to the US Treasury to acquire these bills. The establishment of the Euro gives poor countries the alternative of making low-cost loans to the EU which are then held as reserves. This system, which allows the US and increasingly the EU to borrow cheaply, build up debts and live beyond their means, is an important cause of today's imbalances and instability.

Inflows of capital from developing countries to the US and UK help to lower interest rates and therefore borrowing costs for the people of these countries, and over the last few years have inflated the value of their currencies by about 20%. High-income countries are therefore able to purchase imports from the rest of the world 20% cheaper than they would otherwise have been able to. But despite benefiting immensely from the international financial system, OECD countries are not particularly generous with aid (see part E, chapter 5). So poor countries, while lacking funds to support millions of their own poor, are obliged to finance the overconsumption of rich countries.

Poor countries raise hard currency mainly through exports. While their exports of goods and commodities have failed to generate the resources needed for the holding of reserves and for development, they have discovered one export category that provides a major source of external development finance – but it may also be a cause of instability, for it is the export of people, especially young, educated, highly skilled people (see part B, chapter 3 for a discussion of the health worker brain drain). The money they sent home increased by a remarkable 20% during 2001–3, reaching an estimated US$ 93 billion – nearly twice as much as aid flows.

Against this economic background, the most indebted nations on earth, mostly in Africa, face daunting odds. Not only are they being drained of precious financial and human resources, but their economies are being ruined by a plague: AIDS. Per capita growth is falling by 0.5%-1.2% a year as a direct result: per capita gross domestic product in the hardest-hit countries could fall by a staggering 8% by 2010.

This is the global economic context in which world leaders gathered for the IMF and World Bank annual meetings in Washington in 2004. A furious row broke out over a report which argued that Fund restrictions on public spending in poor countries made it difficult for countries to hire more health workers and to buy medicines (Rowden 2004). It said thousands of health workers

Zambia qualified in 2000 to become eligible to receive up to 50% reduction in its huge external debt of US$ 6.8 billion as a possible beneficiary of the Heavily Indebted Poor Country (HIPC) initiative. First it had to follow the IMF's loan conditions satisfactorily for three years, including a strict cap on the government's wage bill – no more than 8% of its gross domestic product (GDP).

However, the Zambian government – the country's biggest employer – faces a worsening brain drain of skilled professionals. It introduced a housing allowance system that made staying and working in Zambia more attractive. Other measures also increased the wages bill, raising public sector wages to 9% of GDP and exceeding the 8% agreed with the Fund. So Zambia was considered off track with its loan programme and was suspended from eligibility for debt relief. This means it will continue to pay close to US$ 300 million in annual debt service payments to foreign creditors in rich countries. If this issue is not resolved, even larger payments will be expected later.

The Fund says Zambia can get back on track by reducing the budget deficit to not more than 3% of GDP and the public sector wage bill to not more than 8%. It must also privatize its remaining public utilities and state-owned companies in the energy and telecommunications sectors. The monies realized from the sale of the utilities and companies must be used for increased debt servicing, not for investment or consumption.

The Zambian government is at a crossroads. If it pleases the Fund it is likely to provoke industrial unrest by workers opposed to privatization. If it seeks to maintain public ownership it will miss its chance of debt relief. Either way, it cannot raise the wage bill high enough to retain the teachers and health professionals needed to fight HIV/AIDS.

Why? Because the IMF fears inflation.

(*Source*: Bretton Woods Project 2004)

in Kenya were unemployed because Fund economic conditionality reduced government spending on resources needed to tackle AIDS. The Fund's spending constraints might also block poor countries from accepting outside help: Uganda nearly lost a US$ 52 million grant from the Global Fund to fight AIDS, TB and Malaria because it sought to stay within the strict budgetary constraints agreed with the Fund, necessary to be eligible for debt relief and new loans.

Debt relief

The response of Fund staff confirmed that those who dominate the international financial system put the creditor cart before the human rights horse. Their obsession with inflation can be explained simply. High rates of inflation hurt creditors by eroding the value of debts, while deflationary policies maintain or increase the value of debts. By making the interests of creditors and the achievement of 'macroeconomic stability with low inflation rates' the priority (stability that is most often a *consequence* of prosperity, not a cause) the Fund and its rich country shareholders, the G8 finance ministers, subordinate human rights to life and health to inflation targets set in the interests of creditors.

Rich country leaders under pressure

At the same meetings, world leaders were considering a proposal to cancel all the debts owed to the Fund and Bank by heavily indebted poor countries. So far only 14 of the 42 eligible countries have reached 'completion point' of the HIPC initiative since its launch in 1996. Another 28 countries will receive too little too late, the delays largely due to their failure to comply with the rising number of Fund conditions. Twenty seven countries receive debt relief in the form of reduced interest payments. Almost US$ 54 billion of such relief has been 'committed', so some have already benefited, but many still have debts that even the Bank and the Fund deem unsustainable. Hence the call from NGOs for 100% cancellation of these debts.

The debate in Washington became heated. The election was imminent, so Bush's ministers were instructed to get a result on debt cancellation to satisfy US voters concerned at the plight of the indebted nations, but without requesting additional funds from Congress. The official solution was straightforward: the Bank could use its International Development Association resources to write off old debts and as new resources. UK finance minister Gordon Brown proposed an alternative: creditors should use aid to write off all multilateral debts (Bluestein 2004). Both options propose that the cost of writing off debt should in effect be borne by developing countries, which would forgo future aid from bilateral sources or the Bank's soft lending arm. Jubilee Research had proposed a third way (Kapoor 2003): the sale of Fund gold to fund 100% debt cancellation. G8 finance ministers meeting in 2005 told the Fund to examine the proposal and report to a future meeting.

Crumbs from the creditors' table

HIPC debt has now risen to more than US$ 200 billion in nominal terms. Relief has been committed (but not fully delivered) to the 27 countries that have met the Fund's conditions, a two thirds reduction of their overall debt stock – savings that the Bank says have contributed to a 'substantial increase in poverty-reducing expenditures' (IMF 2004).

The HIPC initiative has now reached a dead end, largely because creditors are baulking at the 'cost' of writing off further debts. However this is far less than the Bank and Fund assert, as most of the loans were concessionary with low interest rates, grace periods and long repayment terms. So the HIPCs owe only about US$ 176 billion to governments and multilateral institutions, and the rest to private, commercial creditors. US$ 80 billion of these loans are owed to governments or bilateral creditors, and US$ 45 billion is owed to 27 multilateral agencies of which the Bank and Fund hold the dominant share.

The countries owe the Fund about US$ 7 billion of debt (in net present value terms), of which the Fund has promised or already cancelled just US$ 2 billion. The Bank is owed US$ 13 billion but has only found half the US$ 6.4 billion (in net present value terms) needed for its minimal HIPC debt cancellation effort. Of the sums made available, more than half have come through donor contributions to the Bank, i.e. from aid budgets funded by taxpayers in OECD countries. Yet the Bank and Fund hold a 'wealth of resources on their own balance sheets – about $500 billion in effective capital and $40 billion in provisions for loan losses and reserves' (Kapoor 2003). They could easily marshal internal resources for total debt cancellation, as it represents just 5% of their effective capital and 65% of provisions for losses and reserves. The Fund could sell 20 million ounces of its gold over a period of 3–4 years and raise US$ 5 billion, while the Bank could transfer up to US$ 10 billion from its 'retained earnings', which stand at US$ 27 billion – profits made from lending to developing countries. It could also transfer excessive provisions out of its loan loss provisions, currently standing at US$ 4 billion, more than 1.5 times its impaired loans (provisions made for just such an emergency as this debt crisis).

In other words, these two institutions are rich with the resources needed to help countries like Kenya, Uganda and Ethiopia deal with their health crises. All that is needed is the political will. Jubilee 2000 showed this is strong in civil society. However, just as world leaders are failing to cooperate and coordinate the global economy, so they seem unable to cooperate to solve a problem that is relatively easy to finance. It seems civil society will have to rise up again, and once more remind world leaders of the will of their peoples.

References

Bluestein P (2004). Debt relief plan eludes IMF group. *Washington Post*, 3 October.

Bretton Woods Project (2004). *Bretton Woods Update: Life under the IMF's magnifying glass. No. 39, March–April.* London, Bretton Woods Project.

IMF (2004). *Heavily Indebted Poor Countries Initiative – state of implementation.* Washington, IMF (http://www.imf.org, accessed 16 February 2005).

Kapoor S (2003). *Can the World Bank and IMF cancel 100% of HIPC debt?* Jubilee Research for the Debt and Development Coalition, Ireland (http://www.jubileeresearch.org/analysis/reports/jubilee_canceldebt.pdf, accessed 16 February 2005).

Rowden R (2004). *Blocking progress: how the fight against HIV/AIDS is being undermined by the World Bank and International Monetary Fund. A policy briefing.* Washington DC, ActionAid International US (http://www.actionaidusa.org/publications, accessed 16 February 2005).

Summers L (2004). *The Business Times*, 9 March.

World Bank (2004). *Global development finance 2004: harnessing cyclical gains for development.* Washington DC, World Bank.

E7 | Essential health research

Research has played a central part in improving health and health care over the centuries. In the past few decades, the growth in new technologies and the generation of new knowledge in the physical sciences has been unsurpassed. At the same time, however, and in stark contrast, millions of people lack access to the most basic medical technologies. The discipline of 'health research', and the accompanying institutions of research, have to be harnessed to address the fundamental challenges of poor health and widening health care inequities.

A report by the Commission on Health Research for Development (COHRED 1990), which had been created by a group of 16 donors from Europe, North America, Asia and Latin America, identified health research as essentially linked to equity in development. To evaluate progress in equity-promoting health research, this chapter looks at what has been achieved since 1990, including plans and declarations from the International Conference on Health Research for Development held in Bangkok in 2000 (jointly initiated and organised by COHRED, the Global Forum for Health Research, WHO and the World Bank); the Ministerial Summit on Health Research held in Mexico in 2004 (organised by WHO); and the eight annual meetings of the Global Forum for Health Research held since 1997 (when the Forum was established as an independent international foundation).

Do governments recognize the links between health research and development? Are they taking steps to foster relevant research in their countries? Do governments and donors allocate sufficient resources to health research? Are 'national health research systems' strengthened or forgotten by global initiatives that have budgets many times greater than those of the countries in which they operate? Does the tremendous increase in international initiatives and private investments in health research help the poor? Is research being used to combat the underlying political and economic causes of widening health disparities within and between countries?

In 1990, the Commission on Health Research for Development noted that only 5% of global investment in health research was devoted to problems faced primarily by developing countries, even though these countries carry over 90% of the global burden of disease – a disparity that has become known as the 10/90 gap. It made four major recommendations that can serve to assess developments in health research since 1990:

> ### Box E7.1 Essential national health research and national health research systems
>
> The core of an essential national health research (ENHR) strategy is to promote research on country-specific problems that could underpin national and community decisions on health policy and management. It involves researchers, decision-makers and community representatives, who jointly choose the priorities to be addressed. It is aimed at improving the effective use of existing knowledge and technologies. Country-specific research may have limited transferability to other countries or situations, but it guides the wise use of internal resources and strengthens national sovereignty. It places a country in a much stronger position to judge and, if necessary, seek adjustments to external development assistance. Furthermore, it gives each developing country an informed voice in establishing priorities for research on the global scientific agenda (Commission on Health Research for Development 1990).
>
> For health research to be more effectively aligned to meeting national health priorities, a health research system is needed to plan, coordinate, monitor and manage health research resources and activities.
>
> Health research systems exist to plan, coordinate, monitor and manage health research resources and activities in a way that promotes effective and equitable national health development. It is a concept that 'integrates and coordinates the objectives, structures, stakeholders, processes, cultures and outcomes of health research towards the development of equity in health and in the national health system' (WHO 2002). The concept has been delineated in terms of several components of a system including stewardship; financing; values and ethics; roles and functions; capacity and resources; and strategies for strengthening health research systems.

- all countries should undertake essential national health research (ENHR) (Box E7.1);
- international partnerships to address priority health research questions should be strengthened;
- funding for research focused on the health problems of the South should be increased and sustained;
- an international mechanism to monitor progress should be established.

Developing national health research capacity

Although some progress has been made with implementing the ENHR strategy (Neufeld and Johnson 2001), consultations with various international and national stakeholders leading up to the 2000 Bangkok Conference (International Organizing Committee 2001) revealed several limitations:

- health research was still not sufficiently valued by national leaderships as an investment in development.
- research systems in general, and health research systems in particular, were often poorly organized and managed.
- many countries lacked a critical mass of researchers, a lack that was often part of a wider problem of inadequate human capacity.
- skills development was mainly focused on the 'supply side' (researchers and research institutions) rather than enhancing the capacity of 'users' of research (e.g. policy-makers and community groups).
- research has not often been translated into policy or action.

In evaluating efforts made to implement the recommendations of the Commission on Health Research for Development, the Bangkok Conference also concluded that:

- a much stronger Southern voice was needed to counter the dominance of Northern institutions over global health research.
- research needed to shift from knowledge generation to knowledge management.
- countries, as units of policy, financing and governance, are key to having an impact on health and development through health research – this led to the concept of a 'national health research system', developed further by WHO and other partners (Box E7.1)
- a more unified and inclusive approach was needed to increase synergy and reduce fragmentation.

Four years later, the 2004 Mexico Ministerial Summit on Health Research addressed some of the shortfalls identified at Bangkok and ensured that a high-level ministerial discussion on health research took place for the first time. A major theme of the discussion was the need to bridge the gap between what is known about how to improve health and what is actually done to change policy and practice – the 'know-do' gap.

The Mexico Summit also emphasized better communication, information-sharing and knowledge dissemination as a means of improving national health research capacity, especially in developing countries. One important development was a proposal to establish a global register of all clinical trials, aimed at reducing the selective (and biased) publication of trial results, particularly by the for-profit pharmaceutical sector (Dickerson and Rennie 2003, Dwyer 2004). The idea is gaining support from editors of respected medical journals who will not now publish the results of trials that have not been registered (DeAngelis et al. 2004).

One drawback of these initiatives to expand access to scientific knowledge, however, is that they could make 'Northern knowledge' more accessible to developing countries – knowledge that may not only be of limited use or applicability in developing countries (Rochon et al. 2004, Obuaya 2002) but also may reinforce the general Northern bias of the health sector. Southern knowledge, including traditional and tacit or informal knowledge generated through experience, remains mostly inaccessible and undervalued, partly because there are substantial obstacles to publishing the work of Southern researchers (Saxena et al. 2003, Keiser et al. 2004, Horton 2003). Mechanisms being developed to redress the balance, including SHARED and the Forum

---

Box E7.2 The value of national health research capacity in low and middle-income countries

- Brazil discovered Chagas disease: Carlos Chagas discovered American trypanosomiasis in 1909.
- India developed oral rehydration therapy: H N Chatterjee published the first human study of ORT in 1953.
- Chile led contraceptive development: Jaime Zipper Abragan and Howard Tatum developed the first copper intrauterine contraceptive device in 1969.
- China developed the treatment of malaria: Chinese researchers isolated the plant extract, artemisinin, from a traditional fever remedy in 1972.
- Sudan changed its malaria treatment protocol: the country used national research on resistance to chloroquine.
- Cuba developed the first meningitis B vaccine: Gustavo Sierra and Concepción Campa published the first randomized controlled trial of their meningitis B vaccine in 1991.
- Thailand built up evidence for health systems development: health research and good research management played a pivotal role in reforming the Thai health system over the past decade, and are considered central to efforts to implement, monitor and evaluate further reforms.

for African Medical Editors (Certain 2004), deserve greater support and should go hand-in-hand with the recognition that the South has produced important research (Box E7.2).

Important efforts are also being made to strengthen national capacity in research ethics and in the review of research proposals. But capacity-building for ethics reviews tends to be driven by a goal of speeding up research and minimizing 'ethical problems' when engaging in international health research. As a result, 'just enough' is done to get international trials reviewed but few resources are made available to generate efficient, sustainable national systems or independent regional mechanisms for continued local capacity development.

The statement issued by the 2004 Mexico Summit reaffirmed the need to strengthen national health research systems, to establish and implement national health research policies, and to support evidence-based public health and health care systems (WHO 2004). Disappointingly, however, it defined national health research systems as 'the people, institutions, and activities whose primary purpose is to generate relevant knowledge adhering to high ethical standards, which can be used to improve the health status of populations in an equitable way'. This definition emphasizes 'generators of knowledge' – researchers – while implicitly diminishing the importance of those demanding and potentially using research such as policy-makers, health managers and civil society. This may reflect the tendency for conferences on health research to be dominated by researchers and their needs. Researchers themselves have to ensure that their research is designed and managed in ways that will bridge the 'know-do' gap (see Box E7.3).

International partnerships

The second recommendation of the Commission on Health Research for Development in 1990 focused on establishing research partnerships and networks, in the belief that the right mix of expertise, commitment, local knowledge and excellence could result in progress. Partnerships between researchers in South and North should not only be mobilized around priority health problems, but should also strengthen the health research capacity of developing countries.

A number of so-called global alliances has been set up in recent years, including the Multilateral Initiative against Malaria, the European and Developing Country Clinical Trials Partnership, the Global Alliance for Vaccines and Immunization, and the International AIDS Vaccine Initiative, as well as WHO programmes for research and training in tropical diseases and human

Box E7.3 Bridging the 'know-do' gap

Much of the discussion at the 2000 Bangkok International Conference on Health Research for Development and the 2004 Mexico Ministerial Summit on Health Research focused on the constraints on researchers. However, several issues about the nature and practice of research itself need to be examined as well (McCoy et al. 2004):

- research cultures and incentive systems have changed so that they now encourage researchers to be more concerned with publishing their results in academic journals than with ensuring that their research leads to better policy and practice. Reversing this trend may require changing how research is evaluated and rewarded, as well as allocating more funding to academic and non-government research institutions in poorer countries that work closely with policy-makers, health managers, service providers and communities.
- there should be more funding for action research that involves service users and providers and that ensures that research is embedded in ordinary people's day-to-day contexts and practices (including the fact that health care systems are in a state of collapse in some countries). The use of participatory research methods can also help poor communities shape health systems to meet their needs.
- implementation of health research needs to be aided by a vigorous community of civil society organizations keeping a watch on health policy development and implementation; on the use of research funds to foster civil society's capacity to change the commissioning and priority-setting of research; and on the inclusion of civil society interests in research production and partnerships with academic researchers.
- the capacity of policy-makers, health managers and practitioners needs to be developed to appraise and make use of new information.

reproduction. Collectively these alliances are driven by the research excellence of the North and a focus on a selected number of diseases that cause high levels of morbidity and mortality. While potentially helping to reduce the 10/90 gap, they need to be monitored to ensure that they are not biased towards the development of medical technologies produced by Northern institutions at the expense of, say, health systems research that would directly strengthen the capacity of health services in developing countries.

Neither the consultations leading up to the 2004 Mexico Summit or the Summit itself yielded much progress towards effective research partnerships for health equity and development. Moreover, the dynamics of partnerships that would strengthen the research capacity of developing and transition countries are inadequately understood (KFPE 2001). The statement issued by the Summit does not explicitly address the building of South-South and South-North partnerships to help overcome the barriers to implementing ENHR and to strengthen national and regional health research systems. Global alliances focused on major diseases will be effective only if accompanied by a broad country-based approach to research and research development. An emphasis on piecemeal, disease-based research, rather than on the development of coherent and comprehensive research-systems, mirrors the emphasis on vertical disease programmes at the expense of health systems development, discussed in chapter B1.

At the heart of effective partnerships lies a shared perspective on excellence, relevance and good governance, and a commitment by the Northern partner to emphasize equality in the partnership (Maselli et al. 2004, IJsselmuiden et al. 2004, Chandiwana and Ornberg 2003). But there is as yet no evidence of widespread application of these principles. Most partnerships are implicitly Northern-driven, with few South-South partnerships that have demonstrated any impact.

Increased and sustained funding

The 1990 Commission's third recommendation is probably quoted most often: at least 2% of national health expenditure and 5% of health sector project and programme aid from donor agencies should be earmarked for health research and strengthening research capacity. Despite widespread awareness of this recommendation, funding to support essential health research remains scarce, especially at national levels.

Global spending on health research and development more than tripled between 1990 and 2001, but most of it was spent by high-income countries in high-income countries, with the aim of generating products and technologies tailored to high-income health care markets (Global Forum 2004). The lack of interest in funding regional health research developments, including regional networking and partnerships, is a further problem. In Africa, it has proved very difficult to generate effective and equitable research networks, thereby perpetuating the continent's dependence on North-South links for technology transfer.

Country-specific data indicate that some, but not all, developing countries

345

already invest substantially in health research. However, most of the money is used to maintain the (inadequate) research infrastructure and to pay research- ers' salaries (Murray et al. 1990, Kitua et al. 2002, COHRED 2004). Resources to conduct research are therefore reliant on external funds, giving foreign donors an undue influence on the health research agenda of developing countries.

The growth of the huge global initiatives and alliances also erodes coun- tries' control of their most scarce and valuable research resource: expert staff. Many countries are hard pressed to integrate even one vertical programme into their national health research system. This could lead to further fragmentation of Southern research systems as the number of these initiatives grows.

Evidence suggests that current (published) research carried out in devel- oping countries responds not to national needs but rather to global funding availability, and that research in developing countries is not responsive to future health needs (Nakahara et al. 2003, Farley 2005). To correct this, health research funding will have to strengthen the national research management capacity in the South, and to ensure more appropriate health research.

Building health research capacity is a long-term effort requiring sustained financial support over at least 25 years, if not more (KFPE 2001). The challenge is to ensure sustained research funding in the light of the rapidly-changing short-term interests of political, governmental and private donors.

International monitoring

The Commission's last recommendation was the establishment of an inter- national mechanism to monitor progress and to promote financial and techni- cal support for research on the health problems of developing countries. This has not been achieved. Instead, new but uncoordinated research initiatives and programmes conceived and funded largely in the North mushroomed during the 1990s.

From a Southern perspective, this fragmentation has made access to fund- ing and expertise in health research for development more difficult and more confusing: there are now many small organizations, each focusing on a narrow, specific aspect of health research for development.

The creation of an alliance of national research councils to form an inter- national institute of health, proposed by the US National Institutes of Health (NIH) in 2002, is one approach to the development of an international archi- tecture for health research. A few national health research councils and other interested parties are discussing it but so far without much progress. While this may help provide greater coordination and collaboration internationally, there are concerns that, again, it could strengthen the influence of Northern-

Health research should address the widening inequalities in health and their causes. This requires applying a political lens to research on the more fundamental determinants of health by asking questions such as the following:

- how can health equity be protected from the effects of the current pattern of unfair and unequal economic globalization and the largely unregulated operation of transnational commercial interests?
- why has odious debt not been cancelled? (Odious debts are those contracted by a country without its people's consent and not spent in their interests, of which the creditor is aware.)
- why do many rich countries' development assistance allocations fall short of the UN's 0.7% GDP target?
- why are bilateral and multilateral trade agreements unfavourable, and even punitive, towards the sickest and poorest people?
- who and what are the drivers and effects of the liberalization, segmentation and commercialization of health care systems?

based institutions such as the NIH on research and research systems in developing countries.

The 2000 Bangkok Conference attempted to reduce fragmentation and build consensus among key players. The Conference itself was a collaborative effort of four major players (Commission on Health Research for Development, the Global Forum for Health Research, WHO and the World Bank) and a steering committee of 37 interested organizations. Four years later, however, the Mexico Summit, organized by WHO alone, was less inclusive, marking a step backwards.

Recommendations

Health research and development has progressed to a certain extent since 1990. One important development has been the recognition that health is central in development. A second, reflected at the 2004 Mexico Summit, is the political interest in health research for development.

Other developments, however, may detract from this progress. The current general focus on the Millennium Development Goals (MDGs) is too narrow and pays insufficient attention to key social, economic and political determinants of ill health and inequity (Box E7.4). The Goals are unlikely to be met in the

Essential health research

347

poorest parts of the world, and reflect a Northern look at Southern problems, proposing global solutions without sufficiently acknowledging the diversity of nations or local factors. To counter this, a stronger emphasis is needed on capacity development for 'horizontal' health research, so as to increase the capacity of a country to deal with its own priority health problems and to negotiate the balance between local and global priorities. Implicit in this is the need for greater efforts to improve South-South and South-North partnerships and a commitment to fund and strengthen the voice and capacity of the South.

Other issues that may counter any progress are the enormous growth in private sector health research in the South, mostly from pharmaceutical companies, and the effects of intellectual property rights and trade laws on health and health research (see the more detailed discussion in chapter B2). Neither the Bangkok Conference nor the Mexico Summit adequately addressed these issues, even though the pharmaceutical industry is now the single largest contributor to health research funds in the South – by 2000, its investments were worth over US$ 3 billion. To the best of our knowledge, there has been no concise assessment of the impact on this shift in research funding on research infrastructure, training, ethics, equity and development: it is urgently required.

On a more positive note, it has been increasingly recognized over the past two decades that a strong civil society is a cornerstone of democracy, progress and health (Edelman 2005), not least because of its watchdog function. The role of civil society in health research was recognized at the 2004 Mexico Summit, but was not acknowledged in the final Ministerial statement. Regular review of progress with international declarations, statements, financing, practice and other efforts will be key to the advocacy needed to make health research beneficial for everyone.

This chapter has aimed to outline positive and negative trends in health research in recent years. It concludes with some suggested indicators to measure progress in future:

- national health research systems – progress towards impact and self-sufficiency.
- partnerships for health research – progress toward equitable partnerships, and their impact on national health priorities.
- health research funding – progress towards strengthening local research capacity and addressing national health research priorities.
- effects of health research funded by the private sector – understanding its benefits and harms, globally and nationally.

- global architecture for health research governance – progress towards better but equitable coordination.
- knowledge management and sharing – progress towards increased access to and utilization of knowledge from North to South and South to North.
- health systems research – progress towards developing methodologies, building capacity, and implementing research on health system performance.
- effects of health research related to MDGs – understanding of potentials and limitations, globally and nationally.
- impact on health – documenting and measuring the impact of health research (from any source) on health, health equity and development in the poorest countries.

References

Certain, E (2004). FAME: an initiative to promote local medical research publishing in Africa. *Saudi Medical Journal,* 25, S46.

Chandiwana S, Ornberg N (2003). Review of North-South and South-South Cooperation and Conditions Necessary to Sustain Research Capability in Developing Countries. *Journal of Health, Population and Nutrition,* 21, 288–297.

Commission on Health Research for Development (COHRED) (1990). *Health research essential link to equity in development.* Oxford, Oxford University Press.

COHRED (2004). Health Research expenditures: essential information for rational decision-making (2004.2). *Making Health Research Work for Everyone.* Geneva, Council on Health Research for Development.

Deangelis C et al. (2004). Registration of clinical trials: a statement from the International Committee of Medical Journal Editors. *Ned Tijdschr Geneeskd,* 148, 1870–1.

Dickersin K, Rennie D (2003). Registering Clinical Trials. *JAMA,* 290, 516–523.

Dwyer O (2004). WHO to unveil global clinical trials register. *Bulletin of the World Health Organization,* 82, 714.

Edelman (2005). Sixth Annual Edelman Trust Barometer: A global study of opinion leaders (http://www.edelman.com/image/insights/content/Edelman_Trust_Barometer-2005_final_final.pdf, accessed 14 March 2005).

Farley S (2005). Support to Science, Technology, and Knowledge for Development: A snapshot of the Global Landscape. *The Africa-Canada-UK Exploration: Building Science and Technology capacity with African Partners.* London.

Global Forum for Health Research (2004). *Monitoring Financial Flows for Health Research.* Geneva, Global Forum for Health Research.

Horton R (2003). Medical journals: evidence of bias against the diseases of poverty. *Lancet,* 361, 712–3.

Ijesselmuiden C, Duale S, Nchinda T (2004). *Principles of Good Partnerships for Strengthening Public Health Education Capacity in Africa.* Report of a Consultative Meeting, Geneva, Council on Health Research for Development.

Keiser J et al. (2004). Representation of authors and editors from countries with different human development indexes in the leading literature on tropical medicine: survey of current evidence. *BMJ,* 328, 1229–32.

KFPE (2001). *Enhancing Research Capacity in Developing and Transition Counties.* Berne, Geographica Bernensia, Swiss Commission for Research Partnerships with Developing Countries (KFPE).

Kitua AY, Swai GBR, Urrio T (2002). *Fund Flows to Health Research Institutions in Tanzania.* Dar es Salaam, Tanzania National Health Research Forum.

Masselli D, Lys J A, Schmid J (2004). *Improving Impacts of Research Partnerships.* Berne, Geographica Bernensia, Swiss Commission for Research Partnerships with Developing Countries (KFPE).

McCoy D, Sanders D, Baum F (2004). Pushing the international health research agenda towards equity and effectiveness. *Lancet,* 364:1630–31.

Murray C et al. (1990). A study of financial resources devoted to research on health problems of developing countries. *Journal of Tropical Medicine and Hygiene,* 93, 229–255.

Nakahara S et al. (2003). Research does not indicate future trends in global health. *Lancet,* 362, 493.

Neufeld V, Johnson N, eds. (2001). *Forging Links for Health Research, Perspectives from the Council on Health Research for Development.* Ottawa, International Development Research Centre.

Obuaya C (2002). Reporting of research and health issues relevant to resource-poor countries in high-impact journals. *European Science Editing,* 28, 72–77.

Rochon P et al. (2004). Relation between randomized controlled trials published in leading general medical journals and the global burden of disease. *CMAJ,* 170, 1673–7.

Saxena S et al. (2003). How international are the editorial boards of leading psychiatry journals? *Lancet,* 361, 609.

WHO (2002). *National health research systems: Report of an international workshop.* Geneva, WHO.

WHO (2004). *World Report on Knowledge for Better Health: Strengthening Health Systems.* Geneva, WHO.

PART F | **Conclusions**

Global Health Watch 2005–2006 was initiated by a group of civil society organizations to challenge and act upon the failure of governance, policies and
programmes to improve health for large sections of the world's population.

The preceding chapters have revealed a litany of broken promises and
empty declarations by governments and the international health community
as a whole. Failure to achieve, or to make substantial progress towards achieving, the latest set of targets – the Millennium Development Goals – will only
increase cynicism, fatigue and despair. Keeping a 'watch' on governments,
international institutions and the large and powerful corporate sector is therefore vital – so that current and future promises are not allowed to be broken
so easily; so that current and future efforts directed at alleviating poverty and
injustice are implemented in ways that are effective, efficient and sustainable;
and so that those who block or prevent the fulfilment of basic human rights
can be identified and held up to account.

Keeping a 'watch' is also important in and of itself. The capacity of civil
society organizations who represent the poor and the marginalized (especially
those located in the South), to hold national, international and corporate institutions of power to account is a vital component of democracy and development; a key element of a system of checks and balances required within
national and global systems to enhance fairness and accountability and to
prevent corruption, exploitation and autocracy.

Whilst the voices heard in this report are diverse, there a number of shared
central concerns:

- Intolerable and worsening inequalities;
- A deep democratic-deficit in global governance which underpins repeated
  policy failure;
- Insufficient global health leadership;
- The need to focus on rebuilding the public sector in the face of widespread
  commercialization;
- The need to strengthen synergies between public actions in a diversity of
  fields which benefit health.

This final chapter summarizes some of the major concerns expressed
earlier in the *Watch*, whilst drawing out some cross-cutting themes. Focusing

on the institutions of global governance, it sets out a menu of actions around which civil society, and in particular the global community of health professionals, can mobilize. Political mobilization – especially of those affected most deeply by globalization and the political and economical inequities described here – is at the heart of calls for 'health for all'. Without mobilization, change will not happen.

Intolerable and worsening inequalities

An intolerance of avoidable and unfair inequalities underlies all the chapters in this first edition of the *Global Health Watch.* These inequities, and the fact that poverty is deepening in many parts of the world, are a vivid indicator of the way societies organize themselves politically and economically, and the way the global political economy is structured.

There is plenty of scope for national governments to take action on global inequalities. Appeals to morality, social values and fundamental human rights are key points of leverage. The chapters on globalization and the international movement of health workers point to another emerging pressure point – increased economic interdependency between the people of the world. Acknowledging this interdependency blurs the boundaries between ourselves and others, and can act as a force for change.

However, the *Watch* shows how often the terms of this interdependency are skewed in the interests of rich nations and a global elite: the developing world supplies credit, cheap commodities and human resources which help the developed nations to grow and their people to live comfortably. And in return? Inadequate amounts of development assistance are sent, and actions to cancel unfair and inhumane debt burdens or to implement trade reforms that would assist the development of poor countries remain short of ambition and commitment.

If the developed world is serious about its political commitments towards the world's poor, it can take action to ensure that finances are available. Indeed G8 leaders have explicitly stated that there should not be a failure to meet the MDGs through lack of finances. Efforts to cost the achievement of the goals on a country-by-country basis show that many low-income countries will require complete debt cancellation and substantial increases in aid in order to meet their MDG targets.

Yet, as the chapter on aid shows, whilst the rich countries have more than doubled their wealth in the last forty years, their spending on development assistance has remained stagnant, and most of them are far from achieving the UN target to devote 0.7% of national income to development assistance. The current debt relief mechanism – the Highly Indebted Poor Countries initiative – is slow and its debt sustainability targets unhelpful. Replacing them with 'human development targets' would lead to a more appropriate framework for debt cancellation.

A huge amount of wealth is also created and traded at the global level, with much of it effectively exempt from tax. According to the Tax Justice Network and New Economics Foundation (2005), corporate wealth held in tax havens is costing governments around the world up to US$ 255 billion annually in lost tax revenues. This is not acceptable. An international tax authority could help eliminate cross-border tax evasion and help reduce the outward flow of investment capital from countries most in need of economic development. The World Commission on the Social Dimension of Globalization, convened by the International Labour Organization, has raised the profile of the need for an international tax authority within the United Nations, but there is too little progress in taking this idea forward.

Other potential new sources of revenue include a currency transaction tax; an arms trade tax; a global environmental tax; and an airline tax. President da Silva of Brazil proposed a tax on the arms trade at the G8 Summit in Evian in 2003, and President Chirac of France has been advocating a small tax on airline travel to help combat the AIDS epidemic. Currency transaction taxes, such as the Tobin tax, have received a great deal of attention from academics and policy experts (Simms, Tibbett and Willmott 2005). Other suggestions from chapters in this report include a global Marshall Plan for the developing world (part A) and financial restitution for the migration of health workers from low-income countries with staff-shortages (part B, chapter 3). A global resource dividend – under which governments would be required to share a small part of the value of any resources they decide to use or sell – highlights the idea that the global poor own an inalienable stake in all limited natural resources and can be used to ensure 'that all human beings can meet their own basic needs with dignity' (Pogge 2002).

These ideas require continued creative thought and campaigning pressure. They should no longer be considered unthinkable or unrealistic. They offer a stark contrast to the picture of the Global Fund, UN agencies and NGOs scrambling about with a begging bowl for the replenishment of their budgets. These proposals embody a principle of redistributive justice within the international economic order that must precede the concept of charity that is inherent in 'aid' and ideas such as 'debt forgiveness'. Arguments that redistribution amounts somehow to a punishment on 'success', 'innovation' or 'bold enterprise' must no longer be given any credence in the face of clearly evident

Conclusions

political and economic inequities. Such proposals are not anti-globalization, but are requirements of fair globalization.

Furthermore, aid often brings further problems for developing nations. Described in this report are the ways in which health systems suffer from fragmented aid from multiple donors (see part B, chapter 1); and the loss of national sovereignty that accompanies donor demands. The latter can be addressed by restricting conditionalities on the use of aid to those that deal with financial management and accountability. Donors should work towards sector-wide approaches in the allocation of aid and indicators could be developed to assess levels of national capacity and ownership and government control over decision-making and resource management (LaFond 1995). Conditionalities that further the political and economic interests of donor nations (witnessed recently in the use of aid for privatization and for efforts in the 'war on terror') must be ended.

Fair and just global governance

The vast inequality in economic power between countries results in differential political influence. Richer countries are able to shape international policies and global governance in a way that suits them.

Chapters across the *Watch* reveal the problems this causes – trade agreements skewed in favour of richer countries and multinational corporations, domination of global institutions, interference in poorer countries' social and economic policies. The list goes on. In the absence of major changes to developing countries' economic fortunes, what can be done about this?

Firstly, there needs to be reform of the major economic and trade-policy making institutions, namely the International Monetary Fund, World Bank and World Trade Organization. Part E, chapter 2 gives a comprehensive breakdown of reform measures that must be applied to the first two institutions – increasing representation and accountability are the key measures. The example of the World Trade Organization – ostensibly an institution ruled on the principle of one member-one vote, but where decisions are made by consensus with lots of behind the scenes arm-twisting – points to the need to increase developing countries' capacity to negotiate and for increased coalition-building between poorer countries.

Secondly, some of the existing rules governing world trade need to be revisited. The chapters on globalization, medicines and genome technology have raised the problems caused by global regulatory agreements on intellectual property rights and trade in services. There are strong opinions expressed in this volume about the desirability of renegotiating or abolishing the TRIPS agreement, and taking health and health-related services out of the General Agreement on Trade in Services. Further international accords negotiated under the auspices of the World Trade Organization – such as the Agreement on Agriculture – need to be revisited to assess their impact on food security (see part D, chapter 3). Indeed all international economic policies and agreements should be subject to a health impact assessment.

The UN as a whole needs to be strengthened too. The total annual budget of the entire UN system, including its Fund, Programmes, Specialized Agencies and peacekeeping operations is $12 billion – less than the annual budget of the New York City Board of Education (WCSDG 2004). Reforms to the Security Council to dilute the influence of the US and the other 'big four' powers are critical.

Health leadership

A strong, democratic and effective World Health Organization is important. The same can be said for UNICEF. However, these global health institutions also need democratic reform – for a start, the appointment of their leaders. Leadership elections must be made more transparent and protected from being captured by those representing the rich and powerful, as is the case with the current incumbent of UNICEF. The relationship between the global health institutions with national parliaments, especially those in developing countries, and civil society (who could exercise a monitoring role) could also be strengthened as a strategy for improving their democratic governance. The funding of these global health institutions must also be reformed so as to permit more independence from the political control of the major donors.

At the same time, the management of global institutions must be improved. This edition of the *Watch* describes internal problems facing WHO leading to a range of recommendations (part E, chapter 1), including a renewal of collective ownership by staff, a clarification of priorities, the strengthening of leadership and management skills, a broader representation of staff – from the developing world and beyond the medical profession – and support from donors to ensure that WHO's programmes are functioning and effective.

With better and more credible leadership and management, our global health institutions can assert a more appropriate set of relationships with other institutions that have large impacts on health, such as the World Trade Organization, the World Bank and IMF. WHO needs to ensure that health is given a higher priority in negotiations on economic issues which have the potential to affect health. Given the recent increase in new actors in the health field – led by the new wave of public-private partnerships – there is also a case for asking WHO to lead a global co-ordinating forum which can attempt to resolve differences and avoid duplication between these actors. The example of the Framework Convention on Tobacco Control (part E, chapter 4) proves that health institutions can take the lead effectively.

Strengthening the public sector in the face of commercialization

The history of health care systems worldwide can be read as an ongoing battle to shape and block market forces in the interests of 'health for all'. Cross-national data presented earlier in this *Watch* (part B, section 1) show why: health care systems with greater public financing and provision relative to private financing and provision tend to produce better outcomes. Other chapters such as those on medicines, water and genome technology show the hazards of profit-maximizing behaviour, including the exclusion of poorer households and the destruction of trust and ethical behaviour.

Despite lessons from history about its failures, the rise of private provision and financing in health care and in other health-sustaining services has become one of the most important issues of our time. International organizations such as the World Bank and IMF have facilitated commercialization by cutting or imposing limits on public expenditure and actively promoting privatization. They now need to be lobbied to focus their resources on re-building the public sector.

The chapter on health systems is an attempt to re-focus attention on why and how the public sector should take the lead in health sector development once more. Using the elements of the Primary Health Care Approach as a starting point, it calls for the integrated financing of health systems, special attention to be paid to the plight of underpaid public sector health workers, the development of trust and ethics as a counter-balance to the deleterious effects of commercialization and market-based inefficiencies, and a major investment in strengthening decentralized health management capacity based on the District Health Systems model.

But the public sector must also be kept accountable and constantly galvanized by civil society if it is to perform equitably, efficiently and effectively. This involves structuring appropriate relationships between government and non-government institutions that are able to support and monitor the performance of government bureaucracies. In other instances, explicit social and political mobilization will be required to ensure government accountability or to overcome the barriers towards health equity.

Health care systems do not just 'fall from the sky': they are created through long-term processes of economic change and political negotiation. The majority of the now-developed countries built up universal services from a patchwork of public, private for-profit and charitable providers. This challenge now exists for many developing countries. Whilst resources are constrained, poorer countries do have political and legal muscle with which they can regulate private providers to serve the public interest. They can also mobilize the population to monitor standards of care in all sectors and drive out bad quality, highly-priced providers. The international community should support research which aims to develop strategies for doing this.

The temptation to segment the financing of health care provision – to focus public sector resources on poorer groups, leaving others to buy private care – as recommended by the World Bank, should be resisted. It militates against attempts to create quality universal services, as it takes the money and political voice of better-off parts of the population out of the process of health systems development. Market-led systems tend to force out crucial redistributive mechanisms which protect the poor.

Sympathetic donor governments should put pressure on the institutions that they fund and govern to end support for segmentation and private sector development. WHO should also be encouraged to emphasize principles of fair financing and redistribution. As a first step, the international community as a whole should declare its support for the withdrawal of user charges in health care and for other health-sustaining services.

Most importantly there is a key role for the public in putting pressure on health systems to be more inclusive and effective. Campaigns such as that on the right to health care in India, the participatory budgeting initiated in the Brazilian city of Porto Alegre, and the global advocacy around the rights of those affected by HIV/AIDS are powerful examples – not to mention the multitude of community-based actions around the world. Global impact will only be achieved when a plurality of local actions reinforce the global demands.

Strengthening synergies between sectors

The importance of intersectoral action for health was made clear in the opening paragraph of the Alma Ata Declaration. Yet nearly 30 years later links between ministries of health and other government departments are often weak and concerted action is hard to achieve. So too at the global level, where international agencies tend to represent particular fields of public policy. Even in WHO there is a deep lack of capacity to promote intersectoral action. Part D of the *Watch* re-affirms the need for the health-sustaining services to work together, and also reveals a common set of challenges.

Economic crisis in many developing countries, combined with a pro-privatization push, has had an impact on a range of public services very similar to that experienced in the health sector. The education and water chapters in this volume show the effects: exclusion of the poor due to high charges; the growth of private-for-profit provision; lack of resources to regulate; and decay in public infrastructure.

The forces of globalization and commercialization are facilitating the entry of international corporations particularly in the areas of water and food, where pressures on developing country governments to open space for investments by multinationals are great. Whilst corporations have come up against difficulties in making profits in both the water and health sectors, the food industry appears to be gaining market share year on year, led by vast American and other developed world companies. It is very difficult to reverse such trends, especially when they are accompanied by vigorous lobbying by business and the promotion by developed countries of their own companies' exports.

Two other chapters in the *Watch* are devoted to analysing challenges which demand intersectoral action to guarantee health. They cover two of the most important issues of our time: climate change and war. Conflict already results in a high burden of death, injury and disease, especially in the developing world. Health and health-sustaining services are dramatically affected both by the impact of war and the cost of preparations for war. Essential public services tend to take years to recover after armed hostilities have ceased. Climate change meanwhile appears to be a long-term threat, but new estimates show the impact it has already had on human health and livelihoods (see part D, chapter 1), with the poor affected the most.

Opportunities

How, then, to begin to deal with these enormous problems, and what should the health sector's role be? To start with it is important, from the point of view of advocacy, to highlight the truly integrated nature of the problems. It is estimated that the failure to meet the Millennium Development Goal of gender equity in education will cost the lives of one million children in 2005 alone. The corporate domination of the food industry is leading to expanding distances between producers and consumers and to the worldwide promotion of unhealthy foods, aggravating obesity and climate change simultaneously. The commercialization of water leads to worse health outcomes. The list could go on. But there is plenty of scope for cross-sectoral advocacy to promote healthier futures for all. Potential themes for mobilizing action might be as follows:

Quality public services, free at the point of use Campaigners in health, education and water are experiencing similar problems with the growth of commercial markets in their field. Undertaking joint campaigns around strengthening public services, as well as monitoring their effectiveness, could help to magnify the calls for decent government-financed and -provided services in each sector. Advocates could bring joint pressure to bear on governments and international institutions promoting the imposition of user charges for health-sustaining services. They could share information on multinational activities, encouraging each other to inform their respective constituencies; they could also inform each other about the challenges of responding to small-scale 'informal' private provision, and how local initiatives might gradually be built into universal coverage.

Many would agree that essential services and needs should not be commodified. Using the instruments afforded to them at national and international levels, including human rights law, campaigners should demand that public policy in these areas is free from the influence of corporations; and that international institutions provide good guidance for national governments on regulating health hazards.

Demanding action on international inequalities Campaigners lobbying together for debt relief, increased aid and an end to unfair trade have already shown their power. Nevertheless in many countries, cross-sectoral working on these issues is in its infancy. Efforts should continue, strengthened by messages about the effectiveness of strong public services across the board.

Perish or survive? Lastly, health campaigners can work with those in the environmental and peace movements to reveal the costs of climate change and war. Action on important issues has often occurred because people have begun to consider the health effects – advocates learnt this during the campaigns against nuclear weapons in the 1980s and developed messages which had a worldwide impact.

We end the *Watch* with a reminder of the fundamental message of this chapter – progress towards a healthier world is fundamentally underpinned by political action. Whilst NGOs and those already involved in advocacy may find it easier to link into activities on the issues described above, individual health workers and providers and other members of the general public may find this more difficult.

If the *Watch* has moved you to action, but it is difficult for you to be in touch with others, then consider initiating your own dialogue on these issues locally. Setting up a discussion group on any of the chapters of the *Watch* or conducting small-scale local research on pressing issues in your own locality would be valuable contributions to making change happen. Consider mobilizing people around the production of a local health watch which would embody the principle of holding international and national institutions to account for their policies and actions in your country or region. Without these local actions, global change will never happen.

References

LaFond A (1995). *Sustaining Primary Health Care*. London, Earthscan.

Pogge T (2002). *World Poverty and Human Rights*. Cambridge, Polity Press.

Simms A, Tibbet S and Wilmott E (2001). The Robin Hood Tax: Concrete proposals for fighting global poverty and promoting sustainable development. London, War on Want and New Economics Foundation (http://www.neweconomics.org/gen/z_sys_ Publication Detail.aspx?PID=87).

Tax Justice Network and New Economics Foundation (2005). Tax lost in havens. London (http://www.taxjustice.net/e/press/tax_costs.pdf).

WCSDG (2004). *A Fair Globalization: Creating Opportunities for All*. Geneva, ILO.

Index

Abeyeskera, Sunila, 137
abortion, 135, 137, 138, 141
access to health care, denial
    of, 61–3
accountability, 278, 285; of IMF,
    304; of World Bank, 304
acute respiratory infection
    (ARI), 82
Adam Smith International, 330
Afghanistan: aid to, 327; health
    care structure in, 57
aflatoxin, control of, 31
ageing population, health care
    of, 126
Agenda 21, 165
agenda for health systems
    development, 83–95
Agent Orange, 256
agriculture: in Africa, 232;
    subsidies, 33
Aguas del Tunari, 217
aid, 322–31; and privatization,
    327–30; and the war on
    terror, 325–7; debt and,
    24–8; for political purposes,
    325–30; trends of (allocation,
    325; volume, 322–4)
AIDS see HIV/AIDS
AIDS orphans, 244
Albania, Family Code, 187
alcoholism, among indigenous
    peoples, 169
Alma Ata Declaration on Health,
    1, 53, 55, 56–9, 69, 76, 92,
    191, 272, 289, 357
Anapu development project, 167
Andersen Consulting, 329
Andhra Pradesh, disability
    programme, 186
Annan, Kofi, 295
Anti-Personnel Landmine
    Convention, 260
antiretroviral treatment (ART),
    73, 104, 108, 275, 317
appropriate health technology,
    56
appropriate timeframes in
    healthcare, 89
arms trade, 260–1; control of,
    261; taxation of, 43, 353
Arthur Andersen, 328
asbestos, ban on, 31
Asian Labor Network, 216

Asian–Pacific Resource and
    Research Centre for Women,
    139
Asvall, Jo Eirik, 283

Baby-Friendly Hospital
    Initiative, 316
Bangkok International
    Conference on Health
    Research for Development,
    344–5, 347, 348
bankruptcies, growth of, 37
banks, profligate lending by, 25
Barclays Bank, 328
Batwa tribe, 169
Bauman, Zygmunt, 12
Beijing Platform of Action, 136
Bellamy, Carol, 293, 295
big business, regulation of,
    307–7
bioethics, 186–8; committees,
    187
biological weapons, 260
Biological Weapons Convention
    (BWC), 260
biopiracy, 170
biotechnology, 294; research
    in, 153
birth attendants, 82, 85, 119, 172
birthing, centre in Peru, 172
Blair, Tony, 202
blindness, 208
Bolivia, privatization of water
    in, 217
bonding measures, in public
    service, 128
brain drain from poor to rich
    countries, 42, 334, 335;
    compensation for, 132; of
    health workers, 125–7
breastfeeding, 68, 270, 313, 314;
    promotion of, 316, 317
breast-milk substitutes,
    marketing of, 267, 307, 312,
    313–18
Bretton Woods institutions,
    299–301; influence of, on
    developing countries, 301–2
British American Tobacco (BAT),
    308
British Broadcasting
    Corporation (BBC), 147
British Columbia, sued over

water export restrictions,
    34–5
Brown, Gordon, 336
Brundtland, Gro Harlem, 274,
    287, 308
Bush, George W., 137, 326, 327

Cairo consensus, 134–6, 143
Calgene, 294
California, ban on MTBE
    gasoline additive, 35
Camdessus Report, 218, 221
Canada, trade issues in, 34
Canadian International
    Development Agency, 317
Canavan disease, 153
cancer, 150, 152, 195
Cancer Research UK, 152
capital, flight of, 27, 43
carbon sinks, 200
Carnegie Commission on Pre-
    venting Deadly Conflict, 257
caste prejudice, 244
Center for Reproductive Rights,
    139
Chagas disease, 102, 342
Chemical Weapons Convention
    (CWC), 259
chemical weapons, 259–60
Child Survival Revolution, 68–9
children, 15; child health
    programmes, 70; protection
    of, 293; survival of, 296;
    tobacco addiction, 311;
    undernutrition of, 227–8
    see also malnutrition, of
    children
China: economic growth of, 16,
    17–18; export processing
    zones in, 20–1; inequalities
    in, 19; population policy
    in, 187
Chirac, Jacques, 353
chloroquine, 342
cholera, 218
civil society, mobilizing of, 6–7
Civil Society Initiative, 287, 289
classroom, as site of
    socialization, 244–6
Clean Development Mechanism
    (CDM), 200
climate change, 193–206; effects
    of, 197–8

Coca-Cola, consumption in Mexico, 234
Cochabamba, Bolivia, water protests in, 217
Codex Alimentarius Commission, 235, 236
colonialism, consequences of, 257–8
commercialization of health care, 53, 55, 65–87, 124, 153, 155
Commission on Health Research for Development (COHRED), 339, 341, 343, 347
Commission on Social Determinants of Health, 275
commodification, of water, 209–19
commodity prices, 27
commons, enclosure of, 230
community health workers, 129
community involvement in health care systems, 57, 90–1
community rating, 64
conditionalities associated with aid, 27, 29, 274, 302–3, 327, 336, 354
condoms, promotion of, 141
conflict and militarism, causes of, 257–8
contraception, 70, 342
contract disputes, 68
Corner House, 139
Corporate Accountability International, 309, 311
corporations: donations to health professionals, 314–16; evasion of tax, 318–21
corruption, 6, 26, 277, 284, 300; of academic research institutions, 116; of governments, 76; of health staff, 124; of Western businesses, 26
cost effectiveness analysis, rise of, 74–6
currency crises, 29
cycling, 196; discouragement of, 195; promotion of, 205
cystic fibrosis, 151

Danzon, Marc, 283
de-skilling of primary health care workers, 69–70
death by overworking, 22
debt, 26; and aid, 24–8; as form of neocolonialism, 41; cancellation of, 27, 84, 248,

249, 336; crisis, 23, 300; relief of, 42, 332–8, 353, 359
Decade of the World's Indigenous Peoples, 173
decentralization: of health care, 92; of health financing, 88
democracy, 267; positive correlation with health, 76
democratization, 289–90; of health research agenda, 156
dengue fever, 197
Department for International Development (DfID), 277, 327, 329
depleted uranium weapons, 259
Development Alternatives with Women for a New Era (DAWN), 135, 139
development, as public health issue, 2–4
diabetes, 225
Diang Phoeuk, 168
diarrhoeal disease, 69, 75, 82, 208
diet, globalization and, 234–5
dilution of health care, 88
disabilities, 155; facts about, 180; people with, 7, 179–89 (entitlements of, 186; killing of, 184; self-determination of, 185)
disability: definition of, 180–1; invisibility of, 185–6
disability adjusted life years (DALYS), 183
disability rights movement, 181
Disabled People's International (DPI), 181–2
disabled people see disabilities, people with
disarmament agenda, 258–61
discussion groups, setting up of, 360
distribution of income, 38
District Health System (DHS) model, 58, 92–3
doctors and nurses, density of, 121
dollar–gold standard, 334
donor funding of health care systems, 77–8, 91–2
donors: auditing performance of, 92; desire for quick results, 91
drought, 197
drug resistance, 62
drugs: generic, manufacture of, 105, 108, 114; patented, costs of, 101 see also medicines

education, 239–52, 293, 297; as determinant of health outcomes, 239, 239 (for women, 242); as right for all, 243; expenses of, 11; girls withdrawn from, 63; impact of health on, 241–2; in life skills, 245–6; of girls, 243; of women, 69, 240 (in Mexico, 242); primary, universal, 225, 247; universal, attainability of, 242–4; user charges for, 24, 243, 247 (resistance to, 248)
Education for All, 244
Education for Women's Equality (India), 245
efficiency, meaning of, 75
eflornithine, 102
Eli Lilly, 170
Emerging Africa Infrastructure Fund, 328
empowerment, 241; of women, 142, 225
entitlement, 241
environmental degradation, 193, 201; because of war, 256
equity, 40, 56, 156
essential drugs programmes (EDP), 116
essential medicines, concept of, 100
essential national health research (ENHR) strategy, 340, 341, 345
essential packages of health care, 88
ethical behaviour of health care staff, 94
ethical recruiting of health workers, 127, 132
ethical regulation of pharmaceutical companies, 115
Ethyl Corporation, 34
eugenics, 187
European and Developing Country Clinical Trials Partnership, 343
European Commission, 147, 210
European Federation of Public Service Unions, 222
European Investment Bank, 299
euthanasia, 187
Evian Challenge, 212
export processing zones (EPZs), 20–2; in Mexico, 30

fair trade, 84, 249

family planning, 69, 136, 294, 297
female genital cutting, 241
financing of health for all, 85–6
flexibility of labour markets, 36, 40
Focusing Resources on Effective School Health (FRESH), 246
food, 225–38; as a right, 231–4; dumping of, 231; production of, 5; right to, 5; women's responsibility for, 233
Food and Agriculture Organization (FAO), 235, 236
food production: industry, 358 (in US, corporate control of, 229); systems of, 167; women's responsibility for, 233
food security, 235
food sufficiency, national, shift from, 233
Ford Foundation, 210
Forum for African Medical Editors, 342–3
fossil fuels, burning of, 194
fragmentation of health care systems, 72, 124
free trade agreements, 107, 108
Free Trade Area of the Americas (FTAA), 34–5
fundamentalisms, 140–1; fight against, 144; rise of, 137
funding, of sexual and reproductive health, 142–3

Gefitinib drug, 150
gender equality, 225; in education, 242–3, 358
gender issues, 19, 54
gene technology, 54, 147–59
General Agreement on Tariffs and Trade (GATT), 14, 30
General Agreement on Trade in Services (GATS), 34–6, 87, 212, 355
generic drugs, manufacture of, 105, 108, 114
genetic engineering, and nutrition, 230
genetic modification of food, 294
genetic screening, 151, 153, 154
German, Tony, 323
Ghana: additional duty hours allowance, 129; health care in, 131
girls, taken out of school, 243
Global Action and Information on Nutrition (GAIN), 235

Global Action Week, 249
Global Alliance for the Elimination of Lymphatic Filariasis, 74
Global Alliance for Vaccines and Immunization, 74, 343
Global Call to Action Against Poverty, 249, 250
Global Equity Gauge Alliance, 8
Global Forum for Health Research, 339, 347
Global Fund for AIDS, TB and Malaria (GFATM), 72, 277, 322, 335
Global Health Watch, 134, 351
Global Polio Eradication Initiative, 74
Global Public Private Initiatives (GPPIs), 72–4
Global Tobacco Treaty, 307–13
global warming, 193–4
Global Water Corporation, 212
Global Water Partnership, 210, 221
globalization, 41, 352, 354, 358; and diet, 234–5; and tax avoidance, 320–1; as cause of conflict, 257; as success story, 16–22; impact on health, 11–52
GOBI-FF programme, 69
golden rice, 230
governance, 289–90, 352; fair and just, 354–5
Grant, James, 296
greenhouse gases, 194–5, 199, 203

Hague Agenda for Peace and Justice for the 21st Century, 263
Haryana State Electricity Board, 329–30
hazards of work see wages and conditions of work
health: as human rights issue, 182; concepts of, 170; factors impacting on, 6–7; impact of globalization on, 30–6; impact on education, 241–2; politics of, 2 see also rights, to health care and sexual and reproductive health
Health Action International, 115
health care: approaches to, 55–99; expenses of, 11; financing of, 62; right to, 53, 79; user charges, 24 (abolition of, 86)

health care services, governance of, 53–4
health districts, as basis of health care, 58
Health for All, 58, 269, 275, 279, 283, 288; demise of, 59–60; financing of, 85–6
health insurance, 153, 154, 157
health research: essential, 339–50; global spending on, 345; national capacity, 341–3; North–South partnerships, 343–5
health spending, 59
Health Unlimited, 172
health workers: collecting of data on, 120; crisis of, 119–33; demoralization of, 84, 124; division of labour among, 129; ethical recruitment of, 132; in rural areas, 123; lack of, 121; loss of morale, 60; relation to HIV/AIDS, 124–15; shortages of, 132; valuing of, 83–4 see also migration, of health workers
healthy life expectancy (HALE), 81–2
Heavily Indebted Poor Countries Initiative (HIPC), 27, 42, 335, 336–7, 353
Heb, Cham, 171
HIV-free survival of infants, 317–18
HIV/AIDS, 2, 11, 57, 81, 90, 124, 125, 135, 141, 151, 154, 225, 228, 233, 240, 241, 244, 245–6, 275, 276, 282, 293, 327, 334, 335, 357; and poverty, 22–4; antiretrovirals see antiretroviral treatment; funding of programmes, 123; impact on health workers, 114–15; overmedicalization of response to, 73; rates of infection, 12; related to education, 239
hormone treatment of cattle, 31
hospitals, over-development of, 87–8
Human Genome Project, 111
human resources: management systems, 119; recurring expenditure, 120
Human Resources for Health Development, 119
human rights, 5–8; framework, strengthening of, 144

human rights perspective on health, 58

illiteracy, among women, 243
immunization, 19, 57, 68, 85, 91, 293; against measles, 119; mass campaigns, 70; stagnation of, 70
inappropriate health care, 66
incentive schemes, against migration, 129–30
Inclusion International, 182
independent living movement, 186
India: generic drugs manufacture in, 105; growth in, 17–18; price controls on medicines, 116
indigenous health research, as development catalyst, 176
indigenous peoples, 7, 163–78; health of, 168–73; health services for, 175; organizations and networks, 174; perception of health, 171; resettlement of, 166–7
inequality: as legacy of colonialism, 19; growth of, 4
infant formula, controls on marketing of, 1
inflation, obsession with, 336
informal work, 23
insecurity, work-related, 40
Institutes for Health Research (Canada), 116
institutional memory, loss of, 127
Integrated Management of Childhood Illness (IMCI), 71
integration of clinical services, 56
intellectual property rights, 102, 104–6, 112; flexibility in, 115; overhaul of, 156
Inter-Agency Support Group, 166
interest, payment of, 25–7
Intergovernmental Panel on Climate Change (IPCC), 194, 196, 198, 199, 202
internal markets, 66
International AIDS Vaccine Initiative, 343
International Baby Food Action Network (IBFAN), 314, 316
International Centre for the Settlement of Investment Disputes (ICSID), 218
International Classification of Diseases, 181

International Classification of Functioning, Disability and Health (ICF), 182
International Classification of Impairment, Disability and Handicap (ICIDH), 181; revision of, 182
International Code of Marketing of Breastmilk Substitutes, 314
International Conference on Health Research for Development, 339
International Convention on the Elimination of All Forms of Racial Discrimination (ICERD), 164
International Covenant on Civil and Political Rights (ICCPR), 15
International Covenant on Economic, Social and Cultural Rights (ICESCR), 5, 15, International Decade of the World's Indigenous Peoples, 163, 164
International Development Association, 300, 336
International Finance Facility (IFF), 27
International Labour Organization (ILO), 164, 353; Convention Concerning Indigenous and Tribal Peoples, 164
International Monetary Fund (IMF), 4, 14, 16, 29, 42, 60, 61, 210, 220, 233, 267, 269, 287, 299–306, 334, 355, 356; criticism of, 302–3; governance of, 300–1; reform of, 304–5, 354; riots against, 302
International Physicians for the Prevention of Nuclear War, 261
International Planned Parenthood Federation (IPPF), 139, 145
International Rivers Network, 217
International War Crimes Tribunal, 262
International Weeks of Resistance to Transnationals, 313
International Women's Health Coalition (IWHC), 135, 139
Internet, and job mobility, 126

investment in health care, by poor countries, 127
iodine deficiency, 228
Irish Nursing Board, 125

Jamba, San traditional leader, 171
Japan Tobacco Interational (JTI), 308
Jemaah Islamiyah, 326
Joint Learning Initiative, 119
Jubilee 2000, 337
Jubilee Research, 336
just-in-time systems, 36

Kaprio, Leo, 283
knowledge economy, 152–3
Kyoto Protocol, 199–201

The Lancet, 295–6
land reform, in Mexico, 29
land rights, 166–7, 233
landmines, 253, 260
least trade restrictive practices, 31
Lee Jong-wook, 274–5, 279, 285, 286, 287, 288
leishmaniasis, 102
leprosy, 275
liberalization: of agricultural trade, 233–4; of capital market, 14–15; of health care, 87; of trade, 13 (impact on poverty, 18)
life expectancy, 20, 55, 57, 169, 258
life skills education, 245–6
LINKAGES organization, 317
literacy, of women, 240
local content requirements, 33
Lok Jumbish programme (India), 245

Mahler, Halfdan, 272
malaria, 102, 197, 198, 225, 241, 275, 342
malnutrition, 183, 201, 225–38; maternal, 227; of children, 169, 208, 227, 241, 254, 293
maquiladoras, 21, 30
Marcos, Ferdinand, 26
marginalization, 168; of indigenous peoples, 170
market-driven health care system, 67, 81
Marlboro, 309
Marshall plan, 353
maternal health, 2, 142 see also mortality, maternal

Mbya Guarani people, 167
McDonalds, 234
McKeown thesis, 149
meat industry, rise of, 228–31
Medact, 8
medical information, collecting of, 154, 157
Medical Research and Development Treaty, 115
medicines, 100–18; lack of access to, 101; price control options, 115–16; regulation of, 108; spending on, 101; unauthorised, production of, 111
mega-development projects, impact of, 303
men, responsibilities of, 136, 142
meningitis B, vaccine, 342
Methanex Corporation, 35
Mexico: debt crisis in, 23; imports of US corn, 29; production shifts to China, 22
migration, 12, 13–14, 126, 197; in China, 21; of health workers, 119, 123, 125–7, 128, 129–30, 352, 353; patterns of, 125–7; related to globalization, 127; tax on, 130 see also brain drain
Mexico Ministerial Summit on Health Research, 341, 343, 344–5, 348
Mildmay Centre for Palliative Care, 125
militarism, 41; in developing countries, 258
military spending, 258, 262; reduction of, 58
Millennium Challenge Account, 28, 327
Millennium Development Goals, 28, 72, 85, 136, 143, 145, 166, 207, 217, 220, 225, 249, 274, 293, 323, 347, 349, 351, 358; targets for eduction, 242; underpinned by nutrition, 225
mining corporations, threat to indigenous peoples, 166
MMT gasoline additive, banned, 34
Mobuto, Sese Seko, 26
Mongoven, Biscoe and Duchin company, 311
mortality: in 19th century, 149; maternal, 57, 79, 85, 91,

120, 135, 137, 142, 239–41; of children, 2, 55, 81, 82, 85, 171, 225, 239–41, 314 (reduction of, 69, 70, 71, 72, 293); of infants, 19, 20, 29, 30, 38, 120, 168, 183; rates correlated with health worker availability, 120
most favoured nation policy, 31
motor vehicles, increase of, 196
MTBE gasoline additive, banned, 35
Multilateral Initiatives against Malaria, 343
Multilateral Organizations Performance Assessment, 276
multilateralism, promotion of, 262
multinational companies, 15–16

Nakajima, Hiroshi, 272, 284
National Academy of Sciences (USA), 150
National Human Genome Research Institute (USA), 149
National Institutes of Health (USA), 346–7
national treatment, 31
neoliberalism, 61
Nestlé, 236, 312, 314
Netherlands, euthanasia in, 187
Network for Accountability of Tobacco Transnationals (NATT), 309
New Economics Foundation, 353
New England Journal of Medicine, 111
New International Economic Order (NIEO), 58
New Public Management (NPM), 66
Nixon, Richard, 333
non-government actors, role for, 81
non-governmental organizations (NGOs), 175, 192; role of, 90
North American Free Trade Agreement (NAFTA), 15, 29, 34–5, 212, 231
nuclear weapons, 258–9

obesity, 225; costs of, 235
official development assistance see aid
oil companies, advertising campaigns, 202

oil price rises, effect on health care systems, 59
Omenn, Gilbert, 150
oral rehydration therapy (ORT), 68, 342
Organization for Economic Cooperation and Development (OECD) Convention on Combating Bribery, 26
over-prescribing, 116
over-servicing of health care, 65
ozone depletion, 193

Pan-Sahelian Initiative, 326
paramedical staff, 129
part-time working, 39
participatory budgets, 357
Partnership for Safe Motherhood and Newborn Health, 276
partnerships, between rich and low-income countries, 131, 132
Pastoral Land Commission, 167
patenting, 103, 114, 152–3; auction system, 114; forgoing of rights, 156; myths about, 109–11
patents, zero-cost, 114
patient communication, 94
peace, creating culture of, 263
People's Charter for Health, 286
People's Health Assembly (2000), 1
People's Health Charter, 1
People's Health Movement, 286, 287
People's World Water Forum, 222
periwinkle plant, 170
personnel management in health care systems, 77
Peru, birthing centre in, 172
pharmaceutical corporations, 66, 103, 109–11; contact with researchers, 111; ethical regulation of, 115; revelation of clinical trial data, 112
Philip Morris (Altria), 308, 309, 311
Philippines, privatization of water in, 216
Phiri, Alexander, 184
poliomyelitis, 275
pollution, 39, 169, 193, 195, 196, 199, 228; control of, 30; deriving from war, 256; of water, 209; polluter pays principle, 205

Index

365

poor people, poor care for, 81
Population Action International, 145
Porto Alegre, 357; water utilities in, 214
poverty, 9, 62, 137, 141, 183, 184, 207, 257, 286; AIDS and, 22–4; as public health issue, 2–4; effects on health, 19; growth of, 4; impact of globalization on, 17; reduction of, 249, 262–3; relation to disability, 179 *see also* poor people
Poverty Reduction Strategy Papers, 301–2
precarious employment, 39
PricewaterhouseCoopers, 329
Primary Health Care approach, 7, 55, 56–9, 69, 79, 83, 276, 288, 290, 356; factors undermining, 80; implementation of, 88; obstacles to, 90; sidelined, 280–1
prioritizing of interventions, 88
private health care, 19–20, 60, 65, 82, 138, 357; staffing of, 123
private health insurance, 62, 63, 64; markets, 86
private health sector, regulation of, 86–7
privatization, 24, 322, 335, 358; aid and, 327–30; corporate advisors on, 328; of health care, 20, 82, 138; of water, 209–19; passive, 60; resistance to, 221
Programa Nacional de Educación, Salud y Alimentación (PROGRESA) (Mexico), 242
Pu Tiu, Irma, 171
Public Citizen, 115
public element of health care systems, 79–82
Public Private Infrastructure Advisory Facility, 329
public sector: competition within, 68; failures in, 56, 76–8; for the poor, 64; opposing wage caps in, 248–9; strengthening management, 87; strengthening of, 87, 221, 356–7
public services: incapacity of, 65; politics of, 246–9; provision of, 358–9

public–private partnerships, 355

quality adjusted life years (QALYS), 183, 187
Quinillo, Juana Tzoy, 171

racism, 168
radiological weapons, 259
Randel, Judith, 323
rape, as weapon of war, 254
recuitment of health workers, ethical, 127
REFLECT programmes, 245
reform of health sector, 60
refugees, 254–5
Rehabilitation International, 182
relocation of production, 36, 37
reproductive health, 134–46
research and development of pharmaceutical companies, 101–2, 103, 109–11, 151–2; funding of, 115; new paradigms for, 114
resistance to medicines, 101
resource management and planning, 87–8
restitution, from wealthy countries, 130–1
review articles about drugs, 111–12
rights: to education, 243; to food, 231–4; to health, 42; to health care, 53, 79; to standard of living, 15
risk assessment, 156
risk selection, 157
road injuries, 195
rodent-borne disease, 198
Roll Back Malaria, 74

salaries of health workers, 130
Sanger Institute, 147
sanitation, 207–9
Saro-Wiwa, Ken, 24
schistosomiasis, 208
sea levels, rising, 197
second-hand clothes market in Zambia, 22–4
sector-wide approach (SWAp), 78
segmentation of health care systems, 63–5
selective health care, 55, 68–74
Self-Help Association of Paraplegics (SHAP) (South Africa), 186
Severe Acute Respiratory Syndrome (SARS), 16, 147–8, 275, 276
sex of babies, selection of, 155

sexual and reproductive health, 54, 134–46
sexuality, 141–2
SHARED organization, 342
da Silva, Ignacio, 353
Sinding, Steven, 138
smallpox, 275; eradication of, 68
social ecology of health and disease, 149
social spending, decline of, 37
South Africa, ban on doctor recruitment, 128
Standard Bank Group, 328
Stang, Dorothy, 167
state provision, undermining of, 303
states, duties of, 5
Stepping Stones programmes, 245
sterilization, 187
streptomycin, 150
strikes, by nurses, 130
structural adjustment, 23, 27, 60, 138, 300, 301, 305
Students Partnership Worldwide, 246
suicide, among indigenous peoples, 169
Sun Belt Company, 212
sustainability, 40

tariffs, on agricultural products, 33
Tax Justice Network, 353
taxation, 318–21; increasing, campaign for, 268; of air travel, 43; progressive, 84, 319; reclaiming language of, 321; tax identification numbers, 43; Tobin tax, 43, 353
technological bias in health care, 72
terrorism, 256; definition of, 258; war on, 257, 322, 323, 325–7
tertiary care, 129
Thailand, health worker retention strategies, 129
theft among health staff, 84
thermal extremes, deaths caused by, 197
tobacco: child addiction to, 311; compensation for harm caused by, 310; plain packaging of, 34
tobacco industry: advertising by, 310, 312; control of, 267, 277, 307–13; involvement

of civil society, 312; non-interference in health policies, 310, 312
tobacco-related diseases, 308
Tobin tax *see* taxation
trachoma, 208
trade creep, 31
trade unions, 38, 39
traditional medicine, 165, 170, 173, 175
trafficking, of children, 297
training of health workers, 130
transnational corporations, 267-8, 267
transparency, 278, 285; of financing, 94; of IMF, 304; of World Bank, 304
Transparency International, 26
transport: effect on climate change, 195; reduction of, 204-5
Treatment Action Campaign (South Africa), 90
tribal peoples, 164
TRIPS *see* World Trade Organization, Agreement on Trade-Related Intellectual Property Rights
trust in health care systems: corruption of, 111-12; rebuilding of, 93-5; violation of, 94
trypanosomiasis, 102
tuberculosis, 102, 149, 225, 241, 275; among indigenous peoples, 169
Turner, Adair, 202-3

UNAIDS, 2, 6, 317
undernutrition *see* malnutrition
unemployment, 23, 29, 36, 40
unethical practices among health staff, 84
Union of Soviet Socialist Republics (USSR), collapse of, 14
United Nations (UN), 14, 262, 271, 355
UN Children's Fund (UNICEF), 74, 204, 267, 278, 293-8, 316, 317, 318, 355; *Adjustment with a Human Face*, 296; challenge to, 295-7; creation of, 293; involvement in water issues, 219-21; *State of the World's Children*, 2
UN Committee on Economic, Social and Cultural Rights, 163

UN Conference on Environment and Development (Earth Summit), 165, 198, 322
UN Convention Against Corruption, 26
UN Convention on the Rights of the Child, 186
UN Declaration on the Rights of Persons Belonging to National or Ethnic, Religious and Linguistic Minorities (UNDM), 165
UN Development Programme (UNDP), 140, 210; *Human Development Report*, 2
UN Educational, Scientific and Cultural Organization (UNESCO), 153
UN Environment Programme (UNEP), 196
UN Framework Convention on Climate Change (UNFCCC), 198-9, 204
UN Fund for Populations Activities (UNFPA), 135, 137, 139-40
UN High Commissioner for Refugees, 220, 255
UN Human Rights Commission, 164, 179
UN International Conference on Population and Development, 134
UN Permanent Forum on Indigenous Issues, 166, 173
UN Programme of Action Concerning Disabled Persons Persons, 182
UN Small Arms Action Plan, 261
UN Standard Rules on the Equalization of Opportunities of People with Disabilities, 182, 185
UN Women's Fund (UNIFEM), 140
UN Working Group on Indigenous Populations, 164
United States of America (USA): as aid donor, 326; current account deficit, 333; Food and Drug Administration, 112
United Water, 219
Universal Declaration on Human Rights (UDHR), 15
universal social security, break-up of, 64
US National Institutes of Health, 116

US-Australia free trade agreement, 107
USAID, 317
user charges, 61-3, 358; abolition of, 86, 357; contribute to poverty, 62; resistance to, 248-9 *see also* education *and* health

Vatican, 137
Veneman, Ann, 267, 294, 295
vertical programmes, 55, 56, 68-74, 89, 281
Viagra, 102
violence: against women, 255; armed, prevention of, 261-2; domestic, 241
Virchow, Rudolf, 2
vitamin A, 230; deficiency, 228
vulnerable groups, health of, 161

wage caps in public sector, 248-9
wages and conditions of work, 12, 21, 22, 37, 39, 44; in public service, 83, 248-9
walking: encouragement of, 195, 205
war: impact on environment, 256; impact on health, 253-65
Washington Consensus, 302
water: access to, 75, 207-24, 254; ban on export of, 34-5; commercialization of, 358; commodification of, 209-19; democratic governance of, 221; increased consumption of, 208; investment in, 222; metering of, 214, 215; of glaciers, export of, 212; regulation of private companies, 215; scarcity of, 209 *see also* privatization, of water
water industry, corporate interests in, 211
Water Manifesto, 222
water-related diseases, 208
well-being, 134, 171; nutritional, determinants of, 227
Wellcome Trust, 152
WELSTART organization, 317
White Band Days, 249, 250
WICEJ organization, 140
Wiwa, Ken, 24
Wolfensohn, James, 184
Wolfowitz, Paul, 267
women, 11, 15, 225; and export

processing zones, 20–1; effects of globalization on, 233

Women in Europe for a Common Future, 217

Women's Global Network for Reproductive Rights (WGNRR), 135, 140

women's issues, 134–46

working conditions *see* wages and conditions of work

World Alliance for Breastfeeding Action (WABA), 314, 316, 318

World Bank, 4, 6, 8, 14, 16, 22, 23, 42, 60, 61, 63, 75–6, 136, 166, 202, 210, 217, 218, 220, 233, 248, 267, 269, 274, 278, 287, 299–306, 322, 333, 334, 339, 347, 355, 356, 357; criticism of, 302–3; flawed statistics of, 3, 17; governance of, 299–300; reform of, 304–5; *World Development Report*, 2, 12

World Bank Bonds Boycott, 303

World Blind Union, 182

World Commission on the Social Dimensions of Globalization, 41, 353

World Economic Equalization Programme (WEEP), 43

World Economic Forum, 16, 202

World Federation of Deaf/Blind, 182

World Federation of the Deaf, 182

World Health Assembly, 119, 130, 271, 284, 308, 314

World Health Organization (WHO), 1, 6, 7, 74, 86, 93, 95, 100, 115, 116, 119, 120, 132, 140, 144, 145, 153, 181, 182, 183, 196, 204, 213, 235, 236, 269–92, 296, 317, 322, 339, 343, 347, 357; and health of indigenous peoples, 174; as world policeman, 279; *Changing History*, 282; core budget of, 280; creation of, 271; criticism of, 277–9, 282; definition of health, 170; diminished power in relation to World Bank, 287; election of directors of, 289; core purpose of, 289; funding and programming of, 290; historical milestones, 272–5; importance of, 355; inadequate resources of, 272–82; interaction with commercial sector, 281; involvement in water issues, 219–21; leadership and management of, 290–1; low morale in, 282–3; report on disabled people, 179; *Right to Water*, 220; role of civil society in, 285; salaries and conditions in, 281–2; shift in policy, 275; strengthening of, 285; *Water for All*, 222; *World Health Report*, 2, 285

WHO Framework Convention on Tobacco Control (FCTC), 274, 308–10, 356

WHO Reproductive Health and Research, 140

World Intellectual Property Organization (WIPO), 104

World Meteorological Organization (WMO), 196

World Network of Users of the Psychiatric System, 182

World Panel on Financing Water Infrastructure, 218–19

World Social Forums, 192

World Summit for Children, 70

World Summit on Sustainable Development (2002), 165

World Survey of Funding for Genomics, 152

World Trade Organization (WTO), 9, 15, 16, 30–6, 42, 60, 87, 104, 112, 152, 220, 287, 355; Agreement on Agriculture, 33, 231; Agreement on Government Procurement (AGP), 33; Agreement on Sanitary and Phytosanitary Measures (SPS), 31; Agreement on Trade-Related Investment Measures (TRIMS), 33; Agreement on Trade-Related Intellectual Property Rights (TRIPS), 33–4, 104–8, 112–14, 152, 153, 354 (policy flexibility in, 106, 114); agreements, health concerns within, 32; Cancun talks, 33; Doha Declaration, 106; reform of, 354; Technical Barriers to Trade Agreement (TBT), 31; TRIPS-plus agreements, 107–8

World Water Council (WWC), 210, 221

World Water Forum, 210, 222

youth, rights and health of, 142–3

Zambia: opening of borders, 22–4; suspended from debt relief, 335